Advance Praise for Brando[n Hall's] Web-Based Training Cookb[ook]

M000121951

Brandon Hall has forgotten more about Web-based training than most of us will ever know. This book isn't just the meat and potatoes of WBT's concepts; it's a nine-course, soup-to-nuts examination of one of the hottest topics in the training world.
—Bob Filipczak, Staff Editor
Training Magazine

Brandon Hall has filled the vacuum by creating Web-Based Training Cookbook. *He has developed frameworks, recipes, and guidance that are so necessary for success in training on the Web. We should shout a collective "Hallelujah" as we bring the results of our work to the table. Things would not have been as good as they will be as a result of this important and definitive book. . . .* Web-Based Training Cookbook *will be used often and will remain on my active reference bookshelf for years to come.*
—Gloria Gery
Gery Associates

I found Web-Based Training Cookbook *to provide comprehensive, objective, informative, and thought-provoking coverage of the complex world of Web-based training. It is a wonderful in-depth source of learning done by a wide range of individuals and organizations. Whether you are contemplating testing the waters of Web-based training or have already begun your project,* Web-Based Training Cookbook *is an excellent resource.*
—Nancy Bartlett, Director, Product Development and Educational Services
American Management Association

From technical software issues through ROI to instructional design, Brandon Hall has prepared a comprehensive in-depth source of information, techniques, case studies, models, and examples on all project aspects of Web-based training. It is a valuable resource for experienced computer-based trainers who are looking for information on the new tools and techniques for net-delivered training, for technical Web programmers and Webmasters interested in instructional applications, and for managers concerned with ROI!
—Dr. Ruth Clark, Instructional Psychologist
Center for Performance Technology
Former President of International Society for Performance Improvement

If a cookbook is a collection of recipes with specific ingredients and directions, then Web-Based Training is not a cookbook; rather it is a handbook for setting up a kitchen. It does include general recipes for different kinds of menus—text and graphics, interactive text and graphics, and interactive multimedia. It does include great examples of the type of courses you might cook-up. It will be the standard reference for Web-based training chefs.
—M. David Merrill, Professor
Utah State University

WEB-BASED TRAINING
COOKBOOK

Brandon Hall

WILEY COMPUTER PUBLISHING

JOHN WILEY & SONS, INC.
New York • Chichester • Weinheim • Brisbane • Singapore • Toronto

*This book is dedicated to my wife Vicky, and my children Brian
and Karen. You are what matters most. And to the rest of my family,
Dolly, Kevin, Corinne, Celedra, Leslie, Kristine, and Joe.*

Publisher: Robert Ipsen
Editor: Robert Elliot
Assistant Editor: Kathryn A. Malm
Managing Editor: Carl Germann
Production Assistant: Marnie Shotsky
Electronic Products, Associate Editor: Mike Green
Text Design & Composition: Pronto Design & Production, Inc.

Library of Congress Cataloging-in-Publication Data:
Hall, Brandon, 1951-
    Web-based training cookbook/Brandon Hall.
     p. cm.
    Includes index.
ISBN 0-471-18021-1 (pbk.:alk.paper)
1. Employees—Training of—Interactive multimedia. 2. Employees—Training of—Computer-assisted instruction. 3. Web sites—Design and construction. 4. Web publishing. I. Title.
HF5549.5.T7H285 1997   97-14629
658.3'124'02854678--dc21   CIP

Printed in the United States of America

10 9 8 7 6 5 4 3 2 1

Contents

Introduction ix

PART 1 WHAT YOU NEED TO KNOW ABOUT
WEB-BASED TRAINING 1

Chapter 1 Examples of Web-Based Training 3
  Type 1—Text and Graphics Web-Based
    Training Programs 4
  Type 2—Interactive Web-Based Training Programs 5
  Type 3—Interactive Multimedia Web-Based
    Training Programs 8

Chapter 2 FAQs: Frequently Asked Questions
about Web-Based Training 15

Chapter 3 Internet Technology Basics 31
  The Web 31
  Your Browser 35
  Languages 41
  Resources 55

Chapter 4 Hardware and Software You Need 57
  Hardware 57
  Software 59
  Networking 66

Part 2 PLANNING, DEVELOPING, AND IMPLEMENTING
WEB-BASED TRAINING 79

Chapter 5 The Development Process 81
  Development Overview 81
  The Vision 83
  The Project Team for Custom Development 93
  Where to Find Your Staff 100

Chapter 6 Building a Business Case for
Web-Based Training 103
  Business Concerns 104

v

Return-on-Investment Studies 107
Market Research about Web-Based Training 117
Requests for Proposals/Sample Proposals. 131
Cost Estimates for Web-Based Training 149

Chapter 7 Planning for Technology and
Converting Your Curriculum 159
Developing a Technology Plan 159
Converting Your Curriculum 164

Chapter 8 Designing Courses for the Web 187
Basic Web Design Guidelines. 187
Some Elements of Good Web Design. 189
Choosing an Authoring Tool 195
Authoring Tools. 200
Which Tool to Use? 226
Instructional Design for the Web. 230

Chapter 9 Online Testing. 245
Web@ssessor 245
Decisive Survey. 249
Question Mark. 250
Security 254

Chapter 10 Program Administration 261
LOIS 261
Lotus 263
Oracle Learning Architecture. 265
WBTSystems. 268
Empower Corporation: Online Learning
    Development and Distribution Infrastructure. 273
TeamScape's Learning Junction. 279

PART 3 CREATING WEB-BASED TRAINING 285

Chapter 11 Level 1 Courses: Text and Graphics. 287
How to Determine if Text and Graphics Is
    the Way to Go. 288
Creating a Text and Graphics Web-Based
    Training Course. 290
Creating an E-Mail Course 296

Planning a Discussion Forum and E-Mail Course . . . 298
Creating an Online Course: A Case Study. 300
Creating a Discussion Forum/Board:
  A Case Study 301
Text and Graphics with Live Training:
  A Case Study 303

Chapter 12 Level 2 Courses: Interactive
Text and Graphics 309
Interactive Text and Graphics Course Defined 309
Creating Interactive Text and Graphics 312
Off-the-Shelf Courses 322
External Development 332

Chapter 13 Level 3 Courses:
Interactive Multimedia 341
How to Determine if Interactive Multimedia
  Is Right for You 342
Creating Interactive Multimedia 348
Distance Learning and Computer-Based
  Training in One 377

PART 4 APPENDIXES 381

Appendix A Sample Proposal 383

Appendix B Criteria for Evaluating Programs. 403
The Multimedia and Internet Training Awards
  Criteria for Evaluating Web-Based Training. 403

Appendix C Legal Issues 413
Copyright Law Basics 414
Online Copyright Issues. 421
Licensing 422
Rights of Publicity and Privacy 427

Appendix D Online Curriculum Providers. 431
MOLI. 431
ZDU 434
Logical Operations' LearnItOnline. 438
Gartner Internet Training Group 438

Appendix E Sample Code. 443
   Randysoft's OPIE 443
   Altos Education Network Questionnaire Code 453
   Practising Law Institute Sample Code. 461
   NASA Kennedy Space Center WIT
    (Web Interactive Training). 465

Appendix F About the CD-ROM and Web Site 473
   User Assistance and Information 474

Index 475

↳ Introduction

As we wrapped up the manuscript for this book, down to the wire on our deadline, one of the many people we talked to in the Internet training industry asked if she could submit some information to the book a week late. "No time!" we cried. "We're working in Internet weeks!"

It's true—the fast-paced nature of new information technology means that almost as soon as technology is introduced, it's changed and improved upon. The corporate training world is rushing to keep up with these changes, and has begun to cite the World Wide Web as the way to do it.

Ironically, just when trainers are tripping over themselves to keep employees familiar with new hardware, software, and manufacturing products, companies are slashing training budgets and spreading employees out across the globe. Trainers are responding to the challenge of training in this new environment by using the same information technology that allowed businesses to expand globally: the Internet and the World Wide Web.

The World Wide Web opens up the possibilities of global training, which can be accessed by any user, any time, at any location, as long as he or she has the necessary connection to the Internet. Because all of the training information is housed in one location, updates to the rapidly changing content of many training courses can be issued instantaneously to every user. The development costs are relatively low, compared to the high media development costs of CD-ROM and the high costs associated with delivery for instructor-led training. Online testing software for the World Wide Web also eases many of the headaches caused by delivering paper-based tests, and provides a quick and easy way to evaluate students all over the world with a safe "no-cheat" guarantee. As we move toward the millennium, with a need for more training in more places at a lower cost, fingers begin to point more and more frequently to the Web as a means of delivery. Recent Return-On-Investment studies show that Web-based training, while it may initially have higher development costs because of the need to learn new technology, has lower development costs over time. The delivery is inexpensive, and the programming, because of the simple text-based language used for the World Wide Web known as HTML (Hyper Text Markup Language), is much easier than programming for CD-ROM.

Web training has already been installed in a variety of organizations, many of which are profiled in case studies throughout this book. The Web-based training programs encountered in the process of researching this book spanned the spectrum from simple text lessons sent from instructor to learner via e-mail to NASA's grand multimedia high-tech training program at the Kennedy Space Center. Companies of every nature from Levi Strauss and Charles Schwab to Nike and Federal Express are working on training programs delivered over the Web.

While the Web is useful for training about static or unchanging material, it is most handy for trainers who need to update their courseware frequently. Three areas that have seen generous growth in Web-based training (and will continue to see exponentially greater growth) are software- and computer-related hardware education, training for technologically advancing products, and training in soft skills like management, leadership, and customer service.

The Internet, which has partnered with higher education longer than with the corporate world, is also being used to deliver university correspondence courses. Every possibility for using a rapid-delivery, multimedia-capable, instantly-updatable delivery system for training and education is being explored.

Who Should Read This Book

While some organizations plunge right in to full Web delivery of their training, many organizations we spoke with recommended a tiptoe method. "Get your feet wet, explore the technology, and learn as you go," seemed to be the recurring recommendation. This book will offer some suggestions about getting started, as well as some ways to get your feet wet. While a full multimedia, Web-delivered program might be overwhelming for a company just beginning to explore the Internet, starting with a basic course of a text-and-graphics nature, possibly converted from curriculum already in the company's training program, may make for an easier transition. Other organizations also recommended preparing your training audience for the transition by offering standard instructor-led seminars which are prefaced by a Web-based training module that students take before attending the seminar. This method gives the instructor the insurance that all attendees will have had the same preparation. Learners, trainers and managers all have to be ready to approach the Web as a training tool to make the transition successful.

Whether you are an internal training or IT professional or an external multimedia developer, you have in your hands all you need to successfully get started in this area. Online instruction is likely to dramatically change the field of training. This book is a starting point, a launching pad. What you do with this information will make a difference for you and your organization.

What You'll Find

Even if the technology of the Internet and World Wide Web is foreign to you, don't turn away from Web-based training. Increasingly simplified user tools are being developed even as you read, and the following chapters can bring you up to speed on the basics of these new information delivery systems. A variety of tools for producing online courses and testing are described, as well as hints from the experts about how to most successfully design instruction for Web delivery.

This book will help you decide whether Web-based training is right for your organization and will provide you with specific guidelines covering the major areas and technologies. We will cover instructional design, success stories, funding your project, cost-justification research, hardware, software, networks, authoring tools, and industry resources. We will discuss the trade-offs of creating training internally using outside developers, and purchasing of off-the-shelf programs.

This book is organized into four parts. Part 1, "What You Need to Know about Web-Based Training," will introduce you to the basics. Chapter 1 introduces you to the three types of WBT that will be discussed in the book, and gives examples. All the answers to frequently asked questions about Web-based training can be found in Chapter 2. Chapters 3 and 4 present a general overview of the Internet technology, hardware, and software you'll need to be familiar with to get started.

Part 2, "Planning, Developing, and Implementing Web-Based Training," walks you through all the steps involved in setting up a Web-based training program. Chapter 5 describes the steps of the development process and introduces you to the members of the development team. Chapter 6 builds a business case for WBT—and identifies the business concerns you'll likely encounter. Chapter 6 also contains Return-on-Investment studies, current market research on WBT, a sample request for proposal, and cost estimates for creating and implementing a Web-based training program. Chapter 7 develops a technology plan, and Chapter 8 addresses basic design guidelines and authoring tools. Chapter 9 introduces some of the testing applications already available, and Chapter 10 covers administration tools.

Part 3, "Creating Web-Based Training," integrates Parts I and II into working examples of Web-based training courses. Chapters 11, 12, and 13 cover, in more detail, the three types of training programs introduced in Chapter 1 and how the stages of planning, developing, and implementing are integrated.

The appendixes provide a sample proposal that was received in response to the request for proposal found in Chapter 6, criteria for evaluating WBT programs, legal issues you need to consider when developing a WBT program, and a list of online curriculum providers. You'll also find code from the sample WBT programs covered in the book, along with a description of what each piece of code represents.

The CD-ROM and Companion Web Site

Code for the examples of the Web-based training programs discussed in the book is also provided on the accompanying CD-ROM, along with an HTML interface with the links to the online training programs referred to in the book and some additional examples. There's also a link to the companion Web site (www.brandon-hall.com) where you'll find further information, updates, and links to other resources.

Acknowledgments

A book like this is an effort by many people. Foremost in their contribution is the staff of the *Multimedia & Internet Training Newsletter*. Polly Sprenger brought quality research, writing, and project coordination to this manuscript, as well as great resourcefulness and enthusiasm. John Graham contributed substantial research and writing to the technology chapters. Valerie Merrill pulled the pieces together as the manuscript and graphics coordinator. Karyn Goldstein, Pat Forward, Kristina Allen, and Keri Hayes contributed Web research and editing to many of the case studies. Beth Levis and Sharon Beach provided administrative support. Thank you all for your dedication to this project.

I have been involved in training for twenty years, and what I want to do more than anything else is contribute to the growth and nurturing of this field and to the design of great training.

The way I help is by researching and shining the spotlight on the good work of others, and by providing useful information to those who are beginning or expanding their use of multimedia on the Web for training. The creative and productive people who develop the instructional programs and software tools are the stars of this book. A hearty thank you to all who contributed to the case studies and organizational profiles in the book. Margaret Driscoll, Kevin Kruse, and David Metcalf in particular were willing at every turn to share their ideas with us.

There would be no purpose to the research and writing if there was no one to read it. So to all of you who read the newsletter, who attend the conference sessions, thank you for your interest, your support, and your feedback. But most of all, thank you for caring about this field and for seeing the potential of these technologies to the benefit of your organization and to your own future.

One of the hardest parts of doing research for a book like this is actually locating those programs that are the best examples in the world of Internet- and intranet-based training. The job was made easier by the wonderful 97 entrants to our annual Multimedia and Internet Training Awards Program, several of which are highlighted in case studies in the book.

Thanks to those who provided support during the early days of launching the Newsletter: Dr. Ruth Clark, one of the leading thinkers in instructional design, Lauren Martin of Hewlett Packard, and all the members of our editorial board: Steve Bainbridge of Wilson Learning, Michael Allen and Robert Zielinsky of Allen Interactions, Vincent Eugenio of NationsBank, J. Dexter Fletcher of Institute for Defense Analyses, Gloria Gery of Gery Associates, James Goldsmith of Aetna, James Li of Leading Way, David Merrill of Utah State University, George Piskurich, Consultant, Alexandra Rand of Internal/External Communications, Barry Raybould of Ariel PSS, Allison Rossett of San Diego State University, Roger Schank of Northwestern University and the Institute for the Learning Sciences, and Nancy Weingarten of Inside Technology Training.

Others who helped publicize our work include David Holcombe, founding director of Influent, Gillian Newson of *New Media* magazine, Cinda Daley of the annual Interactive Conference & Expo, Ronda Rosenoff of Computer Training & Support Conference, Bill Brandon of Softbank Institute (a true Texas gentleman), Bob Filipczak of *Training* magazine (one of the most decent people in this business, and an early advocate of technology), Lynn Densford, now of Corporate University Review, and Patricia Galagan, Haidee Allerton, and Sacha Cohen of *Training & Development* magazine; plus the conference committees of the American Society for Training & Development and the International Society for Performance Improvement.

Thanks also to my professors from two short decades ago who taught me about instruction and performance, Drs. Bill Walker, Dick Malott, Jack Michaels, Rogers McAvoy and Dick Walls. And thanks to my early colleagues, who inspired all those around them with their intelligence, wit and humanity: Ansley Bacon, Will Ellis, Steve Bono, Tom Werner, Steve VanderPoel, Lyle Grant, and Don Prue.

And finally, thanks to the group at Wiley: Bob Elliott, Editor; Kathryn Malm, Assistant Editor; and Brian Calandra, Editorial Assistant.

P A R T   1

WHAT YOU

NEED TO

KNOW ABOUT

WEB-BASED

TRAINING

CHAPTER ONE

EXAMPLES OF WEB-BASED TRAINING

Web-based training is making a difference in organizations today by providing a way of delivering training that is often less expensive and more convenient than the alternatives. There are effective programs now on the Web in each of the three main categories of training: computer training, technical training, and soft skills training. The technology for delivery over the Internet or an intranet is improving rapidly and, in a year or so, the state of the art for multimedia Web-based training will be at the level of state-of-the-art multimedia CD-ROM–delivered training. In this chapter we will begin by taking a look at some of the types of training the Web has to offer.

Because this is such a new medium, the distinctions between the various types of Web-based training (WBT) are still forming. In this book, I have used levels of interactivity and amount of multimedia as the primary distinguishing factors between different training programs. This is not necessarily a qualitative judgment, however, because training programs are developed to meet specific training needs, and I don't want to minimize the accomplishments of those programs that don't use the latest multimedia technologies that are available for the Web. If multimedia was not a required element when the program was designed, then a bare-bones approach may be more appropriate. There is, after all, such a thing as too much media, too many bells and whistles. However, training that incorporates too much interactivity is extremely rare. Holding the attention of the student and engaging the user's mind is necessary for learning to occur. Interactivity makes the difference between a program that simply presents information, and one that actually trains the user.

↳ Type 1—Text and Graphics Web-Based Training Programs

Text and graphics programs are sometimes simply paper-based course materials placed on the Web so that students can access them in electronic format. The worst of these programs are throwbacks to the dreaded text-only, mainframe-delivered courses of the 1970s. These courses are assigned the most pejorative of appellations: "page turners." While that is a positive comment for a book, it is a negative one for computer-delivered training, since no one wants to use a program in which one mainly reads off a computer screen, and is engaged only by clicking the forward arrow. On the other hand, some text and graphics programs designed from the ground up for Web delivery can be an appropriate solution for a given training need. Many contain hyperlinks to other material for further study, or to charts and graphs that further illustrate the learning point. These pages usually provide a lower level of interactivity, although not necessarily a lower level of information.

For the majority of sites that utilize the text and graphics approach, no authoring tools were used other than what was necessary for creating HTML coded text.

One example of a text and graphics model profiled later in the book is the Cyber Travel Specialist from New Media Strategies, Inc. The training program is designed to teach travel agents all over the country about how the Internet will be useful to them as a business tool. The curriculum developed for the course is a combination of a Web-based training module, a hands-on workshop, and a lecture. For an audience who may not yet be comfortable with a training course delivered completely over the Web, Cyber Travel Specialist Training eases them into the new technology.

The text and graphics model is the place many people start with development of Web-based training, because it is the easiest to create and is accessible to the most people. However, in many cases it can only minimally be considered training. To gain greater effectiveness from this medium, one needs to move to the next level and add more interactivity.

⬐ Type 2—Interactive Web-Based Training Programs

To engage the learner with stimulating interactivity is the promise and the future of computer-delivered instruction, whether delivered on CD-ROM or the Web. Interactivity and instructional design is to Web-based training as a good storyline is to a movie or gameplay is to a video game. Interactivity at its best is a simulation of the work situation. At a minimum, it can include application exercises, drag-and-drop, column matching, testing, text entry, and even programming code entry. This goes beyond simple text and graphics presentation and brings the learner into the program to engage with the content and practice the skills.

A terrific example of an interactive WBT course is the courseware developed by Randy Hootman of Randysoft (www.randysoft.com). He has designed a series of tutorials that teach programming languages, including HTML, Perl, and others (Figure 1.1).

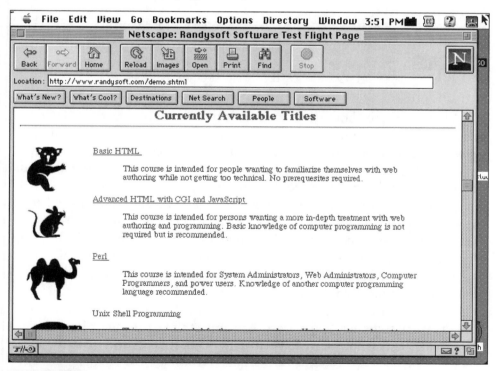

FIGURE 1.1 This page from Randysoft's site shows the available courses.

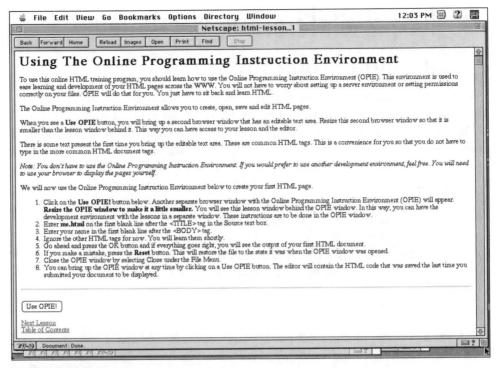

FIGURE 1.2 An explanation screen from the Randysoft courseware describing OPIE—the Online Programming Instruction Environment.

What is unique about these courses is that they provide a simulated programming environment that allows you to actually enter code into an open text area, submit the code, and immediately see the results of your new programming skills. Assessment is done in real-time and the user can see what, if anything, he or she did wrong (Figures 1.2 and 1.3).

The Bank of Montreal's Institute of Learning recently established an interactive WBT course for use by their divisions in Canada and the United Kingdom. The training challenge, discussed in further detail in the chapter on interactive courses, was to provide online training for all corporate users on the bank's CenterPoint system, an object-oriented desktop which acts as a platform for all other applications used by Bank of Montreal's employees. "CenterPoint has changed the way our corporate bankers work together," says Kristi Kustura of the Institute of Learning. "It provides access to external and internal data sources and systems, and enables cross-functional teaming and knowledge sharing. Currently, the only training available for CenterPoint occurs via classroom training and video. New users have no immediate training option other than waiting for a CenterPoint workshop to be scheduled. This, however, is both a logistical and economic problem as it requires flying our facilitator back and forth to remote locations across the world."

The Institute of Learning decided to use the bank's intranet to deliver the CenterPoint training because it capitalized on the existing technology infrastructure. The group put up the initial training, but found a greater level of interactivity was needed. On the basis of a pilot test, they found they needed to redesign the module and add new features like a gauge during feedback screens to tell users how far along they are in the tutorial. The development team at the Institute of Learning is also examining further built-in evaluation and measurement features for additional testing.

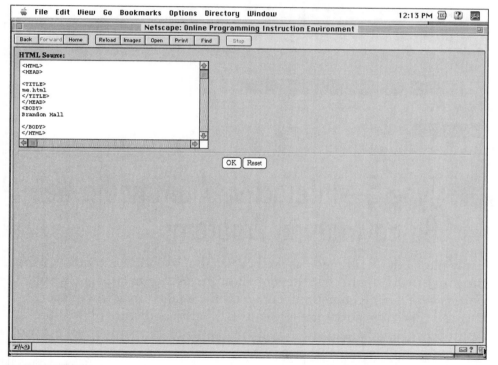

FIGURE 1.3 Screen showing HTML source code in the Online Programming Instruction Environment.

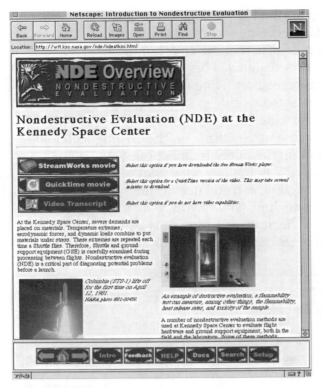

FIGURE 1.4 NASA's Nondestructive Evaluation Overview.

Courtesy I-NET Multimedia and NASA

 # Type 3—Interactive Multimedia Web-Based Training Programs

Truly interactive multimedia is the holy grail of Web-based training. Most programs that fall into this category allow the user to manipulate graphic objects in real-time, sometimes taking on the quality of a game-playing exercise. The simulations are realistic and the situations are often difficult. Appropriate use of audio and/or video helps from an instructional point of view and from the human side as well.

The promise of interactive multimedia training was realized with CD-ROM technology. It allowed the large audio or video files to be stored on a portable disk and presented nicely on the computer screen, without the wait times of the Internet. The Web is following close behind with improved transfer speeds, and is an improvement on the CD-ROM in terms of storage space and ease of update. Once you record data onto a CD-ROM, it is there forever. Information on a Web site can be easily updated as often as necessary.

The interactive multimedia type of WBT programs are usually authored with a software tool that allows for the programming necessary to add the multimedia and manage the high levels of interactivity and record keeping. Java applets can be built to manage this, but most authors prefer the traditional full-scale authoring tools, such as Authorware or ToolBook II, which have plug-ins for delivery over the Internet.

An interactive multimedia course allows the student to enter into a world that attempts to mimic a part of real life, providing immediate, real-life responses to user input. If something goes wrong, such as the student

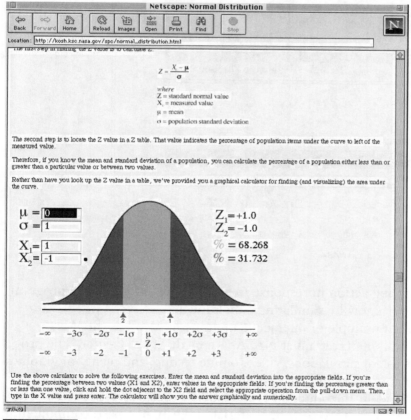

FIGURE 1.5 NASA's Introduction to Statistical Processes.

Courtesy I-NET Multimedia and NASA

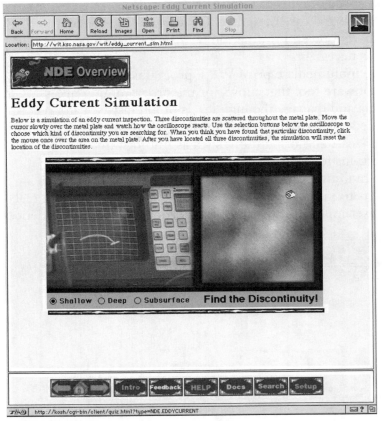

FIGURE 1.6 The Eddy Current Simulation of NASA's NDE Overview is an example of one of the courses designed for NASA managers who work on quality control, safety, and reliability efforts.

Courtesy I-NET Multimedia and NASA

taking the wrong action in response to a hazardous situation, the program lets him or her know by simulating a meltdown.

An excellent example of interactive multimedia WBT is the Web Interactive Training program at NASA's Kennedy Space Center. The program makes use of simulations, video, online testing, and plenty of graphics.

The two courses include the Nondestructive Evaluation Overview (Figure 1.4) and an Introduction to Statistical Processes (Figure 1.5). The first teaches users how to test the material integrity of a part, component, or system without damaging it and the second course presents a method to monitor processes and determine if adjustments in process parameters are

FIGURE 1.7 The office metaphor.

needed. The courses are geared toward NASA managers who work on quality control, safety, and reliability efforts (Figure 1.6).

NASA has evaluated the courses and is reportedly pleased. They are saving money on first-time development costs, in-class instructor costs, and travel costs with the implementation of Web-based training. Lead multimedia designer David Metcalf and rest of the development team are in the process of producing an advanced NDE Radiography course and an advanced Statistical Process Control course.

Another good example of an interactive multimedia WBT course is Oracle Simulator, developed by Empower for database administrators. The program emulates real-life backup and recovery situations for server manager software, from the ringing phone of a distraught user's call, to implementing the software solution.

The simulation takes place in the hotline office of a fictitious company called DBA (Figure 1.7). The user acts as the hotline contact. Customers

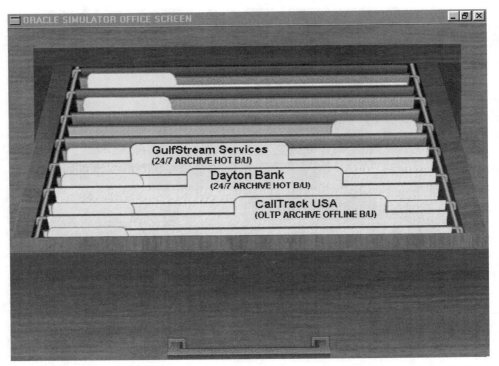

FIGURE 1.8 Users click a file folder tab to choose a customer in DBA office.

call on the phone to report database administration problems that need to be fixed.

The DBA office represents a typical office environment, including a file drawer that contains files of customers and their database problems (Figure 1.8). The desk drawer contains files on DBA hotline customers. The user clicks on a file folder tab to choose a customer.

The file folder contains general information about the customer's company and database.

In the program, customers call you on the speakerphone. The customer outlines the basic database problem, then sends an e-mail detailing the problem (Figure 1.9). You can click on the phone at any time to listen to the customer's message again.

The computer in the simulation is used for video conferences with your on-call expert, for interactions with your customer via e-mail and video

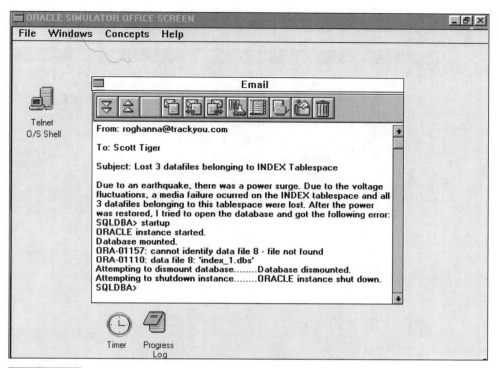

FIGURE 1.9 Customer's e-mail detailing the problem.

conference, and for viewing a log of the information you've received from the expert and the customer (Figure 1.10).

As you solve the database problem using server manager, your on-call advisor, or mentor, guides you through various choices using a desktop video conference window metaphor. A progress log screen records all your interactions with the expert and the customer.

The software simulation includes a series of screens from the actual software program. Certain screens ask you to select commands and show you the results of those commands with instructional feedback. As you progress through different pathways of the simulation, the system keeps track of the steps you have taken to solve the problem.

Web-based interactive multimedia is an effective way to provide training in a risk-free environment. Users can see the result of their actions immediately. The use of graphics, audio, and video provide the multimedia

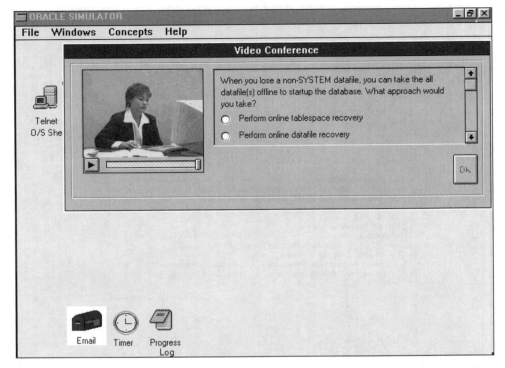

FIGURE 1.10 Video conference window showing discussion with the mentor.

advantage of making the environment more realistic and the training more effective and more enjoyable.

Each of the programs mentioned here will be discussed in greater detail in later chapters. Before we delve into some of the technology needed for Web-based training, the next chapter will answer a few basic questions that commonly arise, starting with "What is Web-based training?"

FAQS: FREQUENTLY ASKED QUESTIONS ABOUT WEB-BASED TRAINING

? What is Web-based training?

Web-based training (WBT) is instruction that is delivered over the Internet or over a company's intranet. The training is accessed using a Web browser, such as Netscape Navigator. Other types of Internet training refer to any program that can be delivered from a remote source, even e-mail correspondence courses, or the transfer of files of course materials. Training over the World Wide Web, and training using an intranet's Web, specifically refers to the readily available, interactive, multimedia nature of Web browsers and associated plug-ins.

? Where can Web-based training be delivered?

To any computer—anywhere—that can access the Internet or a company intranet. This includes a desktop at work, field service engineers on the road, and telecommuters at home.

? What are the advantages of Web-based training?

The technology is cross platform. Unlike other forms of computer-based training, Web-based training can be accessed by Windows, Mac, or UNIX users, usually without requiring additional software. You author the training program once, and deliver it to any machine over the Internet or your intranet.

Widely available Internet connections and browsers. Most computer users have access to a browser such as Netscape Navigator, and are connected to a company's intranet or have access to the Internet. Accessing Web-based training doesn't require much more than that.

Flexibility, accessibility, convenience. Users can proceed through a training program "at their own pace and at their own place." They can also access the training at the time of need, and only as much as they need, known as "Just in time and just enough."

Cost savings and time savings. Because the Internet can be accessed from any location, there are no travel costs for bringing remote employees to a centralized workshop. And, as indicated in my report "Return on Investment and Multimedia Training" (1995, *Multimedia and Internet Training Newsletter*), since the actual time required for training by computer averages about 50 percent that of instructor-led training, additional cost savings are realized.

Inexpensive worldwide distribution. Web-based training can be accessed from any computer anywhere in the world, greatly reducing the distribution costs associated with training in other media.

Ease of update. If changes need to be made in the program after the original implementation, they can be made on the server which stores the program and everyone worldwide can access the update. Courses can be designed to access designated current information, such as the latest new product specifications, from any other server worldwide for on-the-fly update whenever anyone accesses the program.

? What are the disadvantages of Web-based training?

Bandwidth is limited. Limited bandwidth means slower performance for sound, video, and even extensive graphics. These restrictions can cause long waits for download and can adversely affect the learning process. The problem can be serious over the public Internet where more traffic jams occur, but is less severe on a company's intranet, which usually has greater bandwidth.

Are computers replacing human contact? There's a general concern that as we move toward more computer usage, a glowing terminal replaces a friendly face. Decreasing instructor-led training makes some trainees uneasy.

Today's Web-based training programs are sometimes too static. As an emerging technology, the level of interactivity in Web-based training is too often limited. This is gradually improving, and as it does the impact of the training on performance also improves.

Web-based training takes more time and more money to develop than expected. Like any first-time challenge, learning about and implementing new technology takes more resources (and more aspirin) than expected. You can make it easier by starting with a simple program and building on success.

Not all courses should be delivered by computer. Some training topics are not best served by computer-based training and require a more personal touch. Team-building activities and dealing with emotional issues such as downsizing come to mind.

? Why did you choose to call it Web-based training?

Web-based training and Internet-based training are the two most widely used and widely understood terms for this type of training. We conducted a survey of readers of the *Multimedia and Internet Training Newsletter* as well as the subscribers to our discussion-based mailing list, WEBTRAINING-L, to see which term people were using most often. There was no clear first choice and both terms are likely to remain popular. As technology evolves, so does terminology.

? What is multimedia training?

Multimedia training is a type of computer-based training that uses two or more media, including text, graphics, animation, audio (sound/music), and video. In practice, multimedia uses as many of these media as is practical to produce a colorful, engaging program delivered via the computer. A typical program allows users to control their progress and pace through the course so everyone can learn at his or her own speed. A catch-phrase that reflects this impact is, "With Computer-based training, we captured their heads; with multimedia we capture their hearts."

? What are some other terms and technologies used for training?

- *Computer-based training (CBT)*—an all-encompassing term used to describe any computer-delivered training including CD-ROM and the World Wide Web. Some people use the term CBT to refer only to old-time text-only training.

- *Distance learning*—in its most common historical form, this refers to a broadcast of a lecture to distant locations, usually through video presentations.

- *Desktop training*—any training delivered by computer at one's desk.

- *Desktop video conferencing*—a real-time conference using live pictures among two or more people on a network who communicate via computer.

- *Interactive training*—an umbrella term that includes both computer-based and multimedia training.

- *Computer-assisted instruction*—a term used more commonly in education for any instruction where a computer is used as a learning tool.

- *Self-paced training*—training which is taken at a time and a pace determined by the user (kind of like reading this book). Used historically for text or audio/video self-study courses, the term is used by some organizations now to include computer-based, web-based, and multimedia training.

? What are other related terms for delivering training over a network?

There are other terms for remote access training, including Internet-based training, intranet-based training, online training, and net-based training.

- *Internet-based training*—any training that can be accessed over the Internet. Usually this is done with the World Wide Web, but e-mail correspondence courses and file transfers also fall into this category.

- *Intranet-based training*—training based on a company's internal network. Web browsers are used to access company pages, but they are only accessible within the company.

- *Online training*—an all-encompassing term that refers to any training done with a computer over a network, including a company's intranet, the company's local area network, and the Internet.

- *Net-based training*—same as online training.

? What is driving the interest in Web-based training?

New demands in organizations are increasing the interest in Web-based training on a daily basis. The need for less expensive ways to deliver training has led many companies to explore the option of Web-based training. The convenience for users of the programs—at their own pace, at their own place—and the engaging nature of the multimedia delivery are big advantages. The centralized nature of Web-delivered training makes the delivery standardized for all users who take the course. Web-based training is often less expensive and more convenient than the alternatives. Web-based training is a fascinating new field, which will likely have a vast impact on all professionals in the field. And it's fun to use and develop for, too.

? Is this a medium worth investing in?

Yes. More and more information services and programs within organizations are moving to the World Wide Web. The Web can provide the most efficient delivery of information because of its ability to be accessible from anywhere, anytime, and to disseminate a standardized, updatable version to multiple users.

With careful attention to instructional design during the development phase, Web training can be a valuable addition to your company's training and performance support offerings.

The Web and Web technologies have already had a major impact on the way businesses communicate, but this is a dynamic medium, and many more changes are in store.

? How can I justify investing in Web-based training?

People may be wary of new technology, but significant cost savings have a way of catching management's attention. Lower training costs result from the reduction in time and resources for delivery, especially through eliminating the cost of traveling to distant learning sites.

? How can I determine whether Web-based training is right for our organization?

There are several questions you can use to assess the viability of Web-based training for your company:

1. Will management support the effort?

2. Are there enough potential users to justify the cost of purchase or development?

3. Does the target audience use, or can they learn to use, a computer?

4. Will users accept a Web-based program?

5. Will users learn from this particular program?

6. Does the program provide a method of instruction that is easier, faster, cheaper, safer, or more engaging than the alternative?

? What criteria should be used in evaluating Web-based training?

Here are ten criteria we use in judging for the semiannual Multimedia and Internet Training Awards:

1. Content

   Does the program include the right amount and quality of information?

2. Instructional Design

   Is the course designed in such a way that users will actually learn?

3. Interactivity

   Are users engaged through the opportunity for their input?

4. Navigation

   Can users determine their own way through the program? Is there an exit option available? Is there a course map accessible?

   Is there an appropriate use of icons and/or clear labels so that users don't have to read excessively to determine program options?

5. Motivational Components

   Does the program engage users through novelty, humor, game elements, testing, adventure, unique content, surprise elements, and so on?

6. Use of Media

   Does the program appropriately and effectively employ graphics, animation, music, sound, and video?

   Is the gratuitous use of these media avoided?

7. Evaluation

   Is there some type of evaluation, such as completion of a simulation?

   Is mastery of each section's content required before proceeding to later sections?

   Are section quizzes used?

   Is there a final exam?

8. Aesthetics

   Is the program attractive and appealing to the eye and ear?

9. Record Keeping

   Is student performance data recorded, such as time to complete, question analyses, and final scores? Is the data forwarded to the course manager automatically?

10. Tone

    Is the program designed for its audience? Does it avoid being condescending, trite, pedantic, and so on?

? What is the difference between the World Wide Web and the Internet?

The Internet includes all electronic transmissions, including e-mail, file transfers, and the Web. The Web is just one part of the Internet, but it is the fastest growing, most promising part, especially where training is concerned.

? What about the overall impact of the Internet?

Someone pretty bright put it well: "The Internet is being overhyped but underestimated." The Internet will change everything.

? How can I influence decision makers to use Web-based training versus traditional training options?

The costs for a Web-based training program are often lower than those associated with instructor-led training. The biggest hurdle is often the initial costs for the investment in learning the technology and the development time. Companies are finding that the costs associated with the delivery of the training are much lower than for traditional methods.

? How can I motivate employees to use Web-based training?

Any motivation strategies you use now for other training can be applied to Web-based training. In addition, the tracking and reporting available with Web-based training allows you to structure requirements and rewards for completion and mastery. Develop some enthusiastic in-house marketing that will convince students that the perks of Web-based training are just as rewarding as the free coffee and donuts offered at their favorite seminars.

? How can management be assured employees are actually completing the program?

Because Web-based training programs are designed to be "at your own pace," the importance of tracking a student's progress is a concern. The program can be created with specific controls that keep track of where employees are in the course, and how well they are doing. The major authoring tools allow you to automatically keep track of employees' scores, progress, time spent on a lesson, and so on.

? How can I help my training staff, who are used to instructor-led training, make the transition and embrace Web-based training?

To make the transition easier for trainers as well as students, some organizations include elements of both Web-based training and ILT for some programs, especially early on. There are a variety of new roles and career opportunities for those who are willing to adapt to the new technologies.

? What kind of team is necessary to develop Web-based training?

Teams range from just one, very dedicated person who does it all, to project teams of over 40 professionals.

In general, at a minimum you will need:

- A project manager capable of dealing with diverse work styles and personalities

- An instructional designer familiar with computer-delivered instruction
- A programmer or author to use the authoring tool
- A graphic artist
- A subject matter expert
- A Webmaster for maintaining the program on the server
- Someone who can obtain funding for Web-based training from management

The people you use, naturally, will have either one or a combination of the above skills.

? How much multimedia is being used now for Web-based training?

Multimedia on the Web is growing in popularity with languages like Java and plug-ins for authoring tools like Shockwave and Neuron making it possible. Bandwidth is the major limitation and, right now, the vision and the potential are greater than the reality.

? How about multimedia in the future for Web-based training?

Emerging technologies will provide greater bandwidth (i.e., bigger pipes), and greater compression (i.e., lower fat) for delivering audio and video. It is only a matter of time before multimedia over a company's network and the Internet is commonplace. In the meantime, hybrid CDs, also known as Internet CDs, are an alternative in which the program with audio and video are delivered on a CD-ROM, with updates delivered automatically over the Web. This must be what it was like in Detroit in the early 1900s when car makers were trying to figure out basic technologies, such as getting a manual transmission to work. Everyone knew the problems would get solved and just about everyone was working on it.

? How do I determine the appropriate level of interactivity and media?

The type and amount of interactivity required varies with the instructional objectives of a program. It is generally not possible for a program to be "too interactive." However, it is possible for a program to suffer from too many multimedia bells and whistles, when they are gratuitous and don't contribute to meeting the instructional objectives.

? From an instructional designer's perspective, how is Internet-based training different from multimedia training?

Designing for the Internet presents a special problem. Connection speeds can be slow and downloads can be long due to factors over which trainers often have no control. Until bandwidth improves, design out most of the "fat media" in the program, especially video. Design in interactivity, discussion, and access to other resources that are part of the benefit of training online.

? From a student perspective, how is Web-based training different from CD-ROM–based training?

CD-ROM–based training programs usually have their own unique interface. Web-based training requires a Web browser, so the basic navigation scheme is usually familiar to the student. Students who will be receiving the Web-based training should be familiar with how to use a browser. (However, some Web-based training programs are designed to replace the browser window while the course is running.) In general, the student should see little difference in the actual training once it has been accessed. If the training is over an intranet, the difference is not very noticeable, but over the Internet, the connection speeds and download times are often much slower than CD-ROMs.

? I have noticed that some online training programs, especially when offered through a public Web site like Microsoft's On-Line Learning Institute (MOLI), have a learning assistant or facilitator as part of the learning process. Is this necessary?

An assistant or facilitator available online can be helpful but your training can be designed without them. An online assistant can help handle customer service issues or technical problems. A facilitator can help with content issues and can guide discussions. Web-based training, especially when designed within an organization, is usually designed to be a standalone process to be engaged in at any time of the day or night. Even in the latter case, having e-mail access to a Webmaster, course manager, or content expert can be helpful.

? Can existing CBT be converted into Web-based training?

The major authoring tools (described in Chapter 8) allow you to create both a standalone version of the program and a Web version of the program. Depending on which authoring tool you used to create a preexisting CBT program, you may be able to convert most of it for delivery over the Web.

? Can I use Web technology on a company's internal network?

Yes. In many companies, the same technology used for the Internet exists on the internal local area network, which is then referred to as an intranet. While the public Internet is getting all the publicity in the press, the fastest-growing segment of the market for Web browsers and servers are companies' internal intranets.

? What hardware is required by the end user?

- A computer fast enough to handle the training program. For Windows computers, a 486 is okay, but Pentium or better is preferred. For Macintosh computers, a 68040-based machine is okay, but a PowerPC is preferred.

- A sound card capable of playing back any audio files the training program uses.

- A network connection, whether it is a digital line connected directly to the company server, or a modem that can dial into the Internet. If your training were delivered via the company intranet, for example, your users would not need a separate Internet connection.

? What software is required by the end user?

- A web browser.
- Any specialized browser plug-ins or controls that are required by the particular training program, such as audio or video.

? Does the end user need the same computer system as the developer?

No. One of the major advantages of Web-based training over other types of computer-based training is cross-platform compatibility. Web browsers can access Web-based training using a language that is platform-independent.

? What special programming languages do I have to know to create programs for the Web?

Although you need to be somewhat savvy in all things Web-ish, there are no complicated programming languages you need to learn. In general, you should be familiar with HTML, although this is not required if you are using one of the high-level HTML editors, such as Microsoft's FrontPage, which allows you to create Web pages without HTML. The major authoring programs are nearly the same whether you are developing for CD-ROM or the Web. There are also "object oriented" visual tools for programming with Java, such as Aimtech's Jamba.

? I have heard about Java, Shockwave, and other technologies for delivering multimedia over the Web. How much do I need to know technically to take advantage of these?

Java is a programming language that allows the developer to create small applications called applets that control specific aspects of a Web-based training program, such as creating interactive animations. Shockwave is a plug-in for programs developed with Macromedia's Authorware so these programs can be viewed with a Web browser over the Web. There is also the Neuron plug-in, which allows ToolBook II applications to be viewed with a Web browser. You should be aware of what Java is capable of, although the specifics of programming a Java applet are not necessary if you use the right authoring tool. Or send one of your staff off to authoring school.

❓ What kinds of authoring systems are available for Web-based training?

Authorware, ToolBook II, IconAuthor, Quest, IBTAuthor, CBIQuick, and many others are currently available, most with training components built in. If you want to start with a simple program, an HTML editor or Web page layout program like Netscape Navigator Gold, Microsoft FrontPage, Claris Home Page, or Asymetrix Web Publisher may be all you need.

❓ What is Adobe Acrobat? Do I need to use it?

Acrobat is used when existing documents need to be displayed on screen or downloaded in the same format as they appear on paper. Acrobat saves the graphics and font files along with the text of the document so that it always looks exactly the same on the screen no matter where or how it is viewed. Government agencies use Acrobat for electronic versions of reports and papers because they need to make references to specific page numbers. You can use Acrobat to reproduce existing company documents if they need to look the same on the screen as they do on the page. Be aware that HTML has similar functionality.

❓ Should the training be interactive on the Web or should it be downloaded and used offline?

It depends on the type of training and administration that you are after. Real-time administration, as the user is taking the course, can be achieved while the user is online. Offline programs can be set up to send completion information and test scores at the end of the course, and, if necessary, download another portion of the course. But if a student is taking a course offline, he or she may not be aware of any updates to the program that may occur while the course is in progress. If the online course requires a change or update of some part of the data or coding, the student is not disrupted and does not have to initiate another download of the entire course.

❓ Where is the water cooler?

Down the corridor on the right. Just past the cubicle with all the Dilbert cartoons.

? How fast a connection is needed to access Web-based training effectively?

If your program utilizes video, animation, and audio, the connection should be as fast as possible. For home office users, this means ISDN or 56Kbps modems. If the training utilizes limited graphics and no audio or video, then a minimal connection via a 14.4 modem should be adequate.

? What is bandwidth?

The actual speed available at the time of the transmission. The more users on a network, the less bandwidth available for that transmission.

? How can I calculate how fast my program will be delivered over a network?

It is difficult to calculate actual speeds because bandwidth varies so often. One moment, your training might be delivered at 6.5Kbps; the next it may be 1 or 2Kbps or even less. In general, your files are calculated in bytes (MB, KB, etc.) and bandwidth is measured in bits (Mb, Kb, etc.). To determine how many bits your program is, multiply the number of bytes by 8. A program that takes up 4 megabytes of space takes up 32 megabits. If your connection speed is 2Mbps (megabits per second), it would take 16 seconds to download. Alternatively, over an Internet connection of 33.6Kbps (.336Mbps) your 32Mb training would take about 96 seconds. All this is assuming ideal conditions. And, of course, conditions are always less than ideal.

? Do I need a Web server to provide Internet-based training?

A Web server is needed to have the training available to others. The options are a server maintained by your department or information technology (IT) department, or a public Internet service provider (ISP).

? Once a course is developed, how do I get it on the Internet or intranet?

Most of the time it is just a matter of placing your program and its accompanying files on your server, then testing to ensure it works properly. Ask your network administrator, Webmaster, or ISP provider how to upload the files to the Web site.

How can I charge for courses over the Internet?

The most utilized method is to have users pay up front by credit card, then give them a password that lets them into the program once payment has been made. Security for taking payment over the Internet is relatively good. For internal programs over an intranet, course registration software can automate chargebacks to the paying department.

I've heard about viruses, hackers, and so on. What about security?

Your company's intranet should be protected from hacker intrusions from the public Internet by a firewall. Your IT department or network administrator can recommend virus protection software. While these problems exist and make big news in the media, the percentage of incidents is quite small and should not deter your deploying Web-based training.

What is a firewall?

A firewall is a hardware and/or software security measure implemented by companies with internal intranets to keep out unwanted transmissions or visitors from the Internet. An effective firewall will keep out hackers, casual users, and accidental queries while allowing access to legitimate users of the company's intranet from a remote location. Some firewalls limit the ability of employees within the company to download files from the Internet.

Where can I view existing Web-based training programs?

This book provides examples of publicly available training programs. You can access these programs by entering the URL in a Web browser, or by using the hyperlink supplied on the CD-ROM that accompanies this book.

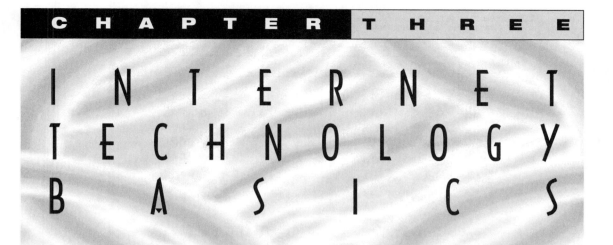

CHAPTER THREE

INTERNET TECHNOLOGY BASICS

One of the great advantages of Web-based training is that the Internet and browsers are becoming so popular. Almost everyone has at least a passing familiarity with the technology. This chapter provides a general overview of the Internet and the technology, as well as the skills you'll need to use this technology properly.

If you are unfamiliar with the World Wide Web, this chapter will provide you with basic information about the Web, your browser, and the different programming languages you'll come across. However, if you have mastered the Web, feel free to skim or skip this chapter.

 ## The Web

The World Wide Web was originally used as a platform for delivering graphics and formatted text over the Internet. Since the single interface for accessing the information available on the Web is the browser, the Web has become an ideal platform for delivering training. Any program created in any format for the Web is accessible through a Web browser.

At its core, the Web is an information retrieval system. The available information can come in the form of text, graphics, animation, audio, video, and multimedia files, all viewable through a browser application. The information for Web pages is stored on computers all over the world,

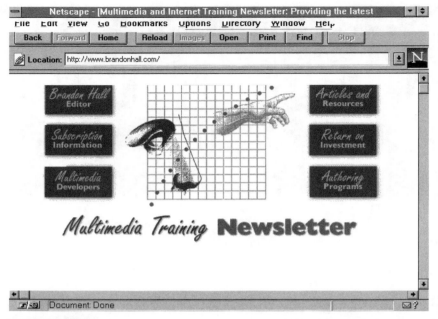

FIGURE 3.1 The *Multimedia and Internet Training Newsletter* home page.

called *servers*. Each server has its own address, or URL (Uniform Resource Locator), so that it can be accessed by Internet users. Each URL points to a particular Web site, which contains files for presenting a viewable Web page. For instance, to access the *Multimedia and Internet Training Newsletter* go to the URL: http://www.multimediatraining.com. Your screen should look like Figure 3.1.

Servers require that you log in with a user name and password every time you access them. However, Web browsers were designed to automatically submit a type of skeleton key called an anonymous ID. Servers recognize these IDs so that people using Web browsers will be given access automatically. Some Web sites, however, do require a special password to access special content, such as a training program which may be available only to paid registrants of that course.

Transferring Information on the Web

The format for file transfer between computers, or *protocol*, for the Web is called HTTP (Hypertext Transfer Protocol). This is the language that

Internet computers use to talk to each other when transferring Web pages. When you enter a URL in a Web browser for a Web page, you type in http:// before the name of the server to let the browser know that you are looking for a Web page. Other designations, such as ftp://, file://, and gopher://, can be used as well, but these do not reference Web pages specifically. Most browsers have a standard default setting of http, so you only need to key in a designation if you want to use ftp://, gopher://, or file://.

The information on a Web site is stored in a format called hypertext, where portions of text, or even a graphic, can be used to call up, or retrieve, additional information. By activating a hyperlink (usually done by clicking on a highlighted word), the user can access another document, which, in turn, has additional hypertext links. The advantage of this is that the user does not need to know the location of the linked files, because they are accessed automatically when the link is clicked. In www.multimediatraining.com you can go to any of the six hyperlinks listed on the screen including Subscription Information, Multimedia Developers, or Authoring Programs. Figure 3.2 shows the contents of the Brandon Hall hyperlink.

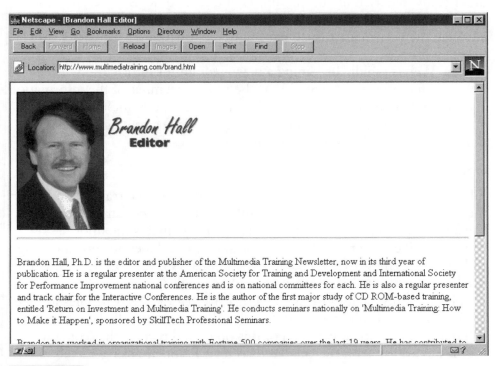

FIGURE 3.2 Hyperlinks can connect you to more specialized areas of a Web site.

Some specialized Web sites take advantage of the linking power of HTML with search engines. These pages allow input from the user about a topic or keyword, and present addresses for Web pages that correspond to the requested topic. Not only are the addresses for the corresponding Web pages displayed, but they are also displayed as hypertext links, so that the pages can be accessed by a simple click of the mouse.

Graphics files can also be displayed anywhere on a Web page, or represented as hyperlinks. The graphics can be static images, animated graphic files, or video files that "play" on the page. The ability to display graphics as well as text is one of the most powerful functions of the Web. The possibilities for combinations of graphics and text are endless. A classic example is the "virtual museum," where art objects are shown with accompanying text about the objects. Links are made to articles that offer criticism or further background on the piece.

This capability allows the Web to lend itself to instruction. Because animations can be shown on the same page as text, processes can be shown as they happen and then explained further in the text. Links can be made to other study materials about the subject and related fields. The Web also has the capability for interactivity with graphics and other types of files, allowing the user to alter the course of the instruction or conduct a simulation of a process.

The Web is rapidly becoming a new medium for information distribution, joining print, radio, and TV as the newest member of the information age. But unlike these other media, the Web is distinctly interactive and individualized. Those training developers who take advantage of the functionality of the Web will likely be the most successful.

FTP

File Transfer Protocol (FTP) is an older standard for file transmission over the Internet. FTP and HTTP are similar in that you use an application, like a browser, to access an Internet server that contains the information you would like to retrieve. FTP was originally developed for downloading and uploading files between computers. Unlike HTTP, however, files don't need to be in any specific format to be downloaded.

The structure of an FTP site is similar to that of PCs, with files located in directories and subdirectories. Usually, there is a file called INDEX.TXT or some variation of this on each directory that contains the list of files available on the current directory. If you are using a Web browser to navigate through an FTP site, you can view the files and subdirectories that are present in the current directory.

Most files available through FTP are not necessarily viewable through a Web browser, although some text files are. To access an FTP site using a Web browser, use ftp:// before the server name. However, the software applications that are available through FTP are not usually intended for a Web browser; they are mostly intended to be downloaded and then run offline. HTTP files are meant to be accessed and run while the user is online. If you try to access a file that cannot be viewed in the browser window, such as a software application or a PostScript file, it will be downloaded to your hard drive. This is also true for files that you access through a Web page. In fact, if you are downloading a file from a Web site, you are performing an FTP.

Another major difference between HTTP and FTP is that HTTP is intended only for downloading. That is, you can access Web pages from a remote server, but you can't send your own Web page to the server from your computer by using HTTP. An FTP application will allow you to transfer, or *upload*, your own files from your computer to an Internet server. But it has to be an Internet server that will let you—some are password-protected and closed to the public for uploads and downloads.

A type of freely available FTP site that does not need a password is called an *anonymous FTP* site, which will allow anyone to download and upload files. If you are prompted for a User ID and password, you type in *anonymous* for the User ID and it lets you in. For some sites, you provide your e-mail address as the password. By accessing a Web page you are actually performing an anonymous FTP.

Your Browser

The browser is your window to the World Wide Web. There are buttons for browser functions, a space for the Web page address, a browser window—where Web pages can be viewed—and a status line. In the space for the Web page address, you can type in the address, or URL, to let the browser know which server and Web page you would like to access.

URLs for Web sites are available in many places. Often they can be located at the signature area, or *sig*, of e-mail messages, for the sender's company Web site. The Web is the best way to find Web pages, because these sites are linked through hypertext on a large number of pages, including some pages that perform searches for other pages.

Bookmarks are also available for automatically entering URLs. When you activate a bookmark, the URL for that bookmark is automatically entered into the browser. This is useful for frequently accessed sites, so that you don't have to keep typing in the same address over and over again. You can create a bookmark while you are at the page you want to save by activating the Bookmark command in Netscape Navigator.

When you specify the server you want to log onto, either by typing in its address or by activating a predefined bookmark that enters the URL for you, the browser then takes you to that server and searches for the Web page you specified. Once you have accessed the server, you can jump from page to page by using any hyperlinks that are provided on the pages. Usually, the page that you have accessed has links that relate to other pages on the same server that contain information about a company or a topic. Often, however, hyperlinks will take you to files that are located on other servers. In this way, you can access other servers without typing in their URLs.

When a hyperlink is activated, the URL of the linked page is automatically entered into your Web browser, and you are automatically taken there. The process of providing hyperlinks to other Web sites is unregulated, so that any Web page can provide a link to any other Web page at any time.

Navigation

The buttons that are available in your browser help you navigate through Web pages that you have already accessed. When you access new pages, a history log is compiled by the browser, and it is placed in a sequence based on when you accessed the page. The Back button will take you to a previous page. The Forward button will take you to a page that you accessed more recently.

The Home button will automatically take you to the home page that is specified in the preferences or options menu. You can change the URL that this button accesses at any time.

The Reload button will tell the server to try and send the page again if there has been a problem or an update. If the page is taking an unreasonable amount of time to load, one of the reasons could be that there was a bad connection, or that something interrupted the transmission (it is possible that the server you accessed has a slow connection). Clicking the

Reload button will establish a new request to the server and may correct the problem.

The Stop button will stop all transmissions from the server. This is useful when the page is coming in too slowly for your taste, or if the information you need is present but an image or graphic element that you do not need is still loading. In general, the server sends the text first and the images next. You can click on the Stop button to let the server know to stop transmitting data you do not need. Or, if the page is in the process of loading and it isn't what you thought it was, or for some reason you no longer need it, you can stop it without waiting for it to load completely.

Plug-Ins

Animation, audio, and video files can be played within the Web browser window, and require proper players for these files. *Plug-ins* are installed into the Web browser software and extend the browser's capabilities to play these specialized types of files. For example, a Macromedia *Authorware* file that can be played as a standalone file on a computer needs a special plug-in from Macromedia called *Shockwave* to play it via the Web. This means that the user does not need to leave the browser application to play the file.

Plug-ins are small applications and files that help extend the capabilities of a Web browser. They work with a Web browser application to translate different kinds of files for viewing in the browser window. Because the browser is used for many different kinds of files, it is possible to view these files without leaving or quitting the browser.

Often, plug-ins take the form of players for different kinds of media files. Players like these normally exist in other applications that must be run separately from the Web browser application.

Plug-ins are widely available for a large number of file types, such as animation, video, audio, document format, graphics, virtual reality, and many others. Sometimes, the Web browser will let you know if a Web page contains a file in a format that requires a plug-in. It will then give you instructions on how to obtain the plug-in so that you can return to that page and view the file as it was intended to be viewed. For example, PDF (portable document format) is the proprietary format for documents that can be read and created by Adobe's Acrobat software. In order to view a PDF file, you must use the Acrobat Reader. But a plug-in available from Adobe called Amber allows you to view a PDF file using your Web browser application. If a Web page contains a PDF file and you do not have the Amber plug-in, you must first download the entire file and then open it up using the Acrobat Reader. If you already have the plug-in, you will see it in the browser window as it is downloading.

Hundreds of plug-ins are available for many different types of files, and many of these are either already incorporated into some browsers or have been planned for incorporation. This means that for some plug-ins you do not have to go to the developers' site to download and install them; they are already installed. Some of the available plug-ins are listed in Table 3.1.

TABLE 3.1 Common Plug-Ins

Plug-In	Company	Description
Acrobat Reader	Adobe	Shows files in the Adobe portable document format (PDF), a standard, cross-platform file format widely used on the Internet for distributing visually rich documents
CMX Viewer	Corel Vector Graphics	Shows high-resolution vector graphics files
EarthTime	Starfish Software	Lets users tell time around the world, displaying the local time and date for eight selectable geographic locations
Envoy	Tumbleweed Software	Shows documents on the Internet exactly as designed; preserves fonts, graphics, and document layout in a compact format for Web publishing
Formula One/NET	Visual Components	Shows Excel-compatible spreadsheets that can include charts, links to URLs, and calculations
Lightning Strike	IION	Uses a compression-decompression algorithm that provides higher compression

Plug-In	Company	Description
		ratios for smaller image files, faster transmissions, and improved image quality over other graphics formats
Neuron	Asymetrix	Plays animations and programs produced with ToolBook II
RealAudio	Progressive Networks	Plays live and on-demand real-time audio files
Shockwave	Macromedia	Plays Authorware and Director files
ToolVox	Voxware	Plays high-quality audio files designed for speech
VDOLive	VDONet	Compresses video images depending on the speed of the user's connection
VR Scout VRML	Chaco Communications	Plays VRML files (virtual reality) and uses multithreading to enable users to view scenes while they are downloading
WebFX	Paper Software	Plays VRML files and runs interactive, multiuser VRML applications written in Java
WIRL	VREAM	Extends VRML with support for object behaviors (such as motion, rotation, gravity, weight, elasticity, and sound), logical cause-and-effect relationships, multimedia capabilities, and links to Windows applications

More plug-ins are being developed for various functions, and new ones are coming out almost daily. The hundreds of types of plug-ins are testimony to the scope and long-term viability of the Web.

Error Messages

As with all computer-related technologies, there are certain errors that you should be aware of. If any of these messages appears on your screen, simply click on the Back button or activate a bookmark to leave the error screen. These messages vary from server to server, but the actual errors are universal.

"404—File Not Found"—This, and similar 404-type messages, indicates that either the Web page that was linked no longer exists, or the original link was misspelled (this happens more often than you might think). This is the most common type of error message.

"403—Access Forbidden" or "You can't log on as an anonymous user"—This means that the server or the Web page was set up specifically for private use. When you try to access a server, your Web browser automatically submits an anonymous ID, meaning that you are logged on to a publicly available server. Some servers do not allow anonymous IDs and will refuse your request for access. These servers require that you register with the owners to be assigned a unique password and ID.

"502—Service Temporarily Overloaded" or "The server is either down or busy"—This means that the server you tried to access is either processing more requests for hyperlinks than it can handle, or is not currently connected to the Internet. Sometimes this message is displayed when the owners of the server are upgrading or troubleshooting the site.

"503—Service Unavailable"—This usually refers to your ISP having problems or to a problem with your own Internet connection.

"Your request has been refused by the server"—This message often appears with the one above or with another message that explains why your request was refused. Most of the time it is because too many people are trying to access it at once. This happens often to the most popular Web pages.

"The server does not have a DNS entry or does not exist"—Domain Name Server (DNS) is an Internet-wide system of cataloging the available, accessible Internet servers. If the server you specified does not have a listing with this system, DNS will generate this message. This most often occurs when the server has been misspelled in the URL. This message also happens when your Internet connection has gone down.

"Plug-in not loaded" or "Helper application not found"—One of these messages appears when you have accessed a page or an object on a page that contains a file that your browser cannot read or play. Sometimes there is a message that tells you how to obtain the necessary plug-in or control in order to be able to read the file.

"Broken pipe"—This is a nebulous communications error that the browser encountered on the network or server. If the message occurs repeatedly while trying to access the same site, then it is a problem at that site.

"File contains no data"—This means that the file you accessed exists, but does not have anything in it. The server administrator who created the file either did it incorrectly or is currently updating it. Try to access the file again after a few minutes or type in :80 before the first slash in the current URL.

Languages

There are Web-specific technologies, or languages, that allow you to provide interactivity and media for your training program. These can add to and extend the capabilities of the Web browser to give it more functionality.

HTML

HTML (Hypertext Markup Language) is the language that Web pages use to communicate with Web browsers. HTML indicates the text, graphic files, and other special functions that the browser can recognize to display Web pages. It also indicates how these elements are to be displayed. HTML files are written in a form of text file called *ASCII*.

ASCII is an international standard for text on all platforms, which means that text in an ASCII file can be read by any computer in the world. E-mail is saved and transmitted in ASCII, so that any computer can send any other computer an e-mail message, which will be able to display it correctly for the user. When you save a file in a word processor as "text only," it is saved in ASCII.

Because of this, any word processor or text editor can be used to create HTML files. To make things easier on the Web developer, the way in which the file communicates with the browser is through the use of text codes, called *tags*. These tags, which tell a Web browser how to display text and graphics, are set off from the readable portion of the text using the greater-than ">" and less-than "<" symbols to form bracketed commands.

For example, to specify an end-of-line, or paragraph mark, you would use the command <P>.

Most of the available commands (there are more than 100) are definition-type commands, which means that they indicate the beginning of a formatted section. A countercommand, using the slash "/", is used to "turn off" the formatting indicated by the command. For example, in the following case you would use these codes to set off the word *bold*: "The <B>bold</B> is set off."

For links to other files, you would use the command <A HREF="filename.ext"> in front of the text to show as hypertext and </A> on the end of it to turn the command off. In this example, the words *home page* are hypertext for the file called homepage.htm:

Click here for our <A HREF="homepage.htm">home page</A>.

Other commands, or codes, available in HTML include: font size, font style, text color, table definitions, frame definitions, transparent titles, window titles, horizontal rules, graphic image mapping, file downloads, input fields, menus, and buttons. Through these codes, the Web page communicates with the Web browser, telling it what to show in the browser window.

HTML is a language with built-in future upgradability: With new technologies come new HTML codes that let the browser display these technologies as they were meant to be viewed. The standard format for HTML commands is determined by an industry consortium of companies and interest groups that meet regularly for this purpose. The current version of HTML is 3.0, and, on its own, has the capability to provide formatting for objects and graphics in many ways. Although most HTML tags are specific to the placement of other files within a Web page, many refer to the organization of these elements. Some advanced HTML effects are:

- Tables—You can view data in a tabular format with a varying number of table displays, such as a raised or sunken look and cells with larger or smaller borders. Tables can also be set up with invisible borders for special formatting effects.

- Frames—You can view more than one Web page in a browser window by splitting up the window into different parts. This allows the user to view some pages all the time in one frame, and change from page to page in another frame. Frames are useful for displaying tables of contents, advertising, page titles, direction buttons, and so on, in one frame while viewing the changing content in the other frame.

- Lists—You can create numbered lists, or ordered lists, and bulleted lists, or unordered lists, for a series of items. The numbers or bullets are automatically inserted when used. You can also specify the numbering used and the type of bullet.

- Forms—You can set up a page to contain input fields of various types, including check boxes, radio buttons, fill-in-the-blanks, text fields, and pop-up menus. You can then specify buttons that either clear the form (if a mistake was made), or submit it to a specified e-mail address.

It is important to choose a browser application that will support the most current version of HTML, so that the latest objects and commands available can be viewed by the user. Netscape Navigator or Internet Explorer are the obvious choices.

HTML Coding

Because HTML uses codes to define formatting commands, Web pages are written for elements as they appear sequentially on the screen. That is, text and graphic elements that appear near the top of the page are defined earlier in an HTML document than elements that appear toward the bottom of the page. This is unlike many WYSIWYG (what you see is what you get) authoring tools that allow you to create a "page" by placing different graphic and text elements in different places on the screen (not only that, but usually, you don't see the "code" used to produce it). With HTML, there is a definite text flow from beginning to end.

The codes for formatting that are used are placed immediately before the element to be formatted. As mentioned in the previous section, some codes that define special formatting commands, like bold text or a URL reference, require termination commands to "turn off" the formatting.

Some sample codes are:

<P> for new line or paragraph.

<B>...</B> for bold text.

<I>...</I> for italics.

<UL>...</UL> for an unordered list (with <LI> at the beginning of each line).

<OL>...</OL> for an ordered list (with <LI> at the beginning of each line).

\<A HREF="link.htm">...\</A> for a hyperlink.

\<IMG SRC="image.gif"> for a graphic file.

\<TABLE>...\</TABLE> for tables and table definitions. Other commands used within a table include: \<TH>...\</TH> for a table heading, \<TR>...\</TR> for a new table row, and \<TD>...\</TD> for a new table cell.

Figure 3.3 shows some example HTML table coding taken from the *Multimedia and Internet Training Newsletter* Web site.

Some characters used as part of the command structure of HTML need to be defined as codes in order to be viewed. For example, the "<" (less-than) sign indicates a command is to follow, and so will not be shown in the browser window. Use the code &lt to make it show up as part of the text. Some of these codes include:

&lt for < (less-than)

&gt for > (greater-than)

&amp for & (ampersand)

&quot for " (double quotation mark)

&#169 for © (copyright)

\<FONT COLOR="000000"> for changing the color of the current font

The color codes range from 000000 (Black) to FFFFFF (White), plus there are sixteen named colors that can be used: aqua, black, blue, fuchsia, gray, green, lime, maroon, navy, olive, purple, red, silver, teal, white, and yellow. Most updated browsers that support HTML 3.x (3.0, 3.1, etc.) will display these colors as well as the following codes for differing shades of blue:

000080	- Navy
00008B	- Blue #4
0000CD	- Medium Blue
0000EE	- Blue #2
0000FF	- Blue
00688B	- Deep Sky Blue
00868B	- Turquoise #4
ADD8E6	- Light Blue
AFEEEE	- Pale Turquoise

```
<HTML>
<HEAD>
<TITLE>Brandon Hall Editor</TITLE>
</HEAD>
<BODY bgcolor ="#ffffff" text ="#000000">
<IMG src = "/images/brandon2.gif" border ="2">
<IMG src="/images/btopbran.gif" align=top alt="Brandon Hall,
Editor">
<hr>
<P>
Brandon Hall, Ph.D. is the editor and publisher of the Multimedia
   Training
Newsletter, now in its third year of publication. He is a regular
presenter at the American Society for Training and Development and
International Society for Performance Improvement national confer-
   ences
and is on national committees for each. He is also a regular
   presenter and track chair for the Interactive Conferences. He is
   the author of the first major study of CD ROM-based training,
   entitled 'Return on Investment and Multimedia Training'. He
   conducts seminars nationally on 'Multimedia Training: How to Make
   it Happen', and Web-Based Training: Design and Development.
<BR>

<p align="center">
<a href="http://www.alink.net/cgi-bin/imagemap/~bhall/newbut.map">
<img src="/images/newbubar.gif" "alt="Button bar menu" border="0"
   ISMAP></a><br>
<a href ="index.shtml">[Home]</a> <a href ="brand.html">[Editor]</a>
   <a href="info.html">[Subscription Info]</a><a
   href="devel.html">[Developers]</a> <a
   href="res.html">[Articles]</a> <a href ="roi.html">[ROI]</a><a
   href="auth.html">[Authoring Programs]</a>

<p align="center"><font size = "2">We value your feedback. Do you
   have any questions or suggestions regarding<br>the Newsletter or
   this web site? <a
   href="mailto:mail@MultimediaTraining.com">mail@MultimediaTraining.
   com</a></font>
<p align="center">
<font size ="-3">Copyright &copy;1996, Multimedia Training
   Newsletter.
All rights reserved</font>

</P>
</BODY>
</HTML>
```

FIGURE 3.3 HTML coding used to create the *Multimedia and Internet Training Newsletter* Web site.

B0C4DE   - Light Steel Blue

B0E0E6   - Powder Blue

There are hundreds of shades of blue alone and over 16.7 million possible colors. Many of these codes can be found at http://www.december.com/html/spec/color.html.

<APPLET CODE=filename width=x height=x>... </APPLET> is used for activating the Java function for the applet called "filename" of Java-enabled Web browsers. When the Web browser sees this code, it causes the Java applet to run in the browser window, allowing the space designated by width and height for the applet. Java and applets will be discussed later in this chapter.

<SCRIPT LANGUAGE="JavaScript">... </SCRIPT> is used for activating the JavaScript function that works in the Web browser window. With this command, you can write small command applets directly in the HTML document instead of calling an external Java file. Using these commands you can control the properties of buttons, open additional windows, scroll text along the status line, and perform many other browser-related functions. For a full description of what JavaScript can do and a description of many of its commands, visit http://rummelplatz.uni-mannheim.de/~skoch/js/index.htm.

Newer codes are being created all the time and are incorporated into the latest version of HTML.

ADOBE ACROBAT

There are certain cases when you may want to use an Acrobat file for greater control of how a document will be displayed. It essentially does the same things as HTML, such as hyperlinks and special formatting, but is more involved and can accomplish text and graphics layout in a more complex way.

Acrobat is used when existing documents need to be displayed electronically in the same format as they appear on paper. Government agencies use Acrobat for electronic versions of reports and papers because they need to make references to specific page numbers.

The main difference between Acrobat and other text-based applications, including HTML coding, is the font files are stored with the document in the PDF (portable document format) file. With other word processing programs, readers must have the same font files in their system as the developer used to create the document—otherwise, substitute fonts are used. This can cause certain documents to appear differently because of font sizes and kerning. The biggest difference turns out to be pagination. For example, a document created in Century Schoolbook, a relatively large font on the page, might be paginated at 50 pages in Microsoft Word. If the reader's system does not have the Century Schoolbook font file, Word may substitute a smaller font such as Times Roman. This would paginate the document to 44 pages, making a table of contents or an index useless.

HTML has solved many of the problems Acrobat addresses: combining graphics and text easily, providing hyperlinks within and between documents, and displaying documents in a standard format. Acrobat does all this and saves the file-required fonts, in order to keep the page looking exactly the same wherever it is viewed. The best HTML can do is to specify first-, second-, and third-choice fonts on the user's system.

An Acrobat PDF file can be read by the Adobe Acrobat Reader, which can be downloaded for free from Adobe's Web site. PDF files are created using the special Acrobat program, or with Pagemaker, if it is configured for PDF files.

With the plug-in available from the Adobe Web site, PDF files can be viewed on Web pages. These may be useful for archiving existing documents for display on the Web, such as those from a magazine

Java

You can incorporate interactive animations and other elements by using the Java API (application programming interface). Java is a low-level language, which means that there is a great deal of control over the functions of the browser and what appears on the screen. Much more powerful than HTML, it is available for Web developers to produce highly complex, interactive programs and simulations.

Java was developed by Sun Microsystems, Inc. in 1995 for use on the Internet and it has taken the computing world by storm, second only to the Web itself in terms of expected impact. With Java, programmers and developers can create small applications, called *applets*. Applets perform certain computing tasks such as background scoring of a test or an automatic update of financial information. Because Java is a programming language with its own terms and processes, it can be used to create applets for a limitless number of functions. This is unlike HTML, which is a code-based system for formatting text and graphics.

Java is made up of a number of different programming commands that can be combined to function in a wide variety of ways. Java applets run in a Web browser window as opposed to directly on your computer. It is possible to write Java applications that run outside the Web browser, independent from it, but these cannot be accessed through a Web browser. Here is a sample of Java code.

```
public void run() {

    setBackground(Color.white);
    // init color array
    float c1 = 1;
    float c = 0;
    for (int i = 0; i < colors.length; i++){
      colors[i] = Color.getHSBColor(c, c1, c1);
      c += (float).01;
    }

    // cycle thru the colors
    int i = 0;
    while (true) {
      setForeground(colors[i]);
      theDate = new Date();
      repaint();
      i++;
      try {Thread.sleep(50); }
      catch (InterruptedException e) { };
      if (i == colors.length) i= 0;
    }

  }
```

The applet that this code was taken from changes the color of a piece of text on the screen in a cycle that moves through most of the colors available on the system. The entire applet takes up about twice as much space as the above example. See http://www.kksys.com:80/members/patrick/Chap10.htm.

Java is similar to C++, which is a programming language used to write applications that run as standalone programs on computers. Where C++ contains commands that relate to non-Internet tasks, such as accessing a disk drive and allocating memory on your computer, Java contains commands that reference Internet-specific tasks and other functions associated exclusively with the Web browser.

Java can take existing functions, such as the date listed on the computer, and manipulate them in numerous ways. The power of Java, however, is that it can take existing functions on other computers, like the server it resides on, and manipulate that data as well. For example, a Java applet could incorporate the current interest rate of various banks and lending institutions into a module for a financial course. Another applet could retrieve information from the company's Web site on a new technology that is being developed. The updated information could then be incorporated into a customer service training course.

Because Java is in direct communication with your Web browser, it is therefore in direct communication with your computer. It has several built-in security devices that keep Java applets from being malignant. That is, when Java was developed, it was designed so it would not be able to mess around with any of the components on your computer, such as the hard drive. This is not true for ActiveX and is one of the biggest selling points for Java. Sun Microsystems has stated they built in this kind of security in order to eliminate the possibility of a Java applet being a virus. That is, it can't access your hard drive, so it can't replicate itself on your computer.

Future versions of Java may change, but for now Java is perhaps the most secure programming language. The major players in the Internet industry have adopted Java as a prime programming language of the Web. It will be supported and in existence for a long time. Many corporations are also looking to it as the language for their general business applications.

Applets

As already mentioned, with the Java application programming interface (API), developers can write small applications that can be run within a Web browser. These small applications, called *applets*, can perform many different functions that add interactivity to Web pages.

One of the major advantages of using Java in a Web browser is that the applet can run on any platform. Because the Java language communicates with the browser application, it doesn't matter what kind of computer is running it.

Java applets download when the Web page is accessed and then run on the user's, or *client's*, computer. The server does not need to monitor the running of the application because all the required code for it has been transmitted to the user's computer. This frees up bandwidth on the server for other things. This is in contrast to the older method of accomplishing interactivity through the use of CGI (Common Gateway Interface) scripts.

Applets on a Web page operate the same way as applications on a computer. Java was developed specifically for the Internet to produce applications that run in a Web browser. There are already thousands of applets, and many more will be produced because of the versatility of Java.

It is possible to write an applet that runs an entire interactive simulation, or administers a test or a quiz. Applets can accomplish the same tasks as computer applications, but on a smaller scale. Two or more applets, each with a specific function, can operate as one application, extending the functionality of both.

The flexibility of the Java language is such that most functions that are possible in a normal application are possible in a Java applet. For example, Java can incorporate user input either in an input field or as real-time input from a mouse, including tracking mouse movements and clicks.

The programs themselves are written and executed in a linear format. That is, the functions that are performed are defined in the first part of the program and then executed, or run, if a certain condition is met in the second part of the program. The following applet displays the current time, including seconds, in a 24-point bold Times Roman font. While it is not within the scope of this book to provide a tutorial on the Java language, it is helpful to see how applets are written.

```
import java.awt.Graphics;
import java.awt.Font;
import java.util.Date;

public class DigitalClock extends java.applet.Applet
   implements Runnable {

  Font f = new Font("TimesRoman",Font.BOLD,24);
  Date d;
  Thread runner;

  public void start() {
     if (runner == null) {
      runner = new Thread(this);
      runner.start();
     }
  }

  public void stop() {
   if (runner != null) {
    runner.stop();
     runner = null;
   }
  }

  public void run() {
   while(true) {
```

```
    d = new Date();
    repaint();
    try {Thread.sleep(1000);}
    catch(InterruptedException e){ }
  }
}

public void paint(Graphics g) {
  g.setFont(f);
  g.drawString(d.toString(),10,50);
  }
}
```

ActiveX

ActiveX is a system of controls that can be used to incorporate external documents—in their native formats—into Web pages. It was designed by Microsoft as a way to display information created in other Microsoft products. ActiveX works only on Windows machines, and is referred to by Scott McNealy, CEO of rival Sun Microsystems, as "Captive X."

Microsoft introduced ActiveX in mid-1996 as a replacement for and extension of OLE. (OLE is the acronym for Object Linking and Embedding and is pronounced *O-Lay*.) OLE was a technology that allowed Microsoft products to interact with each other in real-time. For example, an Excel spreadsheet could be inserted into a Word document with OLE. When the Excel spreadsheet was imported into the Word document, it was imported with OLE codes that told Word how Excel worked. The spreadsheet could then be displayed correctly.

ActiveX works the same way. The Web browser is the main application for the ActiveX platform, which means when it encounters a file format ActiveX supports, an ActiveX control tells the Web browser how to display it. For example, if an Excel spreadsheet is available on the Web, the ActiveX control for Excel—which was previously installed into the Web browser—tells the Web browser how to view the spreadsheet as it was meant to be viewed.

Just like OLE, ActiveX can be written with any low-level programming language, such as C++, Delphi, or Visual Basic. In fact, Visual Basic programmers were targeted by Microsoft to be the primary personnel to write ActiveX controls. Visual Basic is among the easiest of the major programming languages to use and is known by more people than most other programming languages.

ActiveX is commonly viewed as a competitor of, or Microsoft's replacement for, Java. While this may be true, ActiveX accomplishes different parts of the media integration process than Java. In fact, there is an ActiveX control for Java applets so ActiveX-enabled Web browsers can display and run them. Because Java is a low-level programming language, Java can even be used to write an ActiveX control.

ActiveX Controls

ActiveX controls can be thought of as an analogue to plug-ins. In general, when you are using Netscape Navigator, you use *plug-ins* to view external objects. When you use Microsoft's Internet Explorer, you use *controls* to view external objects. A key difference is ActiveX is a Windows-only technology, whereas plug-ins can be written for any platform, and any Java applet can run as is on any platform with a Java-enabled browser.

Another key difference is that because ActiveX controls can display and run files in their native formats, they are not inherently secure from being damaging. An ActiveX control can be written to access your hard drive, your RAM, and all other components on your computer. This is because ActiveX was designed for full functionality on your computer. It has access to the data on your hard drive as well as to the data on the server where the control comes from. This is unlike Java, which has built-in security measures.

A forthcoming type of ActiveX technology, called Active Documents, will allow the browser to act like the application the spreadsheet was created in. This means that when the Excel spreadsheet is encountered, the browser turns into an Excel interpreter, allowing the user to manipulate the spreadsheet as if the computer were running Excel. This will certainly help leverage all the work people have put into mastering and creating Excel spreadsheets.

Table 3.2 lists a sample of the ActiveX controls that currently exist.

TABLE 3.2 Current ActiveX Controls

ButtonMaker	FarPoint	Control the size, shape, and color of buttons—for replacing the standard Windows button
ClearFusionX	Iterated Systems	Play video files in the AVI format as they are downloaded, instead of after they completely download

Control Pak 1	Kwery	Link to external Access databases
CPC View	Cartesian	View images in the CPC compression format
Input Pro	FarPoint	View and edit database field entry features, like currency, boolean, and memo
Lightning Strike	Infinop	View images in the wavelet compression format
mBED	mBED	View interactive applets in the mBED format
PowerPoint Animation Player	Microsoft	Display multimedia presentations in the PowerPoint format
QuickSilver	Micrografx	Display and manipulate vector graphics files
RealAudio	Progressive Networks	Play high-quality audio files in the RealAudio format
ShockWave	Macromedia	View interactive animations in the Authorware and Director formats
Surround Video	Black Diamond	Display 360° images in the SDK format
VDOLive Player	VDOnet	Play video files in the VDOLive format
Whip!	Autodesk	Display and manipulate vector graphics in the DWF format

VRML

Virtual Reality Modeling Language (VRML) is the 3D language of the Web. It is similar to HTML in that its purpose is to provide Web pages with information, but for a 3D format. Just as HTML provides a way for two-dimensional data to be presented, VRML is for three-dimensional data. Because of the complexity of describing three-dimensional space, however, VRML looks more like JavaScript than HTML. VRML Web pages and other virtual reality models are called *worlds*.

This is what VRML looks like (# signifies a comment from the programmer):

```
Separator {
                        DirectionalLight {
  direction 0 0 -1 # Light shining from viewer into scene
  }
PerspectiveCamera {
  position -8.6 2.1 5.6
  orientation -0.1352 -0.9831 -0.1233 1.1417
  focalDistance  10.84
  }
Separator { # The red sphere
 Material {
   diffuseColor 1 0 0 # Red
   }
 Translation { translation 3 0 1 }
 Sphere { radius 2.3 }
 }
Separator { # The blue cube
 Material {
   diffuseColor 0 0 1 # Blue
   }
 Transform {
   translation -2.4 .2 1
   rotation 0 1 1 .9
   }
 Cube {}
 }
}
```

The first VRML projects were home pages with single objects in them. Graphics that are in a three-dimensional space and contain hyperlinks are called *avatars*. An avatar can represent a person or another VRML page, or an additional link to more data, just like hypertext can represent a link to additional external data. These and other three-dimensional objects can be "programmed" to have specific behaviors—for example, floating, bouncing, stationary—and interact on a high level with the user. VRML worlds can have any number of objects and backgrounds in them that behave independently of other objects.

Because objects are defined for a three-dimensional space, they can be viewed at any angle or distance, including closeups. Details are defined by the programmer. The view, or location of the user as the world is viewed, is called the *camera*, meaning that the user is moving a camera through cyberspace while viewing the world.

VRML implies a great deal more than is possible with existing two-dimensional technology. Immediate applications of this include an assembly line training where one "moves" around the factory "operating" the machinery. This could be done with as much interactivity as the instructional designer chooses.

VRML requires a plug-in to be viewed in normal HTML Web browsers. Alternatively, there are also VRML-specific browsers that recognize VRML commands and display worlds created in this language. Superscape VR is a UK-based company which produces virtual reality software for standalone or Web-based worlds. The program has been used to create VR training programs, including Nina Adams' manufacturing simulation for Motorola, and Darrell Farris' telephone system installation program for Northern Telecom.

 # Resources

For more information on the World Wide Web and how it can be used, visit these sites:

http://www.sandybay.com/pc-web/World_Wide_Web.htm

http://www.terena.nl/gnrt/www.html

http://www.albany.edu/library/internet.html

http://www.msn.com/tutorial/faq.html

http://www.openmarket.com/intindex/96-10.htm

For more information on browsers, visit these sites:

http://www.sandybay.com/pc-web/browser.htm

http://www.thru.com/online/

http://www.stars.com/Vlib/Users/Browsers.html

For more information about the Virtual Reality Modeling Language, visit:

www.superscape.com

www.hitl.washington.edu/projects/knowledge_base/vrm.html

www.univ-mlv.fr/VR/VRML/Doc/VRML_FAQ.html

www.graphcomp.com/info/specs/vrml11.html

For more information on ActiveX check out these sites:

www.webtools.atonce.com/pages/activex.htm

www.activex.com

the-pages.com/activex

For more information about Java, visit:

http://www.idgbooks.com/idgbooksonline/java/resources/javalnks.html

http://bass.gmu.edu/~cressdg/javalist.html

http://www.ncc.com/cdroms/web/web_sites_java.html

HARDWARE AND SOFTWARE YOU NEED

Some people say that one of the main drivers of the computer industry is the human desire for things that are new. And there is always plenty of "new" in this industry: new hardware and new software, each product more powerful than the last. On the other hand, one of the constraints in this industry is competing standards: different platforms and different operating systems. The Web helps overcome this constraint. By using open standards and common browsers, the Web speaks a more universal language, using existing hardware and software. In this chapter, we will describe just what hardware and software are needed to create and deliver Web-based training.

 ## Hardware

The computer on which the training program files will reside must be configured for use on the Internet or the company intranet. You do not need a high-powered computer to get access to the Internet, but it is a good idea to get a powerful machine for authoring training programs.

Here are our recommendations for a computer to be used for creating a training program:

For Windows machines, a Pentium or better. For sophisticated graphics and multimedia programs, the Pentium chip should be the fastest you can afford. Generally, anything above 150MHz works quite well. Intel's MMX chip is excellent for multimedia because it includes features that can handle different types of media simultaneously.

For Macintosh machines, a PowerPC or better.

A hard drive with enough space to hold all your program files. Keep in mind that multimedia can take up lots of space, and you may want to store more than one at a time. Plus you need room for the software you will use to author the program.

At least 16MB RAM. The RAM requirements for many programs are increasing all the time. 32MB RAM may become a standard in the near future.

A CD-ROM drive. CD-ROM drives can be categorized in terms of their speed, like 4x, 8x, 10x, and so on. These numbers refer to how much faster than the original music CD players the drive can access the data from the CD-ROM.

A video accelerator card. You may notice that video cards come with something called VRAM. 1MB of VRAM is not unreasonable, and 2MB is better. MPEG compatibility for your video card is a good idea since MPEG is becoming an alternative popular format for video compression. MPEG is a higher quality format, and on a fast system is capable of displaying files at 30 frames per second, the standard for broadcast quality. It does require MPEG playback capability on the user's machine.

At least a 16-bit sound card. You may be tempted to get an 8-bit card because of price, but the quality of 8-bit sound is much worse than that of 16-bit, which can play voice and speech files approaching the quality of radio broadcasts.

Obviously, when it comes to the numbers, more is better. For example, the more RAM you have, the more complex an animation can be and still run smoothly. The better the video card you have, the less "jerky" a video file will run. The larger your hard drive, the more applications and programs can be stored on it.

For running a training program over the Internet, the following is recommended:

For a Windows machine, a 486 or better. Although a Pentium is preferred, for most applications that do not employ large amounts of video or lengthy interactive animations, a 486 should work fine. A 386 can be considered for simpler courses that do not rely heavily on graphics and have no animation, but it is a risk.

8MB RAM (16 preferred). The standard of 8MB on most computers is almost three years old and applications are now being developed assuming that the user will have 16MB RAM. Keep in mind that the more graphically complex your program is, the more RAM you will need.

An Internet connection and Web browser software. If your training program will run over your company LAN, you would not need an Internet connection to run the program, but you would need a connection to the company intranet. Web browser software is standard for Web-based training, and most will use either Netscape Navigator or Microsoft's Internet Explorer.

A video accelerator adapter card.

For running a training program, the main requirement is simply that your computer can access the Web site and run the program. If the training program does not have sound then a sound card is not necessary. If the training program does not have video then you do not need a special video card to run it.

 Software

The software required for accessing a Web-based training program is a Web browser. The Web browser can be running on any platform (PC, Macintosh, etc.), but must be connected to the Internet or the company intranet. Also, if certain Web technologies are used in the course for animations, audio, or video files, those technologies must be incorporated into the Web browser software with plug-ins for the file formats used. See Chapter 3 for information on plug-ins.

The software required for putting together a Web-based training program is known as an authoring tool. Several of the major authoring tools are discussed in detail in Chapter 8. Authoring tools have the ability to combine different types of media into one program. Although many programs allow you to create some animation and graphic effects, it is usually best to first create the media you need and then import it into the training program using the authoring tool.

Once you import the various media, the authoring tool allows you to determine how and when they will be accessed. You can combine many different animations in your program but play only the ones that apply to a specific user input.

Animation and Video

Animations that simulate software, describe physical processes, and are used as attention-getting items are best done with an animation software package. Video needs to be converted from the original analogue source tape to a digital computer file.

The different types of animation/video files include animated GIFs, AVI, QuickTime, and MPEG. Some software studio applications for creating animations and video files are listed in Table 4.1.

TABLE 4.1 Applications for Creating Animation and Video Files

Application	Company	Formats	Comment
AVI Constructor	Michael Caracena	AVI	Easy-to-use but can't incorporate audio
Flash	Macromedia	proprietary	Can create animations with interactivity to be played in a Web browser with the Shockwave plug-in
HyperCam	Hyperionics	AVI	Takes screen shots—which can be continuous—and microphone input to create AVIs
MediaStudio	Ulead	AVI, QT, MPEG	Can convert between different animation formats and includes many different types of effects; multiple input devices are also supported

Application	Company	Formats	Comment
MPEGMaker	Vitec	MPEG	Converts AVI animations into MPEG files
Personal AVI Editor	FlickerFree	AVI	Can create AVIs by editing existing AVIs and BMPs, or by capturing video and audio from any supported device
Premiere	Adobe	AVI, QT	Can edit and create digital "movies" using existing animations and multiple video and audio sources
QuickTime	Apple	QT	Apple's own software for creating video/audio files
RealMagic Producer	Sigma Designs	AVI, MPEG	Includes an MPEG video card, video-tape controller, and software for capturing and editing video from numerous sources
V-Active	Ephyx	AVI, QT, MPEG, proprietary	Can create a number of different animation formats with extensive editing features for audio and video; With a plug-in for Web browsers, files in the proprietary animation format for V-Active can be played over the Web

TABLE 4.1 Continued

Application	Company	Formats	Comment
VideoShop	Strata	QT	Can create and edit Macintosh animations and video files using many different graphics and audio formats, and includes special effects
VidWatch	Neil Kolban	AVI	Can create video files using an external video camera and will only save the video images as they change so that long periods of an unchanging scene will be saved as a small number of frames
VivoActive Producer	Vivo Software	AVI, QT	Can create compressed streaming animations that play over the Web
3DS Max	Kinetix	proprietary	Creates 3D animations that can be run with some Windows AVI players or the Kinetix player

Animated GIF

An animated GIF is a file made up of several different GIF (Graphics Interchange Format) files in a sequence to make a short animation. GIFs are good for attention-getting icons and small animations that don't take up a lot of file space. GIFs are not recommended for longer animations and cannot be made to be interactive. GIFs are often called CompuServe GIFs because CompuServe developed the technology, and animated GIFs are often called GIF89s for reasons that are anyone's guess.

To create an animated GIF, you first need to create each frame of the animation. Then you need to compile all of the frames into a single file. You can use a paint or draw program such as Adobe Illustrator or Corel to produce each frame as a separate file. You can combine the files with a second software application, or you can use an application that allows you to draw each frame and compile them immediately.

Although it seems clumsy to save a lot of Illustrator files before compiling them, most high-end drawing applications can provide the means for automatically altering your image in subsequent frames using such commands as rotate, distort, and lighting effects. Whichever way you decide to create an animated GIF, most GIF applications allow you to both draw separate images and compile existing ones.

One thing to keep in mind about creating animated GIFs is the structure of a GIF file. A GIF file includes a saved set of colors that are used in the file, called a *palette*. The reason a GIF file is so small is because it allocates space for only 256 colors—other formats allow a greater number of colors. If two GIF files in an animation sequence contain different sets of colors, these two palettes won't be compatible and some distortion may occur. This is known as *palette shifting*. It is important to note whether or not the software you are using supports the use of multiple palettes.

Because animated GIFs are comparatively easy to produce and are based on an existing graphic standard, there are many applications that will allow you to create and manipulate this type of animation. The major illustration programs have or are expected to add this capability to their programs. Some third-party editor applications are also available. Two of these are listed in Table 4.2.

AVI

AVI (audio/video interleaved) is the proprietary format of Video for Windows and is the most commonly used video format for general use. It creates frame-based files, like animated GIFs, but does not require that the images be in the GIF format. Unlike animated GIFs, it can also include audio as a part of the file.

TABLE 4.2 Third-Party Editor Applications

Application	Creator	Comment
GIF Construction Set (Windows)	Alchemy Mindworks	For creating animated GIFs from different types of image files with many different features for Web publishing
GIFBuilder (Macintosh)	Yves Piguet	For creating animations from multiple graphic files

AVI was designed for Windows, and a version for the Macintosh is currently under development.

To create an AVI file you must have an application for that purpose. Some applications can automatically take screen captures and compile them into an animation and others can take data from an outside source, like a VCR (with the proper hardware for digitizing a video clip from a tape).

QuickTime

QuickTime is the proprietary video format from Apple for both the Macintosh and Windows systems. QuickTime files are frame-based animation files, like animated GIFs, but do not require that images be in the GIF format. Unlike animated GIFs, it can also include audio as a part of the file.

QuickTime and AVI are similar in that they both achieve the same results in the same way. AVI was designed for Windows, and QuickTime was designed originally for Macintosh. It is possible to create and play QuickTime files for Windows—those that are compatible with Windows have the .MOV extension. To create a QuickTime file you must have a studio application for that purpose.

MPEG

MPEG format for video files is an industry standard for high-end video compression. MPEG (Motion Picture Experts Group) files are video files that have been compressed using a special algorithm. An MPEG compression application compares frames in a sequence and saves only the portions of a frame that have changed from frame to frame. Files saved in this format are normally three times smaller than AVI or QuickTime formats, but require MPEG-capable computers for playback.

There are three different MPEG formats, MPEG1, MPEG2, and MPEG4. MPEG1 was developed as an initial method for video compression. MPEG2 was developed later to enhance compression techniques for smaller and faster files. Most MPEG-compatible cards will play MPEG1 and some will do MPEG2 as well. MPEG4 is still a proposal from the Motion Picture industry for compatibility with future digital television technologies.

Audio and Sound

Audio files can take the form of short alert sounds, lengthy narrative voiceovers, synthesized music, and so on. Synthesized sounds, such as electronic musical instruments, voice simulators, and manually created noises can be created with an sound studio application. For actual voice recording and other real-world sounds, you will need an audio recorder/editor capable of receiving input from an external microphone.

The different types of audio files include aiff, MIDI, MPEG, Real-Audio, and wave.

aiff

The aiff (Apple Instrument File Format) was developed for the Macintosh but it can be run on a Windows machine with the right player application. It is used to simulate musical instruments at a high level of quality.

MIDI

A MIDI (Musical Instrument Digital Interface) is a format that provides a means for synchronizing multiple electronic instruments, including those that are synthesized by computer. MIDI is more of a system than a file format, although music files can be saved in the MIDI format.

Using MIDI, you can connect different electronic instruments together for synchronization, such as a keyboard synthesizer and a drum machine. There are also applications that allow you to create MIDI files (with the extension MID in Windows) with the internal synthesizer on your computer's sound card. These MIDI files can play back on other MIDI-capable computers.

MPEG

The video file format for MPEG is not the same as the format for audio; MPEG stands for the industry group that recommended the type of compression used. In MPEG audio, the sound signal is compressed by eliminating the parts of the sound that are not relevant to the signal. This is a fancy way of saying that the file for the sound is smaller because less irrelevant information is saved than in other formats. MPEG audio comes in three kinds of compression formats, Levels 1 through 3. Level 3 is the most current.

RealAudio

This is a proprietary format for streaming audio over the Web. Streamed audio is a file that is played as it is being downloaded, and not after it has all downloaded. This is analogous to observing graphics files while they are in the process of downloading instead of all at once after they have downloaded. You must purchase the RealAudio Server to create and deliver this kind of sound file.

wave

A wave file is the standard sound file type for Windows, with the extension WAV. It is similar to the aiff file on the Macintosh platform. Most Windows-specific sound cards come with utilities to create wave files and there are hundreds of smaller applications available on the Web.

Many different types of compression schemes exist for wave files—a WAV file that plays in one application may not play in another one. Windows includes the most popular types for WAV compression software. Most WAVs should play in the Media Player that comes with Windows. Some of the most common compression schemes are: A-law, u-law, DSP, GSM, ADPCM, and PCM. All you really need to know about these is whether your sound card supports them.

Networking

The type of networking you need for running Web-based training programs varies according to how your program will be accessed. If your program will be accessed over the Internet, then your students will need an Internet connection. If your program will be accessed over the company intranet, your students will need an intranet connection.

A network is just a mass of computers connected with physical cables. These computers can talk to each other through the connections by using a common software and hardware format for transmission known as a *pro-*

tocol. This means two computers running different operating systems, like a Macintosh and a Windows machine, can talk to each other if they use the same protocol.

A protocol can be thought of as a standardized way of transmitting information. For humans, one protocol, or means of communication, is the voice. A human can speak in English or Urdu, but can't use a language based on sense of smell, like dogs use. If we train dogs to learn voice commands, we are teaching them the voice protocol we use so we can communicate with them.

When the Macintosh and Windows machines talk to each other it means that they are both speaking, but they still need translators, just as someone who speaks only English needs a translator for someone who speaks only Urdu. This is why you can't hook up two computers and expect them to speak fluently with each other. They must be configured with the correct hardware and software in order to be able to communicate. (Then again, there is the Hollywood version of things. In the movie *Independence Day*, the humans defeat the alien invaders by "uploading" a virus from a laptop computer to the computer controlling the alien mothership.)

Servers

A server is a computer that stores files for more than one user. The computer itself is likely to have a processing speed and capacity that is larger than the rest of the computers on a network. The server software is what allows more than one person to access the same data at the same time. Normally, any computer on a network can share files, but a server is designed to manage multiple users.

The type of server is determined by its function. A file server allows users to transmit files back and forth across the network between the server and computers. Mail servers handle internal and Internet e-mail. Print servers handle the printers on a network and set up the queue in which print jobs are managed. Web or Internet servers contain all the necessary files and functions to store Web page files and manage Internet access.

There are networks that do not have servers, or do not require certain kinds of servers. Token Ring networks, for example, are structured as *peer-to-peer* networks, which means that all computers are at the same functional level. AppleTalk operates in this way as well. In this situation, files are sent back and forth to specific locations on the network. A *client/server* network is one where many different computers, called *clients*, access a single *server* for certain functions. Files from client computers are sent to the server, either to remain there or to go on to other computers or devices.

If Internet access is a function your network needs, then you should have an Internet or Web server. Internet/Web servers hold all the files for your Web site and handle all Internet transactions, like firewalls, Internet connections for other computers, and FTP access.

Server Software

Servers can be as powerful as the top-of-the-line computer, on down to just above the processing power that your computer currently has. Server software comes in many different types and runs on many different operating systems.

Server software varies widely in functionality—and friendliness—and the prices can range from bare-bones servers that are actually shareware, to the full-featured, full-functioned megaservers that cost $20,000 or more. Some can be downloaded from the Web and others must be configured by the vendor for your system.

There are many software server packages that run on Windows machines. It is recommended that if a Windows machine is made into a server that it be running Windows NT, which is a version of Windows designed to handle many different functions at one time. Although there are servers that can run on Windows 3.x (3.0, 3.1, 3.11), it is not recommended that a computer running this version of Windows be used as a server. Windows 3.x does not have 32-bit capability and it is more volatile than other versions of Windows—in other words, it's slower and it crashes more often.

Many Macintosh server software packages also exist. It is recommended if a Macintosh machine is made into a server that it be running on a Power Macintosh. The PowerPC chip, which the Power Macintosh uses as its processor, is 32-bit RISC technology and runs quite a bit faster.

Many servers run on the UNIX operating system (OS). UNIX is a relatively old OS that was developed to handle multiple users. The UNIX command set is extremely complex and hard to learn, but very capable. The different types of UNIX include HP/UX from Hewlett-Packard, Irix, Linux (a freeware version), and Solaris from Sun Microsystems.

Other platforms that servers have been written for include OS/2, DOS, VMS, and AS/400.

Web and Internet server software packages that are currently on the market are listed in Table 4.3.

A relatively complete listing of Internet servers and their current prices can be found at http://webcompare.iworld.com/compare/chart.html.

TABLE 4.3 Server Software Packages

Name	Manufacturer	Supported Platforms
Apache	Apache	UNIX
Common Lisp Hypermedia Server, "CL-HTTP"	MIT	Macintosh, UNIX
Cyber Presence	Cyber Presence	Windows
OnNet	FTP Software	Windows
ExpressO (Java-based)	Peak Technologies	Windows, Macintosh, UNIX
IBM Internet Connection Server	IBM	Windows, UNIX
Jigsaw	W3 Consortium (nonprofit industry group)	Windows, Macintosh, UNIX
Microsoft Internet Information Server	Microsoft	Windows
Netscape FastTrack Server	Netscape	Windows, UNIX
Oracle WebServer	Oracle	Windows, UNIX
Quarterdeck WebServer	Quarterdeck	Windows
SCO OpenServer	Santa Cruz Operation	UNIX
Spry Web Server	Compuserve	Windows
WebStar	Quarterdeck	Windows, Macintosh

The Internet Connection

The first part for an Internet connection is the modem or network card (depending on how your company's network is set up). For computers on a network, a connection to the network via a network card is necessary. For standalone computers a modem connection to a phone line is necessary. In either case, the computer itself must be configured for use on a network with the TCP/IP protocol. TCP/IP is used as the format for the transmission of files between computers over the Internet and on company intranets. Other network protocols may be employed for a company's local area network (LAN). These networks are discussed later in this chapter.

The second part of the Internet connection is the Internet Service Provider, or ISP. The ISP provides the connection from your office or company to the Internet. Your company's network or your computer's phone line first accesses the ISP to get access to the Internet. The ISP then routes your request for a Web address to the Internet and monitors your transmission.

Connecting to the Internet

On the Internet, the protocol is TCP/IP (Transfer Control Protocol/Internet Protocol). The Internet is considered one huge network because the many different kinds of servers on the Internet can talk to each other by using TCP/IP. There are two ways to connect to the Internet: via a modem and phone line or over a company's intranet.

A Modem and Phone Line

If the computer the employee uses is a standalone and is not connected to a companywide intranet or LAN, then the computer should have a modem. The modem connects to a phone line so that the computer can dial up an Internet connection. The modem dials an ISP, which is the service that provides the Internet connection. The employee uses a Web browser to access the Web page where your training program resides.

For Internet access, at least a 14.4K modem is necessary, but this is rapidly becoming too slow to access most multimedia applications. A 28.8K modem is preferred, and—if it is cost-effective—a 33.6K or 56K are even better options. As is true with everything on the Internet, faster is better.

If the employee has access to an ISDN (Integrated Services Digital Network) line, he or she must also have an ISDN terminal adapter, or *Internet router*. ISDN lines use normal phone lines, but are higher-speed and more expensive. ISDN is made of two 64K channels: an A channel and a B channel. If the router supports it, the two channels can be combined to form one 128K line. Alternatively, one channel can be used for 64K data and the other as a normal voice line. With most routers, this kind of channel switching is automatic.

A Company Internet Connection
If the employee's computer is part of a companywide intranet that has Internet access, then all is set to go. The employee's computer, however, must be configured for the TCP/IP protocol.

LANs and WANs

LAN stands for local area network, which means that the network is generally located in one immediate area, like a building or company campus. WAN stands for wide area network, which means that the network is spread out over two or more distant locations. WAN requires long distance data lines.

A company's local area network might use any of several alternative protocols for file sharing, printer sharing, and so on. Each has various strengths, and the important point is that all computers on the LAN must use the same protocol. An intranet is a LAN that uses TCP/IP, the Internet protocol, for accessing and delivering Web pages to people inside the organization.

Employees can access an internal intranet training program in the same way they would as if it were on the Internet. The only differences are the address that is typed into the Web browser and the fact that the server the program is located on is within the company's firewall.

Most Web-based training will occur on a company's intranet and be delivered via the LAN. LANs usually have high-powered computers called file servers (not to be confused with Internet servers) that act as storage for files that many people need access to, or that are updated by multiple people in the company. Users can connect to these servers on the LAN to access the files. The files remain on the server or can be copied to the user's computer.

Company LANs can take many forms. Although some network configurations are more common than others, many times an entire company utilizes more than one type of network to maximize speed and minimize cost. For example, most company LANs are Ethernet within one building or campus site, but connections between company sites can be fiber optics to allow for higher speed and increased traffic.

The types of networks to use for a LAN, which then can connect to the Internet, include ATM, Ethernet, FDDI, and AppleTalk.

ATM

ATM stands for Asynchronous Transfer Mode. ATM was originally intended as a high-speed, or high-*bandwidth* alternative to Ethernet. While the top end of an Ethernet network is 100 megabits (Mb) per second (12 megabytes [MB] per second), ATM can theoretically deliver over 2000Mb per second—or around 250MB per second. Actual real-world rates are around 150Mb per second (about 20MB per second), because the hardware has not yet caught up with this type of transmission. In this way, ATM has built-in future upgradeability.

ATM transmission is more or less continuous, meaning that the stream of data is constant. This makes ATM an ideal type of network for multimedia delivery—the transmission is virtually instantaneous and uninterrupted. On an ATM network, two or more computers are hardwired, or permanently connected to each other, making the whole network operate like one machine.

A practical implementation of ATM has been connections between two or more company sites, providing for an almost instantaneous transfer of data between two locations. This is done primarily through the use of T1 lines (24 lines of 64K each, or 1.5Mb per second) or T3 lines (24 lines of 1.5Mb each, or 36Mb each), which are cables that are large in both available bandwidth and physical size. For long distances and general connections to other locations, a Network Access Provider provides the necessary cables.

Once considered the premier new standard, especially for transmitting multimedia over a network, ATM is a technology that has not been widely adopted by the industry. Delays in developing standards have led to other technologies emerging in its place. Because of the hardware required for multiple connections, it is extremely expensive to implement and many companies are reluctant to support a technology that has not come down much in price.

Ethernet

This type of network is one of the least costly and is usually relatively easy to implement. Ethernet was developed by an industry consortium and has been maintained as a standard for data transmission for a number of years. On an Ethernet network, files are broken into smaller "packets" of data, which are sent one at a time to the receiving computer. The files are recreated on the receiving end, checking for any missing packets and letting the sender know if any have been missed, or *lost*. Any lost packets are resent. This ensures the reliability of the transmission at the expense of speed.

The major types of Ethernet networks include 10base2, 10baseT, and 100baseT. The names for these types of Ethernet networks refer to the speed of transmission, or bandwidth, of the cable, and to the physical type of cable.

For Ethernet, each computer should have its own networking card with an adapter that matches the type of cabling you will use. It is possible to combine different types of Ethernet on a single network, but the requirements for this vary with the types of cabling used and the hardware that each supports.

- 10base2 can transmit data at 10Mbps or around 1.2MB per second. 10base2 is configured with coax cabling that looks similar to cable TV wires. The limits on 10base2 include a maximum of 30 devices supported and around 600 feet of cabling without additional hardware.

- 10baseT can also transmit data at 10Mbps or around 1.2MB per second. 10baseT is configured with flat cabling that looks similar to modular telephone wires. The limits on 10baseT include: about 300 feet of cable maximum between devices, two devices per wire segment, and a repeating station, or *hub*, between segments. Theoretically, 1000 devices can be on a 10baseT network if they are all linked properly. With 10baseT, if one point in the Ethernet network goes down, that point is automatically cut off from the rest of the network. This is unlike 10base2, where the entire network would crash if one device goes down.

- 100baseT is similar to 10baseT except that the "100" stands for 100Mb per second—about 12MB per second. There are several different types of cabling schemes, just as with the 10Mb-per-second Ethernet, but all essentially require the same hardware with different connectors. As you might imagine, 100baseT is quite a bit more expensive than most other Ethernet options and is recommended for a network's main segments, or *backbones*, rather than for the computer-to-computer connections.

FDDI

FDDI stands for Fiber Distributed Data Interface. FDDI networking was developed for use on fiber optic cables, although not all FDDI networks use fiber optics. This type of network uses the "token ring" architecture.

This means that all devices are connected to a ring of wires that form an endless chain. FDDI is a high-quality, high-cost type of network that is sometimes used to connect company sites over a wide area.

Communications between computers is through the ring, which operates similar to a highway with meters at all entrances. The data to be sent waits for the metering light to go on and then enters the ring and searches for the right exit, the receiving computer. This means that there is no confusion about which data goes where because only one computer can transmit or receive data at a time.

FDDI employs several different technologies to enhance the token ring concept. There is a second redundant ring in order to minimize data transfer problems. There is no server in an FDDI network, because each computer on the ring has equal access to every other computer. The advantage to having a server is that many people can access the same data at one place, at one time, on a more powerful computer. Technically, you do not have to access other computers beyond the server because everything that you need is there. But with FDDI, each machine is connected to every other machine on the ring, making a server unnecessary.

FDDI allows transfer rates of 100Mb per second, or about 12MB per second, and can support up to 500 devices on one ring. When using fiber optics for the cable, it is possible to create a ring with about 160 miles of wire—a circle with just over a 50-mile radius.

AppleTalk

Also known as LocalTalk, AppleTalk is the simplest and most inexpensive network to set up. Currently, Macintosh computers come equipped with built-in AppleTalk connections, as this is the best way to connect a Macintosh with a printer. But many Apple computers can be connected with each other on an AppleTalk network.

AppleTalk was not originally intended as a major networking system. It was originally developed to link more than one Macintosh machine so that file sharing between hard drives was possible. The disadvantages to using an AppleTalk connection are speed, platform independence, and portability.

AppleTalk connections are extremely slow, too slow to run applications remotely over a network. They are best used for background file transfers among Macintosh computers. They are also Macintosh specific. It is possible to connect Macintosh and Windows computers over an Ethernet LAN using Novell Netware or Mirimar Systems' PC Maclean for Windows 95.

Network Security

For an intranet that is connected to the Internet, there are some security concerns that anyone using a network should be aware of. There are three kinds of problems associated with being connected to the Internet, all having to do with unwanted network traffic:

- Accidental transmissions
- Hostile transmissions
- Viruses

Accidental transmissions usually take the form of someone surfing the Web and happening upon your site. These are easily avoided through the use of password protection. Hostile transmissions, from *hackers*, are harder to stop. In many cases the successful hacker already has one of your passwords or has a good idea what one might be, and therefore has access to your system. Viruses are small applications that are attached to otherwise harmless files. When you try to download and run one of these files, the virus enters your system, sometimes unseen by the user. There are thousands of viruses that exist and protection from them is essential and simple.

Firewalls

A firewall is the primary security solution that protects your company intranet from all unwanted network traffic. It usually consists of software and hardware that contains password protection, encryption, and other types of defense measures. A firewall is based on the assumption that it is easier to configure one system that is impervious to attack than it is to configure all the systems in your company against such an attack.

If a user on an internal company intranet wants to access an external Internet Web site, the computer sends out information about itself, meaning that information about the company's internal network can be collected by an outside server. Therefore, not only must transmissions from the outside be monitored, but transmissions that originate from the inside must be as well.

The two types of firewalls are packet filters and proxy servers.

Packet Filter

On the Internet, data is segmented into "packets" that contain information about the sending and receiving computer, the address it is directed to, the size of the packet, and other information having to do with the transmission.

Because each computer connected to the Internet has its own identity, in the form of an *IP address*, the source of a transmission can be detected by looking at the packet. The packet filter firewall will see if the packet contains an IP address on an internal list of acceptable IP addresses. If it doesn't, the packet is blocked from coming through. This is done on a packet-by-packet basis, so that all packets from a transmission are checked separately.

If a Web page request or FTP download triggers an incoming transmission from a server that is not on an approved list, then that data can be blocked as well. This type of firewall is automatic, because the packet filter will automatically check the incoming data packets' IP addresses regardless of user.

Proxy Server

A proxy server allows network traffic in and out, not based on the data itself, but on a previously entered password and ID. For transmissions coming in, the server checks to see if the user ID matches the password by checking it against an internal list of IDs and passwords. If the password does not match, the entire transmission is blocked.

For transmissions going out, such as when an internal user tries to access a Web page or FTP site, the user logs on to the proxy server, and then the server logs on to the requested Web page. The user and the requested Web page or FTP site are not in actual contact and information about the user and the user's network is not provided.

This type of firewall is the easier of the two to configure because the access level is based on the user, and not the machine. The access that the firewall allows into the system goes only as far as the firewall. That is, the firewall is the only connection that can be accessed from the outside. Internal computers can't be communicated with directly, but only by *proxy* through the firewall. The firewall is the only computer that "talks" with outside connections. This is in case the internal computers have security holes or bugs in them that allow them to be manipulated in unwanted ways. With the proxy, the only system that can be dealt with is the firewall. Therefore, it is the only system that needs a fail-safe security system.

The most important thing to remember with regard to security is that 99 percent of security breaches have to do with the fallibility of people. Common mistakes include users in the company choosing obvious passwords—like "1234", or a birthday—or openly displaying the password somewhere.

Viruses

Viruses are more insidious than other methods of intrusion; often the damage being done can't be discovered until it is too late, and they are often attached to otherwise useful files that the user downloaded. They range in potency from displaying an unsolicited—often unwelcome—message on the screen at a certain time, to wiping out an entire hard drive in seconds (scary, but fortunately rare).

The most effective way of protecting against viruses is not to accept any transmissions at all: files, e-mail, or diskettes. But since this is not practical, virus prevention software is mandatory.

Virus *checkers*, as they are called, monitor your computer system for suspicious activity and search through any new files or diskettes for copies of known viruses and similar files. A list of known viruses is included with the software and many can be updated over the Web. Many virus checkers can run in the background, constantly monitoring your system for suspicious activity, even when the computer is idle.

Suspicious activity, in most cases, is when a file is being created, an unknown command is being executed, or a file or a portion of a file is being deleted. The virus software will suspend all activity and alert you when a suspected virus or process has been found. The activity that a virus checker will report on most often is the installation of new software, so you may have to turn your virus checkers off in order to install new software.

There are many virus lists for the major platforms available on the Web. Here are samples for the Windows and Macintosh platforms:

http://www.ir.ucf.edu/manual/lan/virlist.html—for PC viruses

http://home.pacific.net.sg/~ngerard/virus.html—for Macintosh viruses

UNIX viruses, although rare, do exist despite the belief by some programmers that UNIX systems are safe from attack. It is believed that because UNIX is such a difficult platform to write for, many would-be hackers are hesitant to create a UNIX virus.

PART 2

PLANNING, DEVELOPING, AND IMPLEMENTING WEB-BASED TRAINING

THE DEVELOPMENT PROCESS

The "development process" includes every step you go through to create your Web-based training, from the first gleam in a trainer's eye to the last sigh of relief as the quality assurance engineer approves the final version.

Web-based training development has a lot in common with its CBT and multimedia training predecessors. Many of the same steps are involved, but some strategic differences occur. For instance, coping with bandwidth restrictions means that the costly and time-consuming process of developing extended video and audio is less of a factor for WBT development. On the other hand, new kinds of programming for the Web may be unfamiliar, and even an experienced CBT programming team needs time to get up to speed with this technology.

Development Overview

There are five major steps that make up a development effort: analysis, design, production, implementation, and evaluation. These steps can be further broken down and specialized to be applied to Web-based training development. Nancee Simonson prepared the following schedule in preparation for the development of her company's Web-based project. The steps described below are not all definite requirements for every project, nor will every project manager follow each step in the order they are presented here. Consider these items suggestions to be used or discarded depending on the needs of your client and the demands of the content.

Weeks 1 and 2—Analysis

- Begin outline of the course
- Design "look and feel"
- Select mix of media: text, video, animation, audio, graphics
- Identify necessary development tools for design and programming
- Research software tools

Week 3

- Determine the type of software tool required and how it will be used
- Choose software tool
- Research other similar sites for design ideas, storyboarding, and visual references
- Research/assemble required assets
- Develop content

Week 4

- Choose appropriate media for the course: b/w prints for photos, set of blue buttons and icons for other graphics

Weeks 5 and 6

- Format and code the course

Weeks 7 through 10

- Test program

Weeks 10 and 11

- Testing done; redesigning and debugging happens all throughout the testing phase and is intensified after testing is complete

Week 12

- Final product release

The rest of this chapter will focus on the first steps in developing your Web-based training program.

↳ The Vision

The first and probably most important step in any development process is the conceptualizing of an idea. Most project managers suggest obtaining input from the entire development team, including programming suggestions from programmers, cautionary advice from those who understand the Web's capability to deliver graphics, and interaction between the instructional designer and the rest of the team to decide the best methods for presenting and delivering instruction. Bad training in a flashy package is still just bad training. Remember the overall goal of project: to improve performance.

The Proposal

Some internal developers work on the fly, without a proposal or even a written plan. However, drafting your intentions on paper is important for a number of reasons.

A clear concise plan of action helps explain the WBT development project to a management team that may or may not have a good understanding of the technology and its benefits. By breaking down the elements of the project, you provide an explanation of the project as well as presenting an organized overview. A good proposal will help you get management's approval.

Your proposal can also work as a guide to help you through the project. It's easy to get caught up in the work and lose sight of your original intentions. The proposal can be used as a road map to ease the complications which surround the development of any product requiring various technologies and media.

If your group or department plans on using WBT as a standard, having a record of the original project proposal helps to launch future efforts to create WBT courses. Updating the document as the project unfurls will also be useful in this respect. Documenting problems and mistakes can help your team on their next project. Like sticking to an exercise plan, however, this is usually lost on the pile of good intentions.

The Design Document/Media Design Document

The design document and the media design document describe and explain the overall appearance of the training. Some managers consider the media design document a crucial element of WBT development because of the time and expense associated with preparing the media to be used in a course. Video, animation, graphics, and audio can all be a high percentage of the external costs.

Julie Nolan of Nolan Multimedia in Novato, California, gives this advice for preparing your design documents: "Be sure to state how each objective will be met. Spell out the instructional design strategy including how the content will be presented and what form it will take (video, stills, animation, audio, text), as well as how program users will be tested and what type of feedback and/or remedial loops will be present. Describe how program content will be organized and define all modules that will be produced. Specify all user pathways for accessing content and how the navigation system will work. State how user performance data will be collected and utilized."

Planning in advance the quality and type of media you will use helps with budgeting expenses for the entire project. Bryan Chapman of Allen Communication says the media design document is a way to decide how to make a dynamic interaction with limited media. "The only difference between CD-ROM development and WBT development is making sure people understand the media before they go into it—and design for what's possible. When people are used to having full screen graphics and large video files, the restrictions of WBT are a shock," says Chapman.

Define Standards

Both style and technical standards of the program need to be defined early in the development process. Style standards should be quite specific, including issues like which font will be used for basic text, headings, menu boxes, and any other repeated elements. This also needs to include what colors are used, navigational elements, button design, and so on throughout the course. More than one developer may work on each course; having a set of style guidelines will keep the format consistent.

Technical standards ensure the consistency of the delivery aspects of the program, for example, what color palettes will be used, file formats for media, the minimum speed of network connection, and so on.

Interface Design

Designing the appearance of the standard features of the program may or may not require a separate person, but should be developed alongside the design document and the media design document. The interface design is the graphic architecture which will define all other media elements of a training program, and is the first step in the actual production of graphics. See Chapter 8 for a more detailed description of interface design.

Flowchart

The flowchart is a road map of the program. Nolan says this step is an integral part of the design documents. "You need to understand where you are branching to and from, not only how the program is designed," she says. The flowchart is also used as a reference document for quality assurance testers after the course is completed.

Scripts and Storyboards

The script describes the narration, scene description, and text for each module making up the course, and usually accompanies the storyboarding process. It is important to include exact references to visual materials in the text of the script.

Storyboards are a graphical and text presentation of all the information that goes into each screen of the program. The storyboards will typically include a graphic on the top third of the page, either hand drawn or a screen shot, essentially a rough draft of what the screen will look like. The text portion of the storyboard describes all of the functionality that can occur, on that page. The storyboard should also include technical information such as the name of the graphic files being used, how branching will occur, and other related information. Storyboards are usually prepared by the instructional designer and then handed off to the programmer. Russell Lash of Cavalcade Designs explains, "Author/programming storyboards . . . are used to document the exact content of a multimedia program. They are very detailed and you will typically have one storyboard sheet for every potential screen the end-user would encounter."

STORYBOARDS: WHAT ARE THEY AND DO YOU REALLY HAVE TO HAVE THEM?

Russell Lash, Calvaleade Designs

So, you are designing another CBT program. You have just finished the detailed outline and are almost done developing the CBT script. During a project review meeting, the author (a fancy name for the CBT programmer) asks when the storyboards will be ready. Say what??? "What storyboards? Can't you program from my script and notes?" you reply. The author comes back with, "Sorry, but I really need storyboards to author your ideas correctly. Also, it would be very beneficial to have detailed flowcharts as well." Unfortunately for you, the project manager concurs with the author.

Does this sound familiar? If you are a CBT or multimedia developer and this is not a familiar scene, please give me a call. I'd like to know where we went wrong.

Let's step back briefly and define storyboards.

The two types of storyboards are:

Design storyboards: These are the traditional storytelling pictures that are used during the idea generation of some form of video/movie/TV show production. It can also be used to assist with the idea generation of a CBT or multimedia program. This type of storyboard is used very early in the project lifecycle. It is also not the type of storyboard covered in this article.

Authoring/programming storyboards: These are used to document the exact content of a CBT or multimedia program. They are very detailed and you will typically have one storyboard sheet for every potential CBT/multimedia screen the end-user could encounter.

As you have probably already guessed, there could be a lot of storyboard sheets for a simple one hour CBT program (in the hundreds); however, to properly document the program for the author (and the client), this really should be done.

Now, before we get into the storyboard sheet itself, let me clear up a few things. There are times when a storyboard is not necessary. Now, I know what you are thinking. Didn't I just say storyboards are a must? Well, I might have implied that, but like most rules . . .

There are exceptions. Here are mine:

1. If the program designer and the author are the same person, a communication vehicle between the two is not necessary. Thus, a full set of storyboards may not be necessary. You might want to storyboard difficult parts of the program to see how it would flow before programming, or storyboard the first part of the program to use as a communication vehicle between you and the client.

Exception to the exception: Even though you might be doing the design and development yourself, if your client requests/requires storyboards as part of the project for development review or support purposes later, then plan on buying some binders for the storyboards.

2. If the program designer and the author have worked very closely together on the content and scripting, and have worked together before, storyboards may not be necessary except, again, for those difficult parts of the program.

Exception to the exception: (same as above)

OK, let's talk about the storyboard sheet itself. What is the nature of the beast? There are an unlimited number of variations to storyboard designs. What worked great on the last project may not work so well for the current project.

Personally, I redesign my storyboard sheet to fit the need of the project. There are, however, components to a storyboard sheet that are common to any layout design.

Components common to any layout design:

Storyboard sheet identifier: This is similar to a page number. Frequently, I will use a complex form of identifier like 3-2-32. The first number refers to the module, second number to the lesson, and the last number to the screen number within the lesson.

Placement of the identifier can be anywhere, but should always be in the same place on all sheets. Because I frequently use a word processor to help generate my storyboards, I will let the word processor automatically increment the screen number.

Type of screen: This is usually a bunch of check boxes where I can quickly indicate the type of screen this sheet is for. The various types of screens can include Introduction, Transition Screen (used to move from one topic to another, etc.), Text (presentation of information), Question/Exercise/ Interaction, Remediation/Response to Interaction, Menu, etc., and Next Screen ID(s). Also known as the next storyboard ID, this identifies where the program will go when the user is done with this screen. In many cases, it will simply be the next logical screen or storyboard sheet. However, if the user is required to perform some form of interaction (other than clicking on the NEXT button), then there may be several Next Screen IDs. If this is the case, the storyboard sheet needs to document the action the user can take and what the next appropriate storyboard sheet will be, based upon that action.

Text for the current screen: This is the text that will/should appear on the user's screen when this part of the program is being presented. On the storyboard sheet, you can either copy/paste the text from the script, re-type it, or, from a paper printout of the script, physically cut and paste the paper onto the storyboard sheet. If the program will be using text files that are linked into the program, then the text file name(s) should also appear on the storyboard sheet.

Graphics: If there are one or more graphic images on the current screen, then some representation of the graphics should be on the storyboard sheet. If the graphics are already developed, be sure to include the graphic file names on the storyboard sheet.

Audio segments: If there is one or more audio segments that will be played while on the current screen, then you need to indicate this on the storyboard sheet. If the audio files are already developed, be sure to include the file names on the storyboard sheet. It is also helpful to indicate when the file should be played (i.e., immediately, after a 10 second pause, when the user presses a PLAY button, etc.).

Video segments: If there are one or more video segments that will be played while on the current screen, then you need to indicate this on the storyboard sheet. If the video files are already developed, be sure to include the file names on the storyboard sheet. It is also helpful to indicate when the video should be played (i.e., immediately, after a 10 second pause, when the user presses a PLAY button, etc.).

Rough graphical layout of the screen: This is simply a visual layout representing the monitor screen. I simply draw (always with pencil) where the text, graphics, animations, video will be on the screen. If you have specific screen designs developed for the program, you may simply need to specify which screen design to use. This way the author will know where everything goes based on that screen design.

Special programming instructions: This is a catch-all area for you to give special instructions to the author about your needs for this particular screen.

There are many other things you can add to the storyboard sheet. So, before launching into storyboarding, look carefully at your entire program and try to anticipate the type of information you will need to give the author.

Ideally, the storyboards should be complete enough that once you are done with them, you can give them to the author and then take that well-deserved trip to Hawaii (but don't forget to take your cellular and remember to set the follow-me roaming, just in case).

Media Acquisition

Acquiring the multimedia elements for a WBT course is less expensive than acquiring for CD-ROM–based training because fewer media will be used. Bryan Chapman says this shouldn't change the nature of the training strategies, it only alters the methods used to carry them out. "You can get away with very little media," he says. One strategy of reducing file size for graphic elements is to use the GIF format. "I took the same graphic from the Internet in six different formats and GIF was less than half the size of any other format," Chapman says. "You work along the same lines with other media as well: keep audio sizes small by recording in short segments and use lower sampling rates. Keep video window sizes smaller as well. Another really significant trick in Internet training is to have the program download large graphic files during idle time, like when the user is reading instructions from the screen." Many developers use animated GIFs with audio in place of a video, such as a person talking.

Proof-of-Concept or Prototype

This step involves developing an early test module within the guidelines dictated by the design document. "If you design something, you don't know how it will be received until you get it out there," Nolan says. "Proof-of-concept is a part of a module or representative sample of the program that you deliver to the end-user population to see if you're on target. It's a way of minimizing your risk." Even testing a prototype will not eliminate all the design flaws though: all instructional design problems can't be resolved until the whole program is established. Nolan says that although the concept of building an early prototype is a good idea, it is not used often enough.

Programming

Programming WBT is the most time-consuming factor in the development process. It can be done in-house, but a staff not yet familiar with this type of programming may take longer than an external developer who has the experience and expertise to complete the project quickly and with fewer traumas along the way. However, in-house programming will be cheaper. Authoring tools are becoming more and more user-friendly, and allow new programmers to program WBT more time-efficiently.

Usability Testing

Usability testing requires either direct observation, interviews with users, or some kind of feedback mechanism like a questionnaire or e-mail response button. Testers should also look at the user performance data to see how well the instruction is working. With WBT, observing end-users while they complete the program at distant locations isn't always possible, so some kind of interactive dialog between tester and user needs to be established.

Technical Testing/Quality Assurance

Technical testing is a systematic process in which the development team's QA person examines every link of every screen in the course. Using the flowchart as a reference, the tester works their way through each button and link to make sure the program works as intended. All problems are referred back to the programmer, who makes the changes. The tester must then repeat the entire process, and this will go back and forth between the tester and programmer until all bugs are resolved. QA also involves testing the program on each type of computer the target audience uses, and over the various likely network connections.

Distribution

Distribution for WBT is mainly an installation and a communications effort, letting all end-users know where the course can be found. Links from other sites on the company's intranet or on the Internet can help expedite this process. Valerie Beeman, project manager with Training and Organizational Development at Stanford University, also says it's important to build awareness of the courseware within the organization. "Don't overlook the need to create excitement or communicate frequently about Web-based training, especially if it's new to the company," she says.

MORE THAN TOOLS ARE NEEDED TO MAKE INTERACTIVE MULTIMEDIA HAPPEN SUCCESSFULLY

Vince Eugenio, former manager of AT&T's Interactive Products and Services

Most multimedia developers love fast hardware and powerful software tools. We seem focused on CPUs, RAM, authoring systems, scripting languages, graphics suites, and video editors rather than on the processes necessary for bringing projects in on budget and on schedule. Without sound processes in place for producing product, the odds for failure are increased several-fold. Due to the high visibility, cost, and risk associated with developing interactive multimedia products, you will probably receive one—and only one—chance to make good on the promises contained in your proposal.

In my experience, customers will judge your success not on a complex matrix of variables, but on two easily measured factors: budget and time. If either commitment is exceeded significantly, you will certainly lose any future opportunities to build more product. So for now, forget about the bits and bytes stuff and let's see how a systematic approach to project management can make interactive multimedia happen successfully.

Determining an Estimated Budget and Schedule

Let's assume that a thorough needs analysis has been conducted and interactive multimedia is the recommended delivery media. Your customer is supportive of the recommendation, but demands to know how much the proposed product will cost and how long it will take to produce. Due to the inherent complexity of multimedia, it is strongly suggested that a high-level design document be written outlining items such as the target audience, delivery infrastructure, content, treatment, level of interactivity, sophistication of instructional strategies, media element fidelity, and user navigation features. This document will serve as an initial shaping of the product for both the customer and the development team.

Once approved, the design document can serve as the foundation for developing an estimated schedule and budget. Working from this document, the project team works closely together to produce a project plan. The project plan is a document containing items such as complete task listing or work breakdown structure, task durations, number of resources, work times, task interdependencies, etc.

When estimating task durations and work hours, insist that all estimates fall between worst and best case scenarios as the accuracy of this data directly affects the accuracy of the budget and schedule estimates. It is critical that experienced team members participate in the estimating process or, at the very least, validate the estimates as they will have to live by them. Once the team approves this data, it can be entered into project management software to generate an estimated project schedule and budget. (Don't forget to consider vacations and holidays!)

Having this estimate in hand, meet with the customer to determine if the schedule and budget are satisfactory. Further negotiations may be required as customers often have CD-ROM tastes and a diskette pocketbook. It may be necessary to have several rounds of cutting or expanding the project plan until the customer is satisfied with the estimates. Even though you may be anxious to start, generating sound estimates using this methodology is extremely effective. It provides the customer with a feel for the needed scope and scale of work which would be almost impossible to convey as effectively any other way.

Managing the Project

Determining the budget and schedule is now behind you and the project plan is in place. Now comes the fun part: working with the tools. Granted, they will actually assist in the building of the project, but the project still needs close monitoring or control. Using project management software and techniques, you can generate daily or weekly comparisons of what is actually happening to the planned budget and schedule. During regular intervals, typically at least once a week, team members contribute information such as the task they are working on, how long they have been on that task, and percent of completion. Also, they indicate if there are any roadblocks to the successful completion of that task. In a tightly planned project, any delay of critical tasks can significantly affect the project's schedule.

Having a complete picture of the project's actual performance is a powerful tool. The project team can use this data to readjust customer and team expectations regarding the project's outcome. For example, if the project plan indicates that the schedule or budget may be missed, steps can be taken to get the project back on course. Let's say fidelity of graphics poses a problem. They can be adjusted by moving from 3-D models to 2-D renderings. Do strategies and programming logic need to be simplified? Perhaps canned music clips rather than custom music should be used. Used judiciously, these techniques can be done without significantly affecting the final quality of the product; however, action must be taken fast and firmly. Otherwise, delay will ripple throughout the project, building and magnifying itself to the point where the project is out of control. The end result is being over budget and schedule.

Conclusion

This has been a very simplified model for delivering interactive multimedia projects on time and within budget. Here are several points worth applying to your next project.

1. Perform a good needs analysis.

2. Create a detailed work breakdown structure.

3. Develop a project plan prior to starting work.

4. Include the development team in the development of the project plan.

5. Emphasize that each team member's contributions are essential to the project coming in on time and within schedule.

6. Compare the project's actual performance to the project plan.

7. Take immediate action to avoid delays in task completion.

Having sharp tools and knowing how to use them is only a part of making successful multimedia happen. A systematic approach to project management should be employed to ensure customer satisfaction and your success.

The Project Team for Custom Development

Having assessed the value of Web-based training, the next step in implementing a training system is to assemble a team of developers and administrators. These team members will plan the training, sculpt the training strategies into Web-based system, design an engaging interactive program using a variety of multimedia, and implement and evaluate the system while providing technical support for users.

Roles and Responsibilities

The list of duties and responsibilities that follows describes the many functions that may take place on a Web-based training development project. Some of these jobs might only be necessary for large teams, while on smaller projects one person would likely perform several of the functions. And there is the all-too-frequent hard-working, one-person-band who somehow does it all.

Project Manager

Each team starts with a project manager who oversees the assignment and flow of tasks and coordinates the development schedule. Some project managers might fulfill other roles on the project in addition to management and supervision. For example, Gayle Tansy, a project manager for 3 Dog Multimedia, is project manger plus instructional designer and editor on many projects she works on. Responsibilities and functions for different teams and projects will shift according to the skills and capabilities of each team's members. The project manager keeps the whole team informed of any changes that occur along the away, and will, in the words of Ralph Matlack, project manager for Multimedia Pathways, help the team "stay focused on the big picture and make sure we do not stray off of our intended path."

As a project manager, Matlack stresses that clear communication is of paramount importance. "A lot of times things don't start out well on a project so it's nice when everyone starts with a clear definition or role. This is not *just* for multimedia but it certainly applies to us." Matlack starts his projects with a memo to team members with all the "pre-kickoff project information" they need. This memo describes each team member's role and relationship to one another (see Figure 5.1). This project was for Siemens Business Communications and involved the development of Web-based training for Siemens' sales department delivered over the company's intranet.

MEMORANDUM

Date: October 25

From: Ralph Matlack
Multimedia Pathways, Inc.

To: MDSS EPSS/CBT Development Team:
Mary Baumgartner, Independent—Lead Graphic Artist
Elizabeth Chapman Walker, Independent—Lead Instructional Designer
Jean Cobb, Appintec—Subject Matter Expert
Brad Fietsam, Multimedia Pathways—Lead Programmer
Timothy Johnson, Multimedia Pathways—Programmer
Steve Madeira, Siemens Business Communications—Customer

Subject: Pre-Kickoff Project Information

Well we have finally received the go ahead to start! Before meeting on Thursday, October 31, from 12–1:30 to kick off the project, I wanted to provide everyone with some baseline information about the project, the project team, and the development schedule. Please take some time to review this document and the attached material, and call or e-mail me if you have any questions.

Prior to the kickoff meeting next week, I will fax everyone directions to the meeting site as well as a rough agenda for the meeting.

The Project
Although I have spoken to each of you personally about the project, let me recap. We are tasked with developing a computer-based training/performance support system for Siemens' MDSS (Market Development Support System) software. In general terms, MDSS is a mainframe-based application used primarily by Siemens sales reps to manage customer and contact information. The CBT/PSS will consist of 20 modules programmed using Authorware and delivered over Siemens' intranet. Module 1 (Systems Overview) will be CBT-like, in that it will provide a big-picture view of the system in a traditional CBT format (hierarchical organization of content followed by

FIGURE 5.1 Sample project manager's memo.

testing). Modules 2–20 will consist of smaller "chunks" of training, each one addressing a specific task within MDSS (adding records, for example).

The Project Team

First, let me say a bit about the roles and expectations for each team member.

Project Manager—Ralph Matlack

My primary purpose is to provide you, the team members, with the information and resources that you need to do your jobs in a highly efficient and quality conscious manner. Ultimately, it is also my role to ensure that we, as a team, not only deliver a quality product to our client, but do so in a way such that Siemens will want to return to us for future work. Functionally, while all of you delve into the details of the content, I will stay focused on the big picture and make sure we do not stray off of our intended path.

Subject Matter Expert—Jean Cobb

Jean is our intellectual resource for information on the details of MDSS software. Jean will primarily interact with Elizabeth, but will also play a key role in review and quality assurance. (Jean works for Appintec, the company that creates the software that allows Siemens to create MDSS.)

Lead Instructional Designer—Elizabeth Chapman Walker

Elizabeth is in charge of ensuring the instructional integrity of the system through thoughtful instructional design and clear writing. Functionally, Elizabeth will be the primary contributor to the scripts and storyboards (the blueprints of the system). While most of Elizabeth's work will occur early in the development process, she will remain involved to oversee that implementation of graphics and programming are consistent with her instructional design.

Lead Graphic Artist—Mary Baumgartner

Mary's role is two-fold. First, it is to collaborate with other team members in the design of an attractive and intuitive user interface. Second, it is to create the visual content of the system (i.e., graphics and animation).

Lead Programmer—Brad Fietsam

Brad's role is to integrate Elizabeth's design and Mary's visuals into the final software product. As lead programmer, Brad will be responsible for designing the overall architecture and functionality of the program.

Programmer—Timothy Johnson

Timothy will assist Brad in the programming effort. Timothy will primarily be working on the programming for Modules 2–20.

FIGURE 5.1 Continued

Customer—Steve Madeira

Steve is the voice of the customer (Siemens). Steve's primary role is to ensure that Siemens gets what it paid for. Accordingly, Steve will play a central role in the review/change process, where we tune the system to match the client's requirements. Unless otherwise notified, all questions should be directed to or through Steve.

The Development Schedule

The following pages show an extremely tentative version of the development schedule. The timing on this schedule may change, but the tasks and order of tasks (i.e., the process) will remain fairly solid. We will discuss and revise the schedule in great detail during the kickoff meeting.

Summary

Good communication is essential for this project's success. If we can properly manage the information that flows within the team, our best creative talents will be allowed to emerge and we will produce a product that everyone is proud of.

FIGURE 5.1 Continued

Instructional Designer

The instructional designer of the Web-based training program is the one person ultimately responsible for the program teaching what it's supposed to teach. This is what differentiates a training program from a reference document or a communication program: it is designed to teach, and it incorporates instructional elements, such as remediation loops, which are intended to ensure learning takes place. The instructional designer accomplishes this by conducting a thorough needs analysis, overall design, and often the actual writing of storyboards. Storyboards are a graphical and text presentation of all the information that goes into each screen of the program. The storyboards will typically include a graphic on the top third of the page, either hand drawn or a screen shot, essentially a rough draft of what the screen will look like. The text portion of the storyboard describes all of the functionality that can occur on that page. The storyboard should also include technical information such as the name of the graphic files being used, how branching will occur, and other related information.

Instructional designers sculpt lessons out of a combination of text, graphics, and interactive multimedia. This task usually calls for heavy involvement in the project in the early stages of development which tapers off as the project progresses. As programmers and graphic designers begin to work on the instructional designer's storyboards, the instructional designer makes frequent checks of the work's development to ensure there has been no miscommunication.

Figure 5.2 is a job posting for an instructional designer from 3 Dog Multimedia that may be a useful description of desirable skills for project managers looking to fill this position.

Lead Programmer

Although some teams may have only one programmer for all functions, larger teams will split these responsibilities between a "high-level programmer" and a "data-entry programmer," or some similar combination of those functions. The lead programmer uses an authoring program such as IconAuthor, Quest, or ToolBook to implement the instructional designer's storyboards. The lead programmer writes the code to create the final Web-based training product, incorporating the visual recommendations of the graphic designer and the text recommendations of the editor and instructional designer.

INSTRUCTIONAL DESIGNER

We are looking for an Instructional Designer with experience writing content for CBT courses, including storyboarding. You should have experience scripting, developing, and incorporating both multimedia and interactivity. Ideally, you will also know how to use FrameMaker and be familiar with the UNIX, Windows (all flavors), and Macintosh systems.

Requirements:

- 3+ years experience in Instructional Design field
- Excellent written/verbal communication skills
- Vendor/customer relationship experience
- Project management experience
- Editing experience a plus

FIGURE 5.2 Sample job posting for an Instructional Designer.

Data-Entry Programmer

A second programmer may be required to assist the lead programmer. This "data-entry programmer" is often responsible for entering the course content onto disk as well as building interactive exercises. Bigger projects might require additional programming assistance beyond data entry or exercise building, depending on the work load of the lead programmer.

SQA (Software Quality Assurance)

Once the programming is in place, the team needs to test the applications. Software quality assurance may be a part of the programmer's responsibility but on larger development teams, such as the one headed up by Randy Robinson at Digital Chef, Inc., providing Web-based training to the hospitality industry, as many as five SQA people are on staff at a time.

Administrative Support/Budget Analyst

As with any large endeavor, Web-based training development projects require administrative support. This team member updates production schedules, tracks expenditures, and purchases materials.

Subject Matter Expert/Content Expert

The subject matter expert acts as a consultant on the actual content of the curriculum. Clearly, different subject matter experts (or SMEs, as they're popularly known) are needed for each project, so an SME is often a member of the client group or organization. SMEs are chosen for their area of expertise, and work with writers and instructional designers to create the actual curriculum and training methods that will be used. It is important to clarify the role of the SME up front. Every instructional designer has at least one SME horror story, usually a variation on "They wouldn't sign off on the module because they didn't like the background color."

Interface Designer

Interface design might be performed by the graphic designer, by the art director, or by a separate "interface designer." Interface design refers specifically to the overall look and feel of the program. The interface designer will have specialized knowledge about the way users access software, and what navigational tools are the most user-friendly.

Graphic Designer/Web Designer

The graphic designer takes the recommendations of the interface designer and implements those ideas into the page design. Working with other team members to implement the overall look of the program, the graphic designer assesses what style and look will best fit the needs of the internal or external customer. Some groups, like Sage Interactive of Mill Valley, place all visual-oriented staff members (i.e., video, animation, and still image specialists) under the supervision of the graphic designer or art director. Graphic design and artistic functions are often good candidates for outsourcing, since this specialized skill is project specific. Randy Robinson, instructional designer with Guestware, says that a Web designer is desirable for a Web-based training project. More specialized than graphic designers, these designers must know HTML and be accustomed to working within the confines of a Web page. "In so many ways, you are very limited in what you can do," Robinson says. Having a designer who specializes in Web pages can give you maximum flexibility in the presentation of the training program.

Multimedia Developer

The multimedia developer will work with audio, video, and animation. The project may require more than one of these media to be incorporated into the overall design and programming structure, so more than one person might join the development team in the capacity of multimedia developer.

Writer

The writer (which may be one or more persons, depending on the scope of the project) crafts the text of the training material. This function requires communication among the writer, the editor, the subject matter experts, the customer, and the instructional designer.

Editor

The editing function is a quality control exercise to verify correct grammar and style in the text of the curriculum. This function is especially important if there is more than one writer to ensure a similar writing style throughout.

Webmaster

The Webmaster handles the day-to-day technical support related to delivering your content over the network. If your program is accessed only by a small number of people each week, you may not need a separate person for maintenance, but if you're overwhelmed with e-mail questions, you may want to hire someone to handle the overflow. If your training programs are on their own server, someone will need to maintain the hardware and network connections as well.

Client Contact

Another critical member of the team is the client. The client contact is the primary person representing the concerns of both the purchaser of the program and the end-user. The client pays the bills and therefore calls the shots. The client might have style guidelines which differ from the standards of the WBT development team. For instance, Gayle Tansy describes a situation in which a client preferred the words "click on" to direct the user to select an item using the mouse. Tansy's group was accustomed to using the directive "*select* the item." Small but significant differences like this need to be clarified between the customer liaison and the development team.

Where to Find Your Staff

Many project managers say the best source for finding temporary or permanent staff for Web-based training development projects is through word-of-mouth. "Most of our staff has been friends of friends," Gayle Tansy says. "That's usually how we find most of our good people."

There are several places a project manager can begin to search for skilled individuals, besides networking with Gayle's friends.

- Employment agencies that specialize in multimedia, such as Ronn Rogers' Multimedia Recruiters of Dallas.

- Professional organizations like:

    - ASTD—American Society for Training and Development
      1640 King Street, Box 1443, Alexandria, VA 22313-2043
      Telephone: (703) 683-8100; Fax: (703) 683-8103

    - IICS—International Interactive Communications Society
      Executive Office
      PO Box 1862, Lake Oswego, OR 97035

    - ISPI—International Society for Performance and Improvement
      1300 L Street, NW, Suite 1250, Washington, DC 20005
      Telephone: (202) 408-7969; Fax: (202) 408-7972
      E-Mail: INFO@ISPI.ORG http://www.ispi.org

- SSTC—Society for Technical Communications
  901 North Stuart Street, Suite 304, Arlington, VA 22203
  Telephone: (703) 522-4114; Fax: (703) 522-2075

- Universities and colleges with departments specializing in multimedia or instructional design—project mangers cite this source as a good place to find permanent employees as well as part-time or temporary team members, among students who welcome a flexible schedule.

  - San Francisco State University
    Multimedia Studies Program
    Telephone: (415) 904-7700

  - Georgia Tech
    Center for New Media Education and Research
    Atlanta, GA 30332-0385
    Telephone: (404) 894-2547

BUILDING A BUSINESS CASE FOR WEB-BASED TRAINING

As with any new technology, Web-based training may be met with skepticism from those who don't have a clear understanding of its benefits. This chapter provides information on many levels that will help you focus on your training goals and sell the idea of Web-based training to different members of the client organization, whether internal or external. Included here are return-on-investment studies which help show the cost-effectiveness of multimedia training, market research culled from a number of studies that shows the statistical increases in Internet use, intranet use, and the rise of training, and materials from a number of training professionals or organizations offering advice about how to build a business case and develop support for your WBT project.

The development of Web-based training programs can be viewed as a financial trade-off for one's first program: the cost of purchasing authoring software and learning to author Web-based training programs may cancel out the savings from the less expensive delivery. Some companies take a longer view and see the savings in Web-based training from the beginning. Sherri Rose of Apple Computer said she began using various forms of multimedia for training at Apple due to a shrinking budget and a growing number of employees all over the world who needed training. Rose said Apple began by converting many of their courses to CD-ROM, which they soon found to be costly to update. The company is now working to develop Web-based training for management and leadership training courses.

Lance Dublin, CEO of the Dublin Group, has helped many companies build the business case for a technology plan. His firm specializes in putting together an organizational change effort to make sure technology is implemented effectively. His advice to those seeking funding is make sure your proposal addresses key business concerns because training is only a means to an end, not an end in itself. He says too many plans focus on the features of the program rather than on the benefits to the business. He also believes that most trainers are hesitant to ask for a large-enough budget to really accomplish the task at hand. If you can establish the business case and show a positive return-on-investment, he says ask for what you really need. His final recommendation is to make sure you go through the effort of tracking results and follow through by reporting back to management. They want to know the benefit of their investment.

As you come to the decision to use the Web as part of your training delivery system, you may need to champion the value of this method to several groups: executives, managers, trainers, and especially students. Understanding what each group values will help you persuade all members of the organization to contribute to the development effort.

Building enthusiasm in the organization is important in order to sell and implement a Web-based training program. You have to address concerns of several audiences: for executives, will the training improve productivity and cost less than instructor-led training? For managers, will the trainees complete the training quickly and effectively? For students, will the training be useful to them in their jobs?

This chapter contains examples of return-on-investment studies that will help you demonstrate the cost effectiveness of technology-delivered training. We have also included a sample RFP (request for proposals) sent out by the American Management Association. The actual proposal the AMA received from ACI, used with both organizations' permission, is located in Appendix A. Once you've decided the Web is a good delivery method for your training, begin thinking about what factors will be of concern to different members of the client organization. You can address these issues in the proposal, but first you need to know what they are.

Business Concerns

Steve Roden, president of ITC, one of the largest companies for development and distribution of technology-delivered instruction, has compiled the model of concerns about training at different levels in an organization, shown in Table 6.1.

TABLE 6.1 Heirarchy of Training Concerns

Organization Level	Concerns

Corporate executives	• Profitability
	• Lower costs
	• Higher productivity
	• Return on investment (ROI)
	    Costs
	    Results
	• Skill development ("Prove to me people are learning")
	• Performance improvement ("Prove to me people are doing something differently")
	• Helps for them to see an example or see it in action

Managers	• Want better skilled workers (but don't want to pay to train them) • Want lowest cost for training (student participation time is single most expensive cost of training) • Want people back to work as soon as possible • Privacy for their own training
Trainers	• Want to be more productive • Want to be more responsive to their organization • Want and need power tools • Many don't like CBT when they first see it • Reasonable concerns about job security (replaced by a computer?)
Prospective students	• Make it less painful (easier/less boring/more fun) • Make sure it fits my needs • Make it self-directed (I choose when/how fast/how much/which parts)

Executives

In Roden's model, corporate executives need to be convinced of the profitability of Web-based training. They will be convinced by evidence such as return-on-investment studies, demonstrated improvement in skill development, and cost figures which show that Web-based training has a lower implementation expense than alternative forms of training. Showing this group an example or prototype of Web-based training may help to build your case. Building a prototype as part of the proposal may not be practical, so another alternative is to find an example already on the Web. A number of Web sites that focus on Web-based training contain examples. When building your case to convince this group of decision makers, whether you are an internal or external team, you need to demonstrate that Web-based training has lower delivery costs, is highly effective, and can improve the performance of trainees.

Managers

Managers are concerned about performance but also want to know that they can see their employees back at work quickly. One point you can make to this group is that because WBT allows at-your-own-place, at-your-own-pace access, trainees may be back on the job sooner. Coordinating schedules and transporting employees to remote locations is not a factor for Web-delivered training, as it is for instructor-led curriculum. Even computer-based training can be a logistical nightmare, as trainers try to distribute updates to all branches of the company. The instant-update feature of the Web enhances the efficiency with which the client organization can deliver training.

Another selling point for managers is that with Web delivery, they can have the privacy to complete their own training without any potential discomfort at having to sit through a class with their own employees. Trainees at any level can learn the material on their own time, in a quiet and comfortable environment.

Trainers

Trainers in an organization will also have concerns about the implementation of Web-based training. The most obvious concern is that their function in the company will be replaced by a computer. The field of training is changing, as are many other fields. People need to adapt and there are many other roles besides stand-up training. Trainers will be able to spend their time developing instruction rather than delivering a course to only a few trainees at multiple locations and times. Because many trainers are intuitive, interpersonal-oriented people, the idea of a computer delivering their training may make them uncomfortable. Reassurance about the interactivity and one-on-one delivery capability of a user accessing the training from a desktop can make a difference. Work with trainers and instructional designers to find ways to make the Web-based training more acceptable to them.

Prospective Students

Many of the same issues can be addressed when thinking about why prospective students might like or dislike Web-based training. Students, according to Roden's model, will be attracted to WBT if the training is well-designed, entertaining, and interactive, and allows them to train at their own pace. Talking to students personally and finding out what their concerns are will not only help you craft your proposal, it will help you design your training. Knowing students are interested in a Web-based approach can help sell the idea to trainers, managers, and executives, because the end result is students who are excited by the training product itself. The basic questions to ask yourself about students are: Will they accept the new technology-driven training? Will they learn from the new technology-driven training?

Return-on-Investment Studies

Many organizations are faced with an increasing need for training while their training budgets have been substantially reduced. As a result, training professionals are looking to alternative approaches to meet their training needs. I have conducted a study to document the business advantages of converting traditional instructor-led training to multimedia training. Specifically, this study attempted to:

- Identify and document successful training interventions in organizations using interactive training.

- Identify return-on-investment results (where available) for organizations using interactive training.

- Review academic research to identify the major studies involving computer-based instruction.

Methodology

I identified potential case studies by requesting information from training managers, developers, and end users. Interviews were conducted with project managers of the programs cited herein, and documentation was requested from each organization. Criteria for participation in the study included the implementation of a successful interactive training project and a willingness to allow publication of results.

The literature review was compiled following database searches I conducted at Stanford University and through the American Society for Training and Development's TrainLit. Databases searched at Stanford University included ERIC (Education Resources Information Center), Dissertation Abstracts for 1988 through June 1994, and Melvyl's database of computer-related journals and magazines and the American Business Index, both since 1990. This study was funded by Macromedia of San Francisco; it was based on a comparison of instructor-led versus computer-delivered instruction, and provides some of the most detailed cost comparisons available.

The Findings

Based on a review of these case studies from organizations, and the review of the literature, the following conclusions can be drawn regarding the effectiveness and cost benefits of computer-based, multimedia training:

1. There is very strong evidence that computer-based training reduces the total cost of training when compared to instructor-led training.

    Total cost of training includes cost of development and cost of delivery. Interactive training has a higher cost of development and a lower cost for delivery, while traditional training has a lower cost of development and a higher cost of delivery. The lower delivery costs for interactive training result primarily from a reduction in training time and the elimination of travel. A positive return on investment requires a training population large enough for the savings in delivery to offset the cost of development.

2. There is very strong evidence that computer-based training requires less time for training compared to instructor-led training. The amount of reduction ranges from 20–80 percent, with 40–60 percent being the most common.

Time reduction for multimedia training is usually attributed to a tighter instructional design, the option for participants to bypass content not needed, and the opportunity for participants to focus on those sections of the course not yet mastered.

3. There is very strong evidence that computer-based training results in an equal or higher quality of learning over traditional instruction.

   There are a number of scientific studies cited in the literature review of this report which have investigated this issue. The settings for the studies have included business and industry, the military, higher education, and elementary schools.

The Pattern of Multimedia Training Costs

The study also compared costs for instructor-led training versus multimedia training over a three-year period for Storage Technology and Price Waterhouse.

Storage Technology

Storage Technology provides large storage hardware for mainframe computers. The company employs a field force of 1500 technicians to provide technical support. The technicians traveled to Colorado for a four-to-ten-day training session using a lecture/lab format. Three years ago the company began to convert the format of the training from lecture/lab to multimedia-based training in which the technicians received the training at their local offices on a computer equipped with a CD-ROM. Figure 6.1 shows the cost comparison of multimedia training versus instructor-led training at Storage Technology. The pattern of costs over several years for this course is similar to that found in other organizations. Substantial savings were due to two factors in particular: compression of training time and reduction in travel expenses. A comparison of total training costs over three years at Storage Technology for development and delivery of a program showed costs for lecture/lab format at $3,291,327 versus costs for multimedia format at $1,748,327 (Figure 6.2).

Multimedia training development costs are higher. However, delivery costs are lower, compared to instructor-led training. There was a savings of 47 percent of costs over the instructor-led format.

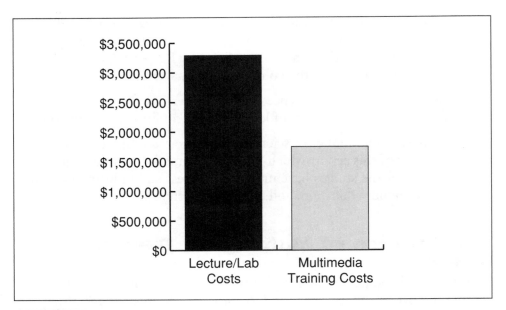

FIGURE 6.1 Total training costs: lecture/lab training versus multimedia training.

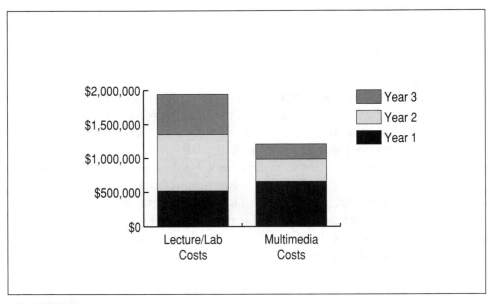

FIGURE 6.2 Comparison of costs for instructor-led training (lecture/lab) versus multimedia training over three years at Storage Technology.

PRICE WATERHOUSE

Price Waterhouse provides audit, tax, accounting, and business consulting services. The company created a CBT program entitled *Terminal* RISK to train the professional audit staff at Price Waterhouse. Staff take the course during their third year of training and it serves as prerequisite training for a week-long residential classroom-based course. The program has been used by 7000 people in 50 countries. To determine benefits to the organization, Price Waterhouse conducted a training effectiveness review. They found that compared to traditional classroom training, the multimedia program reduced by 50 percent the time needed for learners to attain the same standard of knowledge. Price Waterhouse conducted a return-on-investment analysis for the multimedia training course compared with traditional instructor-led training. Total costs for development and delivery over five years were examined. They found the cost-per-learner was $760 for traditional instructor-led training, versus $106 for multimedia training, a savings of 86 percent of costs. (See Figure 6.3.)

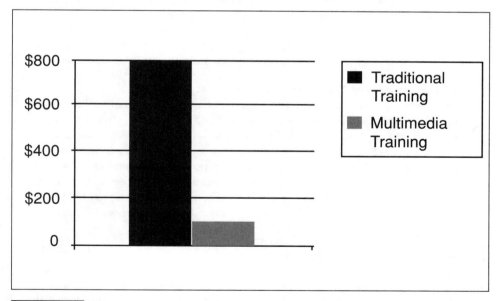

FIGURE 6.3 Comparison by Price Waterhouse of cost-per-learner over five years for traditional instructor-led training versus multimedia training.

CASE STUDY: STORAGE TECHNOLOGY

Abstract

Storage Technology provides large storage hardware for mainframe computers. Cost-per-unit for this equipment can approach one-half million dollars. The company employs a field force of 1,500 technicians to provide technical support. The company typically provided training to the technicians using a lecture/lab format in which the technicians travel to Colorado for a four-to-ten-day training session. Three years ago the company began to convert the format of the training from lecture/lab to multimedia-based training in which the technicians received the training at their local offices on a computer equipped with a CD-ROM. The savings from this conversion were substantial. The savings were due to two factors in particular: compression of training time and reduction in travel expenses. A comparison of total training costs over three years at Storage Technology for development and delivery of a program showed costs for lecture/lab format at $3,291,327 versus costs for multimedia format at $1,748,327.

Background of the Company

Storage Technology designs, manufactures, and markets high-end peripherals for plug-compatible mainframe computers, and is one of the largest suppliers of such equipment in the world. An example of their products is a tape storage device with a robotic arm which can access and load any of up to 6,000 tape cartridges in eleven seconds. Cost-per-unit for this equipment can approach one-half million dollars. There is a field force of 1,500 technicians to service the storage devices and other peripherals at customer locations.

Purpose of the Training Project

The company previously trained field technicians by bringing them to Colorado for regular four-to-ten-day training sessions on new equipment. These sessions used a lecture/lab format in which technicians attended a classroom lecture, then practiced the diagnostic and repair procedures in a hands-on lab with the actual hardware. The multimedia program provides a full simulation of the equipment on a dedicated training platform. Technicians can view the maintenance panel from the target equipment, run diagnostics, see failures occur, then click on pictures of replaceable parts and drag them to the appropriate location to simulate replacement.

Hardware and Software

Field offices around the country were outfitted with computers to provide training. The equipment included a Macintosh Quadra 800 with 20 megabytes of RAM, a 17-inch monitor, and a CD-ROM drive. The courses were developed at headquarters using Macromedia's Authorware Professional. Due to the need for security of company proprietary information, the files on the CD-ROMs are locked. To access the training programs, one must have the matching software key on the hard drive.

Costs

Stephen Ball, the training manager for the training technologies group, used the following costs when computing the total cost of training. These figures are based on several years of tracking actual costs.

Cost factors for multimedia training

Equipment and Development

> Equipment for delivery: $150 per diploma
>
>> (Equipment: Macintosh Quadra 800, CD ROM, 20MB RAM, 17-inch monitors)
>>
>> (Diploma: term used to designate one student completing one course on the computer)
>
> Development time: 550 hours per hour of instruction
>
> Development cost: $30,000 per hour of instruction
>
> Course compression: 60%
>
>> (Training time was reduced by 60% when a course was converted from lecture/lab to multimedia training.)

Staff

> Trainers (contract and employee)
>
> Classes per year
>
> Days per class
>
> Travel cost per class

Trainees

> Number of trainees   1,500
>
> Rate of pay during training   (not used in order to ensure conservative estimates)

Cost Factors for Lecture/Lab Training

Equipment/Development

> Development time
>
>> Lecture/lab: 55 hours per hour of instruction
>
> Development dollars
>
>> Lecture/lab: $3,300 per hour of instruction
>>
>> (55 hours @ $60)

Building & Facilities

    Lecture/lab: $7,000 per classroom per year

Trainers (contract & non-contract)

Classes per year

Days per class

Travel cost per class

Salary & Travel for Trainees

Number of trainees	1,500
Rate of pay during training	(not used in order to ensure conservative estimates)
Days per class	4
Travel costs	$750 round-trip airfare per participant
Per diem expenses	$65/day (2 to a room)

Results

Ball (1994) reported that the dollar savings were substantial when the company converted to interactive multimedia training. This was attributed largely to the elimination of the need for travel and 60 percent less time for training when using multimedia training. According to Ball, the following reasons contribute to the reduction in training time:

- Tighter instructional design
- Users being able to test out of sections
- Varied instructional modes: text, animation, simulation, etc. allow better/faster learning

COST COMPARISON SPREADSHEET

The spreadsheet shown in Table 6.2 was compiled by Storage Technology for comparing costs over three years of a course offered as lecture/lab (L/L) or multimedia (MM).

TABLE 6.2 Cost Comparison Spreadsheet Compiled by Storage Technology

Assumptions	Year 1	Year 2	Year 3
Students to train (#) (The training program was introduced in year 1 with fewer students)	200	480	250

Assumptions	Year 1	Year 2	Year 3
Average round-trip airfare	$750	$788	$827
Training days for L/L course	4	4	4
Per diem + car rental for L/L	$65	$68	$72
Classrooms L/L (internal company charge for use of classrooms)	$6,600	$6,930	$7,277
Burdened hourly labor rate for instructors and instructional designers (includes all administrative expenses for the training department, divided by the total number of hours of direct productive work by instructors and instructional designers)	$60	$63	$66.15
Hours of development required for each L/L instructional hour	55		
Instructor costs for development and delivery of L/L course	$55,000	$57,750	$60,638
Lab equipment (internal charge for depreciation of four machines used in L/L)	$150,000	$150,000	$150,000
Compression ratio (ratio in reduction in number of hours of L/L course by conversion to MM)	0.6		
Training hours per student for MM course	11.2		
Hours of development required for each MM instructional hour	550		

TABLE 6.2 Continued

Assumptions	Year 1	Year 2	Year 3
Platform costs per diploma (prorated cost of hardware for delivery of MM course)	$150	$150	$150
Lecture/Lab Costs			
Travel and living (travel & per diem for 4 days)	$215,000	$541,800	$296,297
Instructor costs	$55,000	$115,500	$121,275
Classroom costs	$6,600	$13,860	$14,553
Development and maintenance costs for L/L course	$92,400	$9,240	$9,702
Lab equipment (4 machines)	$150,000	$150,000	$150,000
Total lecture lab costs	$519,000	$830,400	$591,827
Multimedia Costs			
Development and maintenance costs for MM course (includes cost of L/L course development on which MM course is designed)	$462,000	$46,200	$48,510
MM platform (diploma) costs	$30,000	$72,000	$37,500
Some students will still take the L/L class:			
Travel and living	$64,500	$108,360	$29,630

Assumptions	Year 1	Year 2	Year 3
Instructor costs	$55,000	$57,750	$60,638
Classroom costs	$6,600	$6,930	$7,277
Lab equipment (1 machine)	$37,500	$37,500	$37,500
Total Multimedia costs	$655,600	$328,740	$221,054
Difference (MM minus L/L)	($136,600)	$501,660	$370,773
Savings over 3 years: $735,833			
Internal rate of return: 61%			
Months to payback: 15			

How to Determine Your Return on Investment (ROI)

To compare your cost of training for Web-based training versus alternative means of training, use the following formula:

$$\frac{\text{Total cost of design, development, duplication, delivery and support over the life of the course}}{\text{Total number of students over the life of the course}}$$

Market Research about Web-Based Training

The training industry's use of technology is growing, and the use of the Internet and intranet is growing. In this chapter, we will recap some of the research currently available regarding the growth of these markets. New information will be posted on the companion Web site from the report, "Web-Based Training Market Research Report: Trends, Opportunities, and Risks."

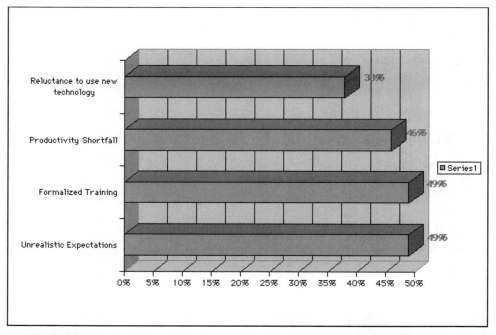

FIGURE 6.4 Possible scenarios anticipated by implementation of Internet technologies.

Source: Infoplex, 1997

Possible Scenarios Anticipated by Implementation of Internet Technologies

The future impact of the Internet upon several general areas was discussed in this study. The four scenarios upon which correspondents were asked to comment are:

- Formalized training of all employees affected by new Internet technologies

- Initial employee productivity

- Shortfall during implementation

- Unrealistic expectations as to the capabilities of the Internet

- Initial employee reluctance to use the new technology

All scenarios were envisioned as being likely by respondents, with the breakdown of responses shown in Figure 6.4.

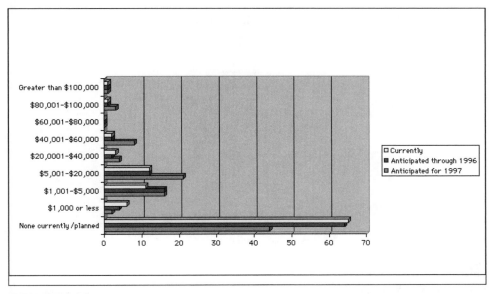

FIGURE 6.5 Current and anticipated training expenses resulting from Internet-related activities.

Source: Infoplex, 1997

Training Expenses Resulting from Internet-Related Activities

Much as respondents view Internet-related activities largely as low maintenance, so too did respondents indicate that such activities could be "self-taught"—training expenses associated with the Internet were said to currently be nonexistent by a clear majority of the survey audience. For the remainder of 1996 this scenario was expected to hold, with 1997 seeing a slight loosening of training budgets specific to Internet activities. To be sure, the majority of respondents still anticipate minimal expenditures and do not appear overly concerned with matters regarding Internet training. Figure 6.5 provides the overall breakdowns for current and anticipated expenditures earmarked for Internet-related training.

Training Markets in 1996 and 2000

Networked training applications already constitute a very important category of the multimedia market. Distance learning, interactive training, and performance support are the primary applications relying on networks for distribution.

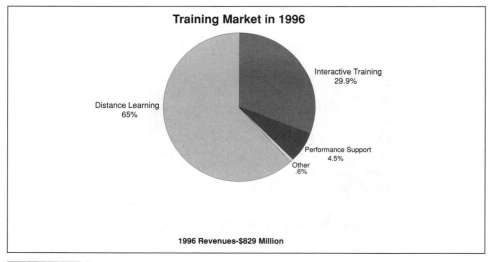

FIGURE 6.6 Training markets in 1996.

Source: New Media Think Tank, 1997

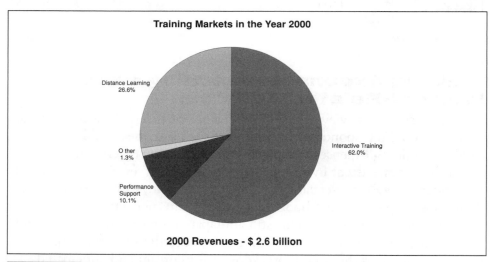

FIGURE 6.7 Training markets in the year 2000.

Source: New Media Think Tank, 1997

Distance learning currently dominates the training category with 65 percent of the market share in 1996, followed by interactive training with 29.9 percent. Local-area networks are growing in popularity for interactive training centers. A growth application is wide-area learning, where most local learning/interactive learning is standalone.

According to Robert Aston of New Media Think Tank, who performed the study, "the real story is that the deployment of interactive training across intranets will dramatically increase as the capabilities currently supported by CD-ROM and standalone applications are extended to the network. When Broadband capability is widely implemented by 2000, the application design will change to take advantage of massive online training resources." (See Figures 6.6 and 6.7.)

Future Intranet Applications

In a Zona market research survey, respondents were asked what intranet applications they anticipated using in the future. More than a single response was permitted. The responses to this question are shown in Figure 6.8.

There is a trend in future intranet use toward expanded use of the intranet for sharing and reviewing documentation. As the documentation-sharing process becomes more structured, use of the intranet as a means to distribute and review documentation will become more formal. This should be the natural evolution of informal document distribution. Functions such as version and configuration control become important.

The sample base also expects to make more formal use of the intranet for structured communications—workgroup forums and video teleconferencing is the initial indication we have seen of mixing multimedia and the intranet.

We anticipate that as the cost advantages of distributing voice via the Internet become more apparent, more sites will use the intranet to move voice, at least within the enterprise as an alternative to traditional telephone suppliers.

There is considerable interest in using the intranet for application interoperability. This may indicate a need for tools which can manage distributed applications, ensuring that they are compatible with the intranet infrastructure. There is also a substantial expectation to use the intranet for enterprisewide training. This appears to be a highly attractive intranet application since it effectively creates a distributed, on-demand training center. Additionally, it should make it easier to create and modify training material. And as multimedia becomes more prevalent, various information types (video, audio, images) can be incorporated into the training material using standard, low-cost development tools, such as Microsoft's Internet Studio. There should be immediate and tangible benefits in providing enterprise and group training via the intranet.

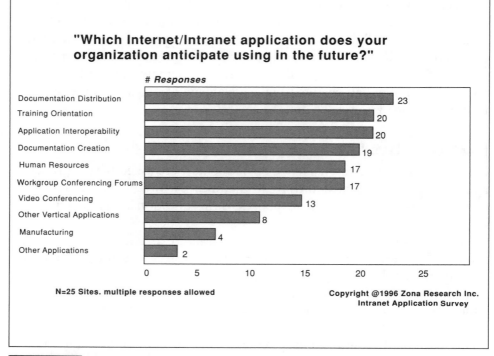

"Which Internet/Intranet application does your organization anticipate using in the future?"

 # Responses

Documentation Distribution	23
Training Orientation	20
Application Interoperability	20
Documentation Creation	19
Human Resources	17
Workgroup Conferencing Forums	17
Video Conferencing	13
Other Vertical Applications	8
Manufacturing	4
Other Applications	2

N=25 Sites. multiple responses allowed

Copyright @1996 Zona Research Inc.
Intranet Application Survey

FIGURE 6.8 Future use of Internet/intranet applications.

Source: Zona Research, 1996

Intranet Applications in Use

Of those 25 enterprises interviewed by Zona Research in this study, 20 sites (80 percent) indicated that they were using Internet technologies and products for internal functions. In the first edition of Zona's report "Internet vs. Intranet," less than 50 percent of those surveyed were currently using intranet technologies.

We are not surprised that intranet use has become more common than external Internet use, but we are a bit surprised at the speed of adoption. The idea of informal and incremental deployment appears to be sound, as organizations are deploying intranets, often without being explicitly aware of the process. This will become more obvious as we study the intranet applications in use.

Within the sample base, we found an approximately equal mix of formal and informal applications in use. The graphic in Figure 6.9 depicts the mix of intranet applications currently being used. From the responses, it seems clear that much of the current intranet use, even at leading intranet users such as Levi's and Visa, is for unstructured sharing of documents and information. This application appears to be the entry point for most organizations using intranets. We interpret these responses to indicate that some users are just starting to deploy intranets, while those utilizing more formal applications have been deploying them for some period of time.

Using the intranet to link to DBMS shows that enterprises are starting to rely upon the Internet as a delivery infrastructure. We believe this use is also a precursor of support for legacy environments via an Internet infrastructure. As users evolve toward supporting legacy environments via the intranet, we would expect to see a convergence of terminal emulation and browsers, with terminal emulation technology delivering their application within a browser, using HTML. This particular legacy compatibility issue represents an interesting path for terminal emulation suppliers, such as WRQ, Attachmate, SCO, and Persoft. Some companies, Simware in particular, are currently offering 327x terminal emulation products which deliver the 327x window inside a browser, converting the 327x output to HTML. DBMS access via the intranet portends the support of intranet-based tools for DBMS access and query. The issue in this area is the conversion of DBMS information and its presentation to browser-compatible HTML format. Some merging of the HTML conversion functions with the DBMS tool capability may be logical. The convergence of the intranet with enterprise DBMS capabilities indicates the potential for new DBMS query and development tools. Oracle is moving in this direction as are Informix, Sybase, PowerSoft, and JYACC.

The paucity of pure vertical applications is expected, given the embryonic nature of the intranet market. An interesting point to consider in this realm is whether ISVs will gain any substantial market share, or whether "vertical" will mean home-brew applications. By viewing the intranet as a computing platform, it is possible to make the case that ISVs could get development leverage. At the same time, the ongoing war between Microsoft and Sun Microsystems mitigates the emergence of a common API for distributed intranet applications. This may hinder the development of vertical intranet applications.

We believe that the use of the intranet for training purposes may be one of the "killer" formal applications that will drive the intranet.

Intranet Market in the Year 2000

Corporations are now undergoing a rapid transition to intranet networks, supporting internal business and business-to-business applications. The amount of multimedia applications delivered over business networks is also

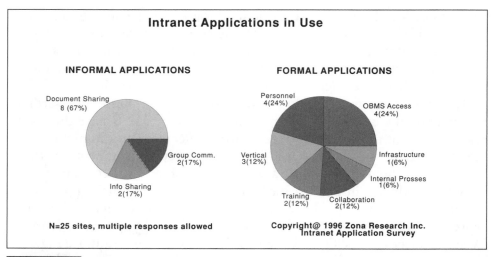

FIGURE 6.9 Intranet applications in use.

Source: Zona Research, 1996

growing. By 2000, the intranet will be more than a document-sharing network: Collaboration will permit real-time interactions between individuals and groups of workers—providing significant productivity gains—increasing a company's global competitive advantage. Figure 6.10 forecasts the breakdown of intranet applications.

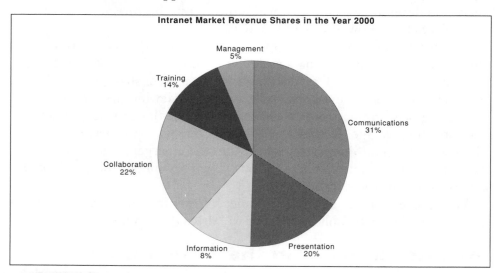

FIGURE 6.10 Intranet market in the year 2000.

Source: New Media Think Tank

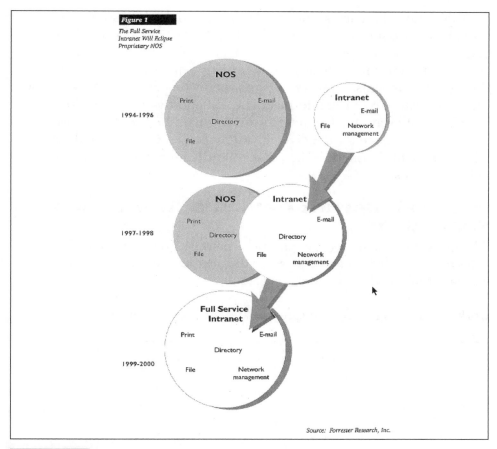

Source: Forrester Research, Inc.

FIGURE 6.11 Applications for internal Web sites.

Source: Infoplex, 1997

Applications for Internal Web Sites

Use of the Web as an external window on a company obviously precedes the use of sites to communicate within organizations. The percentage of companies across a broad business spectrum who have adopted internal Web sites (Web sites accessible to internal employees only) presently lags the proportion with external Web sites. However, a robust start has been made. As of mid-year 1996, 54 percent of Internet-enabled companies have at least one Web site accessible to internal users only.

Furthermore, the survey results indicate this proportion will continue to increase dramatically over the next 18 months. By year's-end 1997 it is anticipated that 79 percent of companies will have at least one internal Web site.

Applications for current internal Web sites (multiple answers per respondent) are shown in Figure 6.11. The answers underscore the very definition of internal Web site, that is, the use of Web technologies to create a tool for internal company communication, indicated by two of every three correspondents. However a high proportion of respondents—48 percent—also cited technical information and support as an application for their internal Web site. The interactive nature of the Web has clearly made it a logical candidate for the dissemination of technically oriented matter. The other natural benefit is the reduction or elimination of hard-copy publication costs.

Intranet Market Revenue Shares in the Year 2000

The market for multimedia applications delivered over corporate intranets will grow to 19 billion by 2000. Over the next few years, the intranet will embrace multimedia tools and applications.

Corporations are now undergoing a rapid transition to intranet networks, supporting internal businesses and business-to-business applica-

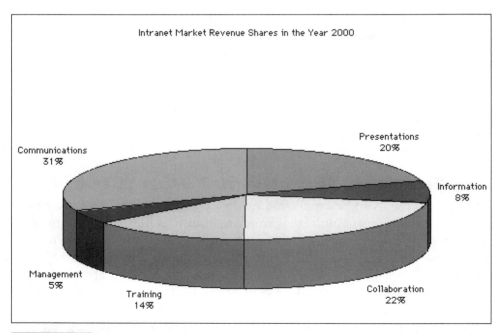

FIGURE 6.12 Intranet market revenue shares will reach $19 billion by the year 2000.

Source: New Media Think Tank, 1997

 Chapter 6

tions. The amount of multimedia applications delivered over business networks is also growing.

By 2000, communications and collaboration applications will account for more than half of the $19 billion business market. (See Figure 6.12.)

Total Revenue for the Intranet

Figure 6.13 shows the revenue for the total sales of software, on-premises equipment, and telecommunications services for the U.S. intranet market from 1995 to 2000.

The revenue totaled $2,700 million in 1995, growing up to $20,096 million by 2000. This gives an overall CAGR (compounded annual growth rate) of 49 percent. However, the growth is much faster at the start of the forecast period, when the installed base is small; then it decreases as the installed base

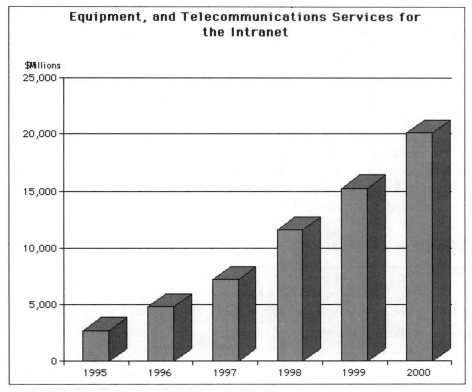

FIGURE 6.13 Total revenue for software, on-premises equipment, and telecommunications services for the intranet, 1995–2000.

Source: Killen & Associates, 1996

increases and more users already have their intranet installed. In 1995 the growth rate for the total revenue from these products was 79 percent. It decreases each year until the end of the forecast period when it is 25 percent.

Note that the revenue growth from 1995 to 1996 was $2,128 million; by 2000 revenue growth is forecast to be $4,844 million, which is more than twice the absolute revenue increase in 1995. Thus, the value of new business generated by the intranet is still growing at the end of the forecast period.

Intranet Market Projections 1996–1999

Market projections from Zona Research indicate that the discrete intranet market opportunity is significantly larger than the Internet market. The projections show that the intranet market, based on revenue, will exceed the Internet market by a ratio of one to two through 1999. (See Table 6.3.)

Specific intranet system components included in the model are system hardware (CPU, disk, memory), communications hardware (modems, switches, hubs), server communications software, authoring technology, search and retrieval tools, browsers, services, online services (dialup), and connectivity (dedicated access). The projections are based upon taking adoption trends from the beginning of 1995 and extrapolating from primary research what type of purchasing plans corporations have over the coming years.

The projections indicated that systems hardware, intranet-related services, and dedicated access server connectivity represent the largest opportunities, while authoring technologies will most likely grow the most in the next three to four years. Growth in the intranet browser market is expected to remain flat at its current $30 million level.

TABLE 6.3 Intranet Market Projections 1996–1999 (millions of dollars)

	1997	1998	1999
Systems Hardware	$2,741.72	$4,605.19	$6,566.90
Communications Hardware	$1,096.69	$1,842.08	$2,626.76
Server Communications Software	$1,0645.03	$2,763.12	$3,940.14
Authoring	$54.37	$117.53	$167.36
Retrieval	$112.97	$179.29	$255.30
Browsers	$31.61	$32.88	$32.58

	1997	1998	1999
Services	$2,791.56	$4,490.11	$6,521.11
Online Services	$903.73	$1,929.55	$2,786.18
Connectivity	$2,724.32	$3,867.02	$506.54
TOTAL	**$12,102**	**$19,826.77**	**$28,402.88**

Source: Zona Research Inc., 1996

Intranet versus Internet Adoption Cycles

Classification of applications has a direct bearing on the adoption rates of the intranet and Internet. The informal nature of the intranet and its deployment cycle makes it a market which will not experience the typical adoption chasm that many technology products experience.

We see consumer Internet use being a classic chasm technology—there will be some early adopters, followed by a fairly lengthy period of digestion and then, hopefully, widespread adoption. The graphic in Figure 6.14 is Zona's depiction of the adoption cycles of intranets versus consumer Internet use.

The differences in adoption rates are related to the following:

- Much intranet deployment is informal.

- Applications are often casual or simply use "raw" potential (i.e., sharing a Web page).

- Intranet applications can be incrementally deployed.

- Using the intranet infrastructure does not require a strategic, enterprisewide consensus or decision.

- There are tangible and obvious benefits, enhancing productivity.

- The technology infrastructure for deployment is already in place.

If we contrast the adoption cycles of intranets versus Lotus Notes, the benefits to the marketers of informal and tactical technology over a potentially superior, but clearly strategic, technology emerge. We believe that the adoption cycle for Lotus Notes at first blush appears to be more akin to that of consumer Internet use than the intranet. We see consumer

Internet adoption differently. Consumer adoption of the Internet appears to be a prime example of a chasm technology. We believe this because:

- There is a lack of technology infrastructure—limited bandwidth and connectivity.
- Use is limited to the technically bourgeois.
- It introduces a lifestyle shift.
- The benefits are not obvious to all potential customers.

Web Servers in Use

The sample base reported a total of 445 Web servers in use for internal and external activities. Of those, 368 were reported to be supporting intranet applications. This represents a substantial increase in the number of Web servers used internally relative to our Webmaster survey of late last

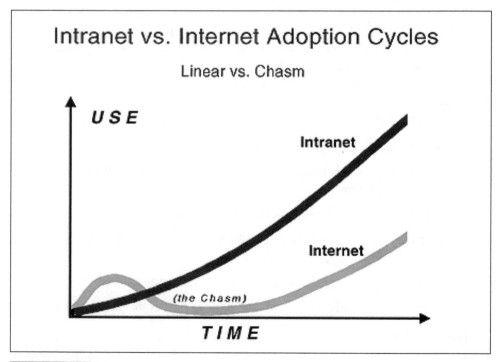

FIGURE 6.14 Intranet versus Internet adoption cycles.

Source: Zona Research Inc., 1996

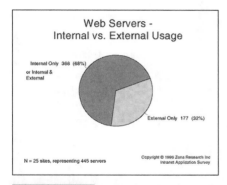

Web Servers -
Internal vs. External Usage

Internal Only 368 (68%)
or Internal &
External

External Only 177 (32%)

N = 25 sites, representing 445 servers

Copyright © 1996 Zona Research Inc
Intranet Application Survey

FIGURE 6.15 Web servers—internal versus external usage.

Source: Zona Research Inc., 1996

year. We believe that this increase in internal Web server use validates our position that the prime business opportunity for Internet technology/product providers lies in servicing the enterprise, not in servicing chance consumers.

Figure 6.15 shows the split between Web servers primarily used for internal purposes and those supporting activities and access external to the enterprise.

Requests for Proposals/Sample Proposals

Once you've assessed how all the members of the client organization will react to the suggestion of Web-based training, you need to address those arguments in your proposal. If you are an external developer, the client may have issued an RFP, giving you some ideas around which to structure your proposal. If you are developing for an internal client, you already know the needs of the organization and can structure your proposal around those requirements. Following is an example of an RFP used by Nancy Bartlett of AMA which gives guidelines for submitting a proposal. When creating the proposal for your Web-based training project, consider the elements in this document. Many of these requirements can be applied to the project you want to develop.

American Management Association
Request for Proposal

You are requested to provide one (1) original copy and three (3) duplicate copies of your proposal to:

The American Management Association

Training Products Division

9 Galen Street

Watertown, MA 02172

Attention: Nancy Bartlett

Please submit by 5:00 p.m., Monday, December 16. All proposals become property of AMA unless otherwise specified in writing. AMA wishes to establish a contract with one vendor, to develop an Intranet-based training product, but it reserves the right to negotiate agreements with one or more companies should AMA deem this arrangement appropriate.

As you will note on the RFP, we have outlined our vision for this product; however, we expect bidders to apply their knowledge and expertise in critiquing and expanding our vision to ensure that the product contains the most effective Web-based features. We will evaluate any alternative proposal in light of its ability to meet or exceed the outcomes we have established for this project. Vendors may elect to submit a bid for fulfillment of any or all of the roles listed under the Scope of Work section of the RFP. You must submit a proposed process or action plan describing how the other sections would be completed if you do not elect to participate in that work directly.

Description of work:

Intranet-Based Training Network (IBT)

AMA Training Products and Services division would like to create on-line learning communities on its customers' intranets. These communities would be on-going intranet-based environments where specific groups (e.g., sales, marketing, customer service representatives, divisional units) acquire skills and information from training programs, SMEs, and peer dialog at their desktop. This community will be part of a larger training solution created by the AMA Partnership Group to ensure a change in behavior so as to positively impact the customer's identified business goal. This product is intended to ensure that training is not an event but a continuous performance improvement process tied to an organization's business objectives. The goals of the product are to: 1) transfer knowledge and develop skills; 2) provide performance support through immediate access and reference information; 3) certify the user's level of learning; and 4) track individual and group's use and performance of the program.

Product Description

The vision for this product is a real-time series of how-to, interactive modules with instruction, exercises, branched proficiency testing, glossary, clipboard, help sections, hypertext links to other modules and references, graphics, audio, and access to chat room(s), bulletin board(s) and e-mail. (Depending upon the marketplace's capabilities video and/or simulations could also be features.) Each module is 10–15 minutes in length and addresses a particular skill or topic area such as closing a sale or facilitation. A series of 50–75 modules would be hyperlinked to create a curriculum in a general topic area such as sales. A customer would purchase either a curriculum or stand alone modules. AMA is providing all content from instruction to SMEs to resources.

Product Features

These are suggested product features; however, based on your knowledge and experience, you are encouraged to suggest alternative or additional features which add value, increase the training effectiveness, or reduce product cost or development time.

Instructional Section

Concepts will be presented in a self-paced (with a possible option for group training), how-to, interactive environment. Each module will be 10–15 minutes in length and indexed by behavioral or skill-based learning objectives. Subject content will be in the areas of sales, marketing, communications, finance, quality, and general management.

Levels 1–2 training evaluations

Level 1 (reaction to training) would be an online survey.

Level 2 (knowledge gained) branching online Pre/Post tests with immediate scoring forwarded to the student and forwarded to AMA for analysis, generation of corporate reports, and certificate issuance.

Glossary

User can pull up a glossary window at any point during the lesson, to get a complete definition/explanation of the term.

Clipboard

The learner can type in notes as he/she proceeds through the lesson. These notes are saved so the student may access them at any time.

Online Reference

Using Hypertext Markup Protocol language (HTML), all (or relevant) AMA self-study modules and other reference material would be hyper-linked.

Online Performance Support Activities (feedback components)

E-mail: Users can use e-mail to ask questions of "Instructor," seek content or tech support, or submit tests.

Chat rooms: Specified time on a weekly or monthly basis will be designated to specific training topics. These virtual workshops will include a specified number of students, centered around an SME who provides information and responds to students' questions. Other chat rooms could be a facilitated "round table" discussion for "invited" students (e.g., sales reps from a particular company) to discuss company-specific issues.

Bulletin boards: Users can post questions or comments to an electronic bulletin board.

Tracking

A student "registers" for a course and chooses a login password; the system will keep track of where they are so that each time they log in, they can resume instruction where they left off. Learners can follow the course in linear fashion or may choose to skip around various courses via hypertext links. Tracking information will also be imported to AMA Educational Services' current registration software program.

Internationalization

In order to accommodate Intranets that cross geographic boundaries, the design of the program should allow for content translation into other languages with minimal impact on cost and schedule.

Scope of the Work

The vendor will work with AMA in the design and development of an IBT product. The vendor will perform all software programming, instructional design, multimedia development, integration with existing AMA systems, and customer tech support. The content of the programs will be culled from AMA's self-paced training product line that includes print, audio, and CD-ROM. The end product may include some or all of the content of these product lines. Other AMA content such as articles, research reports, or newsletters will be adapted to provide reference material. AMA will develop additional content if necessary.

Your proposal should address the fulfillment of each of the roles described below. Specifics for each role should include your definition or description, percentage of time to be spent on this project, status of individual as regular versus contract employee, and whether an individual will assume more than one role.

Project Management

Oversees project from beginning to end.

Instructional Design

Creates detailed design document. Elements must include: organization of content, size and scope, instructional strategies. Ensures the training materials correspond to the objectives of the lesson and that the objectives are achieved.

Instructional Technologist

Creates templates including graphics, interfaces, audio, buttons. Imports content into templates for creation of storyboard.

Writer/Editor

Composes the script of the training program and reviews the script for effectiveness of communication.

Programmer or Authoring System Specialist

Prepares executable code or instructions to be entered into an off-the-shelf authoring system to create the actual program.

Media Expert

Functions as "producer" or "director" to coordinate the activities of others involved in audio and video production.

Graphics Designer

Works with color, graphics, animation, and text placement to enliven the lesson.

Creation of Chat Rooms, Bulletin Boards

Assists in creation of chat rooms and bulletin boards both within customer site and AMA. Has the ability to transfer this knowledge and expertise to AMA staff for future roll outs.

Production Implementation

Distributes prototype and pilot product to end user.

Technical Support

Provides technical support to customers for specified period of time. Has the ability to transfer this expertise to AMA staff if necessary.

Supplier Profile

We are seeking a vendor who can partner with AMA to provide the hardware/software expertise, instructional design, software development, and intranet marketplace experience.

1. Background of your company

    Experience in producing interactive multimedia training programs

    Experience in intranet-based training

    Experience in instructional design of self-paced training programs

    Experience in creation and management of online bulletin boards and/or chat rooms

    Experience in providing user tech support

    Three client references

2. Resource availability

    Biographies of key staff members

    Facility description

Development and Production Schedule

Assumptions:

AMA will provide content according to the needs of developer

AMA staff will be available to review material as necessary

Final product and source code will be delivered to AMA by June 1997

An estimated time to complete the project, including milestones and check-points

Pricing

Pricing must be submitted in a line item format.

All quotations shall remain valid for a period of 6 months from receipt of your proposal to AMA.

Your quotation for the following:

Project management

Instructional design

Multimedia production (includes: scripting, programming, graphic design, creation of design document, creation of storyboard, audio and video production)

Creation of chat rooms, bulletin boards, and training of AMA staff

Production implementation

Technical support and training of AMA staff

Addendum A

Any questions pertaining to the RFP must be submitted in writing and will be responded to within 24 hours in writing. The final submission time for questions is noon on Thursday, December 12.

Questions can be submitted to: American Management Association, Attn: Nancy Bartlett

    9 Galen Street Watertown, MA 02172

    Fax (617) 926-0312

    e-mail nbartlett@amanet.org

Response to RFPs must be submitted by 5:00 p.m., Monday, December 16 AMA will notify all bidders of the status of their proposal by 5:00 p.m., Monday, December 30

A sample proposal which follows the above guidelines is displayed in Appendix A.

LINKING MULTIMEDIA TO PERFORMANCE RESULTS = ROI

Susan Barksdale, Front Line Evaluators; and Teri Lund, Baldwin & Lund Services; footnotes and bibliography as cited in the original work

A major high-tech organization recently recognized that it was losing market share to its competitors. Research revealed that the customer service received at distribution outlets and call centers was inconsistent and not always helpful.

A "Continuous Improvement Team" recommended that a training program or performance intervention be developed by the organization's Learning Services Department. Senior management agreed to fund this program under the following conditions:

Minimal time would be taken away from the distribution centers (call time) as staffing models had recently been implemented to cut costs.

Travel would be kept at a minimum.

The intervention would positively impact customer service levels!

Faced with this mandate, the Learning Services Department investigated how best to meet the business need. Clearly, there was a need to implement some type of evaluation to determine if the intervention was affecting customer service levels.

At this point the client sought our help. Learning Services believed multimedia was a potential solution, but was concerned about how to minimize the risk involved, develop a viable product that met Senior Management's expectations, as well as prove positive results.

In this article we will discuss how the client chose and validated multimedia as a solution, and the implementation of an evaluation process to track the results to link multimedia to Return On Investment. We will also address the following questions:

When is multimedia an appropriate solution for a performance need?

How can you be sure you are utilizing the best media to meet the performance need?

How do you begin to establish metrics and measures to ensure that the multimedia solution will meet the need?

How do you know what to evaluate and when?

The following five-step process was used to determine whether multimedia was a potential solution and to ensure that metrics would be in place to measure the effectiveness and the ROI of the selected solution.

1. Identify and affirm the business drivers forcing the request for the performance intervention and identify the value of the impact on those drivers
2. Define the performance needs and link them to the business drivers and strategy
3. Determine if multimedia is a viable solution
4. Identify potential costs
5. Identify the financial benefits and corresponding ROI models

1: Identifying and Affirming the Business Drivers

The first step in the process is identifying the business drivers, determining whether they can be affected by the performance intervention or training solution. Common business drivers include:

Economic drivers such as recession, inflation, or a shortage of raw products

Human resource drivers such as too few people with particular skills, or a shortage of workers overall

Government drivers which usually involve deregulation or regulation

Public Perception Drivers which are propelled by such things as media, image-making, or outside circumstances

Market/product drivers such as a new product, service, or competitor that forces the organization to change strategies or support

Change in system, process, or key policy drivers which may include new systems or major conversions that affect employees, customers, and generally the manner in which the company does business

Customer drivers which usually are perceptions or things customers influence and that cause organizations to react

Shareholder or financial drivers which usually involve the perception of Wall Street, shareholder perception, or stock price

Business drivers were identified and reviewed with our client's senior management as well as the Continuous Improvement Team. The stated business drivers for this organization were increased competition and customer service levels.

To determine the value of these drivers, the client determined how competition and customer service levels were assessed in the organization. Three key effectiveness measures were determined:

Percent of market share

Customer satisfaction surveys (monitored by an outside company)

Telephone shopping surveys (monitored by an outside company)

2: Defining the Performance Need and Linking It to the Business Driver

Performance needs usually drive a training program or performance intervention. These same performance needs should drive the evaluation approach. In a perfect world, the performance need and the evaluation strategy that will measure the effectiveness of the response to the need will be identified during the analysis stage before the initiation of the project. However, recognizing that this does not always happen, it is necessary to determine the performance need that drives the project implementation before determining what to evaluate.

Keep in mind that not all causes of performance problems are indicative of the need for training or can be solved by training. In our rapidly changing world, problems are often multifaceted and so are their solutions. It is therefore important to determine the actual role of training in contributing to the performance results, especially before investing funds for design and development.

The most common causes of performance needs for which training can provide at least a partial solution include:

A lack of skill or knowledge

A flawed environment (computer system changes, poor procedures)

A re-engineered or changed work environment

A change in market or product/services

A lack of direction or expectations

To define the business need, it is critical to recognize the current skill, knowledge and behavior levels. If an impact is to be made and measured, there must be a "baseline."

The next step in defining the business need is tied to a principle known as the "Balanced Scorecard." There are four basic viewpoints of a performance need using the "Balanced Scorecard." These viewpoints include:

Customer Perspective: What is the performance need in the eyes of the customer? Do employees understand the products and are they able to present the products? Can employees effectively troubleshoot a problem? Is the information provided to customers correct? Were employees timely and courteous when servicing customers?

Define the performance need in terms of how the customers' perspective would be impacted.

Learning Perspective: What skills or behaviors do employees currently lack? How do you know? What skills or behaviors are needed to correctly do this job? How do you know?

Define the performance need in terms of how the participants' knowledge, skills, or behaviors would be impacted.

Business Perspective: What will be the impact "back on the job" as a result of the intervention or program? Will productivity increase? Will job behavior be different? Will costs decrease? Will technology be used where it was not before? What will be improved, changed, or impacted as a result of this program and how will we know?

Define the performance need in terms of the business impact.

Financial Perspective: How is the business need currently affecting the bottom line? What would be the financial result of the performance intervention or training? Would sales increase? Would costs decrease? Would new revenue be generated? Would decisions be made more quickly and with better results?

Define the performance need in terms of financial impact.

Identifying how the performance need would affect the business in all four perspectives and, ultimately, the business driver, are important in considering the value of the solution. If the performance need spans all four perspectives, the results of improving that need are more likely to be of higher value to the organization and thus a more comprehensive media is warranted.

3: Determining If Multimedia Is a Viable Solution

Once the performance need is defined, the solution can be analyzed to determine if it will meet the need efficiently and effectively. To determine if any solution is viable (or how the solution or training will be accomplished), you need to know the following:

- What are the objectives and consequent high-level content that need to be taught or met?
- What are the constraints that need to be considered (no computers available, travel, etc.)?
- Who is the audience (background, learning preferences, etc.)?
- When does the solution need to be implemented and results realized?
- Where does the training or performance intervention need to occur?

To determine if multimedia would meet the characteristics dictated by the performance need, a worksheet was devised, based on various independent studies, for the benefits and disadvantages of delivery methods. Two other options were also investigated, district classroom training and paper self-study [see Table 6.4].

TABLE 6.4 Worksheet for Determining the Key Criteria Dictated by the Performance Need

METHODS:

Self-Paced Paper	District Classroom	Multimedia	Key Criteria for Performance Need Delivery
✓		✓	The content needs to be delivered consistently
✓		✓	The business environment requires flexibility for students to progress at their own pace and revisit any material they may feel less confident in mastering
✓		✓	Maximize learning efficiency
		✓	Required simulations for increased retention
✓	✓	✓	Testing for certification
✓	✓	✓	Ability to baseline learner knowledge and skills prior to learning
	✓	✓	Immediate feedback
	✓	✓	Highly interactive
✓	✓	✓	Lots of practice available
	✓	✓	Fun, appealing, and students will complete
✓	✓	✓	Content of curriculum highly related to job and transfer to reinforced throughout training
	✓		Changes to content are low-cost and can be implemented immediately
✓	✓	✓	Self-efficacy is available
	✓		Opportunity to interact with others in same job

After reviewing the results, Learning Services determined that the best approach to solving the performance need was to provide a computer-based multimedia approach with a follow-up classroom session at district offices. It was also determined that each individual would meet with a District Learning Coordinator before beginning the self-study curriculum as well as after the curriculum is mastered.

4. Identifying Potential Costs

Though initial studies showed that interactive multimedia simulations would improve the quality of the training, the client had to justify the project as if that benefit didn't exist. The organization was willing to fund this project as an experiment to prove that multimedia met the key criteria, but only if Learning Services would also track the costs and benefits of a more traditional method. Hence, costs and benefits needed to be identified.

For the multimedia component, the following costs were calculated:

- Number of hours of multimedia training that would be classified as simple (more text-driven, simple branching, low-level graphics and audio, etc.)

- Number of hours of multimedia training that would be classified as complex (simulations, complex branching, high-level graphics or video clips, animation, etc.)

- Number of hours of video production

- Estimate for content change after storyboard completion

- Total cost per developer-hour (including salary, benefits, and overhead). (This represented an average and was validated as a "charge-back" statistic.)

Additional costs included:

- Participant costs (salaries, travel, lost-opportunity costs)

- Learning coordinator (instruction time)

- Materials (CD-ROMs, disks, paper materials)

- Equipment (videotaping machine, etc.; PCs were already available)

- Administrative support (copying of materials and disks, registration, record-keeping and reporting, distribution)

- Subject-matter expert costs (salaries, travel)

- Pilot costs (facilities, facilitator)

- Supporting material costs (graphics or clip art packages, etc.)

- Installation costs

The final estimated cost for the nine-month project was $870,396.

5: Identifying the Financial Benefits and the ROI Model to Use

There are many benefits (and an equal number of ROI models) to use when justifying or determining the payoff for multimedia. Not all are applicable however, so identifying which are valid and reliable for the project is important. To accomplish this, data gathered in steps 1–3 are used and compared against other variables to ensure that the findings presented are reliable and will be accepted.

Six questions worth one point each were asked for evaluating the reliability of each measure and report. For example, a highly reliable measure, Call Reports, received a "6" which means each question was answered with a yes response.

1. Does the measure reflect program objectives?
2. Is the measure valued by top management?
3. Can the measure be computed for specific employees?
4. Is the measurement output available on a timely basis?
5. Can enough data be collected for reliable measurement?
6. Is the measure free from known bias?

Three ROI calculations were used for this project:

$$\text{Benefit-to-cost ratio (BCR)} = \frac{\text{program benefits}}{\text{program costs}}$$

Measuring for the dollar returned for every $1 invested (for example: $2 benefits for every $1 spent). Benefits and costs are usually calculated on an annual basis.

$$\text{Return-on-investment \% (ROI)} = \frac{\text{program benefits}}{\text{program costs}} \times 100$$

So, for each $1 invested, there is a $2 return in net benefits, an ROI of 200%.

Breakeven = (program benefits for first year $\times$ life of program in years) −program costs

This calculates the point at which the program pays for itself.

And the results were . . .

After a year—the project ran over schedule by three months—the courses were piloted and the final measurement began. The project overran costs by 4.3% (total costs = $907,823). Changes to the course because of unplanned internal reorganization in the company and system accounted for most of the overrun. Had more video development taken place, the overrun would have been greater.

The benefits for the first six months were calculated at $220,732. Using the break-even model, it is expected that the program will pay for itself within two years. The life of the program is currently calculated at five years with an ROI of 243% (not including maintenance costs).

Qualitative benefits that resulted from this project include:

- Participants of the training were better equipped to discuss competitive comparisons with their customers, resulting in additional sales that were monitored as benefits to the project.

- The course reported a Virtual Wall of Fame for anyone scoring 100% on the final exam (within three tries), which became an issue of pride.

- Management was pleased with the "strategic approach" of the measurement and approved a second phase for this project, which will place additional curriculum on multimedia. One of the comments made in the final meeting was that "The ROI for this project was presented as more than just a numbers game, and the results proved it."

- The Project Manager was able to answer the three most commonly asked questions:

    1. How much is this project costing?

    2. Why did you decide to use multimedia?

    3. Why is customer service training being done in this way?

Assessing Your Own Multimedia Need

As you begin to think about the methods that were used in this project and how you might be able to apply them to your multimedia need, consider the following questions:

1. What are the business drivers for your project?

2. Who are the stakeholders who would confirm these business drivers?

3. What are the performance needs and how could you describe these needs using the four "Balanced Scorecard" viewpoints (customer perspective, learning perspective, business perspective, and financial perspective)?

4. What are the key criteria for performance and how does multimedia stack up as a solution?

5. What are the potential costs of this project?

6. What are the potential benefits of this project?

RE-ENGINEERING RFPs

If you find you may need outside vendors for your project, you too will probably want to use the RFP process. Susan Barksdale of Front Line Evaluators and Teri Lund of Baldwin & Lund Services recommend the following procedure.

Increasingly, those who manage and deliver training face shorter time lines and a need to stretch technology in developing multimedia training products. These events often force training and education entities to seek development resources outside of the organization.

Inherent in this need to look outside of the organization for development assistance is the frustration of finding the right person or company to meet the organizational need in a timely, cost-effective, and ethical manner. Most managers have a vendor "horror story" to relate and most surely have spent unnecessary time, money, and human resources managing an external development project that didn't work—not to mention the loss of credibility within the organization for a difficult or failed project!

The case story outlined below is true. The need for a re-engineered RFP process was born from the frustration with and concern over the amount of outsourcing dollars spent—not necessarily ensuring that outsourced development equaled the requested development need.

The process used in this case study emphasizes a link to the business objectives of the requested project and the project owners and key players, outlines parameters for vendors (including constraints) so they are able to match their skills and resources to the objectives (sometimes choosing to select out), syndicates the risk by involving internal clients, and determines the level of commitment required from these clients early in the project, thus minimizing risk and failure. This process resulted in the following five-step model:

1. Identifying the need for the RFP;
2. Cementing the partnership and joint accountability for the RFP;
3. Implementing the request for proposal;
4. Selecting the vendor;
5. Linking the request process to the development process.

Case Study

A large financial institution successfully implemented this re-engineered RFP process. The following case study details this successful experience.

STEP 1: Identifying the Need

Based on a solid training needs analysis, it was determined that a vendor was needed to develop multimedia-based training for a large and geographically separated audience. This training was essential in supporting an organizational need for a computer conversion to a new customer information system. Key conversion project players were part of the process from the beginning.

Almost as soon as the training need was articulated, the Education and Training Department held a meeting to orient these key players to the task at hand. The focus of the meeting was on gaining agreement to the objectives of the training program, identifying additional internal resources for involvement in the selection process and tying the training to project and organizational strategies. Partnership opportunities and accountabilities were identified as the following:

1. Reviewing a draft of the RFP;

2. Attending pre-selection meetings;

3. Attending each vendor presentation;

4. Attending debrief sessions after each presentation;

5. Reviewing vendor nominations.

Additionally, the training budget for this specific training was reviewed and constraints to the training development were identified. These constraints included a short development time, use of a specific authoring system and the organization retaining the copyrights to the training course.

This step established a relationship with key players as they were informed of the requirements of the RFP process and were asked for their support and commitment.

STEP 2: Cementing the Partnership and Joint Accountability

Based on the information provided during initial contacts with key players, the Education and Training Department was prepared to conduct a JAD (Joint Application Design) session for the RFP. The focus of the JAD was on obtaining specific project information to draft the RFP and to identify roles and develop the skills needed for meaningful involvement in the selection process. Key business representatives participated in the JAD, which resulted in a draft of the RFP. The draft was then reviewed by the key players and their feedback was incorporated into the final RFP.

An important transition took place in this stage of the process: key project players became the "Core Team" for the selection of the training vendor. This change signaled a syndication of the risk associated with implementing RFPs. Historically, RFPs have been created in a training vacuum with little true buy-in required by the client. By sharing the responsibility for the selection, the risk was also shared by key project players and project sponsors.

The final Core Team consisted of program managers, subject matter experts, business analysts, and support personnel from business units and Information Systems Development, as well as representatives from the Education and Training Department.

STEP 3: Implementing the Request for Proposal Process

With the final RFP ready for publication, the following activities were conducted by the organization's Education and Training Department:

1. Determined and distributed the vendor list to the Core Team;
2. Drafted a letter to accompany the RFP and distributed it to the Core Team;
3. Sent the RFP to vendors;
4. Answered vendor questions;
5. Determined and distributed the vendor selection criteria to the Core Team;
6. Published a plan for selection and distributed to the Core Team;
7. Reviewed proposals against selection criteria and narrowed to three (3) finalists;
8. Selected finalists and arranged in-person presentations;
9. Notified nonqualifying candidates;
10. Met with Core Team prior to in-person presentations and reviewed the selection criteria, the presentation process, the finalists' proposals, and the debriefing process;
11. Prepared each team member with key information provided in the finalists' proposals.

With these activities completed, the organization was positioned to make an informed and responsible selection.

STEP 4: Making the Selection

While often perceived as the most difficult part of the RFP process, if Steps 1–3 have been successfully completed, Step 4 is relatively easy and this proved to be the case for this particular vendor selection.

Prior to the final selection, the team was once again briefed on the selection criteria, focusing on the following:

1. The content (subject matter) of the proposal presentation;
2. Vendor experience (track record) in doing similar work;
3. Project management skills and preferences;
4. The presentation style to assess vendor personality "fit."

After the presentations, the experience was debriefed. The debriefing focused on the above mentioned criteria and, to the Education and Training Department team's surprise, the majority of the discussion centered on the personal styles of the vendors and their ability (or lack thereof) to inspire confidence in being able to get the job done.

A consensus was reached within 45 minutes. In retrospect, the team's ability to come to a quick decision was directly related to their involvement from the beginning of the process, having a sense of ownership and responsibility in the process and the knowledge that they would make the final decision and have to live with it!

The successful vendor was informed of the selection and contracts were requested at that point. Unsuccessful vendors also were contacted.

STEP 5: Linking the RFP Process to Development

Recognizing that the success or failure of this project was contingent upon the ability to link the entire RFP process to the training that was going to be developed, the Education and Training team closed the "vulnerability gap" by ensuring the organization was getting what it purchased. To accomplish this, the Education and Training Department completed the fifth step. This consisted of the following:

1. Communicating the decision to all involved and interested parties;
2. Establishing the relationship with the vendor;
3. Reviewing the vendor contract and clearly establishing accountabilities with the vendor;
4. Reviewing the Core Team's responsibilities for the success of the project:
5. Establishing a communication plan with the vendor and team;
6. Conducting a kickoff design meeting with the vendor and the Core Team.

Case Study Outcome

One year later. . . .The project was completed on time and under the budget identified in the initial RFP. The Core Team was pleased with the results and the multimedia training product is being implemented and receiving high marks from users. The vendor has contracted to deliver additional products within the organization. It is the opinion of all parties involved—the Core Team, the vendor and Education and Training staff—that the Re-engineered Request for Proposal Process was key to a successful start-up and completion of the training development project.

Conclusion

Obviously, the benefits inherent in using a model, such as the one presented here, are increased organization, time savings, and better vendor selections.

What may not be so obvious is the payoff for the organization in terms of increasing training effectiveness and lowering training development costs.

When following this process, training professionals will be able to identify vulnerabilities in vendor selection, which signal issues and potential problems. If known, these issues and problems can be addressed and hopefully resolved prior to selection. The bottom line benefit to the training organization or entity is the assurance that it has a strategic role to play in the future development of the organization.

Cost Estimates for Web-Based Training

As any project manager will quickly discover, setting out to budget a Web-based training project can be a tricky task. The newness of the technology and the variability of expenses require that the development team have a clear understanding of what multimedia will be used and what the staffing needs of the team will be. Like CD-ROM–based training, by far the biggest expense of developing Web-based training is the programming time. As yet, bandwidth limitations have kept Web-based training to a low level of multimedia, which is a large expense for CD-ROM development. The expense of programming will decrease relative to the complete project as developers become more familiar with WBT programming and as authoring tools become more and more user-friendly and template-driven.

What to Keep in Mind when Costing Out a Project

The following description of the different elements which need to be accounted for in a WBT development budget can help to cost out a project, but because no two projects are identical, no one list can be exact or exhaustive. As a benchmark, I have found multimedia developers who quote CD-ROM training programs at $5,000 per finished hour of training and others who quote $135,000 per finished hour. Like an instructor-led course, a project can be low-cost (and often low-quality) or high-cost (and hopefully high-quality). Depending on the complexity of design, complexity of content, the level of experience of the development staff, and the availability of existing instructional materials, most corporate WBT projects fall somewhere in between. Deborah Blank, Director of Net/Multimedia Services at the Bethesda, Maryland–based company ELF (Electronic Learning Facilitators) says, "The issue of the cost of Web-based training is a bit up for grabs right now—and will remain so. It is akin to the question 'what does one hour of multimedia training cost?' " Blank, an external Web-based training developer, says she is currently working on a project which will cost the client an estimated $25,000 per instructional hour. "This is because the material for this course really doesn't exist," she says. "We have to debrief Subject Matter Experts (SMEs), organize the information, plan the interactivity and work with various IT departments to get it online."

Blank recommends keeping the following questions in mind when figuring out the financing behind a WBT development effort:

1. Does the subject matter already exist in some format?

2. What is the nature of the interactivity—just links or actual simulation?

3. What technology is being used—tried and true, or cutting edge?

4. What multimedia assets exist (sound, photos, animations, graphics) and how many are there?

5. Is the application expected to upgrade along with technology innovation? (If so, it must be constructed that way.)

6. Is the course being developed in-house (where lots of costs are never made explicit but are nevertheless incurred) or by an outside vendor who must price every single cost to avoid cost overruns?

7. Is there scoring, record-keeping, and performance analysis?

8. How reasonable (or impossible) is the schedule?

Where the Money Goes

If your organization plans on producing a number of Web-based training courses, Joan Gregory, Training Director at Texas Instruments in San Jose, California, stresses the importance of understanding that the original development will need a much bigger budget than later courses. "The bottom line is that the initial development always has a greater cost than development after a process and template are in place," says Gregory, who has developed CBT for General Electric as well as WBT for Texas Instruments. "The first courses for General Electric took probably four months to put together, while later ones generally took less than a month. This included interviewing the SME, Subject Matter Expert, storyboarding the course, reviewing the storyboard with the SME again, inputting the course into the templates, 'break-testing' the draft CBT, review by other team members and SME, and then publishing on the network."

BRINGING IN THE BIG ONE

Julie Nolan, Nolan Multimedia, Novato, CA

For some time now, I have been working to convince a group of "investors," consisting of a number of public agencies and foundations, that converting a series of classroom training courses into an interactive multimedia format would greatly benefit their diverse end-user population. In response to their inquiry, "Why does it cost so much?" I developed the following presentation materials, comprised of written speaker support notes and three overheads, which I have modified slightly for this publication.

My objective was to familiarize my audience with what goes into producing multimedia training successfully and to compare the cost of an initial program with the cost of a second, subsequent program of equal length and level of difficulty [see Figure 6.16].

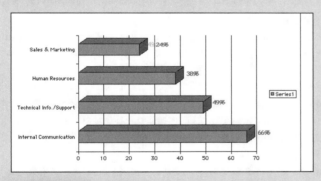

FIGURE 6.16 Costs for subsequent programs.

Source: Infoseek, 1997

I should mention that prior to the first step in developing such a program, a Needs Analysis must be conducted. This involves some fairly extensive research with all participants from the funding agencies, subject matter experts, and classroom trainers to the end users and all other "stakeholders." Then an in-depth report should be prepared to address the issues and present the plan for using multimedia to implement a reasonable and credible solution. Finally, a proposal is written and, with any luck, a contract is issued and the development cycle begins.

Design Documents

The first task to perform is specifying project goals and objectives. Be sure to state how each objective will be met. Spell out the Instructional Design strategy including how the content will be presented and what form it will take (video, stills, animation, audio, text), as well as how program users will be tested and what type of feedback and/or remedial loops will be present.

Describe how program content will be organized and define all modules that will be produced. Specify all user pathways for accessing content and how the navigation system will work. State how user performance data will be collected and utilized.

Content/Script Development

When dealing with content development, assemble all the information (print and graphics in this case) in electronic form. Establish a database for scriptwriting that includes fields for identifying each type of asset that will be used in the program.

Next, you may write the script according to Design Document specifications (narration, scene description, text). Be sure to include exact references to visual materials. Prepare content storyboards for hand-off to the art department.

Art Direction/Interface Design

At this phase, you have reached the point where you need to establish the look and feel of the program content and its navigation. Establish artistic specifications for each type of scene or module called for in the script. Prepare graphic storyboards for client review.

You also should establish an appropriate color palette for use on the project and you should produce (and process) graphical user interface elements for each type of scene or module.

Asset Management

Under asset management, the first thing to do is establish a set of naming conventions for all types of assets and for every module in the program. Determine electronic storage needs and create a file hierarchy for placement of assets once they are produced.

You should also produce a bill of materials for each module that specifies every asset to be developed for the program and that will be entered into the storage system. Log assets into the asset management system as they are produced and/or altered. Ensure that all assets for each module are present prior to importing assets into the authoring software.

Graphics/Video/Stills/Audio Production

Now it is time to produce your 2D or 3D graphics and/or animation as required. Break down the graphic and text elements into appropriate sub-elements for integration into the authoring software. Make corrections or changes as needed.

Record audio with voice talent and/or obtain other audio sources, such as music and sound effects. Shoot stills and have them made into Photo CDs (or use a digital camera). Shoot video and edit into appropriate segments; digitize as needed to meet specification requirements.

Image Processing

Scan all images (such as drawings or print photographs) as required. Process all graphical elements using the color palette for the project. Label each element with appropriate asset names and submit into the asset management system.

Import all the assets on a module-by-module basis into the authoring software for integration. Make corrections or changes as needed during the development process.

Program Coding

First, develop a program architecture for each type of module as per specification. Build a single module for each module type and debug.

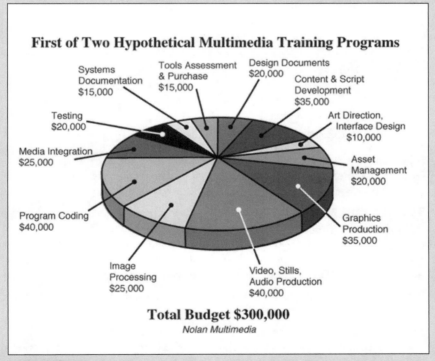

FIGURE 6.17 Cost breakdown of the first program.

Source: Nolan Multimedia

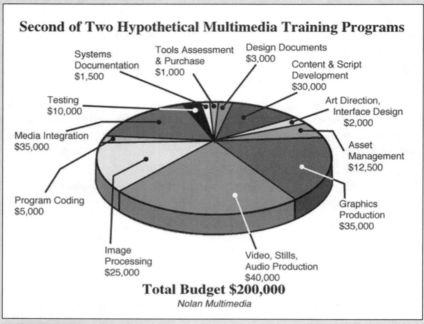

Second of Two Hypothetical Multimedia Training Programs

Systems Documentation $1,500

Tools Assessment & Purchase $1,000

Design Documents $3,000

Content & Script Development $30,000

Testing $10,000

Art Direction, Interface Design $2,000

Media Integration $35,000

Asset Management $12,500

Program Coding $5,000

Graphics Production $35,000

Image Processing $25,000

Video, Stills, Audio Production $40,000

Total Budget $200,000

Nolan Multimedia

FIGURE 6.18 Cost breakdown of the second program. Notice the decrease in resources required for Program Coding, Systems Documentation, and Tools Assessment and Purchase.

Source: Nolan Multimedia

Next, develop a navigation and menu system and link it to the initial module(s). Implement the final computer code (optimization, installer, etc.) for delivery of the finished product (a CD-ROM gold master in this instance).

Testing and Media Integration

For purposes of testing, you should develop a test matrix for each type of module in the program. Develop a bugs database that is customized for the project and development team members. Provide testing and bug reports on an "as needed" basis throughout the development process.

With regard to media integration, link assets to the program architecture for all additional modules and debug.

Project Administration/Systems Documentation

Throughout this process, you should be preparing written monthly and/or quarterly progress reports. Document any changes in scope as they occur and estimate any impact on the budget. Prepare a detailed billing summary (bimonthly) based on percentage of work completed for each line item in the budget [see Figures 6.17 and 6.18].

You should also prepare documentation and provide training for the integration team on program coding. Documentation on specific image processing procedures should also be created. An assessment of technology needs and preparation of written recommendations for long-range technology implementation should also be done.

Tools Assessment and Purchase

Be sure to determine your hardware/software delivery requirements. Make purchases as necessary and establish distance connection for review during the development process.

Conclusion

In any multimedia project—large or small—there will be an overlapping of tasks in the development process. These slices of the multimedia pie are not intended to be discrete categories independent of each other.

Indeed, knowing when to do what can save both the developer and client considerable time, money, and anguish. Suffice it to say that an initial module should be tested with a good sampling of end users as soon as possible and that all other efforts should be minimized until the results are in and the developmental approach can be verified. This, of course, tends to wreak havoc on such things as a schedule and cash flow, but such is the life of a multimedia developer.

Server Hardware

The first item on your WBT development shopping list will be the computers which allow users to access the training and the server which will deliver the instruction. Most corporations developing training on the Web will already have a computer-friendly audience with desktop computers available to access courseware. Stewart Skjerven, account manager at Saratoga Group, an external CBT and WBT developer, says a 486/33 PC with at least 16 to 32MB is the minimum required to run most WBT programs. Though prices and systems are changing all the time, Skjerven says this desktop unit should cost roughly $1,500.

As far as the server computer, Skjerven recommends a machine that has a minimum of 166 MHz speed (preferably 200). The server platform may cost in the range of $7,000, complete with browser software and TCP/IP software, although faster, more robust systems can cost upwards of $10,000. All of the costs associated with hardware assume that there is no system in place. Skjerven says most WBT development should be based on the server platform that already exists within the corporation. "When I go into a company and propose an online solution, I make sure that it will run on the company's minimum platform," he says. "If they don't have a minimum platform that will support the courseware, it's not going to be a viable solution for them."

Development

After paying for client and server software to whatever extent your current system needs upgrading, you can begin to put a price on development of the courseware. Costs will vary greatly based on the sophistication of the training program, the amount of multimedia, the size of the program, and whether you use an internal or external development team. External developers often use a fixed-rate model to estimate the cost of development to the client. Kevin Kruse of Advanced Consulting Inc., an external developer, says his group gathers project team leaders and reviews the proposed project on a lesson-by-lesson basis. "We then estimate the number of days to complete each task, multiply the day count by our daily rate (from $500–$800 per day), and create separate 'media creation and purchase' budgets," Kruse says. ACI then totals all figures to create a project total (Table 6.5). The only additions are shipping, materials, and travel, which ACI bills at cost.

ACI modifies its "day rate" from project to project based on a variety of factors, including:

- Amount of time available to complete the job (i.e., Is this a rush job? Will they be working a lot of overtime hours?)

- Size of project (i.e., Can they achieve economies of scale? Can they streamline a work process?)

- Strength of partnership with client (i.e., Does client have an established, experienced project team in place? Will the client need to be educated about design techniques? Will they have an unusual number of revision cycles?)

"Unlike many other multimedia vendors, we do not price projects using 'screen count' or 'learner time' estimates," Kruse says. "We find these to be very unreliable, and these estimates do not take into account the level of quality, or entertainment value. However, using our standard pricing formula, we have found that most 'one hour' multimedia modules cost between $20,000 and $50,000 to create." (See Table 6.5.)

TABLE 6.5 Spreadsheet Template for Web-Based Training Development Costs from ACI

Cost Factor	Breakdown	Days	Day Rate	Total Cost
Project Management		_____ # days	× <day rate> =	$ _____
Instructional Design		_____ # days	× <day rate> =	$ _____
Graphic Art		_____ # days	× <day rate> =	$ _____
Programming		_____ # days	× <day rate> =	$ _____
Quality Control		_____ # days	× <day rate> =	$ _____
Audio Recording				
	Voice Actors	_____ # days	× $500 =	$ _____
	Equipment/ studio time	_____ # days	× <day rate> =	$ _____
Video Recording	Actors	_____ # days	× $800 =	$ _____
	Equipment/ studio time	_____ # days	× <day rate> =	$ _____
Original Photography	Models	_____ # days	× $500 =	$ _____
	Equipment/ studio time	_____ # days	× <day rate> =	$ _____
Stock Media Purchase			=	$ _____

These are the basic costs for either internal or external development. One additional fee faced by a first-time internal team will be the purchase of an authoring tool. Most commercial authoring tools run from several hundred to several thousand dollars, but there are low-cost, limited function Web-page layout tools like Claris Home Page available over the Internet. "There are inexpensive ways for you to go out and build Web pages and put them on your server," Skjerven says. "Things like Front Page and a couple of other products allow you build HTML pages without forcing you do to the coding; you're just typing in text and the tool converts them to pages for you."

Valerie Beeman, who worked on an internal development team at Stanford University, said that in her current project the categories of costing were similar to those encountered by an external development team, including:

- Instructional design
- License fees for artwork
- Authoring
- Programming
- Actors' fees
- Development fees

"'Development fees' refers to both the content project manager and the project manager for the site development. In my project, I'm the project manager and have contracted with our internal Multimedia/Video Production unit for the site development," Beeman said. "Many companies would have to procure services of a content project manager (someone to determine learning objectives, work with subject matter experts, coordinate with the instructional designers, etc.) as well as the services of a site developer." Combining two positions into one will bring down development cost estimates.

Maintenance/Revision

Whether or not course content is developed by an internal or external team, the client needs to figure in maintenance costs to the overall pricing of the project. Maintenance costs include the continual revision of content (both a programmer and an instructional designer fee need to be figured into this), the maintenance of the server, and someone to handle user problems. A Webmaster can cover most of these technical issues, help users, and input the content revisions as they arise. Stewart Skjerven says that a professional Webmaster's salary currently runs from $75,000 to $100,000 per year.

The frequency and scope of updates are dependent on the nature of the material you are training on, Skjerven says. Highly dynamic technological content that changes often is going to cost more in updates than static content, which requires few changes after the initial program is completed.

CHAPTER SEVEN

PLANNING FOR TECHNOLOGY AND CONVERTING YOUR CURRICULUM

The ease of delivering Web-based training relies on users having access to the necessary technology. Therefore, before deciding to implement a new Web-delivered training program, a company needs to know what kinds of computers its training audience has access to, and clarify what kinds of network will be necessary. The development of a technology plan includes considering all pieces of technology needed to plan, design, author, deliver, and maintain a Web-based training program.

After all the hardware questions have been answered, a trainer needs to examine course content and determine what kinds of instruction will be suitable for conversion to a Web-based course. This chapter discusses some issues to be considered when developing your technology plan, and suggests questions to ask yourself when deciding what kinds of course content can make the best use of the Web's training capabilities.

Developing a Technology Plan

Technology planning is a familiar practice for Information Technology (IT) professionals but might be a new procedure for trainers or instructional designers used to working with traditional training methods. Your technology plan should be developed in conjunction with the IT department. Their experiences and expertise can make the process a lot less painful, and many of the issues are their call.

Your plan should discuss the technology requirements of each phase of development. The first step, of course, is to think about how the training will be delivered and accessed by the end user. Once you've decided on the delivery platform, you can begin to make decisions about the volume and sophistication of graphics and multimedia, which will in turn tell you what other hardware and software to acquire to create those multimedia effects, and the network bandwidth needed.

But a technology plan should be more than just a shopping list of computers and authoring tools; it should also address how changes in technology will affect the future of the training program. Attempt to create a three-year "look ahead" that will assess the likely impact of technology on your training. Enhanced networks within organizations might change the way users access the training or the speed with which training is delivered. Newer, more powerful desktop computers will increase the multimedia capability of every user's machine. The much-touted "network computer," an increased population of laptops, cheaper, easier-to-use Web authoring tools, the rise of the "virtual office," electronic performance support systems—all of these will change the ways Web-based training is created and accessed, and should be considered when the original training is conceived and designed.

Your training organization may want to ease into Web-based training rather than dive into the new technology head first. There are numerous approaches a company can take in the development of Web-based training, but Irene Graff, a training consultant at Arbor Software, recommends an evolutionary approach in which components of multimedia are integrated into traditional training programs slowly, building up to a complete transition to Web-based delivery of training. Graff says one of the biggest obstacles she has encountered in the many companies where she has helped develop multimedia training is the assumption that someone can become a media expert overnight and develop Web-based training alone. Graff says that to be successful, companies have to be willing to collaborate with outside resources that have expertise in certain media types.

One method for progressing slowly into Web-based training might be first adding a WBT module as a precursor to a traditional training seminar, then purchasing commercial Internet courseware and experimenting with more complex Web-delivery, then developing customized Web-training internally.

Another approach is to become thoroughly engaged in Web-based training from the start. This might be more appealing to fast-growing companies that want the flexibility to change with new software releases and new internal developments. Web pages are simple to change and expand compared with other mediums like video and CD-ROM and can be enhanced with new media as it becomes available.

As you decide the way you will make the transition into custom Web-based training development, structure your technology plan around several realistic first-year goals. A skeleton list of those goals might read:

Buy a multimedia computer.

Procure education for yourself, as well as for staff/management/audience.

Examine some commercial Web-based training programs.

Buy a starter Web page layout program and practice creating some pages. Consider Claris Home Page or Microsoft FrontPage.

Select an external developer or hire an internal developer.

Choose a full authoring system for Web-based training.

Develop a pilot project.

Identify your first course for conversion.

Develop away and roll that puppy out!

As you progress in the development effort, with your Web-based training successfully implemented, remember to budget time and money each year for learning about and purchasing technology that may help the efficiency and effectiveness of your Web-based training. The ongoing technology budget might include allotments for new hardware, software, commercial courseware, staff training, and participation in conferences on new developments.

Internet CDs as a Solution

If multimedia is a good idea for training courses and works great off a CD-ROM, how do you overcome the problem of delivering media-rich programs for Web-based training? We all know that the "fat media"—video, audio, and animations—can take forever to download, or choke a company's Ethernet LAN.

One of the main advantages of the Net is the ease of updates, with new data placed on the server and immediately available to all users. How to marry these two? Enter the hybrid CD, known by the preferred name, the Internet CD. In this design, the media and program structure are delivered on a CD-ROM, and hotlinks to the Web are embedded along the way.

TECH TUTORIAL: INTERNET CDs

John Graham

CD-ROM is arguably the best format to deliver multimedia because of its capacity (640MB) and access speeds. One major drawback to CD-ROM, however, is its inability to update information as needed. Once you "burn" data onto a CD-ROM, it is permanently recorded and cannot be updated. To update information on a CD-ROM it is necessary to burn another one and distribute it to your users, making the first one useless and obsolete.

The Internet is arguably the best format to use for information that changes rapidly and often. One major drawback to the Internet, however, is that access times are long and transfer speeds are slow. Large multimedia files normally take an unacceptably long time to download and play on the user's computer.

Enter the hybrid CD. The hybrid CD concept makes use of the storage and data transfer power of the CD-ROM and the updateability of information on the Internet.

Information is stored primarily on the CD-ROM itself when it is first used. When information needs to be updated, because it is out of date or new information is available, it can be done via the Internet.

How It Works

The software that comes with the CD finds updated information either by:

- Accessing a specified Web site on the Internet automatically or through a user command.
- Interacting with a Web site through a Java applet in a Web browser. When the applet runs, it looks for and tells the program that there is updated information available.

The software first recognizes that the information on the CD needs updating by comparing it with the information available on a Web site. Then the software downloads the appropriate information and uses it instead of what appears on the CD-ROM. After the initial download, the software knows to use the updated information from then on because it is marked as updated.

If, in the future, that same piece of information needs updating again, the software goes through the same process to update the information.

How It Can Be Used

Hybrid CD systems can utilize information that changes often, such as stock quotes, headline news, and sports scores. But they can also be used for one-time updates for entire chapters in a book, or the text of a module in a training program.

For example, training for HR employees on CD-ROM may include the laws applicable to exempt and nonexempt employees. If, at any time after the program is purchased and used, some of the laws change, the information would be available on the Web. When the training software accesses the Web to see if any updates are available, it sees that some of the laws have changed, and uses the altered information in the program instead of the older laws that appear on the CD-ROM.

As with many new technologies, the limits of how this concept can be applied are only dictated by the creativity of the developer. Think of what types of data usually need updating: yearly calendars, interest rates, questions and answers on tests.

Because only the some of the information is updated, the CD-ROM can still be used to store the media-intensive elements of your training, such as audio and video files, as well as any information that does not need updating.

Titles can provide links to third-party resources on the Web or to a company's own Web site, sometimes with sections available only to registered users. Training programs can use this technology to update program content, provide additional resources, describe new offerings, collect registration or evaluation data, and set up e-mail or chat sessions with subject matter experts, managers, or other participants.

An example of this technology is the updating of information in the actual program through links to a Web resource. While a program usually looks to the CD for certain information, such as interest rates for a financial services training program, an Internet CD could access today's interest rate data from a public Internet site or the company's intranet server. All of this can be designed to be transparent to the end user. Several market research firms say there will be hundreds of consumer Internet CDs available by the end of the year. A current example is Microsoft's encyclopedia CD, Encarta. After linking once to the Web for updates, a flag appears on the header of an article if new information has been downloaded or is available from the Internet. Visual Home by Books That Work offers links to the Web for updated home design modules as well as new models of appliances.

↳ Converting Your Curriculum

When considering whether or not to adapt courses to the Web and identifying which courses in your training curriculum are best suited for adaptation, you need to consider the audience, the business need, conversion difficulty, course popularity, and course content.

Audience

It is important to consider the audience size and location. Is the audience for this particular course sufficiently large to justify Web-based delivery? If the potential students are geographically dispersed, using the Web to deliver training will be even more efficient—reducing travel time and delivery costs. When choosing a first course to convert to the Web, trainers may want to look for a course with a large audience that is delivered to employees in a number of different locations.

Business Need

Business need often inspires a shift from instructor-led or computer-based training to a Web-delivered product. Trainers may switch to the Web in reaction to a need to reduce costs, deliver training faster, or train a widely dispersed audience without accruing high travel costs.

According to Sherri Rose, a training manager at Apple, a decreasing training budget and new audiences all over the world require that certain courses be adapted to a Web-delivered format. Rose says they have identified the Web as the prime carrier for their management training and this means a big project of converting and adding to the existing courseware to make it right for Web-based training.

New versus Existing Course

Will it be easier to convert existing training or to develop new training from the ground up? If the training already in hand is driven by lots of video and sound or relies on instructor interactions, you may be better off building a new course around the capabilities of the Web. Paul Heacock of Human Dynamics Interactive says that when identifying which course to convert, look carefully at how much media is involved. Heacock's group does technical training for manufacturers and, for them, video-delivered training is successful because learners need to see the product in action. Converting the course to the Web wouldn't be practical just yet, Heacock says, because of the need to provide a long video demonstration of the activity being taught. "There is one advantage the Web has over video," Heacock says. "It would allow the students to be more interactive with the content. They could see and hear the text and answer questions." Once the bandwidth restrictions of delivering video over the Web are resolved, this course may well be a prospect for conversion.

Course Popularity

Undoubtedly, a more popular course will have greater value on the Web than a course that is accessed by only a few users. The cross-platform, unlimited access features of the Web make it easy to deliver a course to a large audience—much easier than trying to deliver the same course in an instructor-led or CD-ROM format. When considering whether or not to convert a course to the Web, address the issue of popularity—will the number of users, both first time and recurrent, justify the expense of converting or creating the course for the Web? And, on the other hand, if it is very popular as an instructor-led course, will your audience accept it being delivered by computer?

Course Content

Many trainers feel that certain training topics are better suited for the Web while others are better suited to instructor-led or CD-ROM programs. Peggi Jewett, president of FRAX Inc. and a developer of technical skills training, shares a belief held by some, that some topics require face-to-face and group interaction for successful learning. "Some types of training do better in a group environment," she says. "CBT [or Web-based training] is excellent for teaching skills, but it's not as good at teaching soft skills like diversity training, and customer support on phones. If we're talking about how to handle an irate customer, sales skills, leadership or supervisory training—in most cases that kind of training requires feedback from other people." Jewett said FRAX has implemented a successful online course which instructs trainees about a specific manufacturing process. The course also has a database for tracking interaction and responses from users.

Others believe a wide variety of a company's courses can be taught through a Web-based approach, as the case studies in this book demonstrate. Through creative analysis and developing interactive technology, instructional design specific to the Web can be used with all kinds of courses. As Warren Anderson of Anderson SoftTeach says, "Almost anything if it's done well can be presented or published in electronic form.

The trick is to make full use of the multiple media available to you when designing."

Very useful and practical interpersonal skills courses were developed on videodisc in the 1980s and on CD-ROM in the early 1990s. The instructional design knowledge is available; these types of courses simply need to be converted to the Web. Since they tend to be more video and audio oriented, bandwidth has slowed conversion of these courses for the Web.

HOW TO CONVERT CD-ROM TRAINING FOR THE INTERNET

Linda G. Marsh, Consulting Engineer/Information Design, Digital Equipment Corporation

The Challenge

When you're designing training, one of the basic questions you need to answer concerns the delivery mechanism. How are students going to access your training? Many design decisions are influenced by the answer.

My group is often asked to convert training from one delivery mechanism into another. Most recently, we've been converting multimedia CD-ROM courses into training that is accessed over the Internet, one lesson at a time. The challenge is to preserve the best features of the CD-ROM training—a task-based orientation with simulated practices, interactivity, and striking graphics—and somehow to translate features that cannot be preserved, namely video and audio.

Converting From . . .

Our client, Global Knowledge Network, Inc., provides multimedia training on CD-ROM to a technical audience. Audio is used on almost every screen, not only to introduce topics, but also to provide instruction. Video clips appear in every lesson, and provide much of the "real life" flavor of the training. A typical lesson that includes audio and video is about 15MB compressed.

We use tools such as IconAuthor and ToolBook to develop the courses, and access external programs from these applications to provide additional functionality. For example, we use CBIquick to present interactive software simulations.

Converting To . . .

Global Knowledge Network also provides a distance learning service in Canada to professionals in information technology: Mentys—The Internet Computer Institute. The Mentys system delivers training via the World Wide Web. Once the client kit has been installed, students can access any of the courses shown in the course list from a Web browser, and select lessons in any order.

Mentys uses a "store-and-forward" approach to delivering training. When a student selects a lesson, a compressed version of the lesson is downloaded locally to the student's PC, where it is decompressed. Ten megabytes on the hard disk are required. About half of that space is used by client kit files, which have been previously installed; the remainder is available for lesson files.

Many Mentys subscribers access lessons over slow transmission lines (14.4 kilobits/second [Kbps]). The Mentys development guidelines therefore recommend a maximum lesson size (compressed) of 275K (100K is recommended) to keep transfer rates under 2 to 3 minutes. The Mentys guidelines also specify a limited number of authoring tools for course implementation. This keeps the client kit as small as possible, reducing student disk space requirements and initial download time.

An Example

Global Knowledge Network recently asked our group to produce a multimedia CD-ROM for a course entitled *Windows NT System Administration*, as well as its Internet version.

To create an effective course on multimedia CD-ROM, my team decided to:

Create task-oriented lessons

Have frequent interactivity

Use audio and video often to deliver content

Include graphics on almost every screen

How did these criteria impact the CD-ROM and Internet deliverables?

Task-Oriented Lessons

The course was designed around a set of tasks that a system administrator would be expected to perform, such as managing users, disks, and files, monitoring the system, and setting up a network. In the CD-ROM course, concepts and tasks were integrated into a single lesson.

A *Try It* button launched an interactive simulation where the student practiced the task being taught. For example, the lesson "Creating and Deleting User Accounts" contained four interactive simulations.

In the CD-ROM course, the software simulations used full-screen graphics. During the prototype phase, we converted the largest simulation to the Internet format. That single simulation approached the 275K size limit. If the simulation alone approached the size limit, we knew we could not deliver the training as designed: one lesson that integrated concepts and simulated tasks.

So, for the Internet version, we provided separate lessons for the concepts (Overview Lessons) and tasks (Exercises). The single CD-ROM lesson, "Creating and Deleting User Accounts," was split into five Internet lessons—one overview lesson and four exercise lessons. [See Figure 7.1.]

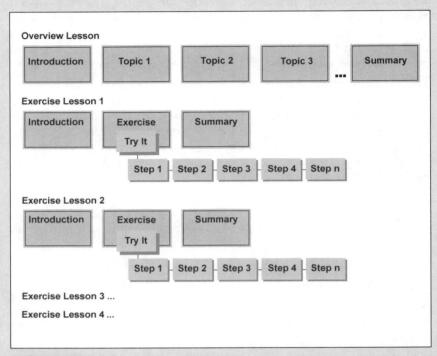

FIGURE 7.1 Internet lesson structure.

Frequent Interactivity

Frequent interactivity holds students' interest and is essential in teaching procedures. The task-based exercises provided "hands on" simulations to give a realistic experience of managing a Windows NT system. To maximize this experience, we built 46 interactive software simulations.

In the CD-ROM version, we used CBIquick (AMT Corporation, 904-913-8354), a tool that allowed us to produce elegant simulations. The simulations opened with a video clip of the system administrator describing the task being taught. Using narration, the system administrator then walked the student through a task. Text and visual feedback were provided for incorrect responses. After two incorrect tries, CBIquick animated the correct response and continued with the next step. CBIquick simulations also captured subtle nuances of the working application, such as the up and down states of a button. When students clicked the OK button, for example, they could see that they had clicked it.

In the Internet course, we wanted to keep the interactive simulations. At the time, however, CBIquick was not one of the development tools supported by the Mentys program. As an alternative, we used screen captures from the CBIquick simulations, and we wrote a simple simulator program in IconAuthor that allowed us to display a graphic, wait for user input, and advance to the next screen if the input was correct. Feedback was limited to a beep if the user made an incorrect response. Although this simulation was not as complex or precise as the one used in the CD-ROM course, it got the job done.

Use of Audio and Video

We used audio and video extensively in the CD-ROM version, but could not in the Internet version because of size restrictions. In the conversion process, the narration was edited and incorporated as screen text. The Internet course developers revised the text so that the conversational and familiar tone of the narration was rewritten into acceptable, grammatical prose.

Use of Graphics

We wanted to create a visually compelling course. In the CD-ROM course, the user lesson interface (navigation buttons and locator graphics) used a 256-color palette. To meet size restrictions for the Internet course, we simplified the user interface. We converted some graphics to the 16-color Windows palette; we removed dithered areas in others to increase file compression.

In researching how to conserve space in the Internet version, we experimented with saving files in different formats. [Figure 7.2 shows two graphics saved in .BMP and .GIF formats, before and after compression.]

GIF files are saved in an already compressed format, so they are small on the hard drive and do not compress any more when run through a zipping utility. BMP files are bigger when uncompressed, but when compressed are smaller than the equivalent .GIF files. Ultimately, we chose to include graphics saved

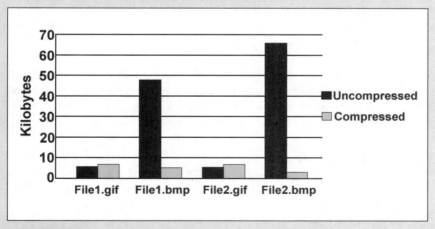

FIGURE 7.2 Compressed and uncompressed graphic size.

in formats that could be compressed as much as possible, because we knew that users needed the space to accommodate lesson files on the hard drive. [Note: The composition of the graphic affects how much it can be compressed. A bitmap using many dithered colors could probably not be compressed very much.]

In Conclusion

As we converted this course from CD-ROM to an Internet deliverable, size considerations impacted our choice of tools and the instructional design. Using the techniques described here, we were able to minimize lesson size without compromising instructional integrity. As new technologies emerge, these considerations may no longer impact Internet deliverables, and you'll be able to deliver the same content regardless of media.

CONVERTING CURRICULUM FOR A WEB-BASED TRAINING PROJECT FOR THE BUREAU OF NATIONAL AFFAIRS: CASE STUDY

Nancee Simonson

Purpose of the Project

The project was to convert a standup training class to an interactive Web site to be posted on our Intranet for access by all employees. The class objective was to familiarize all employees with the three-branch federal government processes and the associated documents that go with the steps in the government activities. This is the basis of our corporate product and activities: we are a private publisher that gathers information on government activities and developments for our professional customers. So most of our employees need to know something about federal government processes, though each in different ways.

The reason for putting this on the Web is the wide range of possible users, the difficulty of delivering standup training to such a wide audience with different locations and time schedules, the just-in-time, need-to-know data of this type for completing job tasks, and the availability of much of the source material now online.

Software/Hardware

Following the principle of "keep it simple," and our budget dictates, which were basically "spend no money," we decided to use Internet Assistant for Word. Word is a powerful word processor that is easy to use and has become our corporate standard. The Internet Assistant is free, downloadable from the Internet, easy to install, provides a seamless interface with Word and is quite easy to use. It does not have the power and flexibility of an authoring tool, but since this is our first pilot for Web-based training, we are going to develop a fairly simple program. (Since it is a pilot, there is no way we could get budget approval for expensive authoring tools. By the same token, most people use 386 and 486 PCs at this time, so they would have a hard time accessing a more powerful program anyway. We must design for the audience and their equipment.) Another reason for using Web technology is that it is multi-platform and the company will be using UNIX as well as Windows and DOS-based machines to access the program.

User Interface

We originally planned a frame-based interface and a "site map" of the main sections and subsections in order to keep users in the program and provide an easy way to navigate. However, it is being postponed until this more advanced feature is needed (see discussion in changes section below). The program is divided into three sections: congressional (legislative), executive (regulatory), and judicial (courts). There are also a brief, entertaining and optional introduction, a fully linked index and a resource guide. Colors are limited to white (background), blue (highlights and graphics), and green (optional). The navigational buttons are blue. The graphics are basically black and white drawings, with some blue highlights, of three federal buildings: Capitol, White House, and Supreme Court. The main frame consists of a horizontal bar with buttons for the intro, three branches, index, and resources. There are also two site maps for the two themes of the program: the sequential government process and the arrangement of corresponding documents will be added later. The six segments will be contained in six scrollable documents: each section will be in one file, rather than using a stacking card arrangement with one screen per page.

Content Outline

Intro: Includes a brief introduction of the course with a link to the Schoolhouse Rock videos online: "Preamble" and "I'm Just a Bill." These video segments were used in the class, but the online site contains audio and lyrics. It's entertaining, but is optional since it is not vital to everyone.

Legislative: Includes steps of the process with links to supporting documents, and flowcharts at each step of the way.

Executive: Includes White House and regulatory steps of the process from bill signing to implementations of regulations with links to supporting documents and flowcharts at each step of the way.

Judicial: Includes Supreme Court and federal court process step-by-step with links to supporting documents and flowcharts at each step of the way. [See Figures 7.3, 7.4, and 7.5.]

Resources: Includes list of resources online.

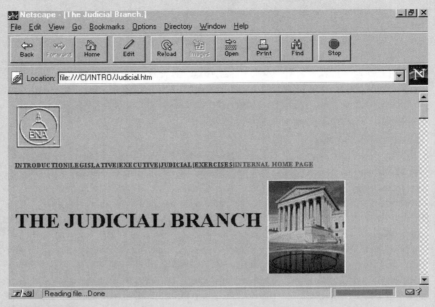

FIGURE 7.3 The judicial branch.

©1997 Nancee Simonson

Index: Includes a map of the program in index form linked to the segments of the program so a user can go immediately to any section or document needed.

The major change, after the class discussion of Electronic Performance Support Systems, was that I began to see this product (and indeed our whole Intranet) as an EPSS and not strictly computer-based training. That is, the goal for the company is *not* to get people to know all the content of this "class," but to have the content available to them in specific pieces at the time they need to use it. This is a fundamental change.

First, this meant that there is no reason to include quizzes or "tests" in the tutorial. While the class doesn't have quizzes, it does have interactive questions to see if the learners are catching on. The quizzes in the CBT would have been a way to "certify" that employees "took the class." In order to do their jobs, employees need access to a glossary of terms, to a flowchart of the government branch, to descriptions of courts or government offices to know which ones to contact or how (phone numbers), etc. So I dropped the quiz part of the design, and dropped the linear "step-by-step" approach in

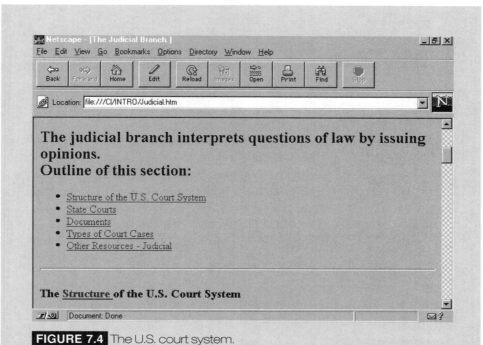

FIGURE 7.4 The U.S. court system.

©1997 Nancee Simonson

describing the government process. Instead, I built the content by "chunks" of information that would be useful for a job task.

Because this is such a fundamental change, the development will be on-going. It means continuing to evaluate the product with users to find out what things they need added in order to do their jobs. This involves a much more thorough job task analysis, rather than just an analysis of users' need for information.

Implementation Description

The implementation, simply, was posting it to our Internal Home Page. The Internal Home Page contains a link to "Editorial Training."

In order to make it easy to access, right under the Editorial Training heading are three links:

1. List of classes

2. Registration form

3. Introduction to Government Process Class

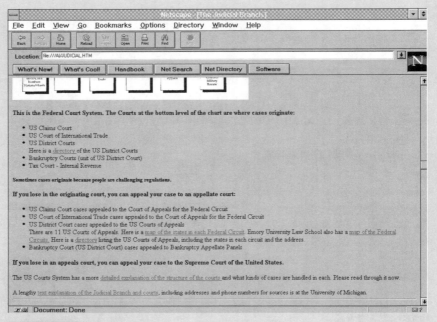

FIGURE 7.5 The federal court system.

©1997 Nancee Simonson

I wanted people to have immediate awareness of the product and not have to drill down to get it. While the class is also linked to the second level where it is described in the schedule, it had to be on the front page as well because it is an EPSS and not simply class materials.

Since, in the time allotted for this class, we only completed the intro page and one of the three sections, Judicial Process, the other two sections were "under construction." Promotion consisted of: first, Announcement to Executive Editor at a meeting Dec. 2; then, second ranking editorial executives; then, a general announcement to all employees. At the same time, testing by users continues. This provides continuous improvement, and, at the same time, a marketing tool. For example, the legal trainer for the research department was already using the Judicial site for her training before the "ink" was barely dry on the coding to get it on the Internal Home Page! I find that the ability to use this product "in pieces," so to speak—rather than using the whole package as you do with a standup class—is one of the major benefits of having this as a Web product or EPSS. Users really can take what they want and use it however it best suits their purposes.

Testing and Evaluation Results

Testing was done continuously by prospective users of the product throughout the company: research, new hires, nonlegal editorial, legal editorial, content experts, managers of prospective users, executive editorial. Testers were given a disk with the prototype, plus a paper printout on which they were instructed to make line-by-line comments on the elements of the product. For many, I also received verbal comments and discussed solutions, recommendations, additions, and deletions. They also had a brief one-page questionnaire with three questions about the overall usefulness, ease-of-use, and suggested changes.

They uniformly found the product useful. My favorite review said it was "awesome." Partly this is because it is the first "just-in-time" training product or EPSS in the company and it is a topic that nearly everyone needs to know something about.

Testers also gave *a lot* of really good suggestions for additions and changes. Some of the critical comments concerned readability—the text in a chart was not clear—and a few typos. These were all corrected. Most of the comments concerned *additions*. This indicated that people found it useful and wanted even more capabilities in the package.

Suggested Changes Based upon Results

A lot of the changes had to do with design issues: adding more information and detail without taking away from the simplicity; giving people the content they needed, where they needed it, without taking away from the purpose of the product, which was to be an overview of the government process. This was solved by adding a few more sections, but mostly by arranging links to solve the access issues. For instance, one person wanted immediate access to information on more obscure tax and bankruptcy courts. While this was in a link to a more detailed discussion later, I added links to these specific sections in the list of courts.

Another person wanted to know about the Bill of Rights. It was a big question. While that did not strictly fit in with the structure—which is the three branch process—it seemed a big enough issue that it was detracting from the usefulness of the product. I made a content connection by adding a short paragraph, with a link to the text, and the explanation that this is the source of a lot of litigation, regulation, and legislation in the three branches. My operating principle here is that since this will be a self-paced instructional piece, used without the guidance or control of an instructor, all individual questions are important, because they are precisely what will come up when a user uses the product on a solitary basis. As a result, I tried to address *every* question or comment by the users in some way.

Others found the directories and telephone numbers in one of the lengthy documents most useful, so a link will be added to the first page of the Judicial section that will give users up-front access without changing the overall format of the first page.

There were no real suggested changes about overall format. Again, I attribute this to my goal of strictly keeping it simple, and to the newness of such a product in our workplace. I suspect, as people become more familiar with this product and other Web-based products, that more suggestions will come up and more changes will be made. The intent is to continually review and update the product to keep up with technology and user needs.

The frames design was not used at this stage, since it was not needed to make use of the product easy. However, I am preparing the coding for that because I feel that as the technology advances and users get used to more sophisticated designs, that will be necessary. For example, for the Internal Home Page as a whole, the design is very plain, and the designers are now only beginning to design a new table format. This product by itself is the most animated and sophisticated item on the Internal Home Page. For consistency and ease of use, the simpler design at this point was more compatible on the Internal Home Page.

Project and Teamwork

I think the loosely constructed team of experts worked very well. Each person had experience working on teams so there was not a long learning curve in that area. We did not have lengthy meetings. We were able to discuss a lot via interoffice e-mail and get things done efficiently. (Having teamwork experience and enthusiasm helps a whole lot on a project like this. I am not a fan of lengthy meetings and discussions.) In addition, we were able to have additional resources—a frames programmer, an interface designer—who were not designated team members, at our disposal easily and enthusiastically! As far as lessons learned, I would do it again that way: a small dedicated team of those who will do the bulk of the work, with easy access to other expert resources as needed.

Lessons Learned

1. *Keep it simple*. One of my goals, of course, was to keep the design and presentation simple. One reason was because the Internet and intranet are very new here and people are not that sophisticated about their capabilities. But the simplicity turned out to be the magic pill. Everyone who tested the product really thought it was valuable, learned something, and found it easy to use.
2. At the same time, keeping it simple yet attractive and easy to use is *very difficult and a lot of work*. I found the design and development implementation took a lot longer to do—to get right!—than expected.

Things change on the Internet, little codes don't work, the design doesn't look right in all browsers. Which leads me to another point:

3. *You must design for all browsers!* It looks different. What looks good, or a difficult execution that looks "OK" on one browser, may come out entirely different on another. Again, a simple design makes this easier to do, but then it's difficult to accomplish the goals in a simple design—a circular problem.

4. Above all else, *you must keep users' needs in mind first.*

5. *Test and test and test some more.* Especially since this is a product on the network for *all* employees, I couldn't get away with overlooking things that I might for a very focused group. The testing on different types of employees was so valuable because it gave insight into how each type would use it, what their particular information needs are, what questions popped up for each. For example, the editors were particularly aware of typos, which might seem like a small thing, but that's what slowed them down! One person in reading about the U.S. Constitution asked about the Bill of Rights. While this was not directly related to one of the three branches of government, it was the first question that popped into his mind. So I added a paragraph and link, with the rationale that the rights in the Bill of Rights prompt a lot of the legislation, regulation, and litigation that churns through the three branches. It became a richer product for everyone's input.

6. *Find some way to include all of the suggested changes.* I discovered that precisely because this is an online product—not standup training—users won't have a trainer to answer questions. Therefore, any questions they have while using the product will slow them down or turn them off if they are not answered. The testing process needs to be very thorough to uncover all of these questions and then the solutions must be incorporated into the product.

7. *It is an interative process.* At this point I don't think the product will ever be completely done. That's OK. I think it is extremely important to add to it what people need to do their jobs. At the same time, design issues and goals *must* be kept in mind so that the additions and changes don't change the integrity of the product.

8. Experience with *teamwork* helps. Learning teamwork should not be a part of the project!

Quality of Software Solution

I think the product more than met its goal of providing just-in-time training on government process. As I mentioned, the project took on the role of an electronic performance support system. Without knowing the technical terms and concepts, users began asking for additional items to make it such. People were thrilled with the *ease of access* to the material. This was one of the goals and the response indicated that it was well met. The "teacher" or subject matter expert involved is a librarian and also one of the maintainers of the Internal Home Page so that it will be easily maintained and updated.

Overall, the original standup training was much-needed and well-received. This product ended up going quite a bit beyond the resource provided in the standup training and gave people an easy desk-reference, telephone directory, subject matter expert, and content review all in one.

It can also be the beginning of building an internal "knowledge base" of frequently asked questions about the process. In other words, it is turning into a dynamic learning tool, resource, and just-in-time training program.

For me, it was an experience in learning the richness of the Web format and HTML to provide a product that can answer many needs at once. Often in standup training you have a group with diverse needs at one time that really degrades the training.

Since the Web and HTML are so robust, the design can be made with links to a lot of information without corrupting the overall simplicity of the original product. It can also be made graphically attractive to use. (See CD-ROM for sample code.)

References

Agada, John, "Analysis of Information Repackaging (IR): Processes Using the Instructional Systems Design (ISD) Model," School of Library and Information Science, University of Wisconsin-Milwaukee, http://www.usq.edu.au/elect-pub/e-jist/agada.htm.

Carleton University, The Tutorial Gateway, http://www.civeng.carleton.ca/~nholtz/tut/doc/doc.html.

Leigh, Douglas, "The Internet and Distributed Learning: Instructional Designer's Medium and Tool," http://mailer.fsu.edu/~dleigh/superfulx/words/dleight/NetDistLearn.html.

McKendree, Jean, Reader, Will, and Hammond, Nick, "The 'homeopathic fallacy' in learning from hypertext," in *Interactions*, ACM Press, Vol. 2, No. 3. pp. 74–82, 1995, http://www.ioe.ac.uk/tescwwr/Homeopathy.html.

SuperCal, Staffordshire University, A joint project of University of Trieste, Italy, and Staffordshire University, UK, on computer-aided Learning materials.

WWW Constructivist Project Design Guide, Institute for Learning Technologies, Teachers College Columbia University, http://www.ilt.columbia.edu/k12/livetext/Webcurr.html.

University of Southern Queensland, Instructional Design for Distance Education, Module 10, Evaluation, http://www.usq.edu.au/dec/88031/M10.htm#Activity10.2.

Is Web-Based Training Right for Your Organization?

As you edge closer to making a decision about Web-based training, issues to consider become more specific. Table 7.1 is a Decision Aid chart that lists all of the possible considerations when deciding if Web-based training is a good option for your training organization. If you have a course in mind, respond to each "consideration" in the Decision Aid and then total the points in the far-right column. According to Nina Adams of Adams Consulting Group, the author of the Decision Aid, a score of less than 135 indicates Web-based training should probably not be considered as a training solution for the project in question; a score of 136ñ200 indicates Web-based training may be worth considering, and a score over 200 indicates Web-based training is most likely an appropriate solution. If necessary, this chart can also be helpful in justifying the implementation of Web-based training to management, and will help start the technology plan development process. An online version of this Decision Aid, with automatic computation, is available on the companion Web site at-www.wiley.com/compbooks/hall.

TABLE 7.1 Web-Based Training Decision Aid

Consideration	Instructions	Points
Number of learners.	If < 50 learners	0
	> 50 & < 100 learners	5
	> 100 learners	10
Number of training sites.	If learners are at	
	1 site	0
	1 to 5 sites	5
	> 5 sites	10
Distance of learners from existing training site.	If the average distance learners are from an existing training site	
	Does not require overnight stay	0
	Requires overnight stay	5
	Requires many overnight stays	10
Number of times program will be offered.	If program will be offered	
	1 time	0
	1 to 5 times	3
	6 to 19 times	5
	> 20 times	10

TABLE 7.1 Continued

Consideration	Instructions	Points
Frequency of integrated updates.	If integrated updates are needed	
	< Every 3 months	0
	Between 3 & 6 months	5
	> 6 months	10
Development time available.	If training must be available in	
	< 3 months	0
	3 to 6 months	5
	> 6 months	10
Preferred learning style.	If learners prefer	
	Group learning	0
	Independent learning	10
Preferred training schedule.	If it is more appropriate to	
	Set training schedules	3
	Allow learner to set schedule	10
Current computer proficiency.	If learners	
	Don't know how to use a computer and don't need a computer for their job	0
	Don't know how to use a computer and do need a computer for their job	5
	Know how to use a computer	10
Current learner skill level.	If learners	
	All have the same skill level	5
	Have widely varying skill levels	10
Need for individualized remediation.	If learners probably	
	Won't need remediation	5
	Probably will need remediation	10
Importance of consistency.	If consistency is	
	Not important	0
	Somewhat important	5

Consideration	Instructions	Points
	Very important	10
Need for performance tracking.	If performance tracking across multiple courses or modules is	
	Not needed	0
	Desirable	5
	Required	10
Content.	If skills are	
	Soft	5
	Hard	10
Content already available on CBT.	If CBT program	
	Must be developed to meet requirements	0
	Can be purchased and modified to meet requirements	5
	Can be purchased for use without modification	10
Management's past experience with CBT.	If past experience with CBT was	
	Not favorable	0
	Neutral	5
	Very favorable	10
General view of technology.	If management views technology as	
	Awful	0
	A necessary evil	5
	Great	10
Budgeting scheme.	For cost comparisons, if development costs	
	Are separated from costs of delivery	0
	Are included with delivery costs	10
Availability of hardware at learner site.	If hardware at learner site is	
	Not available at all	0
	Available but has to be upgraded	5
	Available	10

TABLE 7.1 Continued

Consideration	Instructions	Points
Cash flow. (Can the company spare the cash now for development in order to save later?)	If cash flow is Slow OK Good	 0 5 10
Management's perception of person making recommendation.	If person making recommendation Has a poor track record Has a great track record	 0 10
Availability and skills of project management staff.	If staff Cannot manage a CBT project Can manage a CBT project	 0 10
Availability of production hardware.	If production hardware is Not available at all Available but has to be upgraded Not needed Available	 0 5 10 10
Availability and knowledge of CBT design and authoring language.	If staff Knows nothing about authoring Will buy off-the-shelf CBT Can design and author CBT	 0 5 10
Availability of hardware troubleshooters.	If troubleshooters Cannot be made available Can be made available	 0 10
Availability of content experts.	If content questions must be answered and experts Cannot be made available Can be made available	 0 10
Use of existing trainers.	If existing trainers Will no longer be needed Can be transferred to new positions Can be used on CBT projects	 0 5 10
TOTAL		

CHARLES SCHWAB: A CASE STUDY

Charles Schwab, the investment services company, has been expanding at an enormous rate, both geographically and in employee population. Their main business is called "discount brokerage" in the financial industry and involves making trades for clients who make their own investment decisions. According to the New York Stock Exchange, "The company sets itself apart from the competition in two ways: the level of information it provides (offering materials that help clients decide the direction of their investment programs without giving specific recommendations) and its level of technology (including touch-tone phone trading and software offerings)."

Patrick MacKellan, Training Manager in Schwab's Retail Education department, says the company had over 10,000 employees in 1996, up from three thousand when he joined the company three and half years earlier. "We will probably double again in the next three to four years," MacKellan says. "With this phenomenal growth, our biggest challenge [in training] is how to manage that growth."

"The largest population in our high-growth environment is new brokers. The second-largest population is existing employees for major change initiatives," MacKellan says. "We are constantly upgrading our technology, changing old systems to new systems, getting rid of mainframe systems, changing the way we do business from one model to a newer model. It is an extremely dynamic, change-oriented company."

The Web, MacKellan says, is an ideal delivery method for a company that has been using technology-delivered training for some time. Charles Schwab started with a mainframe system which delivered courseware to dumb terminals, then worked their way toward a multimedia approach with multiple servers delivering training on numerous networks. "The mainframe system was easy to maintain and easy to deliver, but the development time was long, because it was just strenuous coding and very hard to program," MacKellan says.

As Schwab went to a networked multimedia system of training, they found that CD-ROM was not useful for them because the training content they were delivering was extremely dynamic and changed frequently. This system was difficult to maintain because so many servers needed to be kept current. "The advantage of going to an intranet solution is that once again, like the mainframe, you have one box where the training resides," MacKellan says. "Better than the mainframe, though, it is updateable in seconds. It can be used for dynamic as well as static information and distribution is relatively easy. This is really going to solve a lot of our needs." Before preparing an all-out Web-based training approach, Schwab is waiting for the issues of bandwidth to be resolved.

The company has already experimented with its first Web-based training projects, starting with a simple six-module course MacKellan designed. The course, called "Web Basics," was delivered over SchWeb (Schwab's intranet) and as the course name suggests, brought employees who took the course up to speed on Web technology and usage. "It was the first training to be delivered to a general population via our intranet," MacKellan says.

This was the first step in readying the entire Schwab employee population for Web-delivered training. The primary audience for training at Schwab is the huge group of customer service agents or brokers who answer customer questions about stocks and bonds trading. Because this group is large, spread out, and needs to have fairly complicated financial information at their disposal, training is a challenge. MacKellan says that the management of the Schwab corporation is extremely technology-savvy, which has made the process of upgrading client computers for Web-based training that much easier.

The first of those upgrades was to put a browser on every employee's computer. In one department, Schwab has added a RealAudio plug-in to each browser, allowing Schwab employees to access another Web-based training course. Steve Smith, former Director of Business Information Systems for Schwab's Capital Markets and Trading group, worked with his group to update a video course that taught the broad population of consumer brokers about the more specialized role of the Capital Markets and Trading group.

Although most brokers only deal with smaller trades, Capital Markets and Trading handles the more complicated trades. Smith explained that most brokers deal with trades in the hundreds of shares whereas Capital Markets and Trading has a special desk that deals with trades in the tens of thousands of shares. Very few brokers understood the role, responsibilities, and even the language of that group. A video had been prepared by Schwab several years earlier which walked the viewer through a Capital Markets and Trading trade and explained each detail of the process. Smith says that while the video was well-received by the training audience, it was not always available on demand and arranging a viewing was sometimes inconvenient. "We took a piece of the video and put it on the Web in order to get it into a repeat play situation and make it more accessible to the training audience," Smith says.

The result was an HTML page that contained stills from the video as well as a transcript. Through the RealAudio plug-in, users can hear the trade taking place by clicking on the still image that represents the specifics of the trade. With the new Web version of the video training, users can replay any portion of the audio they didn't comprehend fully as well as read the transcript to get a more clear understanding of the entire transaction.

While Schwab continues its speedy growth, trainers are watching the evolution of Web-based training closely and edging the company toward a full-blown online training approach, complete with a testing function which will ease the collection of evaluation data from new employees. Like all fast-paced industries, information in the financial business changes rapidly, and Schwab is looking to their intranet as an ideal platform for keeping their employees up to speed.

CHAPTER EIGHT

DESIGNING COURSES FOR THE WEB

Good graphic and instructional design are both part of building a quality Web-based training program. Without engaging graphics and multimedia, it is difficult to hold a learner's attention on a computer screen. However, nothing but flashy multimedia coupled with weak instructional design is counterproductive for a training program. The goal of the training is to educate the learner, and this must be remembered while designing the graphic elements of the program. Remember also that bandwidth is the primary restriction of the Web and large multimedia files that take too much time to load will distract the learner from the training objectives.

Basic Web Design Guidelines

Designing for the Web in any capacity is different from designing print-based material. In both cases, graphic design needs to catch the eye and yet also inform and educate the reader about its subject. Web design takes this a step further; not only must it be eye-catching and informative, it needs to have a clear conceptual and intuitive path between areas of information. Ease of use comes into play here, as users need to navigate a Web site without getting confused. There should be a logic behind the way screens are linked and the navigational access the user has to each element of the program. Web-based training must take this even a step further; the basic tenets of teaching and learning must also come into play.

Be Aware of What Causes Confusion and Frustrates Users

There are certain design elements that, when not used properly, will frustrate or confuse the reader. Examples are:

- Large, hard-to-download graphics that stall viewing
- Buttons or links that are difficult to use or hard to identify, or that connect to the indicated item or screen
- Lengthy text that requires scrolling to find the buttons at the bottom of a page

Designers also have to take into account what type of Web page they're working on. When working on a training or general business-oriented site, efficiency and clarity are paramount.

There must be clear, rational thought behind the organization of the program on the Web site and the manner in which pages are linked. People who come upon the page and read what is displayed there will probably have lingering questions they'd like to explore. A good Web designer needs to be able to anticipate these questions from an objective point of view, and make the answers easily accessible. Ideally, those answers will be just one mouse click away.

Use Graphics Appropriately

Graphics on the Web should accent the text or subject matter, illustrate a point, or serve a function of their own. They should not overwhelm the Web or distract the viewer from the learning process.

Graphics on the Web should follow the same style guidelines as print-based or CD-ROM graphic design. Nothing detracts more from a good program than bad graphics. In general, consult a professional graphic designer for the graphics in your program.

Color, browser preferences, and the quality of the audience's computers all need to be taken into account when choosing graphics.

Keep Limitations of Web-Based Design in Mind

Graphic design on the Web is limited in certain ways. Because the presentation of text and images varies based on the screen quality and the monitor size, browser, and/or access speed of the client computer, this changes the readability of on-screen text and graphics. Designers need to make sure their images, text, and screen layouts read well on a variety of screens and browsers.

Some Elements of Good Web Design

When one examines some of the best multimedia training programs, there are at least three elements that stand out:

1. Great instructional design

2. Great graphics

3. A metaphor or simulation

A good Web site should also have a clear information structure, be easy to navigate, and follow the basics of design.

Quality Instructional Design

A proper front-end analysis, including clear identification of who is to be trained, what needs to be learned, and a performance analysis of what the job requires for improvement is a minimal starting point. Good instructional design can make up for poor quality of media, but it doesn't work the other way around.

Pertinent and Eye-Catching Graphics

Most internally developed programs and many off-the-shelf programs neglect this area. Good graphic design doesn't have to be expensive, but it does require design sensibility on the part of the project manager, who should value this area and access someone with talent. The state-of-the-art these days is such that, to be considered an excellent program, good graphic design is a must. The graphics of a top-notch program need to be at the quality level of the best printed graphics you see these days, whether it is a brochure or a business-to-business magazine ad. Here's an analogy: When training films were first produced, the fact that anything was on film was innovative. But look at the quality of professionally produced business training videos today. No serious videos are produced that don't approach broadcast quality.

GRATUITOUS USE OF BELLS AND WHISTLES

Margaret Driscoll, University of Massachusetts, Boston

If you have been surfing the Internet and paying particular attention to Web-based training sites, then you have probably noticed the trends in this delivery technology and some of the ironies. As part of a research study at Teacher College, Columbia University, Web-based training trends were explored in a qualitative research study. The following information emerged as part of that study, explaining the pitfalls new Web-based training designers need to watch out for.

Do you remember when desktop publishing was all the rage? Recall the deluge of newsletters that were ugly, memos that made you hunt for the meat, and letterheads that looked like the work of someone creating a ransom note. Well it's back, and it's on your Web browser! The second trend to watch for is training programs that use needless graphics, gratuitous animation, and HTML extensions that don't work for all browsers.

Like the early days of desktop publishing, when everyone could be a publisher using simple tools, now everyone can be a Web-based training developer.

When asked about potential pitfalls that await new Web-based training developers, experts and experienced practitioners agreed that the lure of tools is one of the biggest dangers. Helping developers avoid being "seduced by their own technology" is the mission of a consultant who recently took a job with an Internet service provider. She cautions new developers against both losing sight of the educational goals and using all the bells and whistles just because they can. There are countless stories of developers who spend all night making the corporate logo spin, developing cool but illegible backgrounds, or writing Java applets that do something cute but really annoying.

As the Web development tools become easier to use, and developers search for things that will add "pizzazz" to their sites, expect to see more gratuitous graphics, flashing text, and pointless Java applets. Veterans who have experience developing Web-based training programs suggest that the watchwords for training professionals should be "less is more."

A Metaphor or Simulation

The best programs have an element that grabs users' attention and immerses them in an environment. This may be the metaphor used for the interface, or an extended simulation and is related to what people in the movie business call "the suspension of disbelief." Maybe we should call this "the suspension of training resistance" that occurs when the program is so interesting, or so appealing, or so intellectually stimulating that the users actually like it.

Information Structure

Many designers recommend an interface which has several standard menu options present on every screen. A usual assortment of these options includes "Home, Search, Menu, Contact Us." Having these options available on every screen means that the user is never more than one mouse click away from the main index page. This is a fairly common element of current Web design.

Another option is to include links to other pages within the text of the Home Page. This has the advantage of answering readers' questions as they arise (when a new issue is covered, users notice that it's also a hyperlink). This may be intuitive for some people, but may confuse those who want to read through all the information first, and then find themselves having to wade through all the text again to find the link they want.

A Table of Contents or Orientation Page is also recommended. In addition to having embedded hyperlinks, you may want to give readers the option of seeing a comprehensive description of each link on your site. List clear but brief explanations for each hotlink you provide to make the list a useful resource and still easily accessible.

Navigation

Other navigational items which are rapidly becoming standard include search utilities that help the user browse for specific information. This is particularly useful if your training module is more of an informational support system than an interactive training program. Another useful interface element is a title or logo at the head of each screen in the Web site sequence which keeps users clear on where they are. Because many Web sites have links to external sites which then steer the user back to the home site, these graphic name tags clear up any confusion about which screen is a part of the local site and which is not.

Having the logo repeat through your whole site helps users who arrive from external links on the company's intranet or the Internet. With the logo visible, those external visitors are aware of what your site is and how they can best navigate it. One way of doing this might be to have an image map which is both a menu, linked hypertext, and a pictorial representation of your site and what information is available there. Essentially, every Web site needs to have contact information for the administrator of the page, a copyright date, and should indicate when the page was last updated. Links, a company logo, and a menu bar to direct the user to the local home page or a search engine are also useful components.

Design Basics

There are plenty of resources for Web design that go into further detail. One of those books, *World Wide Web Design Guide* (Hayden Books, 1995) by Stephen Wilson, offers these basic guidelines for Web-based graphic design:

- Create a coherent, consistent layout style. The goal is to create a range of possibilities with a strong family relationship.

- Judiciously use white space. Open space helps set up text and images and makes it easier to focus. Use open space to create an open, balanced feeling and to set off your text and images.

- Use emphasis techniques sparingly. Avoid the overuse of large text, major header tags, bold style, all caps, and colored text.

- Use the whole width of the page.

- Use transparent incline images. They integrate seamlessly into the page.

- Test your page on various browsers. Watch out for conflicts with browser conventions.

THE GOOD AND THE BAD OF WEB-BASED TRAINING

Margaret Driscoll, University of Massachussets, Boston

What do experts and developers perceive to be the qualities of good and bad Web-based training? This article presents the findings of a recent study undertaken to answer that question, as part of a larger study at Teacher College, Columbia University. The survey asked Web-based training experts and developers to describe their experiences with both good and bad Web-based training programs and identify the elements they consider to have the most impact on the quality and effectiveness of design.

These elements appear in the following list, ranked from most frequently to least frequently cited by respondents.

Qualities of Good and Bad Web-Based Training Design

Good	Bad
1. Interactive	Passive
2. Nonlinear	Linear
3. Clear, clean graphic user interface	Confusing, busy graphic user interface
4. Lesson structure present	Lesson structure missing
5. Multimedia	Text-intensive
6. Attention to educational details	Lack of attention to educational details
7. Attention to technical details	Lack of attention to technical details
8. Learner control	System control

1. **Level of Interactivity:** The most frequently mentioned characteristic influencing Web-based training quality is *interactivity versus passivity*. The more interactive, the better. Examples given of good interactivity range from simple to complex. Simple interactivity includes things such as drill and practice, quizzes, hypertext, and hypermedia. More technically and educationally complex examples of interactivity are managed chat rooms, pop-up hints, gaming techniques, and video/audio conferencing.

2. **Linear or Nonlinear Organization:** The second most frequently mentioned issue is whether the training's organization is linear in nature, or nonlinear and based more on "Web functionality." Developer respondents often cite use of "the power of the Web" to its full capacity as a hallmark of good design. The meaning of this may be illuminated by describing its opposite: use or "mimicking" of models based on linear books, conventional classrooms, or traditional CBT, which are considered bad models to imitate in Web-based training. An experienced developer summarizes the problems of using linear models.

   "I feel that this last question addresses the real issue in hypermedia courseware . . . publishers are creating nothing more than glorified electronic books. The beginning has some slick animation or sound file, but the information is still *linearly organized*! In many ways this represents a step backward since most users that I have spoken with dislike reading off a computer screen."

   An expert in delivering training on the Internet shares this perception:

   "The main problem with most Web-based training examples that I have seen is that they are more boring than a book, and difficult to read."

3. **Graphic User Interface (GUI):** This quality is near the top in importance because of the number of times it is mentioned as a *negative* quality due to poor application. It appears that a good GUI is taken for granted, but a bad GUI cannot be overlooked. Frequently cited examples of bad graphic user interfaces are confusing navigation, poor use of color, busy screens, and gratuitous graphics and animation.

4. **Lesson Structure:** While there is ample evidence that developers and experts do not endorse linear or hierarchical lesson structures, respondents indicate a great deal of support for incorporating lesson structure that provides the learner with *guidance*. Developers frequently describe Web-based training programs that they consider poorly designed because they lack guidance-giving structure and thus are difficult for learners to manage.

5. **Use of Multimedia versus Text:** This fifth-ranked characteristic of Web-based training is related to the second category, nonlinear versus linear organization, in the importance respondents place on using the strengths of the WWW and avoiding old, traditional paradigms. Developers express concern that text-intensive Web-based training programs cause learner fatigue and are not engaging. The use of multimedia and hypermedia are seen as ways to avoid fatigue and provide motivation.

   "We wanted to avoid the appearance of being just an 'electronic page turner,'" is the comment of an experienced developer working for a hardware manufacturer, concerned about creating the company's first Web-based training program.

6. **Attention to Educational Details:** Lack of attention to educational details such as cognitive loading, sequencing of information, and feedback, as well as inaccurate content, is cited as representing bad design.

7. **Attention to Technical Details:** Respondents show little patience with Web-based training programs that fail to attend to *technical details* such as broken links, interactions that do not work, or pointers to placeholders for content under development. Developers hold Web-based training programs to the same standards as software development.

8. **Learner versus System Control:** Good programs empower the learner to control navigational paths, sequence content, determine level of detail, and select the presentation mode. An experienced Web-based training developer discusses the problem of a text-intensive program without learner control.

   ". . . it could have been far more engaging and interactive and could have allowed for more student control. Text is linear and you have to 'plow through' it to get to where you want to be. Why not allow branching or

Choosing an Authoring Tool

One of the most common and important questions asked by people interested in Web-based training is, "Which authoring program should we use?" This section is designed to provide an overview of the major Web-based training authoring tools. This section includes:

- A list of criteria for selecting an authoring program

- Descriptions of various authoring programs

Authoring programs allow you to create your Web program. You select the media and determine the interactivity. You are able to set exactly what you want to have happen, exactly when you want it. The amount of control is amazing, and perhaps that is part of the appeal: you get to be the producer and director. Authoring programs are very powerful, but they are only tools; a good Web-based training program still requires expertise in instructional design content, project management, and multimedia design, at a minimum.

The major authoring applications allow the developer to define interactivity and combine the different types of media to make the training program a richer experience for the student. The five media elements available for use are: text, graphics, animation, audio, and video. Media can be combined in a number of different ways for different effects—such as combining audio elements with a video presentation.

There are two types of Web page design used for Web-based training. A *static presentation program* is the simplest type of Web page design. The tools for creating static presentations are typically word processors and HTML editors (an example is the Microsoft Word HTML converter). *Multimedia authoring programs* are designed to do all of the above, plus allow you to include:

- User input
- User interactivity
- Login and user record keeping

Important Issues in Choosing an Authoring System

Once you have made the decision to use an authoring system, it can be a daunting task to determine which one to use. Here are some questions to keep in mind as you wade through brochures and demos.

- Vendor
  - Is the vendor financially stable?
  - How long has the vendor been in this business?
  - What is the profile of the vendor's customer base (commercial versus educational)?
  - What other products does the vendor produce that can be easily integrated?

- Hardware platforms
  - On which platform(s) does the authoring application run?
  - Are plug-ins required for playback? On which platform(s) are plug-ins available?

- Ease of use
  - Is the software user-friendly and intuitive?
  - Can the subject matter expert or instructional designer use the software for the design phase without knowing how to program?
  - What type of interface metaphor is used for the program—page, timeline, icon?
  - Is object-oriented programming or scripting used?

- Development
  - How powerful and flexible is the program?
  - Is a scripting language available for complex interactions or calls to external resources?
  - Which file formats does the authoring program support for graphics, audio, video, and so on?
  - Does the program allow access to an external program or database?

- Computer-managed instruction (CMI)
  - What level of student recordkeeping is available (registration, answer judging, final scores, etc.)?
  - What formats are available for student data (raw data, percentages, ranking)?
  - Is it possible for a student to exit a lesson at any point and later reenter the lesson at the same point (use of bookmarks)?

- Support
  - Is training for the authoring system available locally (vendor or third party)?
  - Are developers available locally (vendor or third party)?
  - Are online technical forums available?
  - What is the charge for technical support?

- Other issues
  - Are there runtime or other licensing fees?

- How recent was the last major upgrade to the product?
- Is a demo copy available?
- Does your organization already employ this authoring system?

Before making your final decision, talk to other recent purchasers of the program. Check out any online technical forums, visit a user group or, if the timing coincides, attend the annual user conference of your top candidate. Use the following checklist when evaluating authoring programs.

CHECKLIST FOR SELECTING AN AUTHORING PROGRAM

As you think about your needs for an authoring program, list your criteria and considerations below:

Platform: _____

Budget: _____

(Consider purchase price, training, technical support, consulting)

Ease of learning: _____

(Consider the skill level of those to use the program)

Power and flexibility: _____

(What must the program be able to do?)

Current use of a tool in your organization: _____

Other: _____

THE "LEARNING CURVE" TRADEOFF:

EASE-OF-USE VS. POWER AND FLEXIBILITY

Presentation programs	Authoring programs	Programming languages
Easy to learn	<- — · — · — — 0 — — · — · — ->	Hard to learn
Easy to use	<- — · — · — — 0 — — · — · — ->	Moderate-hard to use
Less power and flexibility	<- — · — · — — 0 — — · — · — ->	More power and flexibility

Authoring Program Metaphors

Authoring programs typically use a metaphor that makes use of the program more intuitive. The metaphors for authoring programs are:

- Icon-based
- Card-based
- Timeline-based

Icon-Based

Icon-based programs use icons on a flowline to structure course content. Similar to a flowchart, the icon flow determines the logical sequence of a program. Examples of icon-based programs include Aimtech's IconAuthor and Macromedia's Authorware.

Card-Based

Card-based programs are also known as page-based or slide-based. These programs use the metaphor of index cards, or pages in a book for their authoring. Presentation programs often use this metaphor since the series of slides is similar to cards or pages. Authoring programs using this metaphor include Asymetrix's ToolBook II. Presentation programs using this metaphor include Gold Disk's Astound and Microsoft's PowerPoint.

Timeline-Based

Timeline-based programs use the passage of time as the controlling metaphor, much like editing a movie. Events enter the screen for a set duration, then exit. Events can overlap because each event is defined in its own track. Macromedia Director (a multimedia and animation authoring program) is an example of this type of program.

Limits of Authoring Tools

Naturally, not every authoring tool is perfect for every project. There are as many preferences for interfaces as there are multimedia authors and not all multimedia packages were developed for a training audience. Not all of the software authoring tools available have the ability to complete the complex tasks associated with administering training courses. Macromedia Director is an example. It is a highly regarded animation and multimedia tool, but it is usually not the best choice for training. When it is used as the main authoring tool for a training program, it usually means the multimedia developer outvoted the instructional designer.

Keep in mind that authoring with these software tools is usually tougher than it looks. The tools are often marketed as "easy to use" and "no programming required." Here is a useful axiom to remember for all of the tools listed here: "It is easy to do easy things, but hard to do hard things."

Authoring Tools

What follows is an overview of different authoring tools that are available. Remember to use the authoring tool checklist to determine which tool is best suited for your needs.

Authorware

Authorware (produced by Macromedia, www.macromedia.com) is one of the leading tools for creating interactive training programs. It was created years ago by Dr. Michael Allen, now of Allen Interactions in Minneapolis. Dr. Allen was the first instructional designer working on Control Data's PLATO system, the visionary CBT program of the early 1970s. It is sold by Macromedia, one of the major multimedia tool companies, and they regularly update and aggressively market the program. Authorware has been used to create such programs as networked interactive multimedia training, reference titles on CD-ROM, performance support, and online multimedia presentations.

Macromedia also produces Director, mentioned earlier. Authorware can integrate Director movies into training programs, making them more interactive. Director productions can also be manipulated from Authorware programs through the use of native Director commands. Director is better used this way than as the primary tool for authoring training. Developers create a program by placing icons on a flowline (Figure 8.1). The 13 icons define and control the media and logic of one's training program. This "object-oriented" design is simpler for most people to learn than scripting or programming.

Having only a handful of icons for an authoring program may seem limiting, but this is not the case. Each of the 13 icons represents a group of functions, and each icon may lead to multiple dialog boxes to control an aspect of the program. Complex functions are created by using two or more icons in sequence. For example, the Interaction icon provides the developer with numerous choices as to the type of interaction desired, like radio buttons and pop-up menus, but also provides a means for tracking

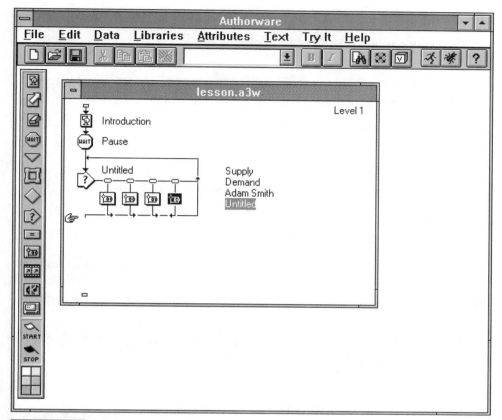

FIGURE 8.1 A sample flowline in Authorware.

the user's responses. So rather than one-icon–one-function programming, Authorware provides one-icon–many-function programming. Alternatively, Aimtech's IconAuthor has more icons, each with fewer functions. Either design works equally well.

The 13 basic icons include:

- Display—imports graphics and text with effects

- Motion—moves onscreen text, graphics, and digital movies from one point to another over a given amount of time or at a specified speed

- Erase—removes objects from the screen by means of special effects

- Wait—functions as a pause

- Navigation—provides hyperlinks, including moving to specific pages

- Framework—controls navigation structures
- Decision—controls path branching, including sequential and random paths
- Interaction—provides user input in the form of objects like buttons and pull-down menus
- Calculation—performs functions using variables, routines, and other files
- Map—organizes the flow of the program
- Digital movie—imports and plays various types of video files
- Sound—imports and plays up to CD-quality audio files
- Video—controls full-motion and analog video sequences and playback

As seen in Figure 8.1, icons are arranged in a flowline to control exactly what happens in a training program. After the developer creates the logical outline of the program, the content is filled in and the function of each

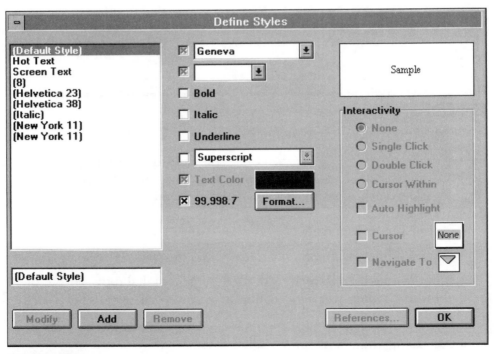

FIGURE 8.2 Options for changing text styles.

Copyright 1996 Macromedia, Inc. Used with permission.

icon is specified. For example, at the start of the program, the developer may want to display the company logo. The Display icon is used to indicate to Authorware that graphics will be imported with the Display function. The developer places this icon in the first position on the flowline, and then opens it up and enters information about where to locate the graphic and how to display it. If text is being displayed it can be further manipulated with a specialized dialog box for effects such as text style and graphic size, as seen in Figure 8.2.

An Interaction icon may be placed next, which can be specified to display a message such as, "Do you wish to continue?" to the student, who then is presented with two choices in the form of buttons: "Yes" and "No." The Interaction icon can be programmed and paired with the Decision icon to continue the training if the student clicks on the Yes button and to quit the program if No is clicked.

The Interaction icon represents user input to either guide the program along the flow or answer preprogrammed questions from quizzes and tests. There are many different types of user responses and automated feedback options. In Figure 8.3, the options for a fill-in-the-blank question type are listed. The developer can specify a number of different characteristics for

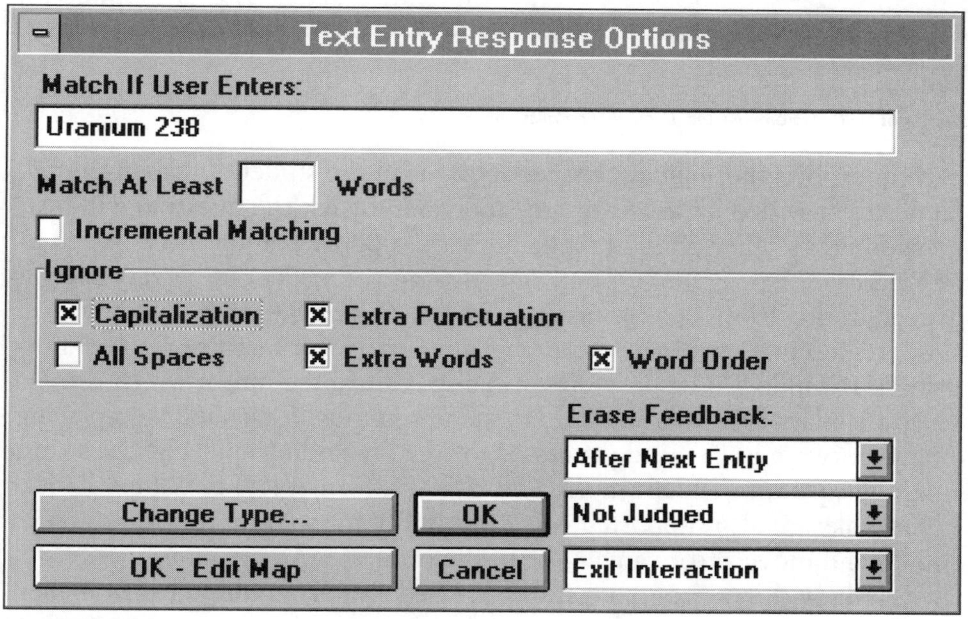

FIGURE 8.3 Options for text entry response.

Copyright 1996 Macromedia, Inc. Used with permission.

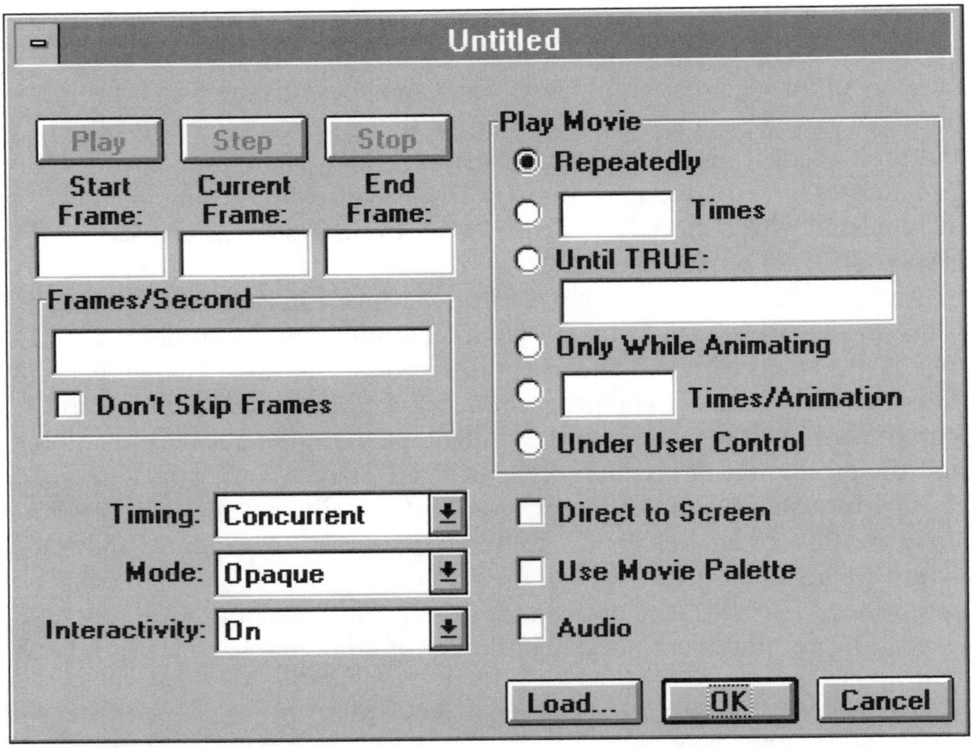

![Untitled dialog box showing video playback options with Play, Step, Stop buttons, Start Frame, Current Frame, End Frame fields, Frames/Second section with Don't Skip Frames checkbox, Timing Concurrent, Mode Opaque, Interactivity On dropdowns, Play Movie options including Repeatedly, Times, Until TRUE, Only While Animating, Times/Animation, Under User Control, and Direct to Screen, Use Movie Palette, Audio checkboxes with Load, OK, Cancel buttons.]

FIGURE 8.4 Options for playing video files.

Copyright 1996 Macromedia, Inc. Used with permission.

each question type, such as what to look for in the student's response, the feedback provided by the program, and what format the question will take.

Numerous other types of media files are supported and can be played in an Authorware program. Options for playback of media can be very specific, as seen in the dialog box for playing video in Figure 8.4. If the video file supports interaction, for example, this interaction can be turned on or off using this window. The developer can also control the rate at which the video file plays and where in the file the program will start and stop playing.

Authorware has a word processor for text, including spell checks, search functions, paragraph definitions, and rich text format (RTF) compatibility. Hyperlinks are also supported, with the ability to navigate to text, graphics, sound, and movies from anywhere in the program. As shown in Figure 8.5, hyperlinks within a program can be directed and programmed as branches to other parts of the program, or as subroutines, which return to the original link location.

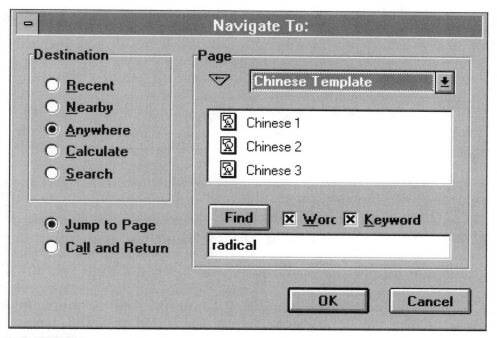

FIGURE 8.5 Options for hyperlink navigation.

Copyright 1996 Macromedia, Inc. Used with permission.

The power of interactive training comes from the ability to branch based on user response. It is this feature that provides the personalized, tutor-style of learning which provides options not available with instructor-led group training. Each of the major authoring tools have ways to manage complex branching. In Authorware, the Framework icon in Figure 8.6 is one of the tools used to manage navigation options.

Authorware is Microsoft OLE (Object Linking and Embedding) 2.0 compliant in Windows, allowing developers to open an OLE server and use the OLE drag-and-drop feature. This means that a developer can open a Microsoft object, like an Excel spreadsheet, and display it in a program. Compatibility with most databases is available through the ODBC standard for database architecture.

Custom transition effects, such as fades and wipes between screens, can be set with Macromedia Open Architecture (MOA) Xtras. Developers can create transitions using plug-in Xtras with embedded sounds and user-controlled durations and sizes. Authorware comes with 50 predefined effects, including those created by third-party companies.

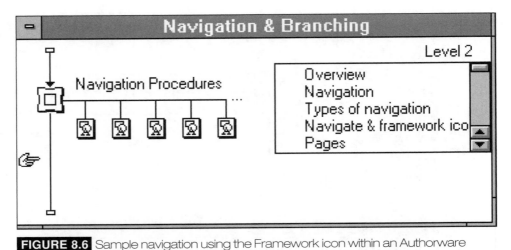

FIGURE 8.6 Sample navigation using the Framework icon within an Authorware program.

Authorware has an online help facility that provides answers to specific questions, Tips and Techniques for creating specialized multimedia functions, and the Authorware Portfolio, which includes program models to be used and edited.

There is also a feature called the "Tech Support Top Ten," which includes templates to demonstrate solutions to users' top-ten questions. The developer determines what the top-ten questions and solutions are about the program, and the templates provide a means for demonstrating them.

Once a program is created with Authorware, it can be used again and again as a template for other programs. Using the icon structure for the original program, the developer can specify other text or graphics that pertain to another program. Although the content may be different from the original program, the program flow is the same. This allows the developer to create many different training programs using the original flowline. There are even third-party templates available, from companies such as Multimedia Learning, Inc. in Irving, Texas, or Tarragon of Sydney, Australia, that offer complete course structures.

Macromedia produces Shockwave, a plug-in helper application for Web browsers, so that Authorware applications can be viewed via the Web. The developer can author an application for use over the Internet or a company's intranet by creating a compressed runtime version of the program for Shockwave-enabled Web browsers. Or an existing Shockwave file can be imported and integrated into an Authorware program (Figures 8.7 and 8.8).

Shockwave plug-ins are platform-specific, meaning that the Shockwave plug-in for Macintosh must be used with Macintosh computers, and the plug-in for Windows must be used with Windows computers. The Authorware authoring program is available for either Windows or Macintosh computers.

ToolBook II

ToolBook II (produced by Asymetrix, www.asymetrix.com) provides tools for authoring, managing, and accessing what Asymetrix calls "distributed learning applications." It is an authoring environment, and a training environment, providing a means to manage and track students. Instructors are

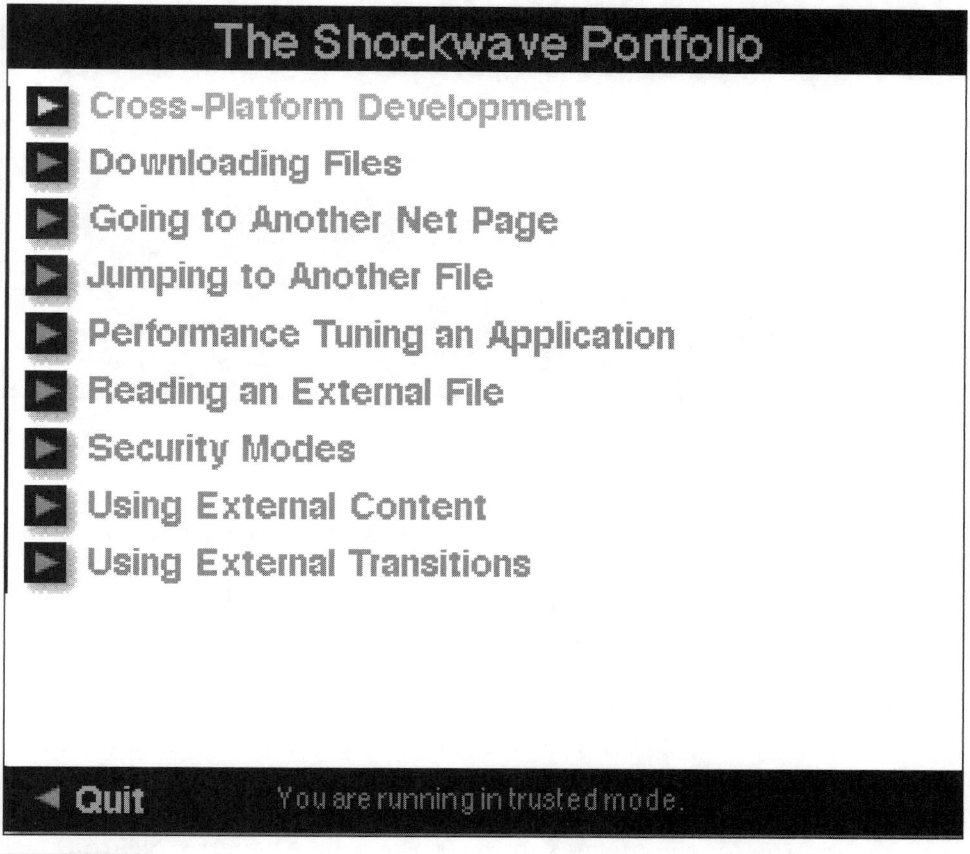

FIGURE 8.7 The Shockwave portfolio interface for making Authorware programs accessible over the Internet.

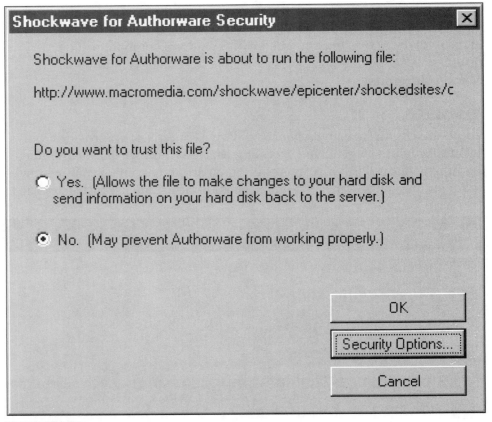

FIGURE 8.8 Security dialog box the user sees when accessing Shockwave files.

Copyright 1996 Macromedia, Inc. Used with permission.

able to determine that courses have been received and the extent to which the content has been understood, through user scores.

Asymetrix produces three applications that work together to form this complete authoring environment. *Instructor* allows developers to create multimedia training programs on the Windows platform. *Publisher* allows the programs to be delivered to users' desktops by such methods as the Internet and CD-ROM. *Librarian* allows administrators to create and manage databases of students and their progress through courses.

ToolBook II courses and the administration features can be deployed over the Internet or a company's intranet using the Asymetrix Neuron plug-in and ActiveX control for Web browsers. The authoring part of ToolBook II allows the developer to create applets—or smaller applications that work with a Web browser—in Java and HTML without knowing how to program these languages. Any Java applet, such as interactive questions and scoring functions, can be incorporated into any ToolBook II program.

ToolBook II runs in Microsoft Windows, meaning that it is compatible with Microsoft technologies such as ActiveX, OLE, Video for Windows, Visual Basic controls, and other Microsoft applications. Paradox and dBase databases can be linked to ToolBook II programs. ODBC database compatibility is also available with the use of all additional packages.

Programs created with ToolBook II can be saved in either the ToolBook format (.tbk) or a native Internet/intranet format (HTML and Java) so that users can access them with a Web browser without a plug-in. Alternatively, programs saved in the ToolBook format can be played through a Web browser using the Neuron plug-in (Figure 8.9).

ToolBook II comes with *Librarian*, which works with the other ToolBook II components for student management. Student progress through the course and scores on quizzes and tests are updated in a Librarian database whether the student is running the program over the company LAN or over the Internet. Administrators can track scores on various tests and progress indicators.

Student functions with Librarian include browsing available courses, taking courses from a centralized library, displaying course descriptions, reviewing personal course activity and performance, and changing personal information such as name, address, and passwords. These features can be added automatically with the use of Specialists, a wizard-like component which helps users customize their programs.

ToolBook II comes with predefined objects and templates to produce more standardized courses with less headache. These objects, called widgets, can be used to enhance the functionality of training programs. Widgets are available for things like question types, action buttons, bookmarks, 3D layout elements, data validation, media clips, navigation, and other interactive objects. There is also a feature that allows developers to create and save their own customized widgets for use in any ToolBook II program.

Question widgets are available for multiple choice, arrange/connect objects, fill-in-the-blank, and other types of questions. Question parameters include scoring options, answer weighing, maximum value, time/try limits, automatic reset, and randomization.

Templates in ToolBook can also be created for company-specific layout design, or *themes*, to ensure a standard look across all programs (Figures

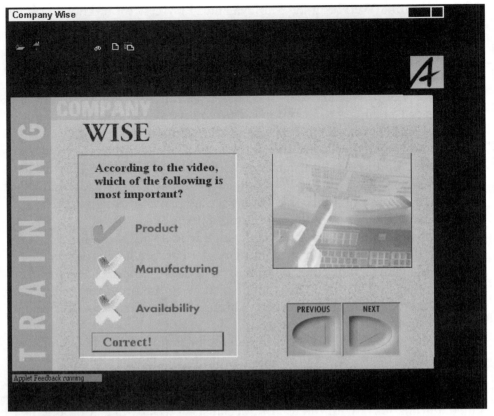

FIGURE 8.9 A ToolBook program running in a Web browser.

8.10 and 8.11). Courses can be customized by creating Book Specialists, which automate certain functions for creating standardized course shells. These features, including widgets and other customized objects, can be reused by copying from one program and pasting into another.

The metaphor for authoring is a book, which means that each page is created as it will look to the user, providing a WYSIWYG (What You See Is What You Get) authoring environment. Developers place objects such as video files, interaction buttons, and text, including RTF files, on the screen where they will appear in the program (Figure 8.12). Text functions such as searches and spell checks are also supported, and TrueType fonts can be embedded in a program. Additionally, hyperlinks can be created and assigned to text, graphics, and other objects in order to link to other files.

ToolBook II can also be used to create hybrid CD-ROM programs. That is, when content on a CD-ROM is tagged with a date of creation, comparable files on the company network or the Internet that are tagged with a later creation date can be retrieved and used in the original file's place. Instructor's built-in FTP (File Transfer Protocol) function allows programs to automatically search specific Internet or intranet locations for updated files. For a complete description of hybrid CD-ROMs, refer to the "Tech Tutorial: Internet CDs" in Chapter 7 or the FAQs in Chapter 2.

Each of the major authoring tool programs has a way to implement scripting or programming to increase the range of what you can make happen on the screen. ToolBook II uses scripting to allow the developer to add special functions to a program and to alter and enhance object properties. OpenScript is an English-like language that includes an auto-debugging feature. Special commands link ToolBook II programs with native Windows files and programs allowing developers to create highly complex and interactive training programs that take advantage of other Windows functions.

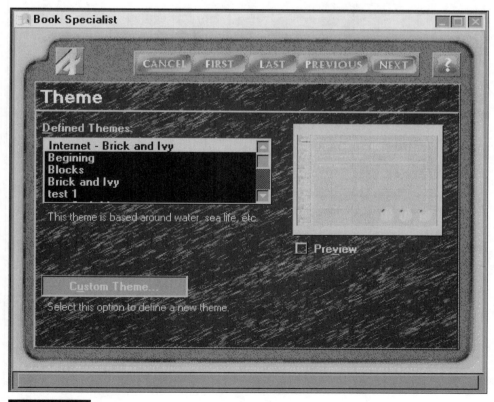

FIGURE 8.10 Catalog for selecting a theme for a ToolBook program.

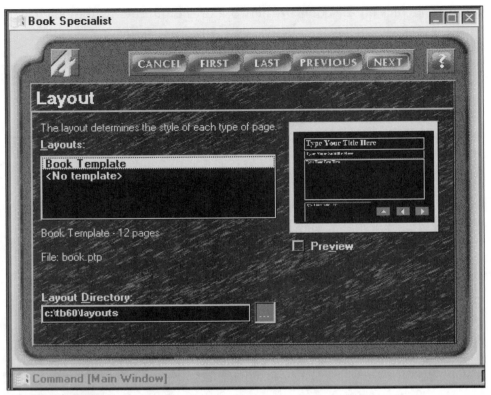

FIGURE 8.11 Selecting a layout for each page.

IconAuthor

IconAuthor (IconAuthor is a registered trademark of Aimtech Corporation, www.Aimtech.com) is an icon-based authoring tool that lets developers create interactive multimedia applications for delivery on the Internet. IconAuthor uses an object-oriented interface to create hybrid Java applications that can be run through any Java-enabled Web browser on any platform Windows, Macintosh, OS/2, UNIX, and so on.

IconAuthor Present is a runtime player that allows IconAuthor programs to be launched from within a Web browser, but it is also possible for the developer to write a control for playback separate from a Web browser. An IconAuthor application can be programmed to run without a Web browser by accessing the appropriate files on an intranet through its own controls.

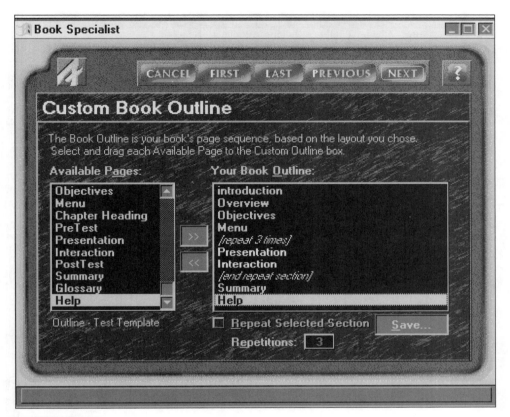

FIGURE 8.12 Editing a ToolBook program's outline.

The programming metaphor for IconAuthor is the flowchart on which icons are arranged to represent events in the program. There are over 60 separate icons that can be used for objects in a program, from display elements to Internet functions. Developers place the icons in the order of the logic of the program, and control their specific functions through a visual interface (Figure 8.13). This design is much like Authorware's. There are differences in approach and for most of the developers I have informally polled: those with a programming background seem to prefer IconAuthor, while those with no programming background seem to prefer Authorware.

Text is supported with a word processor that includes search and replace, spell checks, margin control, and indent and tab control. Graphic objects can also be embedded within text objects, treating them as part of

FIGURE 8.13 The Image Control Center in IconAuthor.

IconAuthor is a registered trademark of Aimtech Corporation.

the text instead of a separate graphic. This is useful for such graphic elements as bullets and buttons.

An ImageLab function lets developers manipulate graphics with image processing functions like color reduction, rotation, resizing, and screen captures. Control of the complicated Windows palette feature is also supported through the Palette Object.

Database functionality is also supported. The Table Object allows developers to use tabular data with a spreadsheet interface. These tables can be linked to database objects, allowing multiple records to be displayed and updated at the same time.

Because programs are compiled in an Internet-native language, the functionality of Internet technologies is supported, including Aimtech's Universal Media Access. With this technology, different Internet-enabled objects can be included in an IconAuthor program, making it easier to create familiar navigational models (Figure 8.14).

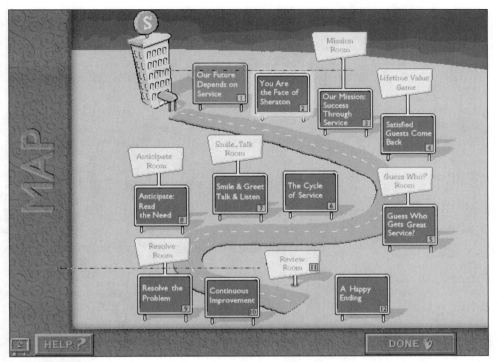

FIGURE 8.14 A sample navigation screen for a course created with IconAuthor.

IconAuthor is a registered trademark of Aimtech Corporation.

Content of the training program is stored separately from the structure of the program. This means that a file location can be specified for text and graphics that is located on any server anywhere. Information updates, such as data on new products or procedures, can be provided by changing the content files, leaving the structure files as they are.

For example, within the training program there might be a control for the first screen of the first lesson. The objects on the screen that will not change, such as placeholders for graphic files and text files, are stored within the structure file. The content objects, such as the graphic and text files themselves, are stored elsewhere, for instance, on the company server (Figure 8.15).

If the text for the first screen of the first lesson changes, only the text file needs to be changed. The program, through its structure file, will automatically access the updated file. Similarly, if the company logo should change in the middle of the training, only the graphic file on the server

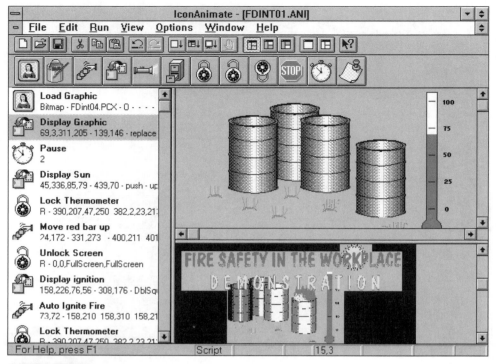

FIGURE 8.15 Animation control features.

IconAuthor is a registered trademark of Aimtech Corporation.

that contains the logo needs to be updated. Alteration of the structure file is not necessary.

Because of this separation of structure and content, IconAuthor's programs can be "thin media." That is, the structure files can be maintained on the student's computer and the content files are downloaded only as necessary. If the student accesses the first module of a training program, only the files necessary for the first module are downloaded at one time— and not the entire training.

Media formats supported are the same as those of a Web browser, that is, JPEG and GIF graphics formats, and also include additional types of files, such as vector graphics and video files.

As with the other major authoring tools, it is possible to produce hybrid CD-ROM applications because the files necessary for the content of the program can be stored either on the CD-ROM or delivered over the Internet or an intranet from the company's server. Hybrid CD-ROMs contain files that are "tagged" with a creation date. If another comparable file exists in another location, such as on the company server, with a later date, then it is grabbed by the program to replace the original file.

Quest

Quest (produced by Allen Communication, www.allencomm.com) offers object-oriented click-and-drag authoring for the development of interactive training, and the latest version comes with full Internet capability. Quest provides strong computer-managed instruction (CMI) capabilities such as real-time updating of course content and centralized data tracking. These features utilize the TCP/IP networking protocol, meaning that they can be used over the Internet or a company LAN.

Once a program is authored in Quest, the program can be Internet-enabled by using the Internet tool tab in the main frame editor. Among the integrated Internet features are: peer communication, URL file access, and centralized data tracking. With the Quest Internet Player, programs created in Quest can be run in a Web browser (Figure 8.16).

The communication models between multiple users of Quest can be peer-to-peer or client/server, allowing two students to interact over the

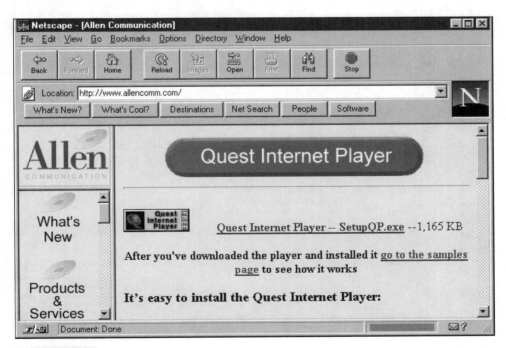

FIGURE 8.16 The Quest Internet Player.

network as well as students with instructors. With peer communication, courses can be developed for team training situations, with each student taking the course communicating with every other student. This feature goes across training titles developed with Quest, so that even students who are not in the same program can communicate with each other. Multiple connections are also possible, allowing the student to maintain more than one communication at a time. Also, with this feature data can be captured during runtime from any other Quest program running on the network.

QuestNet+ is an extension of Quest that makes its programs Internet-enabled. A program can read files stored on any accessible Web site, providing a means to update or add content to a Quest title during runtime (Figures 8.17 through 8.19).

The centralized data tracking feature is called Quest Manager, which allows administrators to manage users and courses from a remote location and allows students to control the presentation of an assigned course.

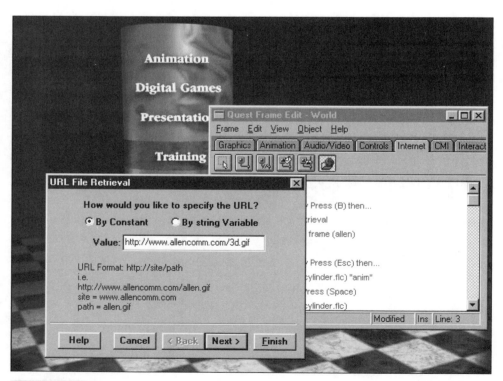

FIGURE 8.17 Specifying a URL to be accessed during a training program.

FIGURE 8.18 Setting a Web site for more information.

Administrators can define users and courses and reports can be generated to track progress through the courses. Students can track themselves through a course using Quest Manager, by viewing which parts of the course need to be completed and in what order.

One of the strengths of Allen Communication is the instructional design focus of the company. As a result, Quest was created with the instructional designer in mind. It offers two modes for development: the Title Design level and the Frame level. The Title Design level allows an instructional designer or developer to organize the course into an overview structure, with modules, lessons, frames, and paths. The Frame level allows a programmer or developer to structure the specific pieces of the course, creating the content that the student will view and interact with. The Frame level also employs WYSIWYG authoring, which allows the developer to see the course as it is written, instead of having to compile it first. Many functions are available through a menu-driven interface for ease of programming.

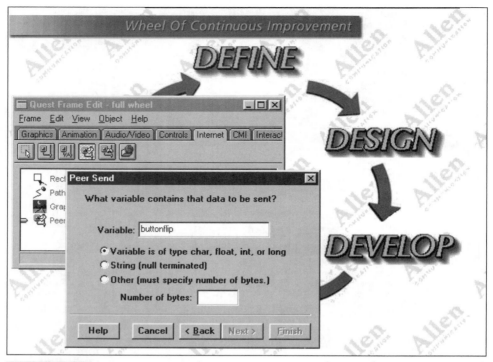

FIGURE 8.19 Options for sending data from one user to another.

Hypertext links are also supported, with the capability of calling up any Quest object, including audio, video, graphics, branching menus, pop-up windows, and other interactive objects (Figure 8.20).

The course is stored with the content separate from the structure and can be managed to control the amount of information transferred over the network at one time. The developer can assign which content elements are required for each unit in the course, so that only the required elements for a unit in the course are downloaded. This eliminates the long waiting periods that are often associated with pulling information off the Internet.

IBTauthor

IBTauthor is a newer, smaller program designed specifically for training over the Internet or a company intranet. The courseware is first written in HTML and compiled further with training-specific objects into a format suitable for delivery through a Web browser. There are numerous training administrative features such as registration and preregistration, assigning

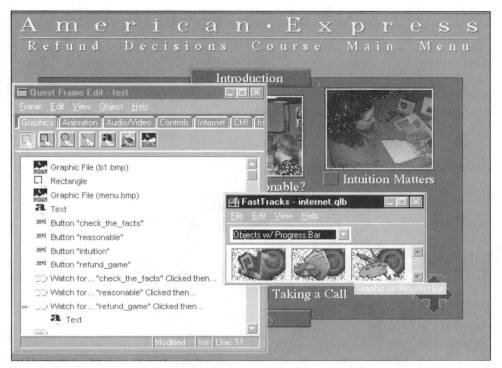

FIGURE 8.20 Selecting the type of object to be displayed in Quest.

users to groups, remote administration, and the export of reporting data to an external database. (See the CD-ROM for a demonstration.)

The authoring process in IBTauthor is the straightforward entry of text (your content) into a word processor or HTML editor with indications to mark the start of question objects, new lessons, and other program-specific functions.

The text of your program and the codes used to mark the start of objects are compiled and translated into a form readable by a Web browser. Because the major authoring element is HTML, any HTML-supported technology can be used (Figure 8.21).

The authoring of the course can be done with IBToutliner, which features drag-and-drop object authoring, WYSIWYG preview, online documentation, and a step-by-step tutorial. IBTmaker is the application software that IBTauthor uses to compile the course. To edit any page of a course, the author highlights the page's icon in the outline, then clicks the

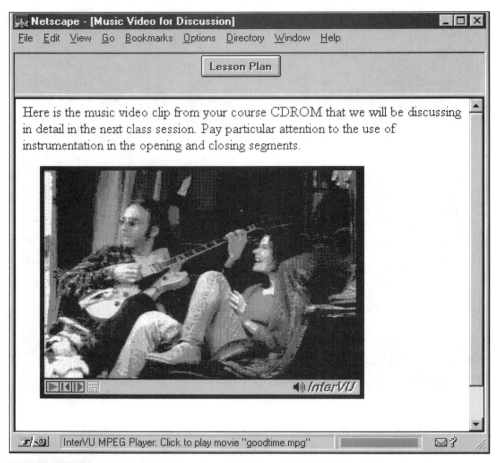

FIGURE 8.21 Video and other Web technologies can be incorporated into an IBTauthor program.

Edit button. IBToutliner uses the author's HTML editor to edit the page. Many existing HTML editor software packages are compatible with IBTauthor.

IBTauthor comes with administration features for managing a training course (Figure 8.22). Students can attach notes to lessons and test answers that are automatically forwarded to the course administrator. Students can choose to run the course in one of three different modes: Training mode, which is a preliminary run-through for casual browsers; Testing mode, which is stricter than Training mode and comes with customizable options as to which materials are required and which are optional; and Certification mode, for students who are required to complete all course materials.

IBTauthor programs can "autograduate" students from one level of a course to the next once one level or course is completed. Students can also view a list of courses that they are required to take for their training. For example, students who are taking clerical training will only view courses related to clerical work, and they won't see other types of courses. It is also possible to set up a prerequisite test in order to enter a particular course, to make sure that students are prepared for the material.

Developers can preview the current course while working on it in IBToutliner. IBToutliner automatically builds a simulated course without having to access it on the Web. When the author clicks on a lesson in the table of contents, the lesson can be browsed in another frame. Page formatting is shown as it is on the final Web-based course, allowing the author to identify screens that need additional work.

To create or modify one of the questions in the course, you highlight the desired icon and click the Edit button. IBToutliner will use your HTML editor to edit the question as it exists on the current Web page.

With IBTreporter, administrators can control aspects of the program remotely via the Internet or a company intranet. Reports of student

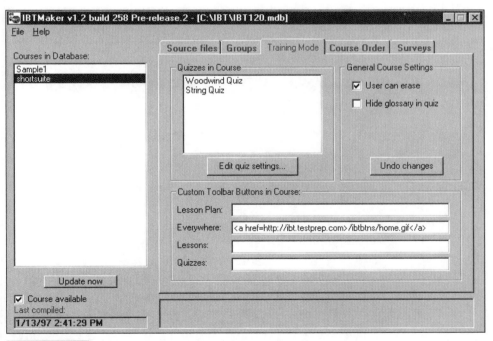

FIGURE 8.22 Dialog box for setting features of training mode.

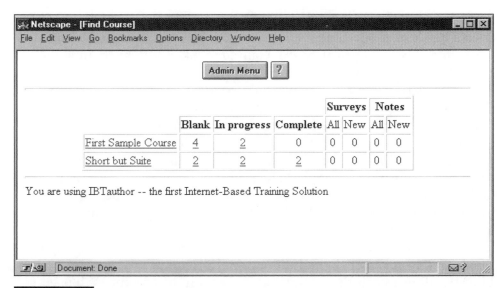

FIGURE 8.23 Sample statistics for a training module.

progress through courses can be viewed using snapshots of a particular student. These reports can be customized to be across students for one course or module, or across courses for one student or a group of students (Figures 8.23 and 8.24).

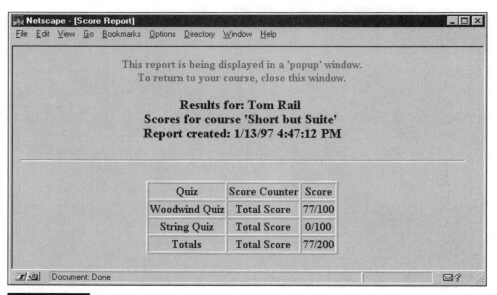

FIGURE 8.24 A sample student report.

It is also possible with IBTreporter to either import student records into the IBT system or have students complete a registration process from their own computer.

If you to allow the trainee to erase his or her work, the course can be retaken as many times as desired. You can also add a custom "return to Home page" button to each screen of the course, or a button that takes the trainee to a discussion group for that course so he or she can discuss the course with other students.

With IBTclass, trainers can "host" a virtual classroom over a Web server with complete administrative control from the server. The Enterprise Edition of IBTauthor comes with Web server software that can be set up for a variety of classroom and administrative options, including notes to and from students (Figure 8.25).

IBTauthor allows for the creation of courses for CD-ROM if students do not have access to a network connection. There is no need for conversion from Internet to CD-ROM because all of the files associated with each can be accessed either online or offline. If the course is taken offline, however, some of the administrative features will not work because of their real-time nature. But the developer need only produce one version of the program for training to be taken either offline or while connected to a network.

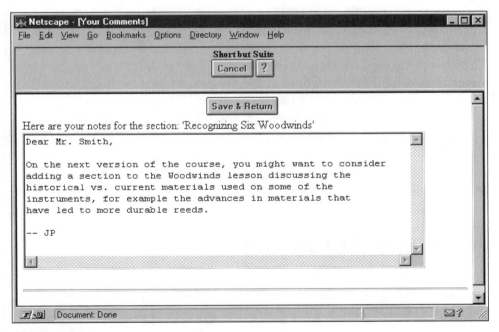

FIGURE 8.25 Students can send notes to instructors about a course.

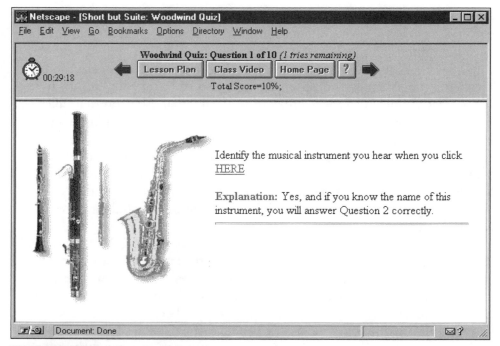

FIGURE 8.26 Sample test question in a Web browser.

Questions can be fill-in-the-blank, multiple-choice, or clickable graphics where each region of the figure represents a different answer choice. The answer choices are treated as separate "objects" by the system and are therefore included in the outline as their own icon, not on the question's HTML screen. The object-oriented nature of IBToutliner allows individual answer choices to be rearranged or disabled, for example, if the trainee is only permitted one or two tries per question (Figures 8.26 and 8.27).

Students can be quizzed on course materials using various media, including audio and video, and automatic administration for the quizzes can be programmed to recognize many different responses.

Which Tool to Use?

The programs mentioned above are five of the 150 authoring programs I have tracked down over the last few years. Authorware, Quest, IconAuthor, and Toolbook II are the Big Four of authoring tools for training. They are

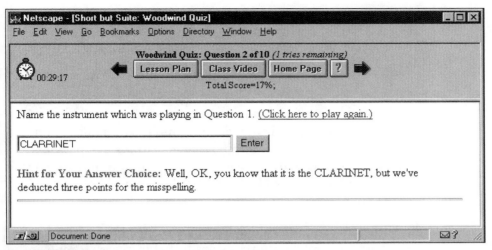

FIGURE 8.27 Sample response to answering a test question.

long-standing, well-respected tools supported by strong companies. You can't go wrong with any of these, for either Web-based training or other multimedia training development. IBTauthor is a new product from a much smaller company but has the advantage of being less expensive and designed from the ground up for Web delivery.

Other Tools

The following authoring tools allow you to create multimedia training though not all have Internet capabilities yet. They are listed here as additional resources for you.

- CBIquick, AMT Corporation—Designed for the simulation and demonstration of software applications. Developer can create simulations automatically by capturing the running screen of the intended software while it is in use.

- CBT Express, Aimtech Corporation—Intended for multimedia training, contains multimedia editors and an interface for the training-specific elements of Aimtech's other multimedia product, IconAuthor. Also includes testing and registration template procedures.

- Course Builder, Discovery Systems International—Can create interactive multimedia presentations, training materials, and simulations. Includes functions for tests, automatic scoring, and student reports.

- CourseWorks, Iprax Corporation—Allows the conversion of preexisting videotape training programs into multimedia training programs, with additions of other media such as graphics and animations. Also has administration capability for multiple students.

- DigitalTrainer, Micromedium—A multimedia training software tool to create "digital books." Developers can integrate many different types of media, including existing video training, with built-in test and question types. Includes some administrative features like performance tracking and ID and password support. Internet functionality is also supported with features like Web distribution and links to Internet/intranet sites.

- Everest Authoring System, Intersystems Concepts, Inc.—A multiplatform object-oriented authoring system that features test and scoring administration. Has built-in multiuser support.

- Learning Processor, Pinnacle Multimedia—Allows for the creation of interactive multimedia learning courses without programming, scripting, screen design, question design, or flowcharting. Developers enter text into various templates to create and administer courses.

- MocKingbird CBT, Warren-Forthought—This computer-based training and authoring system allows multiple authors to work on the same program at once. In addition to multimedia and administrative features, access can be given to training records, operating manuals, manufacturing plant information, and company procedures.

- PowerMedia, RAD Technologies—An interactive multimedia authoring system that supports hyperlinks, imaging, and media control. Also features menu- and button-based authoring control and the capability of playing future media for automatic upgradeability. Internet-and intranet-capable, a PowerMedia production can be viewed on a Web page with the RAD MediaViewer plug-in.

- Rapid, Emultek—A simulation generator that features object libraries and can be used to create software or real-life simulations. Has a feature that will record and play back student responses to a particular module.

WHAT WE HAVE LEARNED FROM AUTHORING COURSES FOR THE WEB

Robert Burton, Recor Corporation

Our Experience

We have been developing and marketing our network-based CBTs for several years now. Our specialty is end-user training for Microsoft and Lotus products. As of December 1996, we have modified two of our most popular courses into Web-based training.

Our Thoughts on HTML

In my opinion, HTML alone is not adequate for creating an effective Web-based training program. There is not enough functionality. The HTML-based programs that I have seen tend to be either simple page-turner CBTs or hypertext-like CBTs. The only advantage of HTML-based courses is that they can run on any browser.

Our Development Tool

We use the Toolbook authoring system from Asymetrix. They provide a plug-in called Neuron that allows a Toolbook application to run over the Net using most major browsers (including Netscape and Microsoft). Virtually the full functionality of the original course is maintained. With very little modification, we can use the same training program that we developed as a Windows application for our Internet-based product. Of course, other major authoring systems also offer plug-ins.

Development Time

The size of the development effort is about the same whether you are creating a Windows-based CBT or an Internet-based CBT. The instructional design, programming, and testing are the same in both cases.

Problems with Plug-Ins

Plug-ins suffer from one major problem, they must be installed and set up. Experienced Internet users have no problems doing this. However, if a training product is aimed at typical corporate end-users, then most of the user population will not be capable of installing the plug-in.

As an example, here is a list of steps needed to install a typical plug-in.

1. Start Netscape and access the Web-page that has the training.
2. Click on a button that says "Download Plug-in."
3. A dialog box appears that asks for the file name and location.
4. User must wait for the download to complete (many minutes on slow modems).

5. User must exit from Netscape.

6. User must locate the plug-in setup file (using the Windows Explorer or the File Manager).

7. User must double click on the plug-in setup file to start it.

8. User must correctly answer any questions the setup routine asks.

9. When setup is done, user must restart Netscape.

As you can see, many steps are involved. Most users have trouble with steps 3 and 6. If your client is a corporation trying to roll out training over the Web, they would probably have their network people install the plug-ins (hopefully). Otherwise, a deluge of tech support calls will flood the help desk or support center. Of course, once the plug-in is installed, you can access any training course that uses that plug-in.

Speed Problem

In actual use, the biggest problem with Internet-based training is connection speed. On a fast intranet, a CBT may run almost as fast as on a hard drive. On a slow modem connection, most courses will run painfully slow. I assume that all developers try to optimize their Internet-based product for speed; however, there is a fundamental conflict between high-resolution graphics and course size/speed.

Database Problem

Many CBT products include a centralized database that records the performance of users. Such products work well on typical local area networks. While Internet-based CBTs do not preclude the use of such databases, the procedures needed to implement them are very different, which may mean that you have restructured your database or its underlying code.

Instructional Design for the Web

Instructional design for Web-based training follows many of the same basic tenets as CBT, multimedia training, or instructor-led training. The basic difference is in the presentation and structure of the materials, and awareness of the constraints of the medium. Arjun Reddy, a training consultant who has worked on numerous corporate training programs, believes it is a common misconception that multimedia or Web-based training is an entirely new realm, when in reality it is just a new medium for delivering quality training. This often causes intimidation and apprehension, but by following good instructional design principles, the process can be quite straightforward.

The following basic model of instructional design holds true for any type of training. This is the fundamental, well-established framework used by professionals in the field to guide them in creating quality training.

- Analysis
    - Who is the audience?
    - What do they need to learn?
    - What is the budget?
    - What are the delivery options?
    - What constraints exist?
    - When is the project due?
- Design
    - Write the instructional objectives.
    - Select an overall approach and the program's look and feel.
    - Outline units, lessons, modules.
- Development
    - Obtain/create media.
    - Program the interactions.
    - Build a prototype.
- Evaluation
    - Test the prototype on technical standards.
    - Test the prototype on instructional standards.
    - Return to and complete development.
- Implementation
    - Duplicate and distribute materials.
    - Provide support for installing and maintaining the system.

Instructional Design Tool

Instructional designers who are not used to developing multimedia instructional materials may want to consult a newly available software assistant. Until 1995, most software that facilitated the production of multimedia training was either an authoring tool or a media editor. In August 1995, Allen Communication of Salt Lake City, Utah, introduced the first tool that provided support to development teams during the design process. When the program was released, we at the *Multimedia and Internet Training Newsletter* named it the Software Product of the Year. It is a powerful and very worthwhile tool. The software, titled Designer's Edge, is aimed at both experienced and novice instructional designers. Experienced designers will find the tool useful to create consistency in and improve productivity of their development projects, while novice users will make use of the structure and training Designer's Edge provides. The program, which runs on Windows 95, uses a "task-driven interface paradigm" to walk users through the instructional design process. The program presents a list of phases and tasks that designers need to complete, and offers a number of built-in wizards, a tutorial called Show Me How, and online support (Figure 8.28).

Rex Allen, Bryan Chapman, and the team at Allen Communication created Designer's Edge based on the industry need to standardize the design

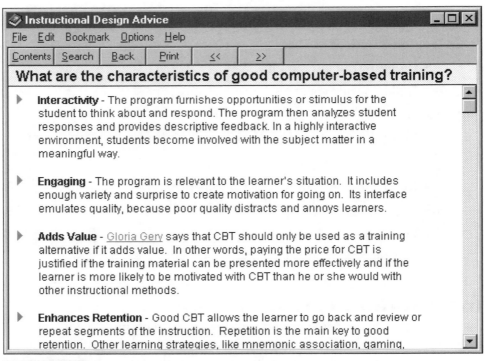

FIGURE 8.28 Instructional Design Advice.

process and reduce the time spent on instructional design. The team identified which tasks are most common for instructional designers and wrote those tasks into the support tool. The company says that while the approaches and methods of instructional designers varies, certain tasks and processes are common to most designers. The team developed the following list of phases that occur in the design process:

- Identifying needs and problems
- Writing instructional goals
- Using a mission statement to define a project
- Understanding the target audience (end user)
- Writing performance objectives
- Outlining the course content
- Creating high-level designs for courses (course map)
- Defining treatments with theme elements, setting, tone, and pacing
- Selecting instructional strategies
- Writing storyboards and specifying screen layouts
- Managing media to be used in the course (whether produced or yet to be produced)
- Generating reports such as Needs Analysis, Design Strategy Document, Storyboards, and so on
- Conducting alpha and beta testing (course evaluation)

The team integrated all of these aspects into the program and linked the different elements so data carries over from one step to another. Another valuable asset of the program is that it makes the instructional design process visual, which eases the problem of keeping all design material organized and accessible (Figure 8.29).

The tool walks designers through the instructional process, and also includes many prebuilt multimedia training templates.

Templates are linked to instructional strategies and can be used as is or treated as an example for modification. There are also prebuilt data collection forms that structure the collection of information from multiple sources. The Objective Writer and Report wizards help designers create important documents quickly. Designer's Edge stores the design files along the way so members of the design team can each access the data.

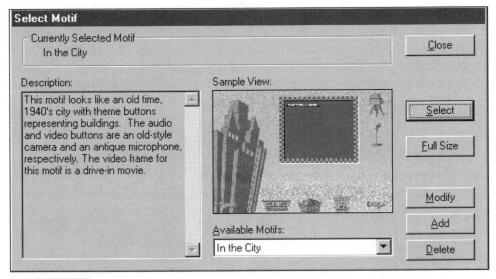

FIGURE 8.29 Sample motif.

Designer's Edge also helps generate reports and documents such as the needs analysis, script and storyboards, audience profile, and the course map. The program also organizes the data into a visual course map for quick access to content, objectives, treatment, instructional strategies, and so on. An autogenerated media log keeps track of the multimedia listed in the storyboards (Figure 8.30).

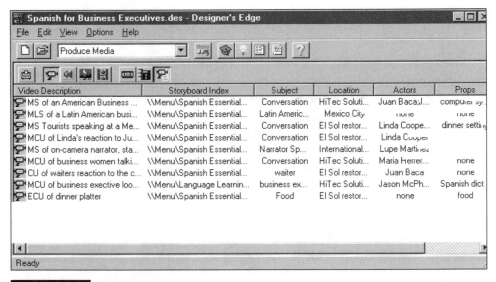

FIGURE 8.30 Media log.

The program can help teach a novice the basics of instructional design through the online instructional design course called Show Me How (Figure 8.31).

Although Designer's Edge works most closely with Allen Communication's Quest authoring tool, it is compatible with any authoring program. The tool will work with any Rich Text Format word processor and users can add or modify forms and templates for their program.

The main interface of the design tool leads the user through 12 phases with tasks to complete. The developers of Designer's Edge recommend using the model as it appears, but users have the option of beginning at any level of development and completing just those tasks most suitable to their needs. The only exceptions are that the Analyze Needs phase must be completed before the Draft Mission phase. Also, you must create a course map before completing the tasks in the Layout Course Map phase. From the main menu, a new task list will appear as you click on each phase of development. Each option is accompanied by a "completed" check box so users can see what tasks remain to be done (Figure 8.32).

FIGURE 8.31 Show Me How options screen.

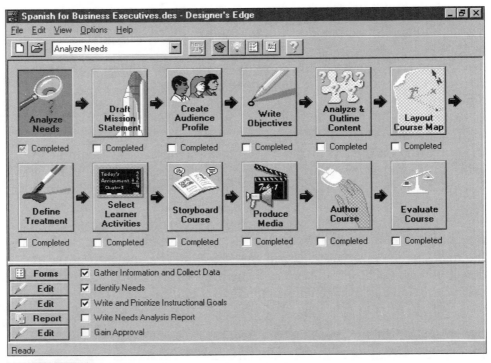

FIGURE 8.32 The main interface—Analyze Needs.

Analyze Needs

The needs analysis step helps designers select a form to collect data as well as collect and analyze all information needed to create a needs analysis statement. Designer's Edge advises the instructional designer to classify and sort each need by type and potential solution, write broad instructional goals for each training need, and then prioritize those goals. The program then helps create a needs analysis report, and asks the designer to record who worked on this phase and who reviewed the needs analysis report.

Draft Mission Statement

The draft mission statement section of the program helps users answer the question, "What will this training accomplish?" The task list includes "Determine Scope of Project (course size), Write Mission Statement, Gain Approval." This phase helps format the mission statement of the project and gives advice on estimating how long the project will take, as well as includes a "report wizard" that walks the designer through the final report (Figure 8.33).

Create Audience Profile

The Create Audience Profile step structures the process of creating audience survey forms, developing a profile of your audience, and recording who created and reviewed the audience profile. The task list for this phase includes "Collect and Summarize Audience Profile Data, Write Audience Profile Report, Gain Approval." When users click on the option "Collect and Summarize Audience Profile Data," a list of forms appears for conducting the audience survey. Once data is collected and entered, Designer's Edge creates an audience profile.

Write Objectives

Objectives clarify how the developer plans to accomplish the instructional goals stated in the Analyze Needs phase. The objectives cover what will be

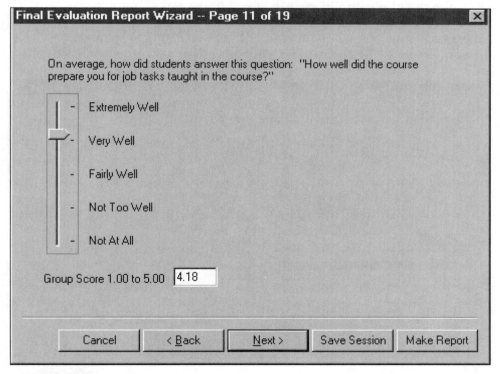

FIGURE 8.33 Final Evaluation.

taught in the course. Designer's Edge displays each instructional goal and asks the developer to provide an objective for how each goal will be met. This phase also includes a wizard that helps write the objective, asking the designer to fill in the blanks (Figure 8.34):

- Who will carry out the objective (i.e., trainees)?
- Under what circumstances the objective will be measured?
- Select an action verb that best matches the desired performance.
- What will be accomplished?
- With what percent accuracy?

Once this has been done for each goal, the tool presents a complete list of objectives and creates a report for management approval.

Analyze and Outline Content

The task menu for this phase includes: "Gather Content, Outline Desired Skills, Knowledge and Attitudes, List Prior Learning Requirements, Gain Approval." This phase has a number of built-in forms to facilitate data collection. There is also a form that can help a designer select a subject matter

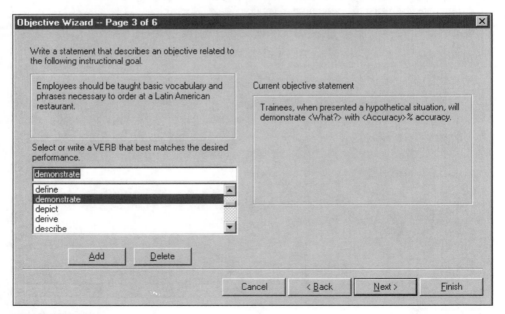

FIGURE 8.34 Objectives.

expert. Once the content data is collected, the program helps the instructional designer create a content outline in which the designer lists the main steps in the process, then breaks each step into substeps, and adds details to describe each substep. The Analyze and Outline Content Phase also suggests one list the required knowledge each trainee must have in order to understand the training. These pieces all become part of the course outline. You know, this is pretty good stuff. These are the kinds of issues the best instructional designers address.

Layout Course Map

Having consulted a SME and decided what the content will be, the next step is making decisions about how to structure the course. Task options for this phase are "Create a Course Map, Assign Objectives to Course Map, Assign Content to Course Map, Write Course Evaluation Plan, Gain Approval." A Course Map wizard helps users with questions about the elements to be included in the course, such as: Overview, Tests, Units, Lessons, Glossary, and so on. Once users work their way through the wizard, the entire course map appears. At this point, the different sections of the map have generic titles (i.e., Unit 1, Lesson 1) so users are then prompted to create names for the various sections.

Define Treatment

In this phase, instructional design begins to merge with interface design as the program prompts users to establish theme, tone, setting, and pace of the training program. The task list includes "Write Treatment (describing theme, setting, tone, pacing, etc.), Select Color Scheme and Motif, Gain Approval." After defining the Treatment, the designer selects a motif from the Designer's Edge library or creates a custom motif. Like most of the other phases, Define Treatment also prompts the designer to "get approval" upon completion of the tasks.

Select Learner Activities

In this phase, designers select the instructional activities that help ensure learning takes place. The first step in this process is the selection of the instructional strategy used by the designer to educate the learner. The program divides the instructional strategies into seven categories:

- Preinstructional
- Information presentation

- Student participation
- Testing
- Follow through
- Instructional games
- Navigational and miscellaneous

For each category, a list of multiple strategies appears. For instance, in the Preinstructional category, the following suggestions appear: "Anecdote, course overview, humorous overview, inform of prerequisite skills required, issue a challenge," and so on. Designers select the option most appropriate for their subject matter. The program then associates that strategy with the selected lesson. After this step is completed, the tool prompts users to write a design strategy document, either on their own or with a wizard. This document is used as a reference to focus the development team on the same design path. All of the data collected from previous steps goes into the design strategy document.

Storyboard Course

Probably the most detailed phase in the instructional design process of course development is storyboarding. Flowcharts are created on external software linked to Designer's Edge. Once the flowchart is created, designers are walked through the creation of storyboards and learn how to adjust font sizes, add frames to the storyboards, add graphics, make buttons for the screen layout, specify where video and audio will appear in the course, and adjust screen templates to fit their specific purpose. Designer's Edge generates the storyboards once the information is entered screen by screen.

Produce Media

The first step in this phase—generating preproduction reports—is completed by the report function in Designer's Edge. Designers access the function, and ask for a video shot list, graphic list, animation list, narrative list, and reports on any other multimedia the training program will use. The reports generated include all media specified in the storyboard. The designer can access a media production form for each media element. The program helps the designer coordinate the collection of multimedia and tracks the media as it arrives.

Author Course

At this point, the designer has established a good instructional design, created a detailed storyboard, and produced all the media that will be used in the final training product. The next step is the authoring of the actual course. Programmers use their chosen authoring tool for this phase.

Evaluate Course

Forms from the Designer's Edge library help start the evaluation process. The program prompts the evaluator to collect evaluation data and conduct an alpha test. The programmer then returns to the authoring program with these results, and changes the course as necessary. A second, beta test is done, and those revisions are completed as well. Finally, the report function helps the evaluator create a final evaluation report. The wizards and report and form functions help educate users about the process and improve productivity and organization of project management.

TIPS TO HELP YOU WITH YOUR FIRST-TIME MULTIMEDIA PROJECT

Randy Robinson, Digital Chef, Inc.

A first-time multimedia training project can be an overwhelming challenge, especially if one is new to the technology. I had spent ten years developing training programs and writing training materials for the hospitality industry, but did not know an ASCII from an INI, or a TIF from a GIF!

Starting one's first multimedia training project is like learning to ride a bike. You look at the bike and think, how in the world am I going to ride that thing? With a lot of help, you get on it and wobble down the street. You may even fall and skin your knees. Eventually, you need less help, the training wheels come off, and you are racing down the street just as fast as you can pedal.

Our first program was challenging, consuming, satisfying and, at times, frustrating. We learned a great deal and, best of all, it was fun. The following top ten list are the most important things we learned on this project. I hope they will be of some help to you.

1. The Storyboard, Our Best Friend.

The storyboard is to the multimedia author what the blueprint is to the construction contractor. I had no idea how important it would be. We spent a lot of time and effort on storyboard design. We designed each page to look as closely as possible like the final screen. Included were all details relating to each screen: templates, colors, navigation button destinations, graphic and sound file descriptions and names.

The return on the time invested in the storyboard was substantial. The storyboard not only expedited the authoring process but was invaluable as a reference when looking for problems in the course.

2. The Bells & Whistles Syndrome.

When first introduced to the powerful multimedia tools, one can easily become like the proverbial kid in the candy store. I wanted everything: spinning logos, flying graphics and flashing text hot spots in as many places as I could put them! Returning to planet earth, one realizes that some of these flashy elements do not enhance the learning, and they may even detract from it.

3. Standardize the Screen Design please!

All anyone has to do is look at one bad training title to understand how important this is. In one screen, the forward button is an arrow in the bottom left corner; later it's a pointing finger in the bottom center. The text on one screen is cyan Arial and on the next it's magenta Times.

It's tempting, and in a few cases desirable, to use multicolored backgrounds and vary the position of screen objects to avoid monotony; however, the ever-changing colors can detract from the content, not to mention give you a headache.

Likewise, it becomes annoying to users if they can't figure out how to navigate or what the buttons mean. If possible, consult with a graphic designer, preferably one with interface design experience.

4. Keep Media Files Organized.

Our first course, The Responsible Service of Alcohol, contains 175 sound files and 73 photo images. We had to create a few slightly different versions of each media file until we chose the final one to use. That's roughly 500 sound files and 300 image files, so it was very important to keep them organized and easy to find.

Creating subdirectories of versions or sessions is a must. It is also helpful to name your files appropriately so you can tell either what it is or where it goes from just the name.

5. The 3 R's.

Review, review, review! We went through the course so many times we could nearly recite it in our sleep, and then we would start over and do it again. Everyone in our company did this. You will become tired of it and so will they, but someone will find a mistake in a place that you have reviewed a hundred times.

6. Have John Doe and Mary Smith take the Course.

We got some of our best feedback from people who knew nothing about computers or the subject matter. You may think your navigation is intuitive and the content is clear and concise, but John and Mary might not—and they should if your project is to be successful.

7. Lock Up Your Ego and Throw Away the Key.

You and your team members are probably a talented group with unique skills. Each of you brings incredibly good ideas to the table, some of which are going to end up on the cutting room floor. Do not take it personally. Some techniques work well in other training media but not multimedia. This is due to the following two main reasons:

It would take too much time to develop.

It would be too costly to develop.

8. All Those Pretty Colors . . . look great on our development system but will they look as good on someone else's system? For example, if our course images are 256 colors (8 bit) and our user's system only has 16 colors (4 bit), the images are not going to show well at all.

Color palettes on the PC are a tricky consideration. Let's say you have two images to place on a screen and you are developing in 256 colors. The first image placed on the screen controls the palette. After placing the second image, you notice that the colors start to change and look strange. The problem most likely is that the two images have different color palettes. When placed together on a screen, they fight each other for colors. The good news is there is software that allows you to merge palettes to correct the problem. Two good programs are Pal Edit, which comes with Video for Windows, and Image Alchemy by Handmade Software Inc.

9. The Alpha and The Beta.

We develop off-the-shelf multimedia training courses for sale to the hospitality industry so we had to make sure the course would run on the lowest common denominator of Windows systems.

In the alpha test, we installed and ran the course on as many different combinations of systems and configurations as we could imagine. This proved to be an invaluable process. We were able to pinpoint and rectify several potential installation and file compatibility problems.

We then beta tested the product in nearly two dozen hospitality sites. This was equally valuable. Although we had tried to anticipate even the most bizarre system configurations, some of the beta sites surprised us! We also received valuable feedback from people through an interactive survey we attached to the course.

10. Go, Team, Go!

The importance of assembling a good team cannot be emphasized enough. We are fortunate to have a small, talented group of people with a wide variety of backgrounds and experience. We place a great deal of value on each other's area of expertise, thereby creating an environment of respect and admiration. If you have the opportunity to choose your team, do so wisely.

The End of the Project.

Our course is finished! The testing feedback was very positive and we are ready to distribute the course. When we look back to where we started and think about all the hard work and how much we have learned, the feeling is exhilarating.

It's just like riding the bike. Your first successful trip starts out a little rough, but the further you go, the easier it gets. When you get back home, you think about where you started and how far you went. It's a great feeling. You have experienced how much fun it is to ride, and you imagine all the fascinating places you can visit. You can't wait to get on that bike again . . . and go farther . . . and faster.

ONLINE TESTING

An integral part of some WBT programs is the inclusion of testing. Whether companies need to certify employees or test their skills and knowledge, Web-based testing is a cost-effective and efficient method in comparison to traditional written tests or to the more common alternative, no testing at all. Following is a description of several tools for Web-based testing. If you plan to create your own testing software, you might want to keep some of these features in mind. Also included are case studies of organizations which have used Web-based testing as part of their performance improvement effort.

 Web@ssessor

Phoenix, Arizona–based ComputerPREP has been in the training business for some years and has developed Web@ssessor, a customizable assessment and data-collection tool written in Java to run entirely on the Web. Companies can develop their own tests without programming; a multimedia quiz or survey can be created using a point-and-click interface. The

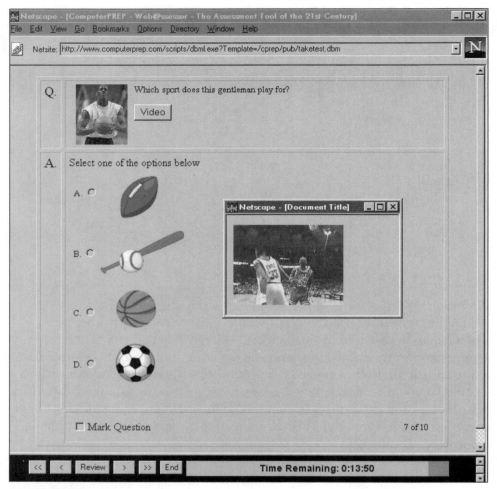

program requires Netscape Navigator version 3.0 or later, Windows 95, NT, or Mac OS 6.0 platform and a Web server application.

The technology for testing and surveying over the Web can be used for a variety of purposes. Trainers can implement a 360-degree feedback system for employees or managers. Tests can be developed for existing instructor-led or Web-delivered courses. Web@ssessor can also be used for screening and aptitude testing of potential employees. Employees can be surveyed on the company's policies and procedures, or customers can be surveyed about their needs or ratings of the company. Because the program is available wherever Internet or intranet access is available, users can access the test anytime and use the program at their convenience.

The program can accommodate an unlimited number of questions, answers per question, and number of users. Tests can be administered in

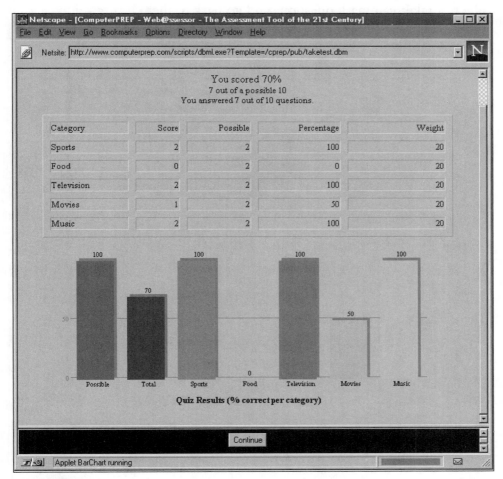

FIGURE 9.2 Test results display page.

any number of languages, with any amount of pictures, video clips, animation, graphics, sound or music files (Figure 9.1). Question types can include multiple choice, true/false, fill-in-the-blank, or short answer. Companies can set time limits for tests, and can access the results immediately if desired. The students can as well. A security system is built in to ensure questions and results are kept confidential.

Navigation buttons let the student taking the test move between questions, see the question number, and determine time remaining in the test. The test taker can mark questions and go back to them if time allows.

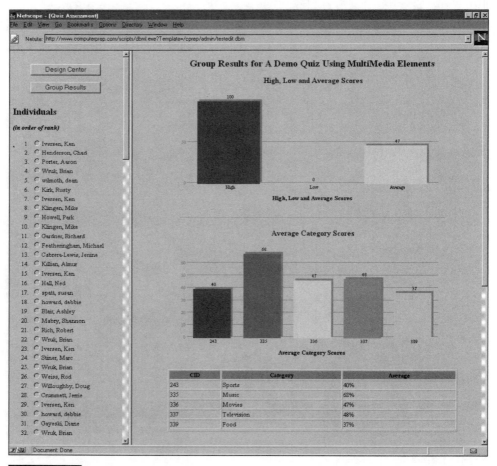

FIGURE 9.3 Group results for quiz.

© 1997 Drake International

Editing buttons allow the administrator to adjust the font, size, and color of the test questions or answers. The appropriate HTML codes are then inserted by the program and the administrator can preview what the answer will look like to the student.

Test questions can be reviewed by clicking the Review button, which provides a graphical snapshot of the entire test on the screen, including skipped questions and marked questions. When the student clicks on the End button, the system grades the test and the results appear in tables and graphs on the screen, as seen in Figure 9.2.

The group scores and the group average are displayed in graphical format by category in the Results Center. Specific individuals' results are available by clicking on the name in the left-hand column (Figure 9.3).

The intranet site license price costs approximately $10,000 per year and the service agreement and upgrades cost $2,000 per year.

Web@ssessor is on the ComputerPREP Web site at http://www.computerprep.com.

Decisive Survey

Decisive Technology of Mountain-View, California, has developed survey software that can be used to administer tests over the Internet. Organizations can deliver questionnaires or tests and receive responses over the Internet or through their own corporate intranet using e-mail. A nice feature of Decisive's software is that it integrates with e-mail systems (Microsoft Mail, cc:Mail, Lotus Notes, Novell Groupwise, DaVinci Mail, and others), and tests or surveys are transmitted in ASCII text messages, so that anyone with e-mail can be included.

Decisive Survey includes a set of templates for developing their tests (Figures 9.4 and 9.5). The program handles the four most popular question types: choose one, choose all that apply, rate on a scale, and fill in the blank (Figure 9.6). In addition, documents, images, and audio clips can be attached to the test on either end of the correspondence.

Once the tests have been completed and returned, Decisive Survey collects the results from a designated e-mail box and tabulates them using statistical techniques. Results are available in either a graphical or tabular format.

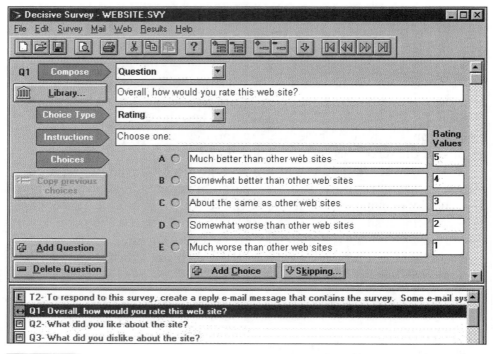

FIGURE 9.4 The development screen for creating an online survey.

Question Mark

AssessNet is a service company that offers online tests for companies to determine their employees' skill level. Once an employee has completed the online tests, a summary of the employee's strengths and weaknesses is provided by the system. Companies can customize their interactive tests and surveys as well. Tests also can be designed to include graphics, audio/video, and hot spots (Figure 9.7).

Once a test is completed, the employee pushes the Submit button to send it to AssessNet for grading. After the test is graded, results are sent back to the company. (See CD-ROM for demonstration.)

The tests and surveys are designed with the Question Mark software tool. The developer can make true/false, multiple choice, multiple

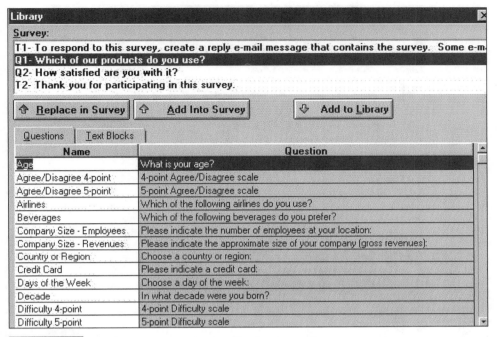

FIGURE 9.5 The Survey Library for creating test questions.

© 1996 Decisive Technology Corporation. All rights reserved. Decisive, Decisive Survey, and Decisive Feedback are trademarks of Decisive Technology Corporation.

response, fill-in-the-blank, selection, and hot spot questions (Figure 9.8). Hot spot questions have the correct or incorrect answer hidden behind a graphic, which can be revealed after the question is answered.

The graphics can be drawn with tools included in the program or other Windows-based applications. The Question Mark software allows the creator to make interactive study guides, tests, and surveys without programming.

All tests are created using Question Mark and then converted for Web use. Test questions can be created using any word processing software and may be designed to change the course of the program depending on which answer is chosen. The test may be taken in the order presented or designed so the student/employee can skip around. Introductory and explanatory information can be displayed throughout the test. If a certain layout is used repeatedly, a template can be saved.

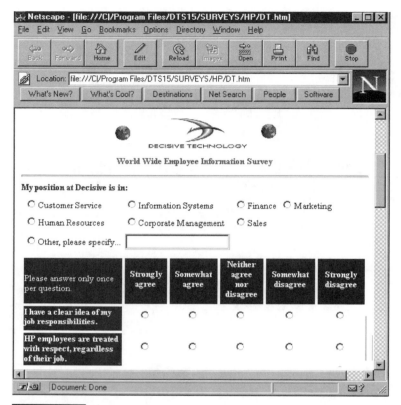

FIGURE 9.6 Sample of an online survey on a Web page.

A file is created where the questions are stored, with up to 1,000 questions. All of these files become one library, which can be accessed to re-create tests out of previously-used material. Files can be combined to make tests as long as desired, and the questions can be programmed as to how they are given (questions can appear randomly or in a defined series). Test questions can be multiple-choice questions, multiple-response (student/employee chooses one or more answers), hot spot questions (i.e., drag-and-drop), text questions, numeric question, and essay questions. Feedback on student performance can be delivered at the time of test completion and a time limit can be set.

Question Mark can transfer previously used material from word processors into the Question Mark format, such as cutting and pasting from another program. Tests can incorporate colors, graphics, photographs,

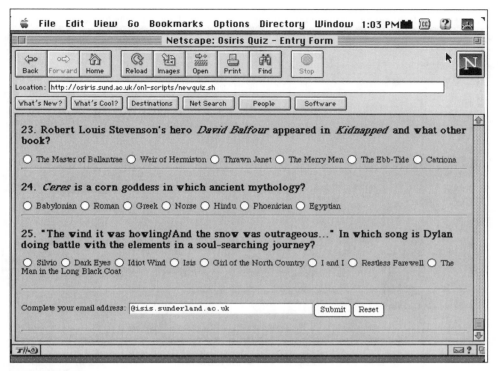

FIGURE 9.7 Online quiz.

QuestionMark America

sound, animation, video, and other multimedia into the test design. The MediaCall function can run AVI, FLI, FLC, WAV, or EXE application files. From the Edit menu you select a media option which will provide you with a Command and Parameters field for how the media or executable file is to be run.

When questions are entered into Question Mark, the QM Web Converter converts the questions into HTML with GIF or JPEG graphics. The test then can be loaded on to a server. Each question has a "map file" where the answer is stored, which cannot be seen by the student/employee. These files provide information such as who has taken the test, a summary of answers, scores received, and different types of analysis (e.g., what percentage of answers people are choosing). The developer supplies the possible end-of-test feedback, feedback to individual questions, test scores, and additional informative text (e.g., introduction or acknowledgment), and the student sees the automated response.

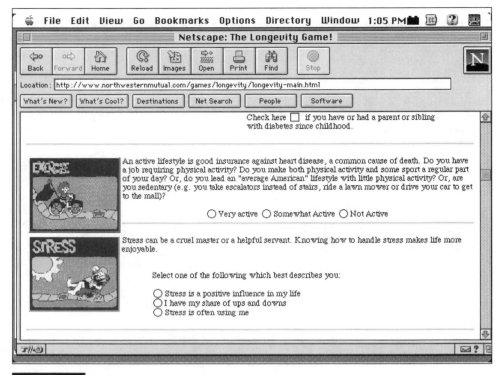

FIGURE 9.8 Sample AssessNet Survey.

Question Mark America

 Security

One of the important considerations with testing software is security. Safeguards to help prevent mistakes and cheating are built into the software. Tests are stored in an encrypted format and then computer-scored instantly. Not all tests that are given are the same because the questions can be mixed and randomized for each student, making answer sharing difficult. There is also a QM Guardian which distributes passwords and allows control over who takes the test and how many times. Some organizations require test-taking at a monitored location.

Be aware that once the test is on the Web, everyone can have access to it. To make administration easier, it is possible to upload the questions just before the test.

DELL UNIVERSITY: CASE STUDY

When Dell University made the decision to deliver some of its courses via the company's intranet, it opted to have an Internet Service Provider administer computerized tests associated with its Dell Business Model Course—a basic course on Dell's business practices which is taken by every company employee.

AssessNet helped develop the computerized quiz to determine how much employees know about the company prior to the course as well as a post-course test and a course evaluation survey.

AssessNet's Web server is accessed via a link from Dell's Intranet. Question Mark testing software then administers the tests and immediately scores them.

After the tests are completed, they do extended analysis, histograms, and frequency of distribution reports on a monthly basis. When employees' pre- and post-course test scores are compared, they can see how much students

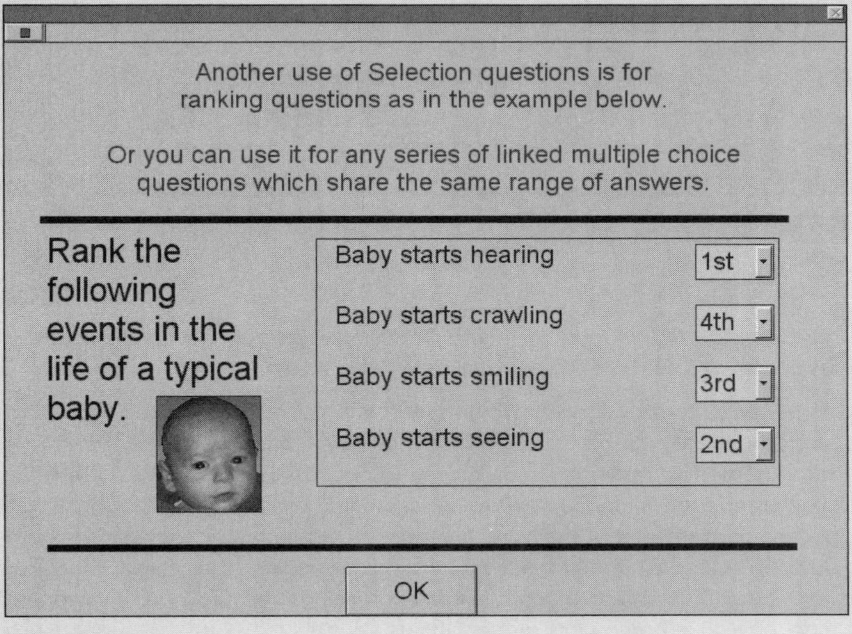

Another use of Selection questions is for ranking questions as in the example below.

Or you can use it for any series of linked multiple choice questions which share the same range of answers.

Rank the following events in the life of a typical baby.

Baby starts hearing	1st
Baby starts crawling	4th
Baby starts smiling	3rd
Baby starts seeing	2nd

OK

FIGURE 9.9 Ranking.

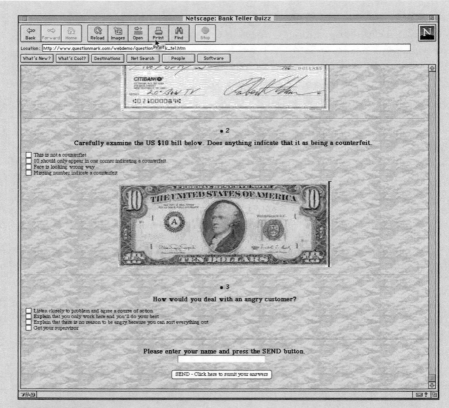

FIGURE 9.10 Bank teller quiz.

have learned from a course. It lets Dell know how successful the course is and where improvements can be made [Figure 9.9].

"With computerized surveys we find that when people are asked for a comment they really do comment," says one of the project leaders. "Using the intranet, the feedback has been more thorough than before." As a result Dell is getting better guidance in tailoring courses for their employees. Some people are concerned that their employees will be intimidated by having a computer ask them questions, but they are finding the opposite to be true—people seem more comfortable expressing their opinions via computer than they do in person or on paper [Figure 9.10].

Dell used Question Mark's question formats, which include question types for

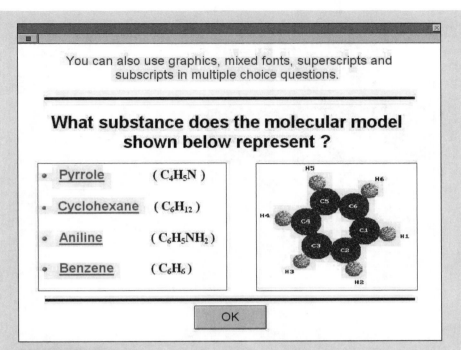

You can also use graphics, mixed fonts, superscripts and subscripts in multiple choice questions.

What substance does the molecular model shown below represent ?

- <u>Pyrrole</u>   (C_4H_5N)
- <u>Cyclohexane</u> (C_6H_{12})
- <u>Aniline</u>   ($C_6H_5NH_2$)
- <u>Benzene</u>   (C_6H_6)

OK

FIGURE 9.11 Multiple choice questions.

matching, fill-in-the-blank, true/false, multiple choice, and word or short-phrase answers [Figure 9.11]. The questions were then converted to HTML using the Web Converter software, and formatted to fit the look and feel of Dell University's Web site. They were then uploaded to the AssessNet Web Server.

The interactive tests that were created for Dell can function as instruction tools or as formal tests. The company is looking to develop online study guides as well, since they can provide explanations, information, and instructions as well as tests. They believe these types of interactive tests and surveys will be increasingly important tools in corporate education programs.

The Question Mark authoring tool can be used to create a variety of interactive quizzes, tests, study guides, and surveys [Figure 9.12]. Quizzes, tests, and surveys can be delivered via network, intranet, floppy disk, or CD to individual workstations or the Web.

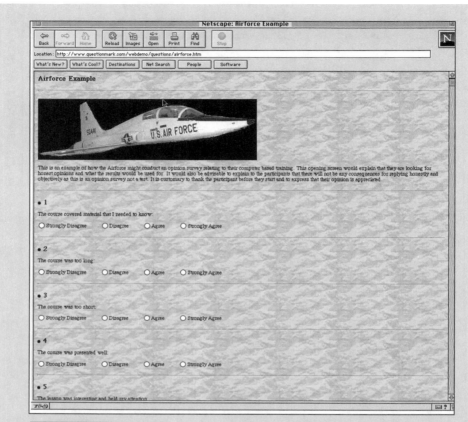

FIGURE 9.12 Airforce quiz, an example of Question Mark–created quiz in action.

KEMET ELECTRONICS: CASE STUDY

Kemet Electronics Corporation, one of the largest manufacturers of capacitors in the United States, is using Question Mark for internal training and skills assessment.

Kemet has won many supplier awards from its customers, and one aspect of maintaining high quality is training for the manufacturing plant workers. Computer-based testing is part of this process.

Kemet used Question Mark software to create tests that are designed to test knowledge of safety procedures as well as the use of equipment. Some

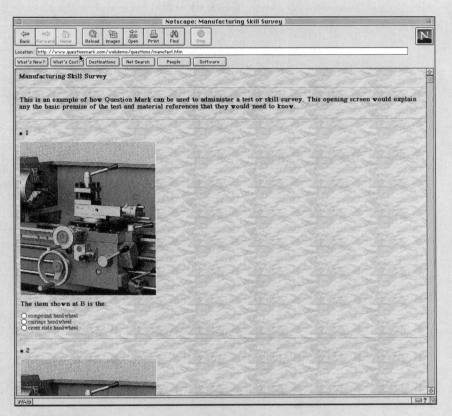

FIGURE 9.13 Part of a manufacturing skill survey.

questions include graphics and require the employee to identify the correct parts or functions of the equipment [Figures 9.13 and 9.14].

The first implementation was in Matamoros, Mexico, at Kemet de Mexico S.A. de C.V. AssessNet provided training, in Spanish, for six staff members responsible for developing assessments for the manufacturing plant workers. The test developers were computer literate but not programmers. Kemet offers training along with the online testing to employees who would like to learn new skills and be able to rotate throughout the plant when needed to balance production and staffing.

Anne Pinkerton, Human Resources Manager, says they have developed over 50 exams and now can more accurately document the effectiveness of job skill training for 600 manufacturing employees. Implementation in the one plant was so effective they plan to develop over 500 exams for a total of 4,000 employees.

FIGURE 9.14 Part of an electronic skill survey.

PROGRAM ADMINISTRATION

As you begin to offer courses over the Internet or your intranet, the issue of program administration rapidly becomes important. Listing your offerings, defining which employees can access which courses, registering students, accepting payment information, and tracking usage and scores all need to be handled. Luckily, these activities can be largely automated through the magic of computers! (Well, that's the way it's supposed to work, anyway.) Rather than develop such administration software yourself, there are a number of tools available to address this need for your organization. Some have been "ported" from earlier versions of software available for Windows and run on a LAN to administer instructor-led courses and some are new ventures using the latest JAVA-enhanced technology. Some are simply registration software, while others provide an architecture for delivering a curriculum of courseware.

 ## LOIS

Knowledgesoft, Inc., a ten-year-old information technology company, has developed one innovative Web-based training administration tool. LOIS (Learning Organization Information System) is "knowledge management software" that helps coordinate the learning process as well as monitor and assess it. A client/server application, LOIS maintains tracking and measurement databases for large-scale learning programs (Figure 10.1). LOIS version 3.0 allows Web browser access for end-users, management, and training administrators, so there is no need to install software on desktops.

LOIS version 3.0 runs on a company's existing network, with or without an Internet connection. The program itself is organized into three subject areas: a Competency Management System, an Assessment System, and a Training Management System.

The Competency Management System maintains a job skills database classified by organization, department, or job profile. LOIS can identify skills gaps based on competencies that a company distinguishes. Career-planning capabilities are also featured; employees can periodically access LOIS through a Web browser to determine what skills are required to move to a new job profile and then plan a course of study to achieve the skill set required.

The Assessment System allows companies to do skills assessments and track certification programs. Management can create tests and surveys to test knowledge or receive general feedback about skills.

The Training Management System maintains an electronic catalog of learning events, which can vary from live instruction to a WBT program.

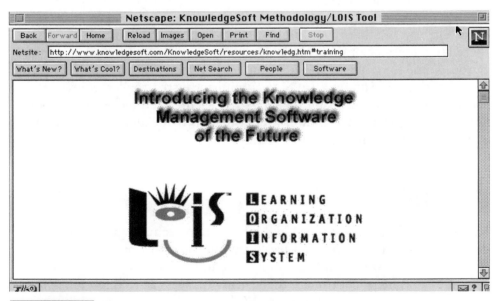

FIGURE 10.1 Learning Organization Information System.

Employees can register for events over a company intranet or the Internet. The program can also generate bills and invoices.

LOIS allows any user on a desktop to access course schedules, outlines, career plans, and transcripts. Use of the program should result in a decrease in the amount of time traditionally spent in running training programs, since the program automates scheduling and related activities. ZDU, the Web-based training offering from Ziff Davis profiled earlier in this book, uses the LOIS system to deliver its courseware, as does UOL Publishing, Inc. (formerly University On-Line) and United Defense.

UOL partners with universities and corporate trainers to provide courses for professionals and traditional students and uses LOIS in the delivery and administration of its interactive online courses. UOL manages the courseware delivery systems, grading, and student services that allow their partners to launch online training programs.

United Defense, an army tank manufacturer, uses LOIS to organize Web sites and computer-based training. They are looking into developing a WBT program with LOIS to handle their ISO 9000 certification.

Lotus

As is true for all of the major software companies, Lotus has a division dedicated to customer training on its products. Lotus Education is charged with the development and delivery of programs and products to maintain a consistent level of competency of technical professionals and end-users. The organization offers participants learning programs such as instructor-led training, computer-based and self-based training, curriculum development and customization, education needs analysis, and professional and instructor certification. There are over 450 Lotus Authorized Education Centers and 230 Lotus Desktop Training Companies worldwide. In addition to LearningSpace, described below, Lotus has developed a computer-based training course for integrating Lotus SmartSuite applications and a library of computer-based training courses for Lotus Notes. The courses are designed for participants to work on their own desktops at their own pace.

Lotus LearningSpace

In addition to the instructor-led and CBT courses mentioned above, Lotus has created an architecture for delivering courses which is uniquely Lotus' and therefore uniquely collaborative. Lotus LearningSpace is a product

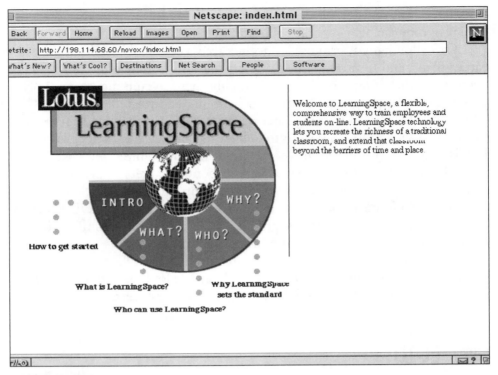

FIGURE 10.2 Lotus LearningSpace.

and set of services that will enable instructor-facilitated and collaborative learning using Lotus Notes. LearningSpace provides training for users who cannot attend classes or who want to benefit from the advantages of WBT (Figure 10.2).

LearningSpace and the related services were created to help corporate training and management development departments, graduate and continuing education programs, and training and education companies delivering services to corporate customers.

Current Lotus Education courses train participants in how to design and adapt curriculum for online delivery in LearningSpace with the *Introduction to Courseware Development in LearningSpace* course. *Teaching in LearningSpace* helps participants facilitate and teach in the LearningSpace environment as well as learn how to utilize LearningSpace as end-users with an online tutorial and how to set up and implement technical services for LearningSpace.

LearningSpace includes tools that support instructor creation and student access to educational content. A virtual classroom is provided for student-to-student and student-to-instructor interaction. This use of media allows students to work with others to better understand the curriculum. LearningSpace has the capability to perform graphical interfaces, agent technology, Web integration, and other enhancements.

LearningSpace offers a multidatabase application suite in which course content is delivered to participants.

The Schedule database is a central module for participants to use to obtain course materials. The schedule is organized by time frames or by modules so that participants can create a self-paced instruction schedule. The Schedule database keeps participants informed on assignments, readings, and quizzes.

The MediaCenter database holds articles, newsletters, chapters, abstracts and summaries, and multimedia, as well as access to external sources such as the World Wide Web and other content repositories for participants' use.

The virtual CourseRoom acts as an interactive environment for participants to engage in public and private discussions with other students or their instructor. This allows participants to share information and to complete team tasks and assignments.

The Profiles database includes contact information, photographs, education and experience, and interests from participants.

The Assessment Manager is an evaluation tool for the instructor to privately test and receive feedback on participants' performance. Quizzes are posted in the schedule database and are sent via e-mail to the Assessment Manager database, accessible only by the instructors. Instructors can review, grade, and provide feedback to participants.

Oracle Learning Architecture

Oracle, another major software company, has created an architecture for delivering WBT as well. Oracle Learning Architecture (OLA) is an Internet course delivery and management system with more than 75 training titles. Users can receive training on a variety of topics. OLA is an open, Internet-based, online training environment that allows users to access and customize information technology training courses (Figure 10.3).

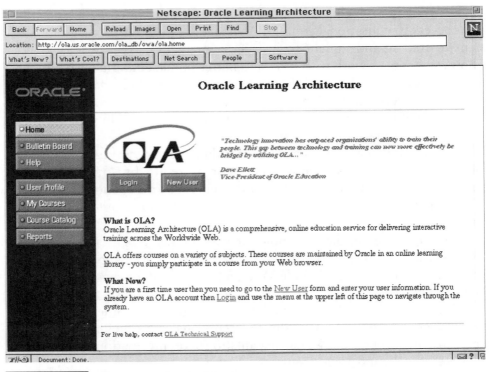

FIGURE 10.3 Oracle Learning Architecture.

Oracle technology makes up the architecture of OLA, including WebServer and Oracle7 Server. Users can access OLA from any Web-compatible platform—for example, the Network Computer, UNIX, Macintosh, Microsoft Windows 95, or Microsoft NT—using any of the standard Web browser programs: Netscape Navigator, Microsoft Internet Explorer, Oracle PowerBrowser, and Mosaic.

OLA courses are maintained by Oracle in an online learning library—participants can access the library through their Web browser. Standard courses and curriculum can be selected, or the user may develop a personal course structure. The Administration option provides tools to manage user information and allows the student or training administrator to determine an individual training plan.

All visitors to OLA are welcome to browse the system; however, users must be registered with a valid license code to take courses and to view free demo courses. Registering requires the user to fill in information on the New User Registration page. The system will validate the information and make notification of a successful or incomplete registration. Once registration is complete, users are able to log in with a username and a password. Registration information can be updated at any time.

Understanding the OLA Main Menu

The OLA main menu provides access to the OLA offerings. The main menu appears as a vertical bar of blue buttons on the screen. Each button represents an administrative feature, as described below:

Home: Takes the user to the Home Page, which explains the overall purpose of OLA and gives instructions on how to get started. Clicking the OLA logo on the Home Page brings up an OLA facts sheet.

Bulletin Board: Allows users to submit comments about OLA and specific courses, as well as read through comments submitted by other users. A user can also search for comments on various topics. All comments are reviewed and, if appropriate, posted to the Bulletin Board.

Help: Provides an online user guide for navigating through the system.

User Profile: Contains the information (such as name, address, etc.) entered on the registration page by the registered user. Information can be updated or changed on the profile at any time by accessing this page.

My Courses: Lists the courses the user is authorized to take provided that the license code has been entered. The site administrator or OLA representative will issue the license code to access these courses. The license code must be entered to obtain the authorized courses.

Course Catalog: Gives access to a list by title, subject, language, or price code of all available courses on OLA. Clicking any of the course titles will bring up course detail information, including vendor, abstract and objectives; prerequisites or follow-on courses, estimated time to complete, whether the course requires downloads or helper applications, and ordering information.

Courses can be searched out by topic or users can match courses to their personal profile. More advanced searches can find courses with specific attributes, such as Java, audio, and so on.

Reports: Provide statistical information such as the top-ten OLA courses, test results, progress reports, and administrative reports.

Different Types of OLA Content

The types of courses available on OLA include:

- **Web-based courses:** These courses cover the World Wide Web and represent over half of the instruction on OLA. RCI is the main vendor for this type of content. Some courses include simulation, Java, audio, and so on.

- **Download courses:** These courses are stored in OLA and are accessed by downloading course modules to a personal computer. Vendors for these courses include NETG, CBT Systems, PTS Learning Systems, and Kelly Services.

- **Vendor demos:** These programs demonstrate the capabilities and potential of Web-based training. They showcase the technology of specific vendors and point to future OLA content.

- **Assessments:** Courses from multiple vendors, such as NETG and RCI, have questions and tests built into individual course sections. Some courses are linked to a testing system that offers tests that can be taken before or after completing a course. The system suggests which course sections should be taken based on the users' responses in assessments taken at the beginning of a course. An assessment taken upon completion of a course is graded and returned to the user with a percent correct score. When multiple choice, true/false, or fill-in-the-blank questions are answered within each course topic, the user is notified whether the answer is correct or incorrect. Most OLA content vendors have built assessment capabilities into their courses.

Users can browse descriptions of all OLA courses by clicking Course Catalog from the main menu. When the OLA Course Catalog page appears, users select an individual course title. A course detail page is brought up, which provides information such as the vendor, course description, objectives, and estimated time to complete course. Statistical information such as the top-ten OLA courses, test results, and progress reports can be obtained in the OLA reports option.

 WBTSystems

WBTSystems, formerly known as WEST, offers a server for managing and delivering courses. Their product, TopClass, is the company's effort to combine the best qualities of one-on-one instruction with the convenience of self-paced computer training. Developed in 1995, the server software TopClass creates an environment designed to provide enabling tools for the creation, delivery, and management of training and training material over the World Wide Web.

The TopClass Environment

TopClass emulates the instructor-led environment of personalized and supported training by providing bulletin board systems for course announcements, e-mail for electronic submission and correction, and conference forum areas for discussion groups. It also allows the instructor to take standardized course material and tailor it for each student on a dynamic basis according to the student's progress (Figure 10.4).

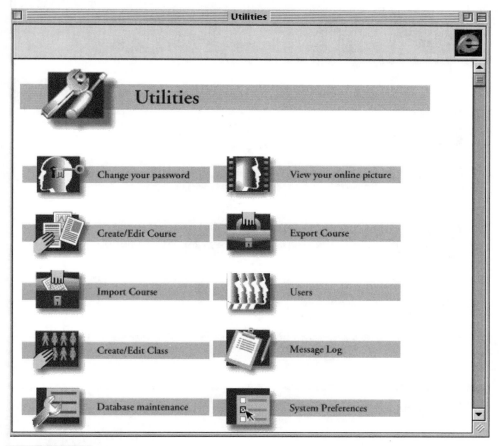

FIGURE 10.4 Utilities.

TopClass was developed on Power Macintosh 6150 and 8100 and Macintosh Quadra 950 and 660AV computers, using AppleScript, FileMaker Pro, and BBEdit for the HTML text editor, CUSeeMe, and Netscape Navigator for the Web browser. TopClass has been developed to run on all platforms, running WebSTAR software on a TCP/IP Ethernet network.

The TopClass environment is built or layered on top of a standard World Wide Web Server (such as the Netscape Communications Server, Microsoft's Internet Server, or WebSTAR). These servers are in turn built on top of TCP/IP, the network protocol of the Internet. A user's request is passed via a Web browser to a Web server using TCP/IP. On receiving the

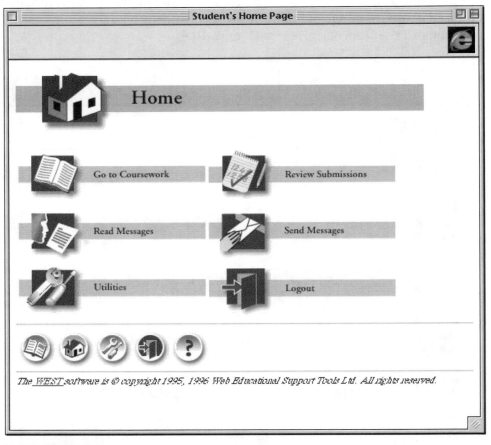

FIGURE 10.5 Student's Home Page.

request, the Web Server will pass it to TopClass, which will process it, construct the appropriate information/pages dynamically, and pass them back via the server to the user.

As servers and TCP/IP follow open, nonproprietary standards, this allows TopClass to work across many different client platforms (e.g., Apple Macintosh, Windows 3.1, 95, and NT, and UNIX) and with many different Web servers and Web browsers without a significant investment in developing these servers or clients.

TopClass has a database at its core which stores and manages all information on users, classes, courses, submissions, and so on. This database is constructed to allow all administration and authoring to be done remotely using a standard Web browser. The database also manages the information/pages for each course including maintaining the integrity of forward and backward links. None of the information/pages delivered by TopClass to a user exist as static HTML files sitting on a server. They are all created as they are needed and custom tailored to the particular user requesting them.

The TopClass server knows who the student is, who the assigned instructor is, and the assigned classes and course material. This, coupled with built-in messaging and conferencing, which provide one-to-one and one-to-many communication, means that TopClass is a personalized and supported learning environment (Figure 10.5).

Content or courses which take advantage of tools such as Java, Shockwave, VRML, and so on are TopClass-compliant. TopClass will also interface with major authoring tools such as Macromedia's Authorware and Director, Aysemtrix's Toolbox, and other tools such as Adobe's PageMill or SiteMill. TopClass utilizes standard communication tools of the Internet to complement it: these include e-mail, bulletin board services for class announcements, and newsgroups for group discussions (Figure 10.6).

The administrators' interface includes management of total environment, including classes, courses, and students (users). They may assign instructors and create/edit courses. Instructors may manage classes and courses, post class announcements, assign material, and create/edit courses. They can correct submitted classwork and perform automated testing. Students (users) may register for and take supported courses, send/receive messages to/from instructors, send/receive personalized class material to/from instructors, and discuss problems and issues with class and instructor in conference forum areas.

TopClass emulates the instructor-led environment of personalized and supported training by providing:

- Bulletin board systems for course announcements
- E-mail for electronic submission and correction of exercises, allowing instructors to correct exercises and return results and comments to students
- Automated grading of exercises with multiple question types
- Conference forum areas for discussion groups, allowing students and instructors to collaborate
- A means of customizing standard course material to each students' needs and progress
- Information on the product and its applications can be found at http://www.Wbtsystems.com/showcase

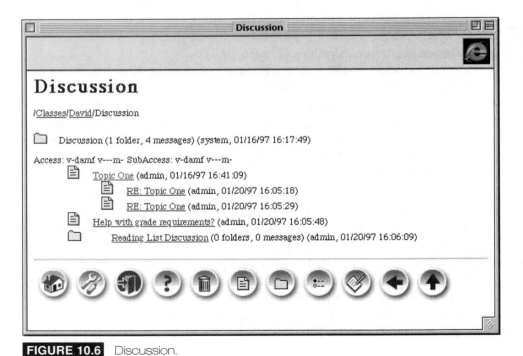

FIGURE 10.6 Discussion.

Empower Corporation: Online Learning Development and Distribution Infrastructure

The Online Learning Infrastructure (OLI) developed by Empower Corporation is based on the corporate intranet (client/server) system and deploys a relational database as a central repository for courseware or collection of learning objects (Figure 10.7). The different components of OLI architecture include the common user interface (standard Web browser), plug and play tools, authoring tools and templates, administrative, assessment, and distribution tools, the Multimedia Learning Object Broker, and the Distributed and Replicated Learning Object Repository.

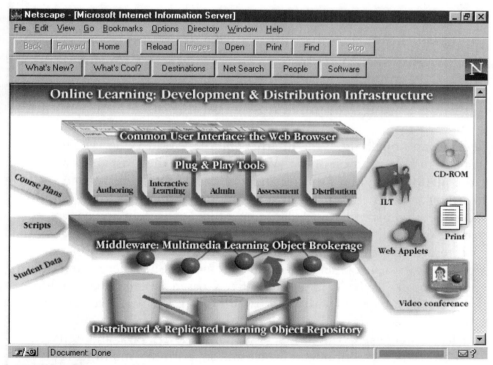

FIGURE 10.7 Online Learning: Development & Distribution Infrastructure.

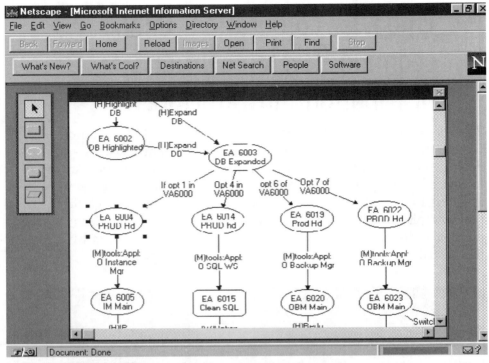

FIGURE 10.8 How a complex interactive software simulation can be created by using a software simulation builder applet (written in Java).

The vast popularity of the Internet and the World Wide Web has resulted in the evolution of the Web browser into the most consistent cross-platform solution for browsing multimedia data. The Online Learning Infrastructure provides a common user interface to the authors, students, administrators, and management in a consistent and convenient manner from any location on the Internet or intranet.

Interactivity can be achieved through widely accepted cross-platform languages and development environments such as Sun Microsystems' Java and Microsoft's ActiveX. Java- and ActiveX-based applets (small applications) can be integrated with Web-based HTML (Hyper Text Markup Language) files.

Most widely used Web browsers support HTML, Java, and ActiveX. Web browsers will continue to evolve and support new multimedia and collaborative technologies. The learning infrastructure will naturally benefit from these advancements.

OLI architecture provides a framework for many types of tools to be plugged into the infrastructure depending on an organization's specific needs. Tools can vary from simple forms or applets to very sophisticated interactive multimedia development environments. The open OLI environment, based on industry-standard components (data formats, languages, and protocols), allows tools from different vendors to be deployed as the needs dictate and as the technology advances (Figure 10.8).

Authoring tools and templates assist the content producers and instructional designers in creating learning objects.

Tools provided in the architecture include instructional analysis and design templates and wizards, question and answer editors, a media object browser, and a simulation editor (Figure 10.9).

Instructional analysis and design templates allow the learning object authors to analyze and specify their audience profile, topics, and learning objectives.

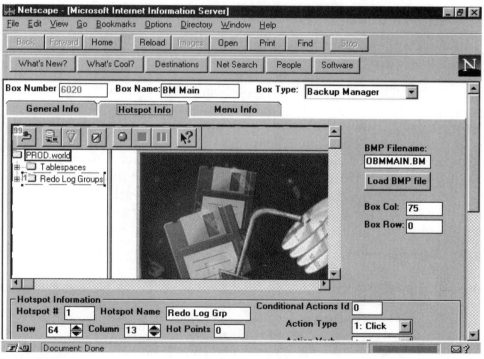

FIGURE 10.9 How hot spots can be defined on a screen from the software application to be simulated.

The Q&A Editor is a set of forms and wizards that allows the author to create a variety of learning activities including:

- Multiple choice questions
- True/false questions
- Drag-and-drop exercises
- Click to identify objects
- Connect the points with lines
- Match the columns
- Simple interactive "challenge" games

Feedback, scoring, and linkback to course content options can be specified in the Q&A Editor.

The OLI Media Object Browser allows the author to reuse media elements (graphics, animation, text, audio, and video). It supports:

- Selection by object type
- Drag-and-drop feature to drag media elements from a visual browser into a lesson

The learning tools provide presentation, navigation, feedback, and search capabilities. A Java-based search engine can be used to scan the instructional content for specific key words.

OLI's Software Simulation Editor provides a framework for building software application simulations using a visual and iconic framework. The author creates a decision tree using a visual flowchart editor. Each node in the tree represents a state of the software systems. At each node, the author can specify hot spots, menu events, mouse events, actions a student can take, and the subsequent outcomes. Along the decision tree, the author may also include hints, instructions, and advice using different media types: text, audio, or video.

The administrative tools allow OLI administrators to register students using a forms-based interface and generate attendance and progress reports. OLI assessment tools provide management with different views (with password protection) about students' performance such as vital statistics about usage, progress, evaluation, and course success measures. The OLI distribution tools allow the learning objects or the courseware to be exported out of the repository for distribution in a variety of formats

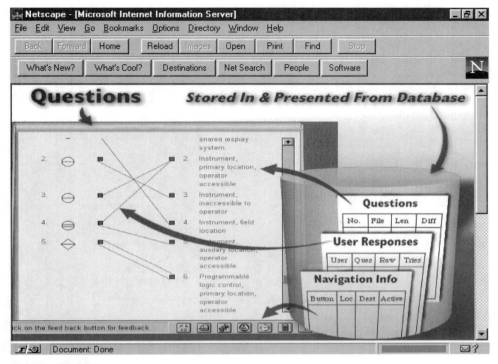

FIGURE 10.10 Shows complex interactive questions being queried from the database and displayed within an Internet browser.

including online (for Internet/intranet delivery), CD-ROM, print, and instructor-led classroom presentation (Figure 10.10).

Between the tools layer and the learning repository is the layer called middleware—Multimedia Learning Object Broker—a software layer that maps data in and out of the tools and the database repository. The data is displayed in the browser window in the form of dynamic HTML and applets. Data is then mapped out of the tools as relational data to be stored in the repository (Figure 10.11).

OLI stores all the learning objects, student progress/performance data, and administrative/management data in an open-architecture relational database called the Distributed and Replicated Learning Object Repository.

The database repository stores:

• Student preferences

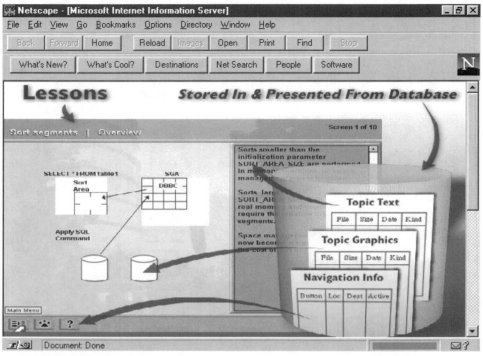

FIGURE 10.11 Shows the training content being pulled out of a relational database scheme.

- Passwords, security information
- Results, scores, levels, progress
- Clips, reusable multimedia elements
- Catalog of lessons
- Links between nodes of training (as in hypertext environment)
- Query index for specific searches or fact-finding

According to Harvi Singh of Empower, the benefits of a relational database are as follows:

Open: Relational databases are based on time-tested, industrywide, accepted relational models. Most application development environments support SQL (Structured Query Language) through ODBC (Open Database Connectivity) and JDBC (Java Database Connectivity) interfaces and therefore can be used to supply, query, and manage the content stored in the repository.

Sharable data: Learning objects such as questions, simulations, and lessons and media objects such as graphics and animations are stored in the repository; they are not tightly coupled to or embedded inside the training applications. The learning objects can be shared between multiple training applications or learning situations.

Cross-platform: The popularity of a relational model ensures its availability on almost every server platform. The learning objects repository, based on the relational database, can therefore reside on any intranet server.

Enterprisewide client/server support: The relational repository provides a multiuser environment that can support collaborative authoring and learning activities throughout the enterprise.

Scaleable: The database also serves as a *scaleable* storage system which can deploy a large library of learning objects and support a large number of simultaneous users on the enterprisewide network.

Ongoing and incremental updates: As the enterprise's learning needs expand, the learning object repository allows the content to be added or updated in an incremental manner without impacting the existing objects.

TeamScape's Learning Junction

TeamScape's Learning Junction is also an Internet-based training system, targeted at training departments and institutions serving the needs of students, employees, and customers. The company was founded by several ex-Oracle employees and benefits from being designed in Java and from the designers' experience with database management, which is the foundation of a registration system. The system, a Java-based software application, covers several areas of training administration, delivery, and personalized training services.

"A key challenge in training organizations today is the volume of administrative work that's associated with typical training functions," TeamScape reports. "Training activities include training administration, for

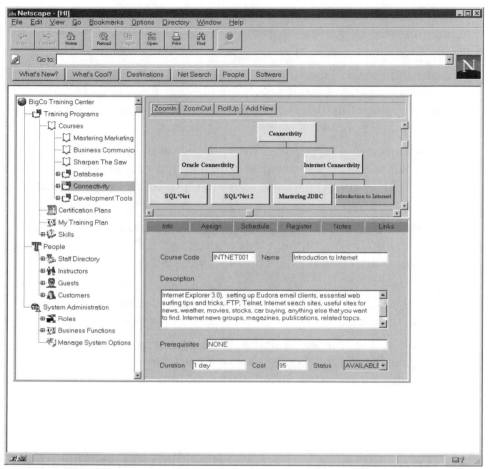

FIGURE 10.12 A graphical list of courses.

example, how to develop and maintain a course catalog, support student registration, schedule instructors and classes at various locations. In addition, there is training content development and delivery through various media, student pre- and post-testing and performance assessment, and (re)certification and compliance tracking to meet federal and state standards for specific job functions. Several training organizations rely entirely on outside instructors and consultants to deliver their training courses. Managing outside interactions and relationships has also been recognized as being very time-consuming."

TeamScape's Learning Junction is designed to provide the user with an integrated, online environment for training management, delivery, and personalized training services for use by training departments and businesses. The system is built on a three-tier architecture and supports industry-standard databases like Oracle. There is an out-of-the-box support for all traditional client platforms, as well as upcoming Network Computers Online Kiosks, Webstations, and other client services. The architecture enables centralized software upgrades on a single server or a small set of server machines across the enterprise. The system provides ongoing management and maintenance of the application, without requiring the assistance of the corporate IS organization.

This product has an online course information repository which displays a graphical list of courses (Figure 10.12), certification plans, and

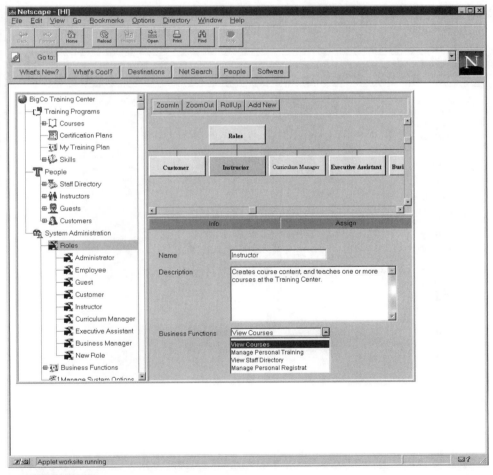

FIGURE 10.13 View Roles.

needed skills. Students can register online and develop a personalized training plan, and keep track of their skills assessment. The system enables the user to maintain course- and class-related information like class notes, handouts, tests, and quizzes. Some training administration functions include support for a range of business functions that are attached to one or more roles. These functions include: manage courses, view staff directory, manage personal profile, manage personal training plan, manage reports, and others. There is a function to maintain an instructor and skills repository. This provides annotation and tracking capabilities for maintaining public and private notes about courses and people. (See Figures 10.13, 10.14, and 10.15.)

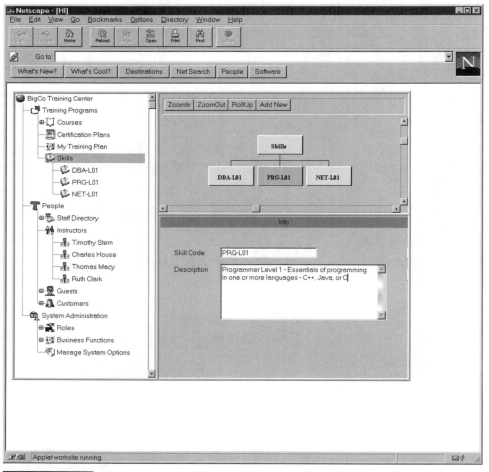

FIGURE 10.14 View Skills.

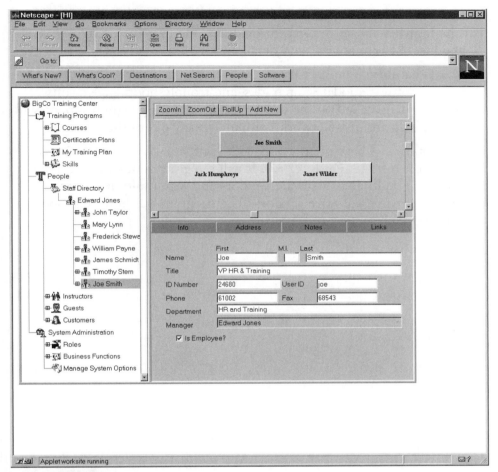

FIGURE 10.15 View Staff Directory.

The architecture of the Learning Junction has the following system benefits:

Extensible: Comprehensive customization of end-user screens, labels, and visual icons to effectively represent the specific organization. Provision for a complete range of system defaults that can be overridden at the level of one or more "objects."

Object oriented: Completely object oriented. Supports over 30 object types, including courses, course groups, instructors, customers, certification plans, locations, addresses, HTML links, and so on.

Interface: Java-based applets for administrators, managers, end-users. The Java-based user interface provides a Windows-style explorer view, graphical hierarchy view, and detail views.

Manageability: The Java-based three-tier architecture allows for centralized software updates, upgrades, and troubleshooting. No software needs to be installed on the client platforms. This program supports all client platforms; it is network-computer-ready out of the box.

Capabilities: This system works with Netscape Navigator 3.01 and Microsoft Internet Explorer 3.0. It will integrate courseware and content from multiple courseware vendors and with multiple test and student assessment software vendors. The program was built to support multiple Web servers and databases.

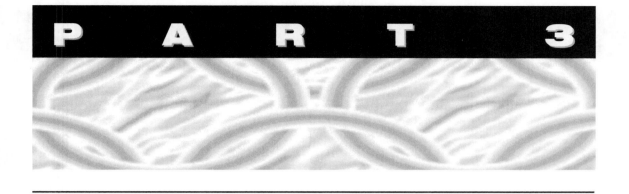

PART 3

CREATING

WEB-BASED

TRAINING

CHAPTER ELEVEN

LEVEL 1 COURSES: TEXT AND GRAPHICS

Text and graphics courses make use of the basic capabilities of the World Wide Web. These courses tend to be primarily informational and are an easy starting point for new WBT developers. Similar to instructor-led classes that rely on lectures, these courses do not use instructional design elements. While not exemplary in terms of the potential of Web-based training, the reality is that this type makes up the bulk of the courses now available. Presented in this chapter are examples of courses that represent a cross section of text and graphics courses delivered over the Internet.

The term "text and graphics," as you will see by the range of examples presented here, covers a fairly broad territory. E-mail courses that are merely a sharing of text-based information fall on the most simplistic end of the spectrum, while related text and images with an instructional bent delineates to the far, or more complicated, end.

Simplicity is not necessarily a recipe for lack of value, however. As you will see, e-mail courses can be very flexible in that the instructor can easily control the rate at which the training is digested. As with Clearly Internet's e-mail course described later in the chapter, instructors can also tailor the course as they go, giving customized information to each student. When the primary goal of the course is to merely disseminate information with all activity taking place offline, e-mail courses are easy to use and inexpensive to develop and deliver.

Cost issues might come into play for other text and graphics courses as well. What drives up programming costs are the multimedia and interactive aspects of online courseware. Multimedia also makes the material considerably more engaging and enhances the learning benefit, but if keeping costs down is of paramount importance, easily designed and programmed text and graphics courses may be a short-term answer for your organization.

A step up from e-mail-delivered courses is the online discussion forum or bulletin board. This delivery method allows instructors and students to interact and keeps all messages viewable to anyone involved with the course. In this way, students can scroll back through the instructor's messages from the previous lesson, or the instructor can look back to see how the students' understanding of the subject has improved over the course of the program. Students can read each other's messages and gain insight. The discussion forum is one definition of the "online classroom."

Used alone, the online forum can help facilitate discussion, but can't provide the depth of information of a full online course. In later chapters you will see how the discussion forum is incorporated into training programs as a feedback tool, supplemented by other materials, either paper-based or online.

Programs that use the Web in conjunction with other delivery methods can also fall into the text and graphics category. Additional resources like workbooks, standup seminars, or other traditionally delivered training can support and be supported by the online text and graphics course. One of the examples described below depicts a situation where course participants are required to access the online training prior to attending an instructor-led seminar. In this way, the instructor can ensure that all attendees have a similar level of understanding and can save time during the standup portion of the course.

How to Determine if Text and Graphics Is the Way to Go

Before deciding on text and graphics as a good format for your Web-based training program, think about the options this format can offer. Examine the purpose of the training program you'd like to put online and decide if this relatively limited functionality can meet all of your needs. Are you going to use the program in conjunction with other traditionally delivered training? Is an online discussion forum a suitable way for students and instructors to interact? Do you need the day-to-day flexibility an e-mail course can offer? Are development and programming funds limited? Overall, think about the range of functions you need to deliver to your online students and decide if those needs can be met by the simple presentation of text and images. If online assessment is not necessary, if multimedia doesn't suit the material, if costs are limited, or, as one of our case studies shows, if you just want to get your feet wet in the prospect of more involved training down the road, then a basic text and graphics course might be the way to go.

A Caveat

The quality of training is often defined by the amount of interactivity. An experienced instructional designer can generate low-cost, easy-to-implement activities or exercises to engage the student. Creativity and imagination don't have to be expensive. If you are up to it, and the instructional need requires it, set your target a little higher. Learn from the examples in this chapter and then add interactivity, as in the next chapter.

Costs Involved

The costs associated with an e-mail course can be relatively minor. Essentially, if the infrastructure for sending and receiving e-mail is already in place, the only costs are for content development (and content may already exist in the form of instructor-led or paper-based training) and instructor preparation and response time.

With full online courses, programming costs begin to come into play, as well as further development time for instructional design. These courses are cheaper to build than a multimedia course because fewer tools are needed (i.e., no assessment tools, audio players, Shockwave, etc.). User computers need to be equipped with a Web browser and your training audience needs to know how to use the browser interface. Assuming this architecture is already in place, content development and programming along with minor site maintenance will be the primary costs. If no assessment or interactivity is involved, online courses can be very inexpensive, to the point, one developer found, of being able to produce an online course with no budget whatsoever (see the Bureau of National Affairs case study). Similar considerations need to be made for hybrid courses of any nature, factoring in the type of online course to supplement the traditional training and the costs of developing and delivering that traditional instruction.

The online forum or discussion group requires a larger time investment in its finished phase from the class instructor, but again, is inexpensive to establish if the company's online infrastructure is already available. Content development costs may be incurred, but actual hardware and software expenses are minimal. See Chapter 7 for a complete breakdown of online development costs.

Staff Involved

Clearly Internet's e-mail course described later in the chapter was developed by a staff of one, who then contracted with outside instructors to develop the training content. For most online courses, however, a programmer, artist, writer/editor, instructional designer, and project editor can be used. In less complex courses, one person fills more than one position. The instructional designer may also write and edit the content, while the programmer serves both as project manager and artist. After surveying many development teams involved in Web-based training, we found that no two look exactly alike. From a staff of 30 to a single person performing all functions of development, it is difficult to generalize the staffing needs required by a Web-based training project. For a complete breakdown of the elements and staff involved in development, see Chapter 6.

Creating a Text and Graphics Web-Based Training Course

MediaPro, Inc. provides instructional design and development services to corporate clients. The Seattle-based company has worked with traditional CBT projects and is currently involved in a large intranet-based training project for a Fortune 500 company. This case study focuses on the development plan for this project and the tools and procedures to accomplish this plan efficiently.

Planning

From the inception of the project, the most important thing the client emphasized to MediaPro was that the project was conceived as a response to a business need and not merely as an experiment in new training delivery methods. The use of the company intranet to deliver training to workers' desktops was a way to avoid extensive classroom training and its consequent demands on workers' time. The company has important production schedules to keep but at the same time, training must take place, which impacts the production methods as they change in response to the market.

Other considerations for the client company were the large and widely distributed target audience for the training and the need for frequent updating of the training content. When all of these considerations were weighed, the company management decided that they were ready to commit to an intranet-based training solution. Further analysis of the business needs of the company drove the requirements for the performance and functionality of the intranet-based training package and were the primary consideration in shaping the training development team and the methods that they used to build the courseware. Here are some examples of the business needs and the requirements they generated:

- The target audience has access to computers on the desktop but is not required to have experience using Web browsers. Also, the company intranet is heavily trafficked and the delivery of multimedia elements is discouraged. For these reasons, it was determined that the training should have text and graphic content and should conform as closely as possible to Internet standards. Any solution requiring that users configure their browser with a new plug-in was also unacceptable. This means that solutions such as Shockwave were not useful, because of the bandwidth needed to deliver useful multimedia and the need for a plug-in.

- The training materials are extensive and need to be delivered over an extended period of time. This indicated the need for an in-house team with a production line approach to developing the courseware. This production line approach also indicates the need for a team consisting of specialists such as instructional designers, graphic artists, and programmers.

- Students needed to receive credit for completing courses in the company's training database. This required that students log in to the training with a unique password and that their completion status was monitored. Whenever they complete a course, the data was passed from the intranet-based training system to the company's training database.

Development

After the initial team members were assembled, two priorities dominated the agenda. One priority was the creation of a prototype to demonstrate what the intranet-based training materials would look like. This prototype was used to gain approval and buy-in from relevant people within the company, mainly upper management and IS. The other priority was to establish and document a plan for the development process for the team to follow when building the courses.

The detailed development process plan was useful for a number of reasons:

1. A variety of team members participated in the development of every unit; members needed to understand their role and the timing of their deliverables.

2. The target audience needed the training content as quickly as possible. The planning stage helped eliminate any potential bottlenecks from the development process. This in turn helped ensure that the most current content was delivered and that development hours were kept as low as possible.

3. While most team members had experience in CBT development, Web development was a new experience for some. A model process alleviated the uncertainty about how to proceed in this unfamiliar endeavor.

4. What proved very important was how the development process plan facilitated project management and deliverable scheduling. Gantt charts with milestones and deliverable dates were constructed using the tasks and phases of the process plan. This allowed for accurate project management despite the unfamiliarity of many aspects of the development process.

The development process was initially mapped in a flowchart format, but as the amount of detail associated with each task increased, a spreadsheet was eventually used to document the process. Task details included responsible team members, deliverables, reference materials, and outstanding issues. One area that needed particular attention was the graphic request and tracking process. The communication lines between the instructional designers and the graphic artists were mapped out in detail to avoid any confusion and to bring new personnel up to speed quickly. The plan indicated such things as when graphic request forms were due, where to deposit graphic files when ready for review, and how revision information was communicated.

A detailed plan was also very important for the distributed draft reviews that occur during course development. These reviews provide formative evaluation of course design and content. Two different reviews of draft materials take place for each course, with the initial review using paper-based storyboards of the course and the final review taking place with an intranet-based version. The development process documented the plan for implementing the reviews, including information about the review audience, team roles for the review, and feedback collection.

Creation

The main challenge for the instructional designers (IDs) was the design and development of the training content for this project. This was not a case of converting existing content such as classroom training into Web pages. The business processes that constituted the training content were either new or still under development. Instructional designers derived content mainly from interviews with subject matter experts. This content was gathered and designed right from the start to be delivered on the Web. The instructional designers had the dual challenge of gathering the content quickly and efficiently as well as designing the page sequences, exercises, and tests so that the content was effectively delivered via the Web.

One of the primary constraints of the project was that the instructional designers who were building the course materials were not experienced in HTML programming. The company did not wish to hire a cadre of HTML programmers to provide this service, so different options were examined. One possible solution was the use of Microsoft FrontPage97, a WYSIWYG HTML editor. Ideally this tool would provide authoring capabilities that would allow the instructional designers with little HTML experience to create HTML pages. In reality, even the most sophisticated of existing HTML editors cannot insulate authors from the need to deal with the conventions of HTML layout and file handling. This became a problematic issue on the project because FrontPage97 and other WYSIWYG editors are touted as products that allow easy authoring. In addition, HTML itself has a reputation as an "easy" language to learn. "After all," the logic goes, "it is a markup language, not a programming language." From this perspective, it seemed reasonable that the instructional designers could author the HTML themselves. However, the issue proved increasingly complex as the project requirements and the development process came into sharper focus.

Another element of the project that facilitated the HTML development was the creation of template pages. During the creation of the prototype course, the instructional designers met often to design a standard structure for courses and standard navigation and layout for pages within courses. These designs were encapsulated in templates. These templates were pre-built in HTML to provide instructional designers with a starting point for every page they needed to build. A catalog of the templates was created to provide quick reference to the various pages available for course construction. These templates were valuable in standardizing the design of courses and streamlined the creation of course HTML pages.

While no particular task involved in creating HTML pages is extremely difficult, it is the cumulative effect of many different programming-oriented tasks that combine to make HTML development much like other more involved programming endeavors. On this project, as the time deadlines and the myriad other responsibilities of the instructional designers became evident, the bottleneck potential of having the IDs do the HTML programming was more obvious. The cognitive overhead of all the minor tasks associated with HTML development combine to make it a very involved endeavor for team members who have to juggle other responsibilities. In particular, the file management and linking add complexity to HTML development. Every page and every graphic on each page is a separate file. These directories and files must be logically ordered so that the Web server can use them effectively. HTML developers must have an understanding of how the Web server uses these files and must be careful to use the directories as established on the Web server. Managing links between pages can also be a tedious process that is less related to content and more of a programming task. While instructional designers could be expected to eventually become adept at these tasks, on this project the priority for them was to develop content. Time spent on HTML tasks took away from this important activity.

Although the addition of HTML programmers to the team was suggested, this was not an acceptable alternative to the company because of headcount considerations. The successful compromise was reached by examining where the challenges occurred in the process. The concern was that HTML was not an easy and flexible environment for the course development in the early stages. Laying out ideas on pages was just the starting point because the content needed extensive work as the course took shape. Manipulating all of the necessary HTML and graphics files, adjusting links, and working within the constraints of HTML layout conventions was a burden when the task was just to flesh out the content on the pages. There was a need for a storyboarding tool that would let instructional designers assemble a course in a less constrained manner before it went into HTML.

Implementation

Microsoft PowerPoint provided instructional designers with a familiar and simple tool for storyboarding the pages of a course. The entire course was contained in one file and graphics were sketched or described in the correct location before the graphic artists delivered the final files. In addition, the initial draft review was paper-based to avoid the labor of preparing the materials for intranet-based delivery when content could change significantly after the review. PowerPoint provided a useful environment to mock up the course content and distribute a paper version for the first draft review. The only remaining problem was the effort involved in converting the materials from PowerPoint files to HTML. It was determined that PowerPoint text content could be easily cut and pasted into FrontPage97. By setting up a set of PowerPoint templates which matched the HTML templates, the instructional designers had a powerful set of tools. They could develop the materials for the first draft review with the flexibility and ease of PowerPoint. After the materials were approved, the conversion to HTML was a matter of creating an HTML file in FrontPage97 for every page in the PowerPoint file and then cutting and pasting content from PowerPoint into FrontPage97. Graphics could be sketched or described in the PowerPoint file, and then when the finished graphics files were available from the graphic artists they could be placed into the correct HTML page using FrontPage97. This system allowed the flexibility required at the design phase and facilitated the creation of HTML-based courseware by non-HTML programmers.

The preliminary design and documentation of the development process was essential to the success of this project. Although the intranet delivery of training met the business needs of the company, this was still an unfamiliar approach that was greeted with resistance in some quarters. The ability to deliver materials quickly and on schedule was necessary as a proof of concept for Web-based training in the company. This would not have been possible without basing the schedule on a well-designed development process. Lacking prior management experience on this type of project, because of the newness of the technology, trial and error would have been the only way to proceed. By the time an efficient development process was in place it would have been too late for the survival of the project. By allocating the up-front time to designing the development process and by drawing on the experience of consultants with backgrounds in CBT and Web development, the company was able to successfully achieve their objectives.

The issues surrounding the need for the instructional designers to program HTML were very illuminating. Depending on the circumstances of a particular project, there are situations when it would make sense for IDs to program HTML. Just as some CBT projects utilize instructional designers programming with tools such as Authorware, some Web-based training projects could make sensible use of IDs who can program HTML. However, it is crucial to examine the project priorities. For example, if an Authorware-based CBT project requires cutting-edge technical features or if there is extensive and involved programming needed, then it makes sense to have a skilled Authorware programmer on hand who is dedicated to the programming tasks. In the same way, any training program which uses Internet technology should examine the technical and workload requirements to determine whether dedicated HTML programmers are necessary.

Creating an E-Mail Course

The most elementary level of usage for providing training over the Internet is a simple question and response format such as that used in an e-mail course from Clearly Internet (Figure 11.1). The title of the program is "Using the Internet as a Business Tool." Subtopics of the program include Introduction to the Internet, Accessing the Net, Communication with the Net, Using the Internet for Research, and Using the Internet for Marketing.

The e-mail course is self-paced, including five lessons each with questions at the end. Each lesson/set of questions takes about 30 minutes to complete. An assessment of current use and recommendations for future use is delivered to the participant within a week of completion. No graphics or multimedia elements are included since the course is taught via e-mail, but URLs to relevant Web sites are included throughout the course.

Participants answer questions related to the topic of each lesson, with respect to their own use of the Internet and their business in general. After completing the course, they receive a personalized plan, based on their answers, which includes an assessment of their current Internet use and recommendations for future use.

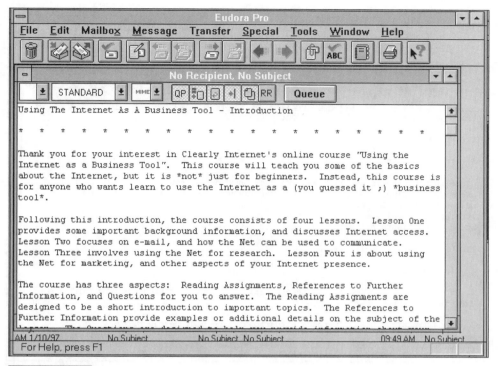

Using The Internet As A Business Tool - Introduction

* * * * * * * * * * * * * * * * * * *

Thank you for your interest in Clearly Internet's online course "Using the
Internet as a Business Tool". This course will teach you some of the basics
about the Internet, but it is *not* just for beginners. Instead, this course is
for anyone who wants learn to use the Internet as a (you guessed it ;) *business
tool*.

Following this introduction, the course consists of four lessons. Lesson One
provides some important background information, and discusses Internet access.
Lesson Two focuses on e-mail, and how the Net can be used to communicate.
Lesson Three involves using the Net for research. Lesson Four is about using
the Net for marketing, and other aspects of your Internet presence.

The course has three aspects: Reading Assignments, References to Further
Information, and Questions for you to answer. The Reading Assignments are
designed to be a short introduction to important topics. The References to
Further Information provide examples or additional details on the subject of the

FIGURE 11.1 Clearly Internet's online course.

Copyright 1996, 1997 Clearly Internet and Ira M. Pasternack

In the first lesson, the user signs up for the course, and answers the first
round of questions, which is basically a questionnaire about his or her business. The first actual learning lesson is an introduction to the Internet and
covers Internet access. The questions at the end are used to make sure users
understand the basics, and find out what they use for access. Lessons on
communication, research, and marketing explain how the Internet is used
for each topic, include URLs to relevant Web sites, and ask questions about
the participant's use of the Internet with regard to the topic of the lesson.

Creator Ira Pasternack says the program is useful for businesses because
it is e-mail based, and therefore simple and efficient to use. "By using e-mail for this course, they gain experience using e-mail in new ways—in
addition to the material they learn in the course itself," Pasternack says.
(Figure 11.2.)

Pasternack goes on to say, "This course solicits feedback from the participant throughout. It gives them a way to ask a question and get a quick
answer if they really need it, but most of the time, I only have to get

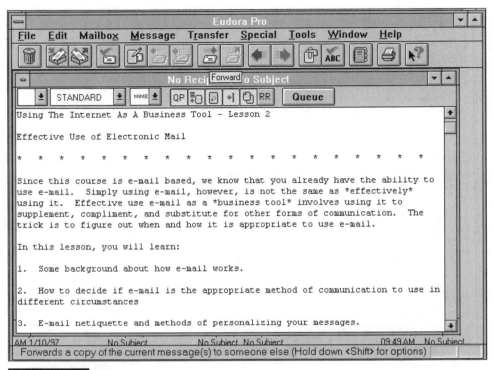

FIGURE 11.2 Effective use of electronic mail.

Copyright 1996, 1997 Clearly Internet and Ira M. Pasternack

involved when they are all done, in order to read their answers and write their plan."

This process and design is fairly simplistic by today's standards, but may represent a viable business option for those who only need the Internet as a delivery mechanism, not as a platform for hosting the training in full. It does represent one end of the spectrum of online technology for course delivery.

Planning a Discussion Forum and E-Mail Course

When planning an e-mail course in conjunction with a discussion forum, it is important to take your audience into consideration. The type of course you create should be one with the potential for most use. It should be tailored to the needs of the audience.

NIIT, Ltd., whose transnational corporation headquarters is located in New Delhi, India, specializes in this. Their employees are scattered among 100 offices in 50 different locations. Abraham Tharakan, the head of Research and Development in the Instructional Research and Development business group at NIIT realized this challenge when setting up an e-mail-based discussion list.

"It was noticed that in our company, geographically distributed as its employees were, there existed discrete pockets of knowledge and experience on the one hand, and enormous need for these qualities on the other. The first initiative taken by the President's Club group at NIIT was to set up an e-mail-based discussion list connecting all employees together across the globe so that they could share their knowledge and experience, help one another, foster cross-functional collaboration, and discuss common problems," Tharakan relates.

NIIT found that training all their employees was a drain on their resources. Internal training was considered especially important considering the high number of personal training days (11.3 training days per person in 1996) allotted to each employee.

The idea behind distance education for internal training at NIIT was to foster an atmosphere conducive to learning, and to enable the employee to learn at his or her own pace, and at his or her workplace. Since most of NIIT's 3000 employees at present do not have easy access to the Internet, it was decided to use e-mail while combining the capabilities of the Web.

Some of the perceived advantages were:

- Self-paced learning, enabling the participant to learn at his or her own time and pace

- Lower cost implementation since employees already had access to e-mail

- No interruption of branch activities as employees are not called away for training

- Ease of creating and maintaining training material

NIIT's training is done by creating material on Web pages which are then zipped and sent as attachments via e-mail. Animated GIFs are used to demonstrate onscreen procedures. Participants then use a browser to go through the course.

The current plan is to set up a Web server at each location. Training material, when received, will be transferred to the server and participants will connect to their local server to go through the program. This way, records can be kept of the names of participants who have gone through and successfully completed the course, how much time they took to complete it, and so on. Also, interactive exercises and tests can then be included and performance tracked. Once a month, data from all offices will be centrally collated.

This will combine all the advantages of the Web with the ease of use and vast reach of e-mail. The program is titled VAST, which stands for the initials of the members of the project team, and also to denote the vast reach of the project. It can be run on e-mail or an intranet and the external training program is on the Internet at www.niitnetvarsity.com. Currently, stage 1 of the program, forum and distance training, is completed, and stage 2, Web servers and tracking at unique locations, is in the design process. The program is an ongoing learning process for the participants.

"Most people love to share their knowledge and experience, and by giving people the means to communicate, true synergy happens, horizons get broadened, and people can pick up ideas from other people in different disciplines," Tharakan says. When users and managers were asked their opinion on the program, the users were generally thrilled by the fact that they now had a "one-stop" location to go to for answers to their problems. There was a problem earlier across the company of teams trying to locate subject matter experts in a particular area. With the e-mail forum, they now can use a whole range of such people across the globe. Finding people with the requisite knowledge became a lot easier—in one case, a team found a person with the requisite skills via the forum in the adjacent room.

Tharakan says NIIT managers were happy about the distance training part of the project as they could keep their people on site and still have them trained. Also the problem-solving capabilities of the e-mail forum were seen as a great boon to productivity (and helped cut long-distance phone bills).

The program is on a PC development platform and requires Windows 3.X/95/NT, Netscape Navigator, or Internet Explorer version 3.0 or any other Web browser that supports frames and Java. This project, along with other President's Club projects, was created by the six-member team in their spare time.

Creating an Online Course: A Case Study

ISIM University, based in Denver, Colorado, has taken the traditional continuing and corporate educational environment to an online level. ISIM is an accredited provider of distance education and training, with numerous courses available for credit and/or general education. ISIM University also offers graduate degrees in Business Administration and Information Management. The faculty consists of business executives, consultants, university professors, and other specialists, with most courses geared toward the professional adult.

ISIM offers their courses in online interactive formats as well as traditional print-based, self-guided study. The online courses are taught over the Web on ISIMnet, an electronic network for computer conferencing. Students participate in discussion forums, which they can download and save for future reference.

The ISIM Executive Education program consists of courses such as Finance and Strategic Management. The Finance course is an introduction to corporate financial management and investments, with major topics including capital budgeting and analyzing financial decisions. The Strategic Management course includes topics like strategic thinking, environmental change, and industry events. Both courses last eight weeks and recently cost $1,350.

ISIM has also partnered with other corporations to develop and administer custom training programs. OmniTech, a consulting firm, has partnered with ISIM to create new business and management courses. ISIM also worked with Xerox and the Department of Defense to create online training courses. The corporate Web site for ISIM is www.isim.com.

Creating a Discussion Forum/Board: A Case Study

The Altos Education Network provides business education and training for managers, professionals, and entrepreneurs over the Web. Students are assigned to groups when a class is formed so there is a greater sense of community. Through use of a class discussion board, questions and assignments can be posted by faculty and students at any time, encouraging one-on-one interaction with an instructor or group learning with other students (Figure 11.3). (See Appendix E and the CD-ROM for sample code.)

The class content covers the basics of starting a business and takes place over a four-week period of study (Figure 11.4). The course includes an ongoing threaded discussion on the topic.

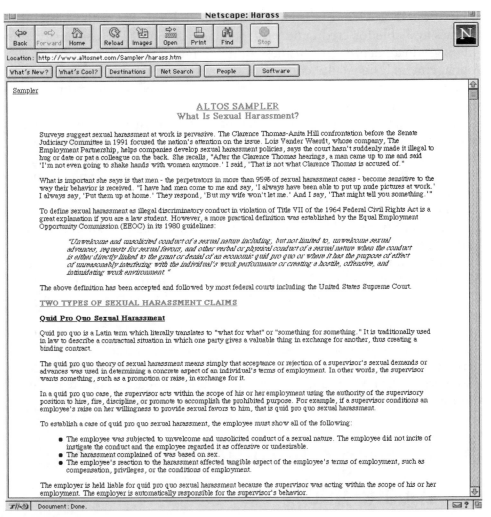

FIGURE 11.3 A sample page from the module entitled "Avoiding Sexual Harassment Claims." The material defines sexual harassment and provides case study examples.

Figure 11.5 shows a course catalog which includes the start date, instructor name, course length, cost, and outline, as well as student comments on each class.

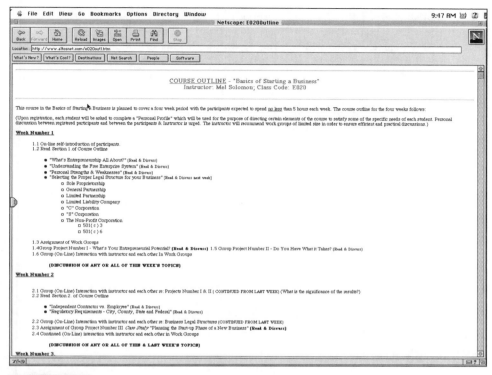

```
 🍎  File  Edit  View  Go  Bookmarks  Options  Directory  Window                    9:47 AM  🔳  ②
                                    Netscape: E0200utline
 ⇦⇨      ⇔⇨     🏠      🔄      🖼     📑      🖨     🔍      ⊗
 Back   Forward  Home   Reload  Images  Open    Print   Find    Stop
 Location:│http://www.altosnet.com/e020out1.htm                                                    │
 What's New?  What's Cool?  Destinations   Net Search   People    Software

            COURSE OUTLINE - "Basics of Starting a Business"
               Instructor: Mel Solomon; Class Code: E020

 This course in the Basics of Starting a Business is planned to cover a four week period with the participants expected to spend no less than 5 hours each week. The course outline for the four weeks follows:

 (Upon registration, each student will be asked to complete a "Personal Profile" which will be used for the purpose of directing certain elements of the course to satisfy some of the specific needs of each student. Personal
 discussion between registered participants and between the participants & Instructor is urged. The instructor will recommend work groups of limited size in order to ensure efficient and practical discussions.)

 Week Number 1

      1.1 On-line self-introduction of participants.
      1.2 Read Section 1 of Course Outline

        ● "What's Entrepreneurship All About?" (Read & Discuss)
        ● "Understanding the Free Enterprise System" (Read & Discuss)
        ● "Personal Strengths & Weaknesses" (Read & Discuss)
        ● "Selecting the Proper Legal Structure for your Business" [Read & Discuss next week]
               o Sole Proprietorship
               o General Partnership
               o Limited Liability Company
               o "C" Corporation
               o "S" Corporation
               o The Non-Profit Corporation
                    □ 501( c ) 3
                    □ 501( c ) 6

      1.3 Assignment of Work Groups
      1.4 Group Project Number I - What's Your Entrepreneurial Potential? (Read & Discuss)  1.5 Group Project Number II - Do You Have What it Takes? (Read & Discuss)
      1.6 Group (On-Line) Interaction with instructor and each other In Work Groups

           (DISCUSSION ON ANY OR ALL OF THIS WEEK'S TOPICS)

 Week Number 2

      2.1 Group (On-Line) Interaction with instructor and each other re: Projects Number I & II ( CONTINUED FROM LAST WEEK) (What is the significance of the results?)
      2.2 Read Section 2. of Course Outline

        ● "Independent Contractor vs. Employee" (Read & Discuss)
        ● "Regulatory Requirements - City, County, State and Federal" (Read & Discuss)

      2.2 Group (On-Line) Interaction with instructor and each other re: Business Legal Structures (CONTINUED FROM LAST WEEK)
      2.3 Assignment of Group Project Number III  Case Study "Planning the Start-up Phase of a New Business" (Read & Discuss)
      2.4 Continued (On-Line) interaction with instructor and each other in Work Groups

           (DISCUSSION ON ANY OR ALL OF THIS & LAST WEEK'S TOPICS)

 Week Number 3.
```

FIGURE 11.4 Course outline for basics of starting a business.

Text and Graphics with Live Training: A Case Study

Delivering courses over the Web opens up many alternatives for the design of courses. Some trainers prefer to combine WBT with the more traditional classroom instruction. New Media Strategies (NMS) of Boulder, Colorado, is in the process of developing a training program which combines elements of Internet training with instructor-led seminars. They believe many travel agencies and vendors are making significant investments in the Internet and the World Wide Web but that the productive and profitable use of the Internet by the travel industry depends upon developing Internet skills and research expertise among travel professionals.

FIGURE 11.5 A course catalog.

Planning

NMS is therefore developing a program for this group called Cyber Travel Specialist Training, designed to provide travel agents and agency owners with skills on using the Internet in their work. The curriculum has three components:

Hands-on workshops—Half-day training workshops will be held in major cities at CompUSA training facilities with high bandwidth T-1 Internet access.

Web-based training—The CTS Web-based training course will provide students with a self-paced program on Internet usage at http://www.newmediastrategies.com.

Context seminar—The New Millennium Travel Agency.

To promote the series and the importance of gaining knowledge of the Internet and the Web, a series of presentations around the country will be conducted to provide an overview of the position of travel professionals in the new information age. The hands-on training facilities used for the live portion of the program will be provided by CompUSA, a computer retailer with 116 locations in the United States. Each store has three to four classrooms, each equipped with 12 to 14 IBM-compatible PC workstations. Currently, 26 of these locations have classroom settings with T1 high-bandwidth Internet access.

Development/Creation

The Web-based training courseware will be authored using Stanford Training Systems' IBTauthor. This program will handle the qualification, registration, lesson administration, and testing aspects of the program. The company plans to add to their curriculum by having travel industry experts author courses on additional aspects of Internet-related programs. Authors will be paid a fee plus royalty and will be under contract to update their courses regularly to secure royalty income.

Implementation/Follow-up

Participants in the program will be linked with an Internet-based follow-up program. It is designed to build a sense of community among alumni of the program. As additional lessons on new Internet features are developed, participants will be notified through e-mail of their availability. Discussion groups based on various specialties are planned so that participants can learn from each other on using the Internet and the Web.

The hands-on sessions are designed to include 14 participants per session at a price of $299 per trainee. The initial hands-on, half-day workshop, and the follow-up self-directed training, will require about 16 hours of training for the average agent.

SMALL-CHUNK TRAINING AT NATIONSBANK

Jeffrey Adamson, Assistant Vice President, Nations Bank

The powerful and flashy tools that modern technology offers often have a seductive appeal to professionals in the area of multimedia training. These tools can add value and functionality to a training project. The high costs which are often associated with cutting edge technology, however, must be balanced against the benefit they provide. Audio, video, 3-D Graphics, and

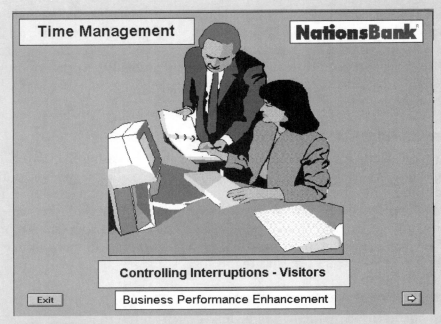

> **Time Management**
>
> **NationsBank**
>
> **Controlling Interruptions - Visitors**
>
> Exit   **Business Performance Enhancement**

FIGURE 11.6 Opening screen for a module on controlling interruptions caused by visitors. This module is part of a series on time management.

other media may require expensive hardware and software in addition to steep learning curves for developers.

There are other ways to get high-impact that do not require high costs. At NationsBank, we have recently completed a pilot program of a technology that fits this description. We refer to this concept as Electronic Distributive Learning (EDL). Basically, EDL modules are small, computer-based training modules which are distributed and brought to the learner's desktop as files attached to our current WAN-based e-mail. An average module takes only about ten minutes for the user to complete.

The idea was brought to us by Brian O'Brien, now President of Myriad Performance Services in Columbia, Maryland. Working with Brian, we developed templates for rapid development, worked out the technical details, and piloted an assortment of modules. Using a standard template programmed using Macromedia Authorware, a module can be developed and distributed in less than a day by a team of two or three.

This method of delivering training is not meant to replace our current CD-ROM–based training or any other training method. Rather, it adds one more tool to our Performance Support toolbelt.

During the pilot program, we developed modules designed for four primary functions:

1. Delivering new training (e.g., time management, product knowledge, compliance, etc.)

2. Reinforcement of prior classroom training (e.g., sales skills, system training, etc.)

3. Sharing of best practices among job functions (e.g., success stories, sales tips, etc.)

4. Survey implementation (e.g., training evaluation, assessment, etc.)

There are several key characteristics of this delivery tool which we found appealing. It brings training to learners at their desktop. It also provides brief learning "chunks" that do not interfere noticeably with participants' workday. The training provides the ability to create tracking reports which confirm completion by individual, responses to interactions (multiple choice, matching, text entry, etc.), and any other information desired. Finally, it leverages existing technology (i.e., "low cost") with which participants are already familiar.

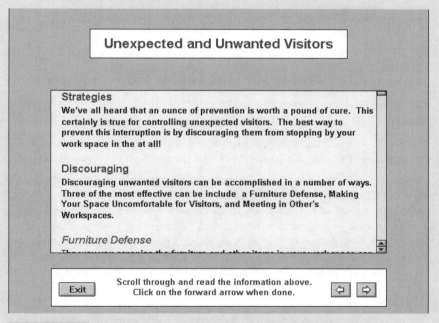

FIGURE 11.7 Use of scrollable text fields to present content helps to reduce file size.

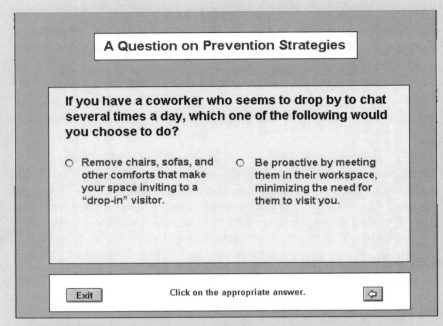

A Question on Prevention Strategies

If you have a coworker who seems to drop by to chat several times a day, which one of the following would you choose to do?

○ Remove chairs, sofas, and other comforts that make your space inviting to a "drop-in" visitor.

○ Be proactive by meeting them in their workspace, minimizing the need for them to visit you.

Exit   Click on the appropriate answer.   ⇦

FIGURE 11.8 The best practices module was very simply designed and contains only five screens.

There are, of course, some limitations inherent to EDL. Most notable are:

File size must be kept very small to avoid overburdening the e-mail system.

Small file size limits use of complicated graphics, sound, etc.

The modules must be developed to the lowest common system capabilities. For instance, PCs on some users' desks may be displaying only 16 colors.

Although these characteristics can be a bit frustrating if you currently design for CD-ROM–based training, the ease and speed of development and distribution can be refreshing. Like any other delivery method, training professionals must look at the problem first, then choose the method that is most appropriate. At NationsBank, we have found this to be another effective way to provide training and performance support to our audience at their desktops—bells and whistles not required! [See Figures 11.6 through 11.8.]

LEVEL 2 COURSES: INTERACTIVE TEXT AND GRAPHICS

What is interactivity? It is the most important component in an instructional program. It is the means by which people learn, by having their brain engaged and interacting with the content. It is what makes the difference between a communication program and a training program, between online documentation and training, between reference material and training.

Many training programs do not include interactivity. As the standards in online training become more established, corporations and end-users will demand effective instruction, not just information. Much of the appeal of the Web is the technology, and the earliest programs have included limited interactivity. If we as Web-based trainers focus solely on the technology without keeping our users and the need for interactivity in mind, the Web as an instructional tool will never reach its full potential.

If we continue to focus on the magic of the technology without including interactivity (real interactivity, not just navigation), we will not benefit from the full potential that Web-based training has to offer as an instructional tool.

 ## Interactive Text and Graphics Course Defined

According to one popular dictionary, the definition of *interact* is "to act on each other." Unfortunately, there is a thin line between interactions and navigation as we look at most Web-based training in the marketplace today. But true interactivity goes much deeper. Robert Zielinski of Allen Interactions, Inc., an experienced developer who has been working with interactive training for over a decade, says, "Much like a conversation between friends, there should not be a restricted path for the dialogue, but simply a series of responses as each one acts on the other."

The design of a training program that incorporates interactivity may be time-consuming and the development of such a system may be complex. So why should we strive to develop interactive multimedia applications? The answer isn't always obvious, but Zielinski offers these rationales:

Motivation—By providing a learning experience which incorporates curiosity, suspense, and surprise, motivation for the user to participate may be increased. Educators acknowledge that when a student is motivated to learn, retention of the material increases. This is due in part to the fact that the user is dedicating greater concentration to the material, and, in part, to the fact that the user is willing to participate in the experience repeatedly.

Individualized instruction—One way to create motivation on the part of an end-user, and thereby increase retention, is to create a system which presents information in an individualized manner according to the user's interests and existing body of knowledge. A system which looks into the eyes of its user to determine understanding reduces the possibility of presenting information which the user is not ready for or has already mastered.

Decreased instructional time—By focusing on elements of the subject matter which the user has demonstrated a greater need for and eliminating the elements which the user has already demonstrated sufficient mastery over, the overall time required to reach competency may be reduced. In fact, most studies show that the time required to master an objective using multimedia is roughly 50 percent less than the time needed to master that same objective when it is taught with traditional media.

Decreased required testing—When a system is designed to promote a dialogue, it must first determine that the user clearly understands foundational instructional objectives before it proceeds with the presentation of more complex objectives. Following this pattern, the multimedia system may then ensure that any prescribed level of mastery is achieved.

The challenge—The challenge now is not to find new multimedia technologies. While technological advances will provide greater opportunities to distribute or communicate information, they will more than likely have little impact on the instructional value of the content. The challenge for us is to design, or think, interactively. The challenge is to produce systems that, while actually having parameters in which the user may roam, provide a seemingly endless conversation in which the user is carefully and gradually brought to the point of understanding through experience.

While the text and graphics courses are the minimal entry point for doing any kind of online training, the next step is to add substantive interactivity for instructional effectiveness. This is to ensure that students respond to the content of the course, and do not just read their way through successive information screens. Because of the limitations of bandwidth, the media and interactive state-of-the-art level of Web-based training is still at the level of sophistication that CD-ROM programs were about seven years ago. While some aspects are less advanced, the ease of administration and capacity for fast, worldwide updates makes the technology worthwhile. In addition, the rapidly advancing technology of the World Wide Web ensures that bandwidth limitations will quickly be eliminated, paving the way for CD-ROM-like media and interactivity delivered over the Web.

The use of striking multimedia may be overkill, but use of good interactivity can enhance the learning experience provided by many training programs. Programs that ask learners to do nothing more than read and turn pages are less effective from an instructional standpoint. Interactivity allows the trainer to ensure learning is taking place, track a student's progress, provide remedial strategies, and, by tracking responses, gain understanding about the success of the program and the speed with which it can be completed successfully.

Situations in which interactivity is especially needed includes simulations like software training or manufacturing applications. Software training programs in which a student can read a screen, digest the information, and then apply the new knowledge to the actual activity are one example of this. For manufacturing processes, one use of interactivity was in a mechanical training course in which students were shown examples of components, read about their function, and then performed several simulations of placing each component in its correct locations on the overall product.

Interactive Web-based training programs are important and needed. As tools develop they are becoming easier to administer. The first step in choosing this level of training is looking at the needs of your program. Are you dealing with heavily technical material? Does your content require more than just a basic dissemination of information? Will the interactive factor improve the learning and performance of your training audience?

The costs associated with interactive WBT don't necessarily rule it out for organizations on a budget. Like any kind of Web production, budgets can range from nothing into the millions. Without the built-in expense of multimedia, interactive training programs can still come with reasonable sticker price. Programming may be more costly than for simple text and graphics courses, but the greater range of functionality and benefits of enduring learning may make up for that.

For advanced site administration like data-tracking mechanisms and assessment, more software, more administration, and more staff time will be required. As discussed in the chapter on costs of Web-based training, one Webmaster who can maintain the online service and one trainer who can update content may be the only postproduction staff required.

Creating Interactive Text and Graphics

Following are several examples of this middle ground of Web-based training programs. The programs profiled here represent an assortment of commercially, internally, and externally developed programs.

Bank of Montreal's CenterPoint Electronic Workbook

Although off-the-shelf courseware like that available from Outbound Train and InfoSource (see below) is a large sector of the Web-based training market, organizations with large in-house training development teams are also tackling online delivery of courseware. One of these groups is the Bank of Montreal. They've developed a training program called "The Electronic Workbook."

The Electronic Workbook provides technology training and performance support across Bank of Montreal's intranet. The focus of the training is the features and functions of CenterPoint, the Relationship Management desktop.

CenterPoint is an object-oriented desktop in place in all North American and United Kingdom locations of the Bank of Montreal's Corporate Banking division (a user base of over 850 people). CenterPoint acts as a platform for many other applications (MS Word, Netscape). This application has transformed the way Bank of Montreal's corporate bankers work together by providing access to external and internal data sources and systems and enabling cross-functional teaming and knowledge sharing.

In 1992, the education strategy for the initial rollouts of CenterPoint was classroom-driven. Given the large groups of people requiring training, this was an effective and economical solution. By 1996, the training needs had changed. CenterPoint was now a businesswide platform, and all new employees to Corporate Banking were using it to perform daily business functions. As classroom training was the only available option, each new user had to rely on the availability of a facilitator for training, and often waited for a workshop to be scheduled in their business location (facilitators must travel from Toronto). The facilitated workshops were no longer logistically and economically appropriate, and a new and distributed approach to CenterPoint education was required.

There are two relevant user profiles:

1. New users (requiring a complete tutorial)

2. Existing users (who require "refresher" learning, or have reference needs)

Kristi Kustura at the Institute for Learning at Bank of Montreal said the user profile dictated the approach the development would take. "Given our widely distributed client base and the infinite uses of the technology, we required a medium that would allow modular-based learning materials to address the needs of both new and existing users while providing access to this learning from any location," Kustura said. "Additionally, the application changes would periodically require that 'add ons' and modifications be made, so the training materials required a reusable and sustainable design."

The team looked at several methods of distribution before settling on the bank's intranet. They explored video, but decided the maintenance would be too difficult due to changes in CenterPoint and inconvenient since users would have to have simultaneous access to a VCR and television. They also explored CD-ROM, but similarly decided that maintenance was difficult, it was inconvenient to require users to have a CD-ROM drive in their computers, and expensive, time-consuming simulation would be required for users to practice tasks.

"We chose the Bank's intranet to develop and deliver our CenterPoint training since it enabled us to capitalize on the client's existing technology infrastructure, which supported a Bank-wide intranet," Kustura said. CenterPoint, a desktop application which acts as a platform for other applications (MS Word, Netscape), provides users with immediate access to the Bank's intranet at any time through an icon on their desktop.

With this structure in place, a training program could be developed to enable users to log onto the intranet for guided instruction and switch to their regular desktop application for actual practice and exploration (replacing the need for simulation of the application). "Essentially, we are using the intranet as a 'wizard' requiring users to use the Window's ALT + TAB capability to move back and forth between the real CenterPoint environment and the Netscape tutorial," Kustura said. "In this way, we have been able to utilize the intranet as an actual performance support tool, as opposed to just a static information browser."

With their user group in mind, the team chose the metaphor of an "electronic workbook" to bridge the gap between a format the users were comfortable with and the new technology of the intranet. "We felt the word 'workbook' would reinforce the performance support characteristics of the piece while not overselling the level of interactivity," said Kustura.

"Additionally, we were aware that the user environment is dynamic and fast-paced, and users often do not want to spend time reading a lot of information and would need to access the learning they require quickly and easily. Our users needed a multifunctional tool for learning: one that can provide users with immediate access to the procedures they require; and also one that can, if needed, provide the details required for them to understand new concepts behind these tasks."

Development Process

An initial prototype (one chapter of the Electronic Workbook) was constructed.

Design reviews were conducted by the design team, with instructional design input from colleagues at the Institute for Learning, and an interface design consultant.

The design was revised based on feedback and internal usability tests. Some of the revisions made included the following:

- Navigation was initially designed to reside within three frames (top, main, and side bars). In addition to taking up too much real estate on a page, this also managed to inundate the user with too many navigation options. A solution was to create one main navigation bar at the top of the page with the options deemed necessary for operation of the workbook. Focus was then applied to the organization of the content, to provide the user with navigation options within the main page information, as opposed to all over the screen.

- The original frames were replaced by a navigation bar at the top and bottom of the each page to increase performance and lessen the time for the frames to update with changes in their content (this decision was reversed at a later date).

- A pilot study was conducted in London, England to examine the effectiveness of the pilot Electronic Workbook on a group of new users. Fourteen CenterPoint users were asked to complete the third portion of a three-part learning workshop using the Electronic Workbook. Data for the pilot was gathered using direct observation as well as feedback obtained from users during focus group discussions. The qualitative results of the pilot indicated users enjoyed an overall comfort level with the intranet as a learning vehicle. Questions, concerns, and difficulties encountered and expressed by the pilot users served as a guide for instructional design changes within the workbook.

- Further usability tests were run (participant Internet experience ranged from naive to expert; all were naive CenterPoint users) . Users were required to navigate through the Electronic Workbook without interference, and all observations and feedback were recorded.

- The pilot design was revisited based on feedback from both user groups.

Workbook Structure

The Electronic Workbook is currently organized into five chapters, each divided into sections or stages. Each section contains three types of information: background information, procedures, and practice opportunities. These are described in Table 12.1.

Feedback screens also contain a number of optional "challenges" combining business scenarios with specific technical tasks (requiring higher order thinking skills for completion).

Additional Features

Optional "quicktip" icons which give a hint or tip and additional linked procedures when required include:

- Hotlinked table of contents—includes a button for an "expanded" version

- Overview and review screens at the beginning and end of each chapter which present the user with an advance organizer for their upcoming tutorial and also provide a summary of objectives and tasks learned

- A gauge on each feedback screen at the end of a practice exercise which tells users how far along they are in the tutorial

- To be added: a hotlinked index for reference at any time

- To be added: glossary of terms

TABLE 12.1 Types of Information in the Electronic Workbook

Section	Function
Background information	Outlines new concepts, CenterPoint technology definitions, and advanced organizers.
Procedures	Outlines all steps the user must perform to complete certain tasks in CenterPoint. The procedures are written in action steps with accompanying screen captures to give users visual guidance.
Practice opportunities*	Provides the user with a practice exercise and they can use the Window's ALT + TAB function on their computer to switch ("toggle") between their intranet workbook and their CenterPoint application to practice the procedures they were taught on the actual application.

* The practice opportunity screen contains an optional "feedback" button where users can receive an additional information screen which provides them with an overview of the correct procedure and the result users should have found when completing the task. This screen was left optional so that users who are using the workbook for a quick tutorial and reference do not have to go through an extra screen of information.

Navigation

A navigation bar at the top and bottom of each page contains five icons:

1. Link to CenterPoint Learning Web home page (the education site for the client)

2. Link to table of contents

3. Link to chapter overview (a quick glance at what is contained in the chapter you are currently in)

4. Back and Forward arrows (page forward or back)

5. Link to the index

It was determined during pilot and usability tests that users would prefer fixed navigation that does not scroll off the screen. Therefore, the navigation bar was placed in one borderless frame at the top of the screen.

Critical Development Tools

A multimedia vendor assisted with the interactive design of the content, and provided graphic design, production, and HTML coding services.

Graphics were done using Adobe Photoshop 3.0.

Intranet browser is Netscape 3.0.

A style guide was constructed and will be revised on an ongoing basis for any consultants or additional personnel who join the team. This will assist with client maintenance of the workbook when complete. The guide contains information such as font sizes, screen capture sizes, table values, graphics programs used for certain graphics, and original file formats.

Site maps were used to flowchart content and procedures, as well as user navigation options and tutorial guidance (points where segues and guided text were applied).

HTML editors—a number of different editors were used at different points during development (Hotmetal Pro and Microsoft Frontpage), so as not to be limited by the layout and coding capabilities of one particular editor. Due to the use of multiple frames in the current site, a range of tools was required for editing. The team plans to use Microsoft Frontpage as a site management tool to keep track of the pages and links.

Current Status

Bank of Montreal is in the process of redesigning the pilot chapter of the workbook based on findings of the pilot test. This will form a model for the rest of the workbook.

This is how they are proceeding:

Redesign of the pilot adding new features which were suggested in the pilot (e.g., a gauge during feedback screens to tell users how far along they are in the tutorial, and indexing capabilities).

Some modification to the graphic look has accommodated the user preference for more visuals (less text), and a "cleaner" look to the navigation bar (consultation with graphic designers had confirmed that consistency of fonts and typeface would improve the look, as well as give a more professional/conservative look to the page).

Assessing current content for areas where graphics may be used to replace or enhance text (overview pages and process flows), and recurring icons may be added as signposts for important information.

In response to client/user feedback the team is attempting to increase the level of interactivity in the program. They have redesigned the organization of the workbook pages, providing additional frames within a page so that users have brief and condensed information available, with options to click for more detail or graphics to explain procedures and concepts when needed.

Scripting of remaining content (four chapters), and interactive design (storyboarding).

Media production, and authoring of remaining chapters, index, and glossary. To meet the delivery deadline, the development team is operating on a staggered production schedule of interactive design, media production, and authoring.

Continuous usability testing and documentation as part of the production process.

Rollout to users.

Postimplementation evaluation of user response and overall effectiveness.

Postevaluation potential modifications to site.

Advanced modules added to the workbook.

A built-in evaluation and measurement feature for additional testing will be examined.

Largest Challenge

In August of 1996, when the initial design sessions were conducted, the development team did not have a large knowledge base of intranet training. Through consistent user practice, feedback, and documentation, they are creating the theories they need to go further. The process of design, development, user testing, and feedback have generated a greater understanding of the capabilities of the Web, the user requirements for navigation, graphics, and guidance (language) in order for learning to occur. "It has been crucial to our design process that all activity be documented in order for us to learn from all attempts and feedback," Kustura said.

Interactive Development Tool: The Navus Gadget

The Navus Gadget (by Galileo Systems, LLC) aids internal development teams like the one at Bank of Montreal with the development of online training. The tool uses the strengths of the Java programming language to deliver performance improvement to the desktop. Java provides both platform independence and a Webcentric orientation to training. Instructional content built for specific needs can then be reused in performance support systems. While the Navus Gadget itself is written in Java, content is written in a superset of HTML. This allows content to be created (or imported) by course designers using familiar HTML editors or word processing programs.

Navus provides students the ability to access courses locally as well as over the Internet and intranets. Courses can be organized in a Library/Course/Module hierarchy, building on students' familiarity with traditional training. Typically, several modules make up a course; courses can be collected into "libraries." Course developers can further segment Modules into a series of Lessons for ease of organization and design. A history list keeps track of the most recent frames the student has seen; this information is used for course bookmarking as well.

The software allows for the interspersing of evaluation elements (and remediation) anywhere in the course. Students can be engaged after each frame of information; or evaluation can be left to the end of a module. This feature provides for engaging the student appropriately at each step in an instructional sequence.

Navigation

The needs of the students and the course always define the interface; that interface is simply layered on top of the Navus Gadget. Once the interface

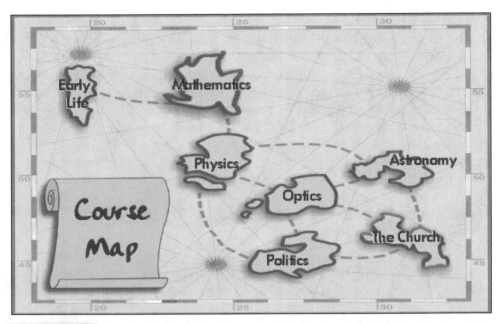

FIGURE 12.1 An example of a graphical map.

has been defined, templates help speed the creation of training or performance support. The interface pictured below (designed for a tutorial on the inventor Galileo) uses the compass rose in the lower-right corner to provide navigation for next frame, previous frame, more detail, and overview/table of contents (less detail).

Course maps can be either textual or graphical, though often both are used (Figure 12.1).

New dedicated windows can be called up as needed to display additional related information such as illustrations, a glossary, or hints.

As previously mentioned, evaluation questions can be interspersed as often as desired. The Navus Gadget provides for several kinds of cognitive-based questions: multiple choice, short answer, drag-and-drop, and matching. Performance-based questions can also be utilized to accurately assess that the student can perform the job-related tasks, not merely answer questions about them. The Java underpinnings of the Navus Gadget allow for interactive illustrations, demonstrations, and simulations.

Information Organization

Students access the content of a course through several different means, reflecting the various metacognitive organizational strategies that individual students may elect to use. Three main mechanisms define the information access paths: table of contents (TOC)/index, hyperlink, and search.

Typically, courses are organized with a table of contents and an index as in the traditional print model. Often a graphical course map is also available (this is an interface design decision). (See Figure 12.2.)

Extensive hyperlinking is also usually present, relating text-to-text, text-to-illustration (which may be graphical, animated, or interactive), text-to-audio, and (eventually) text-to-video. Usually these hyperlinks are implemented with both text highlighting and margin icons; often the illustration, audio, and video components are available through other screen icons as well. A globe icon opens a window into the whole world, indicating access to the index and search functions.

A topic/text search function provides access to whatever information the student requests. Searches can be restricted to courses or modules. Searching is designed as a two-step process. First the student identifies the search term; the search engine then replies with a list of likely topics and their context (hits). The student then selects from the topic list and jumps via hyperlink to the appropriate location in the course. Upon arrival, the searched-for term is highlighted.

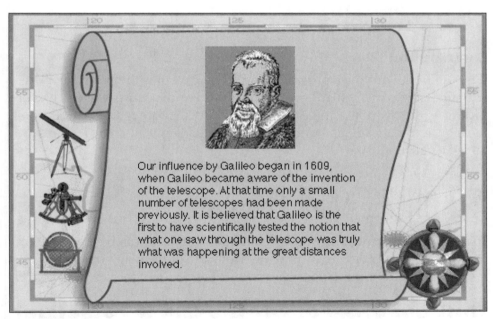

Our influence by Galileo began in 1609, when Galileo became aware of the invention of the telescope. At that time only a small number of telescopes had been made previously. It is believed that Galileo is the first to have scientifically tested the notion that what one saw through the telescope was truly what was happening at the great distances involved.

FIGURE 12.2 The telescope icon can be clicked on to provide a more detailed view by opening an index. Index and search functions can be combined.

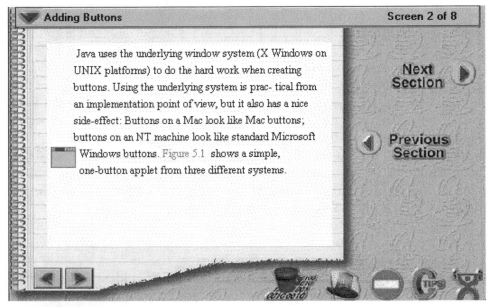

Java uses the underlying window system (X Windows on UNIX platforms) to do the hard work when creating buttons. Using the underlying system is prac- tical from an implementation point of view, but it also has a nice side-effect: Buttons on a Mac look like Mac buttons; buttons on an NT machine look like standard Microsoft Windows buttons. Figure 5.1 shows a simple, one-button applet from three different systems.

Next Section ▶

◀ Previous Section

FIGURE 12.3   The illustration shows the Navus Gadget LaTEX and graphical courses. While the interfaces look appreciably different, the underlying software is the same.

Distribution

The use of the new Java programming language holds the promise of distribution across many platforms while authoring the content once. The use of Java as the distribution mechanism can also alleviate maintenance problems by automatically upgrading the Navus Gadget when new features are added (Figure 12.3).

Off-the-Shelf Courses

If internal development isn't possible, maybe your needs can be met by selecting a commercially developed program from one of the many vendors servicing the market. For more information on choosing a vendor, see Appendix D.

Outbound Train: Off-the-Shelf Technical WBT

Technical training classes have been one of the more popular topics for computer-based training, and some training companies like Outbound

Train now offer Web versions of their courses. Outbound Train's Train Depot offers custom multimedia courseware for training requirements from Electrostatic Discharge Control (ESD) (Figure 12.4) and Safety Training to Sexual Harassment and Cultural Diversity education. Billing is done on a per-student basis

ESD Training Online has a variety of Web-based training courses available for companies who want to provide training and testing for all their employees without classrooms or instructors. The course costs $39.95 per student up to five students and $10 per student beyond. Orders for 1,000 or more students include a customization option which lets companies incorporate company or site-specific photos, graphics, and ESD policies and procedures.

To sample what a training course may offer a company, users can visit the demo on the Outbound Train Web site and learn "How Much Static Does It Take to Damage a Component?" (Figure 12.5). Text and graphics are combined to provide a complete learning experience for the user. If your organization has specialized needs or training requirements that can't

FIGURE 12.4 ESD Training Online.

Outbound Train™

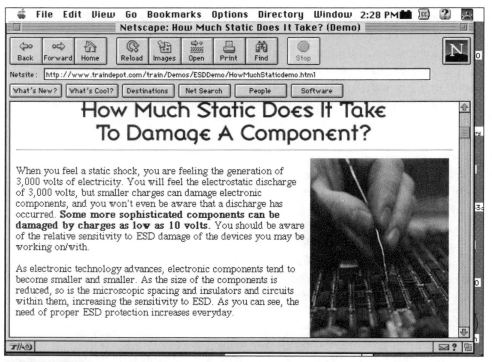

FIGURE 12.5 "How Much Static Does It take to Damage a Component?" demo.

Outbound Train™

be met by ordinary courseware, the Training Depot courses can be customized to fit the users' needs. The Training Depot instructional design team can help the user with training objectives, then recommend a media format (e.g., Web-based training, company intranet, interactive CD-ROM) perfectly suited to the users' needs and budgets.

This training is designed to run on any system with access to the World Wide Web. The program will guide users step-by-step throughout the content and testing process. Employers can create the training information with photos of the actual workplace environment. There are "Knowledge Checks" (Figure 12.6) at the end of each section to test the employee on what was covered and provides instant feedback of the student's progress.

The "Knowledge Check" asks general questions about the information previously presented. After the student completes the test, the test is automatically graded and results posted. If the employee does not answer all questions correctly, he or she has the option of returning to the text information for review or to proceed. The ESD training course teaches the

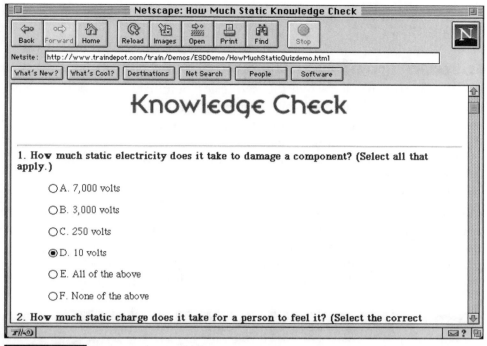

Netsite: http://www.traindepot.com/train/Demos/ESDDemo/HowMuchStaticQuizdemo.html

What's New? | What's Cool? | Destinations | Net Search | People | Software

Knowledge Check

1. How much static electricity does it take to damage a component? (Select all that apply.)

    ○ A. 7,000 volts

    ○ B. 3,000 volts

    ○ C. 250 volts

    ◉ D. 10 volts

    ○ E. All of the above

    ○ F. None of the above

2. How much static charge does it take for a person to feel it? (Select the correct

FIGURE 12.6 Knowledge Check.

Outbound Train™

basic concepts of ESD, how it occurs, proper precautionary measures required to avoid static damage to sensitive electronic components, how to control ESD by working in ESD-protected areas and workstations, proper handling techniques, and use of personal grounding devices.

Other courses available through Outbound Train are:

• Electrostatic Discharge Control Training Online

• ISO 9000

• Clean Rooms

• Sexual Harassment

Outbound Train is the exclusive distributor of all products and services featured at the Train Depot. It also distributes interactive multimedia courseware, specializing in the areas of OSHA Compliance/Health and Safety Training, Electrostatic Discharge Control (ESD), IS0 9000, Professional/Personal development, basic skills, and ESL/EFL. To visit the Outbound Train Web site and the Train Depot go to http://

www.outboundtrain.com or link to the site from the URL provided in the accompanying CD.

InfoSource: Conversion to the Web

InfoSource, Inc. produces a disk-based series, Seminar-On-A-Disk, which is part of a curriculum of self-paced instructor-led and skills assessment tools. In business since 1983, InfoSource delivers disk-based and multimedia programs, and has now added a network version of their programs.

A link to InfoSource, Inc.'s home page is located on the CD-ROM. Their URL is http://www.infosourcenet.com.

The tutorials teach people how to use office applications at both beginning and intermediate levels. Material is covered in seven to nine topics, and each program takes three to five hours, depending upon the pace of the student. The lessons in the set build upon each other to a final completed project. The tutorial duplicates the look of the real application, while providing feedback and hands-on capabilities (Figure 12.7).

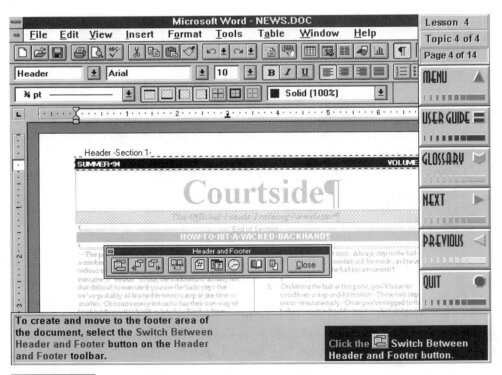

FIGURE 12.7 The tutorial duplicates the look and feel of the application.

The program consists of 35 percent graphics and 20 percent animation, not including simulation.

The basic program simulates a real application and an incorrect action brings feedback showing the error, and help in resolving it. The lessons are self-paced, with quizzes available to test comprehension when the student is ready. A glossary is included as well as location jumps to that particular term in the lesson.

The opening screen prompts users for name and ID number and additional customization of the screen (to add log-in fields, for instance) is available as well. After log-in, users select lessons and topics from menu screens.

A navigation bar is used with Next, Back, Glossary, Exit, and User Guide buttons. Topics usually begin with a series of screens explaining the application's features, and the application environment itself. Following each lesson, there is an optional quiz.

Excel 7.0 Fundamentals

An example of the structure of their Web-based training programs is Excel 7.0 The first step to using this tutorial is to click on the Excel 7.0 Fundamentals package. A security notice from Shockwave will immediately appear (this tutorial is developed with Authorware and Shockwave). A yes or no response is needed. A yes answer is the agreement that Shockwave and Authorware will write information to the hard drive on your computer.

The Excel 7.0 Fundamentals screen (Figure 12.8) appears on the main menu and lessons 1 through 9 are listed. Within each lesson is a series of topics you may select. To the right of this area there are navigational buttons which are consistent in each function. The program uses adult learning principles of information chunking (i.e., breaking down learning into chunks or pieces that are more easily learned than entire sections of information).

The program follows three principles: concept, story, and a hands-on student exercise application. As you go through your lessons, a series of tickmarks are entered next to the subjects completed.

Within each lesson there are a number of topics, always followed by a quiz. There are two types of questions in the quiz, multiple choice and interactive, indicating that the student needs to do something. The pattern of concept, story, and interaction by the student is repeated in each lesson. There is an index glossary available to look up any terms, and users may search by keyword or letter of the alphabet. The user can use the GO TO button to access the specified subject.

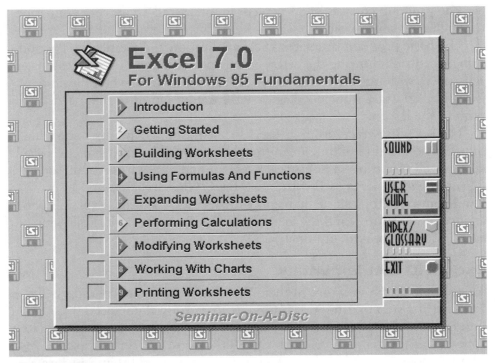

FIGURE 12.8 Excel 7.0 Fundamentals.

At the conclusion of the tutorial, the user may click on the Exit button and return to the browser.

Software for Development and Playback

According to the developers, the authoring software used in this product was Macromedia Authorware. In addition, the following software was used for development:

- Macromedia Shockwave
- Netscape Navigator
- Internet Explorer
- Adobe PhotoShop
- Microsoft Word
- Afterburner for Authorware

- Animator Pro

- Macromedia Freehand

To run the program, end-user workstations require a minimum of 486MHz, 8MB RAM, and Windows 3.0 or higher. Software required is Netscape Navigator 2.0 or higher or Internet Explorer 3.0 or higher, and Shockwave for Authorware. Network access should be at least a 14.4Kbps modem or faster (28.8Kbps recommended).

Randysoft: Skills Training for Programming Languages

Randysoft's Web-based training provides training in programming languages such as Perl, C++, Java, JavaScript, HTML, and UNIX Shell Programming. This program has a unique standalone programming environment that allows the student to interactively write and test code. The training program runs on any hardware platform, but it requires a JavaScript and forms-aware Web browser such as NetscapeNavigator 3.0 or Microsoft Internet Explorer 3.0.

The program is designed to be used by company employees on an intranet. The programs are designed for the Web, but have also been used in a computer lab workshop. (See CD-ROM for a demonstration.)

To use the program, students log into the corporate server with a JavaScript and forms-aware browser at their convenience. Each course is broken down into lessons and each lesson contains a small lecture with exercises that test the student's knowledge at a progressive pace. All lessons use a programming window called OPIE which allows students to write their programs in their browser and get immediate feedback. Student and trainee questions can be sent to the Randysoft training support staff via e-mail. There is also access to an FTP site where students can get the answers to the questions about programming assignments, plus there is a Frequently Asked Questions (FAQ). One can also arrange for on-site mentoring by a trained instructor.

To install the program the user runs a script and answers a few questions. Randysoft gives technical support over the phone to help the user with the installation if there are any problems.

Users can browse the course catalog and view what will be learned in the different available classes (Figure 12.9). Program training courses include Basic HTML, Advanced HTML with CGI and JavaScript, and Perl.

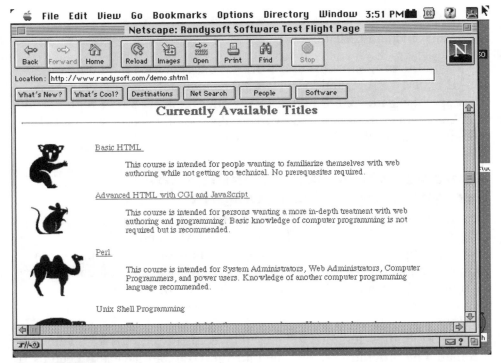

FIGURE 12.9 Currently Available Titles.

In the Basic HTML course, students learn programming tools including text character formatting tags. The screen shown in Figure 12.10 teaches the user how to format and use text tags.

Students taking the Perl course learn how to manipulate numerical scalar data as in figure 12.11 (which I am sure is very important, whatever it is). The entire source code for this program is provided in Appendix E and the Randysoft Web site can be accessed from www.randysoft.com or from the attached CD.

Practising Law Institute: Audio Web-based Program

Another approach to program design is the use of audio as the primary medium. Although there are limits on this as an instructional method, the technology is worth investigating.

In this approach, learners log onto the Internet for an audio-based training program delivered in real time. The program, Keeping the Fire:

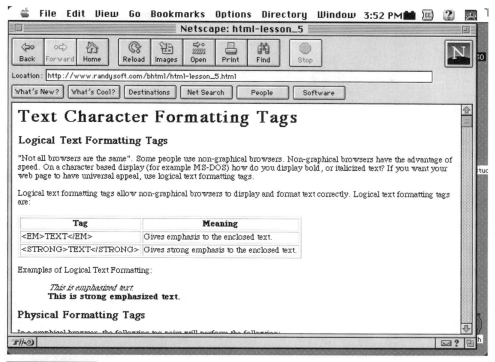

FIGURE 12.10 Formatting tags.

From Burnout to Balance, uses RealAudio software (Figure 12.12) to deliver the program on demand (while users are online, rather than requiring them to wait until the audio is fully downloaded).

Keeping the Fire focuses on lawyer burnout and uses personal case histories, written materials, and self-assessment exercises. The program was designed and produced by attorney-turned-multimedia-developer David Simon and helps learners recognize symptoms, redefine values, and develop coping strategies.

The course is designed as an alternative to traditional CLE credit programs delivered through audio cassettes. While an advantage of cassettes is the ability to listen while driving, the Internet course provides supplemental written materials on the screen.

Simon said one of the biggest obstacles in developing and promoting this course has been getting lawyers to accept the Internet as a way of obtaining CLE credit. "Lawyers are not early adopters of technology," he said.

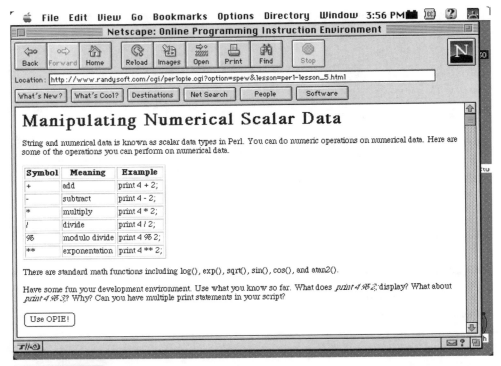

FIGURE 12.11 Numerical scalar data.

Access the program through URL link on the accompanying CD-ROM or at www.cle-net.edu. (See Appendix E and CD-ROM for sample code.)

External Development

Some companies may want to use an external developer to provide the training for them. The following case study also explores the use of Shockwave in the development of Web-based training.

Motorola with Tobin Erdmann & Jacobsen

The development team at Tobin Erdmann & Jacobsen (TEJ) developed one of the first interactive training modules for client Motorola using Shockwave over the Web. "When converting an instructor-led training

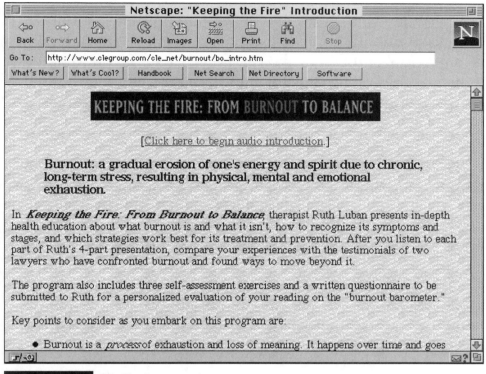

FIGURE 12.12 RealAudio example.

© 1996 Ruth Luban

program to interactive Computer Based Training, adjustments in the presentation of concepts must be made," wrote David Johnson of TEJ and John Manion of Motorola in an article in the *Multimedia Training Newsletter* (March 1996). "In our case, the 'hands-on' approach used in Motorola's Design For Manufacturability course simply couldn't transfer because of the tactile nature of the exercise. Learners were given Tinkertoy components that had values attached to each part. They were instructed to build a Space Tower and maintain the inherent trait that defines Motorola: quality. Learners had to implement concepts learned in the course, apply Six Sigma standards, and ensure that the manufacturing process was feasible."

In initial discussions between TEJ and Motorola, the external developer and the internal client jointly assumed that the CBT course exercises would replicate the Space Tower and Solar Tower exercises in the current classroom course, though with the understanding that we would not incorporate a simulated "gravity" factor as the environmental test for towers "constructed" in the exercises.

In preliminary design efforts aimed at adapting the Tower exercises from their current classroom-based operation to computer-based versions, the team defined an approach that provides opportunities to maximize the veracity of the exercises while also increasing the sophistication, as well as interest value, to the learner. Moreover, the approach which TEJ defined has the additional benefit of placing less risk and pressure in regard to calendar time for development.

The approach involves replacing the Tower design and development activities with ones aimed at designing a Water System for multiple user sites within a tract of land. Rationale for this approach is based on the following.

While TEJ and Motorola were in agreement that the CBT exercises would not incorporate simulated gravity, this does not eliminate the need to test the soundness of learners' designs.

The Tower exercises derive much of their interest on the part of the learner, and possibly instructional value, from the fact of the Tinkertoy media being actually live and tactile. "Handling the Tinkertoys may be necessary for learners to perform well in design," Manion and Johnson write. "While TEJ could have rendered Tinkertoy 3-D graphics of exceedingly high quality, they remain graphics, and not the 'real thing.' We saw some risk of learner frustration regarding this issue."

The Water System exercise (Figure 12.13) was potentially more interesting and engaging. Given the types of graphics TEJ would use, and the types and interplay of variables, this exercise could have a gamelike look and feel, somewhat like the popular simulation game, SimCity.

A key reason for selecting the Tower/Tinkertoy approach for the classroom exercise was its "neutrality" in regard to actual Motorola design activities; it is quite obviously a "pretend task," completely separate from any engineering focus in any part of Motorola. As such, there is no risk of confusion with learners' actual work tasks. The Water System exercise enjoys this same advantage.

The Water System exercises can also unquestionably focus on the same learner objectives as the Tower exercises and do so at least as well. These objectives (applying to both exercises, except as noted) possess engineering soundness and meet marketing specifications, cost effectiveness specifications (not a priority in the first exercise, but is in the second), time effectiveness specifications and installation criteria.

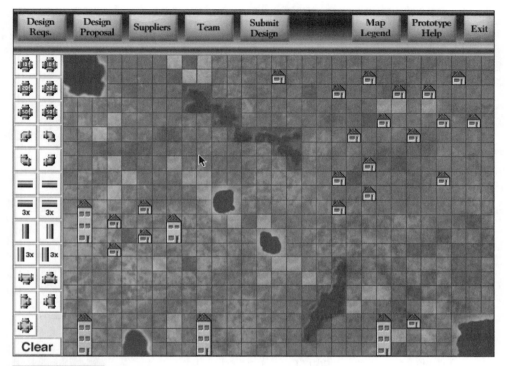

FIGURE 12.13 Water System exercise.

Copyright 1996 Tobin Erdmann & Jacobson

USING A WEB-BASED TUTORIAL TO TRAIN YOUR STAFF TO SCREW IN LIGHT BULBS: A TONGUE-IN-CHEEK WBT DEVELOPMENT PROJECT

Steven Kirk, Sage Interactive

Like any self-respecting instructional designer, I have always wanted to develop training programs that have real value and impact. In early January, I found myself sitting by the phone waiting for corporations to call with engaging and consequential projects for our company to develop. But the phone, as they say, wasn't exactly "ringing off the hook," so I decided to take matters into my own hands and determine what training was most needed by the companies I have worked with.

After a significant needs analysis spanning approximately 15 minutes, I came to a momentous conclusion: very few people in corporate settings know how to effectively screw in a light bulb. I know this because time and again I have overheard the following question whispered between cubicles: "How many people does it take to screw in a light bulb?"

So I set out to solve this evidently universal problem. I initially attempted to sell the idea to corporate contacts, but, incredibly, no one seemed to have room in their annual budgets. But when you really believe in the value of something, you stick with it. Consequently, I convinced my partner that this tutorial, developed for the Internet, would help both mankind and America's competitive position, and she hesitantly moved her head in a way that I interpreted as a form of approval. (The fact that my partner also happens to be my wife has absolutely nothing to do with her apparent acquiescence.)

Selecting the Web as a Delivery Platform

We soon discovered that developing instructional materials for Internet or intranet environments is no easier than producing the CD-ROM–based programs we were used to churning out. The good news was that it isn't any more difficult, and it has considerable advantages. In fact, we've now fallen in love with Web-based training approaches, and are consequently shifting our emphasis toward development of online instructional programs. Among the key values that became quickly apparent are immediate and universal access for users; true interactivity through hot text, hypertext, and hyperlinks; genuine multimedia, integrating voice, music, text, graphics, and animation; and straightforward and universal updates for developers. In a word, we found that this stuff is "sexy" (and at 48, I needed a lift).

Development Approach

It turns out that there is nothing magical about the design and development approaches required for Web-based training (WBT) production. We essentially followed the same methodologies used in developing our "old world" programs (Figures 12.14 and 12.15). Our key steps were:

Identify terminal and enabling performance-based Mager-type objectives.

Terminal Objective: effectively screw a light bulb into its socket.

Enabling objectives: identify all necessary tools and personnel required to screw in a light bulb, ascertain how to position each individual for maximum effectiveness, and recognize the correct direction to screw a bulb into its socket.

Develop test items.

What materials are needed to screw in a light bulb? How many people does it take to screw in a light bulb? What is the correct direction to screw in a light bulb?

Develop Design Guide.

Define target audience (typical corporate management and staff). Define

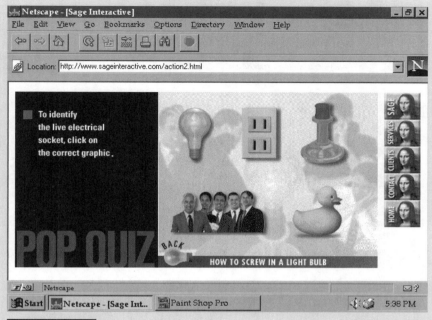

FIGURE 12.14 Sage Interactive quiz.

Sage Interactive, Copyright 1996, 1997

technical/physical context (online networked microcomputers in cubicle corporate mazes). Define media approach (Internet and enterprise-wide Intranets using text, sound, graphics, and animations).

Outline course content.

Develop budget.

Eleven liters of French roast coffee plus $7,000 in salary and expenses.

Establish development timeline.

Four weeks with bathroom and snack breaks every third hour.

Develop storyboards.

Determine development platforms and tools.

Hardware: Power Macintosh 7100/80—because Macs make the best multimedia development platform. Syquest EZ Drive—to store and transport large files between laborers. Polaroid SprintScan 35—to capture and digitize graphic images. HP LaserJet printer—to print text and storyboards.

Operating System: Macintosh OS 7.5—because this project was produced in January and version 7.6 wasn't released yet.

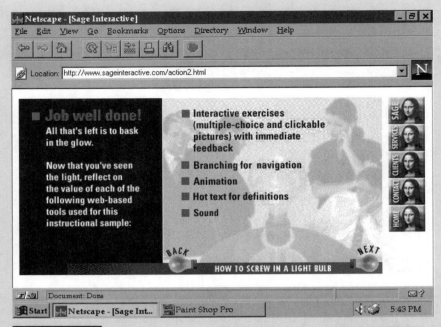

FIGURE 12.15 How to Screw in a Light Bulb: screen from Sage Interactive mock WBT program.

Sage Interactive, Copyright 1996, 1997

Software: *Macromedia Director 4.0*—because *Director* is a very capable multimedia development environment and, more importantly, an *Authorware* version of *Shockwave* hadn't been developed at that time. *Microsoft Word*—for the design document and storyboards. *Adobe PhotoShop 3.0*—to manipulate photos and graphic effects. *Adobe Illustrator 6.0*—to create icons and manipulate text. *Strata Studio Pro 1.75*—for the light bulb animations. *Macromedia Afterburner*—to "Shock" the *Director* files into compressed sizes of only 50 percent of their pre-*Shockwave* formats.

Key Challenges

Staffing—I am blessed with the native ability to determine optimal methods of screwing in light bulbs, but less talented at a number of other things including art, animation, photography, interface design, programming, Internet protocols, color palettes, digital sound, hybrid instructional approaches, budgeting, storyboarding, scanning, photography, HTML, digital sound production, scheduling, marketing, tech support, project management, and, embarrassingly, unscrewing light bulbs. As a result, I brought in reinforcements to help with virtually everything except pouring the coffee. For this nonexistent budget, it added up to a grand total of one overworked and gifted artist/developer named Jeff Chen.

Bandwidth—The only thing really keeping the Internet from becoming the obvious choice for a lot of training applications is the time delay caused by inadequate bandwidth. Numerous promising technologies are being reported for 1997, but for now video is completely unreasonable except in low-volume, high-bandwidth intranet environments and sound should be used sparingly unless Shockwaved or sent via real-time audio. For this tutorial, for example, we developed a "high-bandwidth," full voiceover version for a T1 corporate intranet environment; but for typical 28.8bps modems, even the low-bandwidth Shockwave version takes up to four minutes to download. To alleviate download times, we broke the tutorial into two smaller files of approximately two minutes each. We could have segmented the files even further, but determined that the constant minor disruptions would be more intrusive than a few larger downloads that allow smooth running of full modules.

Real estate—Browsers love to take up valuable screen space and there's little you can do about it. Just remember to design your interfaces with an ongoing awareness that your content needs to fit within the space your browser allocates.

Color palettes—Someday corporations will upgrade computers to today's standards. Until then, realize that many computers read only 256 colors, or even 16 colors. We have found that 16 colors is unreasonable unless necessary, so 256 makes a good compromise. Always optimize color palettes using Debabelizer.

Platforms—One of the beauties of the Internet is that the protocols are designed to fit virtually all platforms. You can develop WBT programs using your favorite authoring and tools programs on the platform of your choice, but experienced developers often embrace the Mac due to its stability, robustness, and established development community.

Browsers—Beware, not all browsers are created equal. AOL and CompuServe fall far short of meeting all the important capabilities important to the Web. MS Explorer is coming on strong, but still has a good distance to go. Netscape sets the standard, and since it holds 80 percent market share and allows you to play with all the latest toys (plug-ins and helper applications) you should build for it and pray for the others to someday catch up. If you do need to build for all browser environments, you're best off staying with text-based HTML instruction for now.

Tech support calls—Because of the various tools and protocols required for Web-based applications, the issues are often unrelated to the programs you develop. Sticky problems caused by online glitches, earlier versions of browsers, or difficulties downloading plugins such as Shockwave are not uncommon. At least you can pass the blame onto everyone else.

Recouping costs—You don't want to develop Web-based tutorials and make money too, do you? Adequate security measures have yet to be implemented to provide reliable methods of charging others for the use of your programs. Until electronic transmission of funds becomes a standard, develop Web-based tutorials for internal training or introductory demos for marketing purposes.

Learning curve—Nothing to it. Just combine all that you've learned building programmed texts, audiocassette tutorials, video-based training tapes, CBT programs, multimedia tutorials, and hyperlinked Web pages, then glue them together, compress them into Internet-ready packets, and call it a day.

Measurable Results

In case you are interested in knowing how effective this Web-based tutorial has proven to be, our available measurable results are fairly encouraging. Statistics gathered by the virtual VP of Efficiency we hired to monitor our light bulbs 24 hours each day indicate that our office is now fully lighted an average of 21.5 hours a day, 6.2 days a week. Put in terms more common to instructional designers, 90 percent of our trainees can now effectively screw in a light bulb 80 percent of the time.

You can access the light bulb tutorial from the Sage Interactive Web site at www.sageinteractive.com as well as from the accompanying CD-ROM.

LEVEL 3 COURSES: INTERACTIVE MULTIMEDIA

With this highest level of Web-based training courses reviewed here, elements of multimedia are added to enhance and upgrade the learning environment. Video, sound, animation, and improved graphic legibility change the possibilities for training, encouraging users to learn with more of their senses than just their eyes. Interactive multimedia also opens the way for conversion of video-delivered training to a web-based format which improves the convenience of distribution for these materials. Audio can be especially useful for soft skills training like customer service, or for servicing the needs of audio students, who have a stronger response to information they hear than information they read. Overall, the more engaging nature of multimedia has been a hit in the CBT market, and as the Web adapts for larger files and bigger bandwidth chunks, it will be a useful, if expensive addition to training in this medium as well.

As mentioned in Chapter 12, because of the limitations of bandwidth, the multimedia state-of-the-art level of Internet training is still at the level of sophistication that CD-ROM programs had more than seven years ago. While the interactive and media aspects are less advanced, there are several reasons to pursue multimedia training over the Web rather than using a CD-ROM:

1. Ease of administration, including updates instantaneously delivered worldwide.

2. The rapidly advancing technology of the Web ensures that bandwidth limitations will quickly be eliminated, paving the way for CD-ROM-like graphics delivered over the Web.

Many of the state-of-the-art programs are custom-developed and are available only on company intranets. Case studies in this chapter include both commercial programs that can be viewed on the public Internet and some private, internal programs which can only be described here, because of the proprietary nature of the content. But first, a look at the technology which pulls these programs away from those discussed in earlier chapters.

↳ How to Determine if Interactive Multimedia Is Right for You

Macromedia's Shockwave technology, now just over a year and a half old, can assist in the leap from computer-based training to Web-based training and allow for a hybridization of both. Brandon Carson of Multimedia Pathways, Inc., a Redwood City, California, development firm, says that the move toward Web-based training using Shockwave is greatly enhanced by the ability to repurpose existing programs authored in a Macromedia product for Internet delivery without starting the development process over. "You can convert your *existing* training material to 'shocked' programs that will run over the Internet or your company's intranet with the full interactivity of your computer-based program," Carson says.

"The promise of Web-based training is in the ability to deliver training to individuals anywhere at any time," Carson says. "The two primary Web browsers both support the required Shockwave plug-in, and with current advances in computer technology and bandwidth, the capabilities of delivering rich, fully interactive Web-based training materials is a reality today. These tools provide developers the ability to construct unified *on-demand* delivery of up-to-date educational training and other information systems."

In the process of developing computer-based training (CBT) you have to consider the various delivery methods available to you. Should you create and optimize your training for CD-ROM, floppy disk, local hard disk installation, and/or the local intranet or the Internet? And to make the decision even more complicated, what technological limitations do you need to succumb to when you make your decision? Basically, what are the advantages and disadvantages of WBT, and where does Shockwave fit in?

Once you have looked at your options and decided if WBT is for you and fits comfortably in place with your educational goals, you must look at the development tools available to you.

"Advanced authoring tools such as Macromedia Authorware reduce the time required for developers to create rich, fully interactive multimedia productions," Carson says. "With this and other tools, developers and subject matter experts can focus more on the instructional paradigm and methodology and less on programming. If you have already used or chosen Authorware or Director as your development tool, then you are on the right path to converting to or creating WBT. Studies have proven and shown that effectiveness and return on investment of well-implemented CBT is superior to other training methods, and now WBT takes that cost-effectiveness and adds timeliness, easy modification, and cross-platform compatibility to the picture."

Using Shockwave in Web-Based Training

Shockwave allows you to create fully interactive multimedia productions for playback through Web browsers. Shockwave is available for both Macintosh and Windows computers and works with the two primary Web browsers, Netscape Navigator version 2.0 and higher, and Microsoft's Internet Explorer version 3.01 and higher. To view applications created using Shockwave the user must download and install the Shockwave plug-in from Macromedia's Web site at http://www.macromedia.com/shockwave.

There are several versions of the Shockwave plug-in. The user must download the correct version to view programs created in different Macromedia products. Shockwave is compatible with Windows 3.1, 3.11, Windows 95, Windows NT 3.5.1, Windows NT 4.0, Macintosh 68K machines running System 7.1.2 or higher, and Power Macintosh machines running System 7.5.1 or higher. Shockwave for Director is also an ActiveX control in Microsoft's Internet Explorer. In the following discussion, Brian Carson explains the ins and outs of creating shocked programs using Macromedia Authorware as an authoring tool. The processes to convert existing packaged files to shocked files are somewhat different from burning Director files.

Converting Authorware Files to Shocked Files

To create a "shocked" piece that will run through a Web browser you will need an application called Afterburner. (It is available to developers for download at Macromedia's Web site.) Afterburner will compress and segment your Authorware file so it can be delivered over the Internet. The various segments created by Afterburner allow your Authorware piece to "stream" to the student's browser, thereby allowing large files to look and work exactly like your packaged piece.

When you shock a piece with Afterburner, two types of files will be created: one or more "segment" files and one "map" file. The segments are the actual program compressed into several files. The map file is the file the Shockwave plug-in will access from the HTML tag and direct to the segments to start streaming the shocked piece. If you use any external functions or libraries the map file will also store the information allowing the segments to retrieve the necessary external data needed. These files are what you will upload to your server. Once you have burned an Authorware piece you will not need the packaged file with which you began.

To burn an Authorware piece into a shocked Authorware piece start with a packaged file:

1. Make sure you have packaged "without runtime." The plug-in the browser uses will serve as the runtime for the application.

2. Launch Afterburner.

3. Select the packaged file from within Afterburner.

4. When you are prompted to save your map file, create a new directory. This will ensure you upload all the necessary files to the server and don't miss any. All the segment files created will need to be uploaded or errors will occur.

5. When you are prompted for a "segment size" a default is entered. "I have found that with most applications the default works fine," Carson says. "But if you want your segments to be larger or smaller, change the default to the desired size. Remember, if Authorware encounters icons with audio or video it cannot break them up, so some segments may be larger or smaller, and you may get disturbing breaks in the presentation. It's always best to start with the default and experiment."

6. Upload all the segment files and the map file to a server configured for Shockwave delivery. Be sure to transfer the files as binary files, not ASCII files. Carson suggests checking with your Internet Service

Provider or with your Webmaster to make sure your server is configured properly for Shockwave.

To add your Shockwave piece to an HTML Web page, use the HTML tag EMBED. This tag will specify the location of the map and segment files and will create an area in the browser to display the piece. An example tag may look like this:

```
<EMBED SRC="trainingpiece.aam" WIDTH=640 HEIGHT=480 WINDOW=OnTop>
```

The WIDTH and HEIGHT tags are important because they specify the width and height of the display area created in the Web browser to view the shocked piece. This setting should reflect the size of your packaged piece's presentation window. The WINDOW tag instructs the Authorware runtime how to display the presentation. You currently have three choices for Windows platforms:

- InPlace—Displays the piece within the web browser. This option is not available on the Macintosh.

- OnTop—Displays the piece in a separate window on top of the browser.

- OnTopMinimize—Displays the piece in a separate window and minimizes (or hides) the browser.

For Macintosh you have the two latter options.

Palettes

If you know ahead of time that you will be delivering your program through a Web browser you can address the palette issue from the beginning. If your presentation uses the system palette, you can either load the Netscape palette into your Authorware file before you convert to Shockwave, or you can use the PALETTE tag to specify either the browser palette or the palette currently in the Authorware piece. The arguments to use with the PALETTE tag are "foreground" or "background." If in your EMBED call you use "PALETTE=background" the shocked Authorware piece will default to the browser's color palette. This will avoid any noticeable color shift in images inside the browser if when your shocked Authorware piece loads it uses a different palette. You must be careful to realize that if you used a custom palette while authoring your presentation, and allow the shocked piece to default to the browser palette, you might change the appearance of your shocked piece.

To optimize for Web browsers while you author you can load the Netscape palette directly into your Authorware file. The palette is available in the Director 5 Xtras directory, or for download at http://www .killersites.com.

Preparing for Non-Shockwave-Enabled Browsers

If you are delivering your shocked piece over the Internet to various users and not a company's intranet, you don't have control over what Web browser a prospective user may have. If students are using a browser that is not Shockwave-compatible there are steps you can take in programming the HTML to alert them to the fact that they can't view the presentation. You can display an image in place of the shocked piece and/or a message informing students they are using a noncompatible browser. To do this you use the NOEMBED tag.

The following example shows how to place the NOEMBED tag in your HTML page so a non-Shockwave-enabled browser can display an image and/or a message:

```
<HTML>
<HEAD>
<TITLE>My Training Piece in Authorware</TITLE>
</HEAD>
<BODY>
<CENTER>
<EMBED SRC="mytrainingpiece.aam" WIDTH=640 HEIGHT=480 WINDOW=InPlace>
<NOEMBED> <IMG SRC="alternateimage.gif">
<p>
Your browser is not enabled to view Shockwave
<p></NOEMBED>
</CENTER>
</BODY>
</HTML>
```

In a nonenabled browser students will see the image and the message, instructing them that they cannot participate in the training.

Cross-Platform Compatibility

One of the advantages of using Shockwave is the ability to deliver your Authorware piece over the Internet regardless of the end-user's platform.

The same rules apply though, when authoring shocked pieces as when authoring for other forms of delivery—namely, to create a Windows-compatible shocked piece you must start with a Windows Authorware file, and to create a Macintosh shocked piece you must start with a Macintosh Authorware file. For all users (Macintosh and Windows) to have access to your piece, you will need to convert the piece to both platforms (you need both the Windows and Macintosh versions of Authorware) and "burn" both versions to create two groups segment files and two map files. You can then have two links in your HTML page to either version so Macintosh users can call the appropriate Macintosh-compatible shocked piece and likewise with Windows users.

Macromedia realized that developers may want their presentations to seem platform-independent to the end-user, so it is possible to edit the two map files created by both the Windows and Macintosh Afterburners into one map file. This way when the user clicks on the link in his or her Web browser, the map file calls the appropriate segments based on the user's platform. All you need to do is open both map files and copy and paste the information from one file into the other and resave it with the same name. Then upload *all* the segment files produced by burning both presentations. This way the shocked piece will run on either platform and the compatibility issue is hidden to the user.

Other Development Issues

If you are developing a piece for delivery over a company's high-speed intranet, you can be assured that download time may not be an issue for your end-users. Remember: *Each time a segment is downloading the user cannot interact with the program*. So the quicker the download, the more seamless the presentation. Although the local network may be ultrafast, the download time over the intranet may still be slower than that of a CD-ROM. Network traffic may also dictate "burps" in the stream. Regardless of whether or not you know your delivery may be over a local corporate intranet you should develop your shocked piece with the lowest common denominator in mind: a 28.8Kbps modem. A well-crafted presentation optimized for this speed will blaze over a high-speed intranet. The challenge is in creating professional-looking multimedia-rich pieces that have to load with a 28.8Kbps modem. You may have to reconsider some of the instructional philosophy of the piece. Audio files can add tremendous size to your Authorware piece, and can literally stall the presentation as it downloads.

You may want to provide the user the ability to turn off the sound and view the audio as text. Try to emphasize Authorware's built-in interactivity features. These do not require lengthy downloads and work well at all modem speeds. Consider using 4-bit images instead of 8-bit images.

"Interact with other Authorware developers to learn tips and tricks and view their pieces for interesting examples of workarounds for everyday bandwidth problems," Carson suggests. "Try not to be discouraged; bandwidth limitations are diminishing with time. Soon, delivering full streaming audio and video will be taken for granted and we'll all be using CD-ROMs for coffee cup holders."

Additional Resources

For more in-depth technical explanations, and for a downloadable developer's handbook, visit Macromedia's Web site at http://www.macromedia.com/Shockwave.

To engage in discussions with other Authorware developers about Shockwave and other issues, join the Authorware Discussion listserv by sending a message to LISTSERV@CC1.KULEUVEN.AC.BE. In the body of your message type: SUBSCRIBE AWARE YOUR NAME. The listserv's companion Web site is located at http://www.hvu.nl/aware/.

In the developer's forum at the Macromedia Web site you can view examples of Shockwave at Macromedia's Shockwave gallery. You can also request that your Shockwave pieces be posted there. If you search the Web search engines using keywords "authorware" and "shockwave" you will be presented with URLs of various shocked sites to check out. You can also check out the Multimedia Pathways corporate site athttp://www.mpathways.com, or Brandon Carson's personal site at http://www.carsonmedia.com, for examples of Shockwave using Authorware and for more up-to-date information and links to other Authorware-related sites. All of these URLs are accessible from the accompanying CD-ROM.

Creating Interactive Multimedia

Following are studies of different organizations' approaches to developing an interactive multimedia Web-based training program.

The Interactive Patient CME Simulation

The Marshall University School of Medicine's Continuing Medical Education program has developed a wonderful example of a Web-based training program. Available to anyone at no charge, "The Interactive Patient" is a valuable resource for physicians who want to continue their training or for lay people wanting to learn more.

"The Interactive Patient" is intended for use by physicians and medical students to learn to assess and diagnose different types of abdominal pain and then develop treatment plans for specific illnesses. Since many states require participation in Continuing Medical Education for license renewal and hospital privileges, "The Interactive Patient" has the potential to be an invaluable tool for rural doctors and/or those who find attending conferences and workshops inconvenient.

"The Interactive Patient" consists of a multimedia interactive patient encounter over the Web. Physicians can interview the patient, conduct an examination, order lab tests and X-rays, and then submit a diagnosis and treatment plan. The program then evaluates the user's performance automatically.

The program uses sound, video, text, and pictures in the simulation. It begins by issuing the patient's complaint and then allowing the user to submit questions for the patient via forms. The program's server recognizes more than 1,700 questions. If the question is recognized, the patient responds to the question; if not, the user is asked to rephrase his or her query. The Interactive Patient's answers are designed as realistically as possible, with the idea that many patients have a limited knowledge of medical terminology. This also helps sharpen the physician's ability to ask the right questions.

The user can then examine the patient by clicking on any body part (the patient is presented as an image map). Ordering lab tests and X-rays can be done at any time by clicking on a menu. Whenever the user feels confident of a correct diagnosis, she or he may submit a diagnosis and treatment plan via e-mail. The system responds with an evaluation within a short period of time.

The Interactive Patient is still in its prototype phase, with significant improvements being made by the original developers, Kent Hayes and Christoph Lehmann, M.D.

Copfer and Associates and Cutler-Hammer

Cutler-Hammer's training program was developed for their Intranet Institute on the subject of circuit breaker technology. The audience is made up of sales associates for their Series C Circuit Breaker product line.

Many of these sales associates have little prior knowledge of electrical circuitry. In order for the sales associates to be competent at selling the product to electrical contractors and vendors, they must know the product and be able to compare and contrast it to the competition.

The authoring tool used was NetShow by Microsoft. NetShow is a unique product at the moment because it is designed exclusively for the Internet- or intranet-based delivery media and as such it streams audio and still graphics while executing a script on a timeline basis. One-third of the screen is devoted to images compiled as a movie that are shown to reinforce the topic at hand. Certain images may be clicked on for further information, which gives the user control and the program its interactivity. These clickable image maps are within the ASF movie (Microsoft's proprietary file format). The program utilizes VBScript, Perl, HTML 3.2, and NetShow's ASF Editor for developing the source code, although other languages were used as well. Another third of the screen remains constant, as it provides navigational information, or shows the student, "you are here." The final third of the screen is used to display text heard simultaneously in

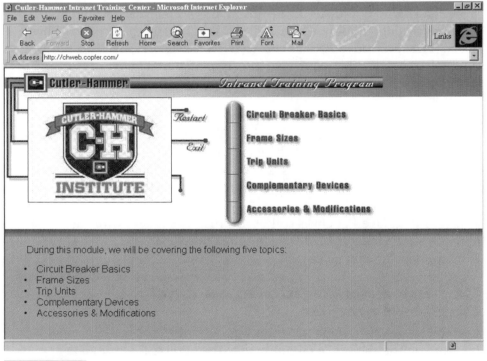

FIGURE 13.1 Training menu for the Cutler-Hammer Institute.

a voiceover audio track. The audio is strictly synchronized with the pictures. Reading the text reinforces what is heard for users with audio capabilities, and for those who do not hear the audio it presents the basic material. This space is also utilized to present questions to students and any appropriate feedback.

There are five topics covered on the subject of circuit breaker technology, including: Breaker Basics, Frame Sizes, Trip Units, Complementary Devices, and Accessories & Modifications (Figure 13.1). The student must begin with Breaker Basics and view all topics in the order in which they are presented. Each successive topic builds on the content of the previous one. In Breaker Basics, the definition of a circuit breaker is given. It continues to identify the six basic components of a molded case circuit breaker. The components are listed and may be clicked on for further information (Figure 13.2).

This is a good example of a clickable image map. Afterward, selection criterion are discussed for a molded case circuit breaker. There are three questions at the end of each topic that reinforce the material presented. As

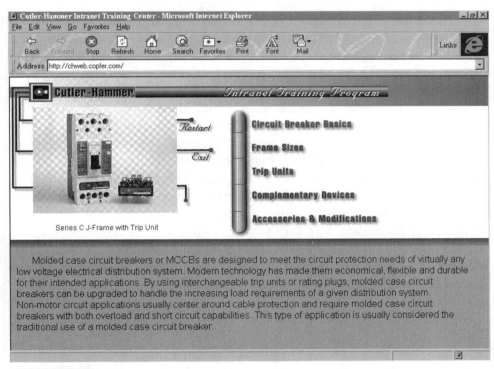

FIGURE 13.2 The components may be clicked on for further information.

soon as a student submits his or her answer, feedback is given as to whether the answer is correct. If the student was incorrect, the correct answer is given. In the event that two or more questions are missed, the student has the option to review the topic before moving forward.

The development process for the content was a basic brainstorming session of the three subject matter experts (SMEs) from Cutler-Hammer and the Copfer & Associates' instructional designer. According to the developer it was a marathon seven-hour meeting, where most of the content and all of the questions were written. There were two earlier drafts from which to borrow content and that were used as a guide. The earlier drafts had been made up by the SMEs and refined and organized by the instructional designer. Each had a copy of the latest version of the content for the seven-hour meeting. The SMEs are engineers and perform various functions at Cutler-Hammer.

A graphic designer was assigned for developing the interface to the program. The Copfer & Associates Webmaster worked with an engineer from Microsoft to develop the source code. The team had a strict deadline of three weeks for developing and implementing the application. Our developer also wrote many of the CGI scripts that were needed to keep track of the answers submitted by students in order to give a score, not only at the end of the topic, but also at the end of the training session. A score of 7 out of 9 earned a certificate of completion that was forwarded to Cutler-Hammer's Human Resource Department (Figure 13.3).

Once the structural layout has been established for the program, it is a matter of setting up the synchronization. The application timeline orchestrates the video, audio, and text together. The author must put the picture and sound files in sequential order and allow enough time between each so that they make a instructional point, but they are not presented for such a long period of time that the attention of the student is lost. NetShow does not allow a picture file and a sound file to begin simultaneously. The author must decide which to start with and leave a fraction of a second between the start of each. We see faster than we hear, simply because light travels faster than sound. Knowing that, an author may choose to begin the picture file first because we are used to seeing before hearing, even if we are not aware of it.

By using interactive multimedia for a simulation a student can acquire not only facts, but also job experience. "There are some very sophisticated programs that allow a student to practice within a simulated work environment. These programs allow the student to make decisions and witness the

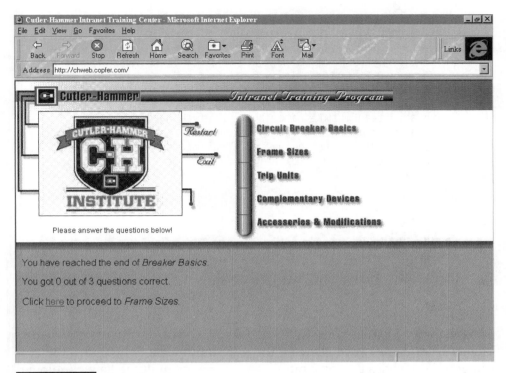

FIGURE 13.3 End of lesson.

repercussions with positive or negative feedback. Positive feedback from a correct decision builds confidence, a knowledge base, and experience. Whereas negative feedback teaches a student what not to do, without incurring damage or loss of property or even life. Computer technology allows one to truly learn from his or her mistakes," says Ron Copfer.

Here is some sample code from the program.

```
<HTML>
<HEAD>
<TITLE>Cutler-Hammer Intranet Training Center</TITLE>
<frameset frameborder="0" border="0" framespacing="0"
rows=51,225,16,*>
  <frame src="head.html" name="header" frameborder=0 marginheight=0
marginwidth=0 scrolling=no noresize>
    <frameset frameborder="0" border="0" framespacing="0"
cols=38,240,68,*>
      <frame src="left.html" name="leftofmovie" frameborder=0 mar-
ginheight=0 marginwidth=0 scrolling=no noresize>
```

```
        <frame src="movie.html" name="asfmovie" frameborder=0 margin-
height=0 marginwidth=0 scrolling=no noresize>
        <frame src="right.html" name="rightofmovie" frameborder=0
marginheight=0 marginwidth=0 scrolling=no noresize>
        <frame src="buttons.html" name="buttons" frameborder=0 margin-
height=0 marginwidth=10 scrolling=no noresize>
    </frameset>
    <frame src="beans.html" name="buttons" frameborder=0 margin-
height=0 marginwidth=10 scrolling=no noresize>
    <frame src="intro.html" name="textarea" frameborder=0 margin-
height=10 marginwidth=10 scrolling=auto noresize>
</frameset>
</HTML>
```

NASA's Web Interactive Training

The Web Interactive Training project (WIT) at Kennedy Space Center
uses multiplatform interactive media to more effectively and efficiently
deliver training to NASA employees over the Web (Figure 13.4). "The first
phase of this project is the conversion of an existing course on
Nondestructive Evaluation (NDE) and a new course on Statistical Process
Control," explains David Metcalf, the lead multimedia designer on the
project. "The project incorporates state-of-the-art multimedia technologies
to meet the defined objectives."

The primary users of the system are NASA personnel at Kennedy Space
Center and other NASA centers. The objective of the project is to efficiently and effectively train a large base of NASA staff using state-of-the-art
technology to enhance learning. Training modules consisting of text, graphics, animation, video, simulations, and tests are delivered over the Internet
through a Web browser interface. The project is expected to reduce training costs and associated travel and time-off task costs. The training is available 24 hours a day, seven days a week for student convenience with
follow-up job performance support after the training is completed.

The WIT project spans several years and will continue to evolve as new
technologies that enhance learning and meet course objectives are developed. The project began in July 1995 and has continued through 1996
and now into 1997.

A feasibility prototype and two full courses were completed to verify and
validate the design and technologies incorporated and developed. The first
course was the Nondestructive Evaluation (NDE) Overview (Figure 13.5).
The second was the Introduction to Statistical Process Control course.

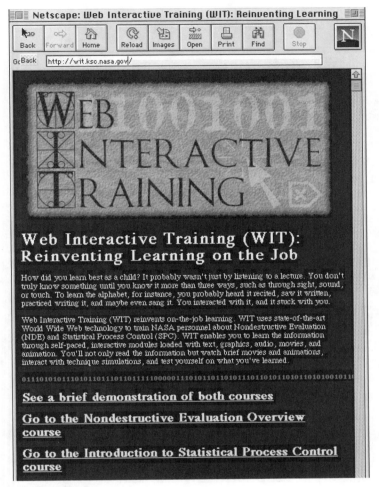

FIGURE 13.4 Web Interactive Training.

Courtesy I-NET Multimedia and NASA

The next phase of this project is the conversion of two advanced courses. One will be Nondestructive Evaluation-Radiography and the other will be Advanced Statistical Process Control (Figure 13.6). The project incorporates state-of-the-art multimedia technologies to meet the defined learning objectives.

Instructional Design

"In order to develop an effective WBT system that accomplishes the goals of providing sound instruction over the Web, it is necessary to understand

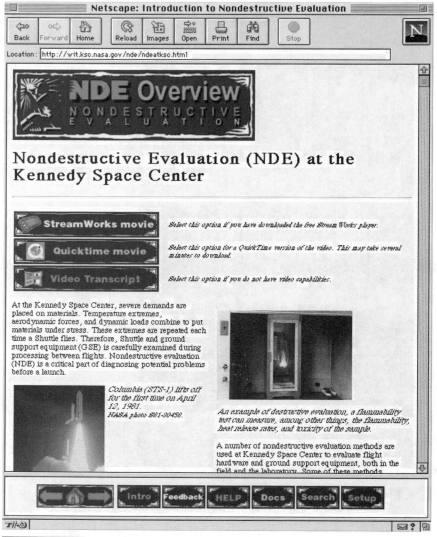

FIGURE 13.5 NDE Overview.

Courtesy of I-NET Multimedia and NASA

key instructional features that will contribute to the development and deployment of the WIT system," Metcalf wrote in describing the program. "Using multimedia in an effective way on the Web and especially in Web-based training applications is a challenge. The project also defines a functional educational design model that takes into account the advantages and

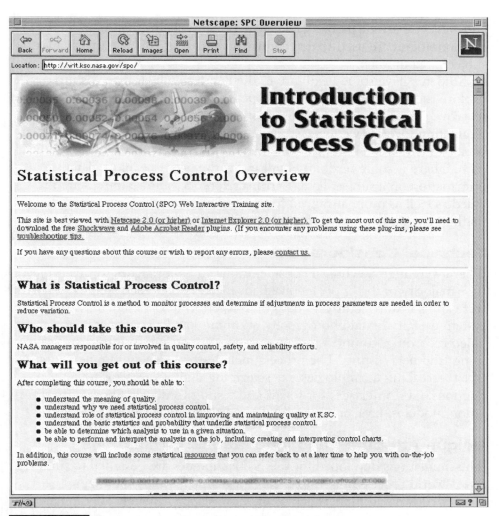

Netscape: SPC Overview

Back | Forward | Home | Reload | Images | Open | Print | Find | Stop

N

Location: http://wit.ksc.nasa.gov/spc/

Introduction to Statistical Process Control

Statistical Process Control Overview

Welcome to the Statistical Process Control (SPC) Web Interactive Training site.

This site is best viewed with Netscape 2.0 (or higher) or Internet Explorer 2.0 (or higher). To get the most out of this site, you'll need to download the free Shockwave and Adobe Acrobat Reader plugins. (If you encounter any problems using these plug-ins, please see troubleshooting tips.

If you have any questions about this course or wish to report any errors, please contact us.

What is Statistical Process Control?

Statistical Process Control is a method to monitor processes and determine if adjustments in process parameters are needed in order to reduce variation.

Who should take this course?

NASA managers responsible for or involved in quality control, safety, and reliability efforts.

What will you get out of this course?

After completing this course, you should be able to:

- understand the meaning of quality.
- understand why we need statistical process control.
- understand role of statistical process control in improving and maintaining quality at KSC.
- understand the basic statistics and probability that underlie statistical process control.
- be able to determine which analysis to use in a given situation.
- be able to perform and interpret the analysis on the job, including creating and interpreting control charts.

In addition, this course will include some statistical resources that you can refer back to at a later time to help you with on-the-job problems.

FIGURE 13.6 Introduction to Statistical Process Control.

Courtesy I-NET Multimedia and NASA

disadvantages of the Web." The instructional model for each section includes introduction and definitions, key concepts and theoretical foundation, practical application and case studies, an interactive simulation or practice exercise, and testing or evaluation.

Students have a clear learning objective presented in each module and their path choices are limited to pertinent information. A structured approach is determined in each course by instructional system designers and subject matter experts. The instructional objectives, content, and methodologies are used to determine the best approach for a particular subject area module.

Students have some flexibility in the depth to which they wish to explore the information, but an acceptable level of proficiency must be met to prove completion of a module. For example, in the Nondestructive Evaluation Overview course, students must take a test with results posted back to a database in order to advance to further sections by the specified path. There is some flexibility built in for the user to explore detailed information on a subject area. Further references and resources are provided as well as more advanced follow-on modules in a particular NDE method currently under development.

Technical Considerations

There were many technical considerations and approaches to this project. The majority of the effort involved advanced HTML scripting, and hardware and software setup and design. This effort also included instructional system design, digital photography, scanning, media conversion, audio and video recording, compression, animation, formatting, scripting, programming, and beta testing. The process includes research and implementation of late-breaking technologies like streaming digital video for topic introductions, CGI interfaces for forms and testing feedback, Shockwave simulation modules, Java, and other advanced client/server features.

Unique Attributes and Innovations: Simulations

The simulations developed for the NDE modules are designed to simulate a real-world process in a simple, elegant manner while minimizing the learner's download time. (Each simulation is approximately 30 kilobytes in size.) Each simulation follows the same general model: using the technique under study, the student searches for discontinuities randomly scattered throughout a test object. The Eddy Current simulation (Figure 13.7) shows a sample plate on the right and the feedback screen on the left. These simulations were designed and developed using Macromedia Director and its native programming language, Lingo. While most of the simulations are currently produced using Shockwave, future efforts will explore interactivity in standard Web pages without requiring a plug-in. Embedded Java, persistent connections, and built-in browser multimedia capabilities are example technologies that may prove useful in future simulations

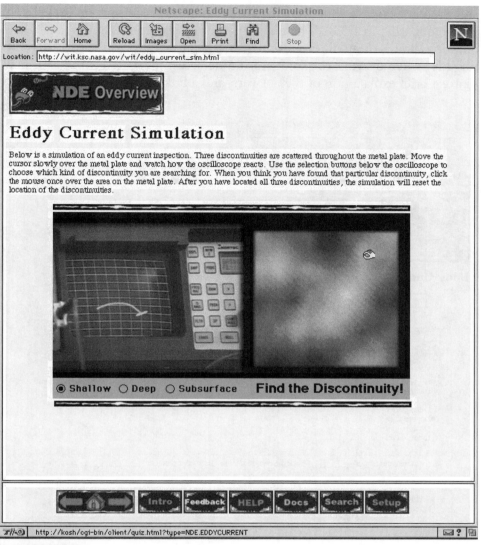

FIGURE 13.7 Eddy Current Simulation.

Courtesy I-NET Multimedia and NASA

Testing

Testing will aid in comprehension of the information presented on NDE and SPC and reinforce the most important points in the section of training presented. Test answers will be cataloged in a database to show student progress and adequate completion. Students are presented with a short multiple choice quiz (Figure 13.8). The quiz is randomly generated from a database of questions and is different every time the student takes the quiz. After submitting his or her answers, the student is immediately presented with his or her score, a brief explanation of the answers, and a link to the place in the course

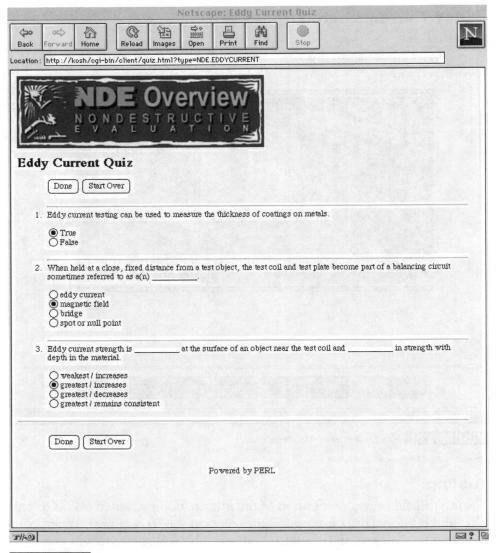

FIGURE 13.8 Eddy Current Quiz.

Courtesy I-NET Multimedia and NASA

where that topic was covered. Students cannot cheat. The program prevents them from returning to the same quiz and retaking it. The testing database was written in Perl and partially converted to Java. Metcalf says that the program will eventually be entirely converted to Java for ease of future expandability and possible cross-platform server deployment.

Security and Student Tracking

The system is available only to the NASA centers unless special password authorization is granted by NASA. The courses may be opened up to a broader audience in the future at NASA's discretion.

Current activities include enhancing student tracking to include a placeholder for reentering the training space at the same point of exit from the last use. This will avoid unnecessary navigation and the disorientation often associated with large hypertext systems.

A good CMI (computer-managed instruction) database to track completion of sections is an essential component of the WIT system. Instructional designers will have a much clearer idea about the effectiveness of the instruction from the answers received. Tracking could be automated to send an electronic mail reminder to individuals who need to finish instruction by a certain date for certification.

Performance Support

Some of the interactive calculation simulators like the normal distribution calculator shown in Figure 13.9 provide performance support after the training. The system also contains an electronic version of relevant reference material and procedures used for each discipline. A search engine allows users to pinpoint specific information and get to it in seconds. This makes the modules usable as a reference after the training has been completed.

Future Developments

Future efforts at NASA will involve advanced security functions, enhanced student tracking capabilities, additional performance support functions, adaptive learning through dynamic Web pages and objects, integration into centralized NASA training activities, front-end "push" technology (Figure 13.10), synchronous instructional communication aids (videoconferencing and live bulletin boards), and research in just-in-place training using mobile communication technology. Current Web-based training is geared toward the individual. Team-based learning using Web communication tools will also be explored to enhance interactivity and the learning experience in the WIT system. (See Appendix E and CD-ROM for sample code.)

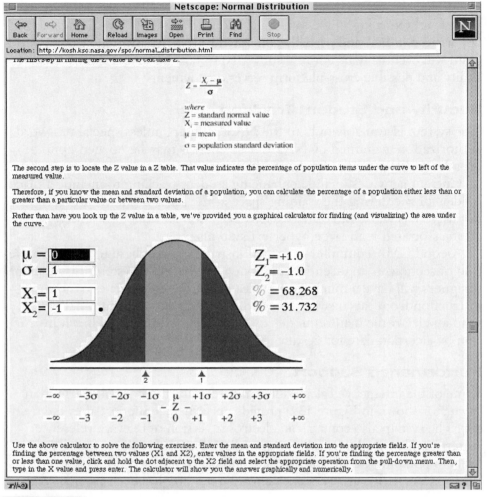

Location: http://kosh.ksc.nasa.gov/spc/normal_distribution.html

The first step in finding the Z value is to calculate Z.

$$Z = \frac{X - \mu}{\sigma}$$

where
Z = standard normal value
X_i = measured value
μ = mean
σ = population standard deviation

The second step is to locate the Z value in a Z table. That value indicates the percentage of population items under the curve to left of the measured value.

Therefore, if you know the mean and standard deviation of a population, you can calculate the percentage of a population either less than or greater than a particular value or between two values.

Rather than have you look up the Z value in a table, we've provided you a graphical calculator for finding (and visualizing) the area under the curve.

$\mu = \boxed{0}$
$\sigma = \boxed{1}$
$X_1 = \boxed{1}$
$X_2 = \boxed{-1}$

$Z_1 = +1.0$
$Z_2 = -1.0$
$\% = 68.268$
$\% = 31.732$

$-\infty \quad -3\sigma \quad -2\sigma \quad -1\sigma \quad \mu \quad +1\sigma \quad +2\sigma \quad +3\sigma \quad +\infty$
$- Z -$
$-\infty \quad -3 \quad -2 \quad -1 \quad 0 \quad +1 \quad +2 \quad +3 \quad +\infty$

Use the above calculator to solve the following exercises. Enter the mean and standard deviation into the appropriate fields. If you're finding the percentage between two values (X1 and X2), enter values in the appropriate fields. If you're finding the percentage greater than or less than one value, click and hold the dot adjacent to the X2 field and select the appropriate operation from the pull-down menu. Then, type in the X value and press enter. The calculator will show you the answer graphically and numerically.

FIGURE 13.9 Normal distribution calculator.

Courtesy I-NET Multimedia and NASA

Empower's Oracle Simulator

This program closely approximates the state-of-the-art CD-ROM programs through the use of simulations, audio, and graphics. Oracle Simulator is a Web-based training program that demonstrates the power of Java as an interactive programming language for developing Internet/intranet-based training applications. The program is an interactive learning tool for database administrators. The simulations allow users

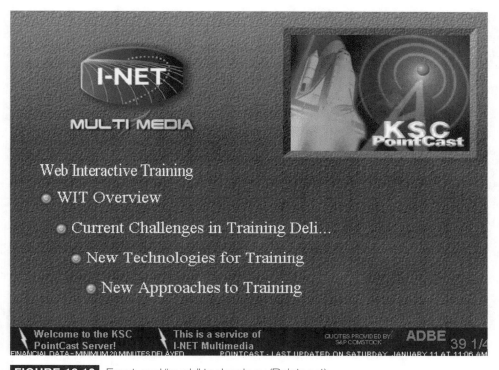

FIGURE 13.10 Front-end "push" technology (Pointcast).

to develop their skills through scenarios that emulate real-life backup and recovery situations.

The simulation takes place in a fictitious company's (DBA) hotline office (Figure 13.11). The user or student acts as the DBA hotline contact. Customers call on the phone to report database administration problems that need to be fixed using software tools such as Oracle server manager.

In the office is a letter from the mentor, a file drawer with customer files, a phone, a computer terminal, a bookcase with reference books, a certificate on the wall, and a framed personal photo. The office door stands slightly ajar with an exit sign on it. You can go to any object in the office by clicking on it. To exit the object and return to the office screen, you can either click anywhere outside the item or double-click on the close bar if there is one. Through the DBA hotline office interface, you have a file drawer that contains files of customers and their database problems (Figure 13.12). You select a problem type by clicking on a folder.

FIGURE 13.11 The office metaphor: The DBA office represents a typical office environment.

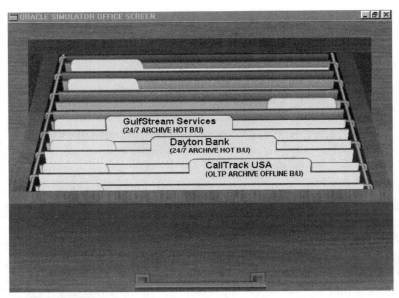

FIGURE 13.12 The desk drawer contains files on DBA otline customers.

Click on any file folder tab to choose a customer (Figure 13.13). In the folder is a customer's profile and a list of situations that exist in the customer's database environment. Click anywhere outside the desk drawer to return to the office environment.

There is also a color-coded list of DBA administration situations, from relatively simple to fix, to moderately challenging, to difficult. Here are a few of the working elements:

- Overview screen: The overview provides an synopsis of each database situation in a customer's file folder. Click on the close bar or click anywhere outside the window to return to the office environment.

- Phone: The customer calls you on the speakerphone. The customer outlines the basic database problem, and promises to send e-mail detailing the problem. You can click on the phone at any time to listen to the customer's message again.

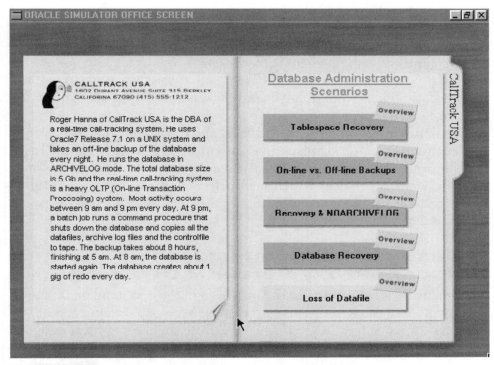

FIGURE 13.13 The file folder contains general information about the customer's company and database.

- Computer: The computer is where you video conference with your on-call expert, interact with your customer via e-mail and video conference, and view a log of the information you've received from the expert and the customer (Figures 13.14 and 13.15). In addition, you can tell how long it took you to solve a problem by using the timer which compares your time with that of the expert's.

As you solve the database problem (Figure 13.16) using server manager (Figure 13.17), your on-call advisor or mentor guides you through various choices through a desktop videoconference window metaphor. A progress log screen records all your interactions with the expert and the customer.

Timer window: You can keep track of the amount of time it takes you to solve a customer's problem by using the timer.

On each screen, the simulation engine traps user actions such as clicks, double clicks, menu selections, and command selections and either executes the action or provides instructional feedback if the action is incorrect. Cue cards provide additional information to guide the user to the optimum solution (Figures 13.18 and 13.19).

Certain screens ask you to select commands and show you the results of those commands with instructional feedback.

As the you progress through different pathways of the simulation, the system keeps track of the steps you have taken to solve the problem (Figure 13.20).

Software simulation provides the chance to learn new skills in a risk-free environment. The simulations are a refreshing change from text-based ("page-turning" metaphor) CBT. Users see the results of their actions and learn from correct choices as well as incorrect choices. The audio-based guidance provides additional insights into problem solving based on expert experience and knowledge (Figure 13.21).

Multimedia Learning and NetscapeProxy Server 2.0Training

Multimedia Learning of Irving, TX has been in the development business for a number of years, and is now developing Web-based training. The Netscape Proxy Server 2.0 training course from the company was designed to reduce in-class training time for one of Netscape's server products by introducing fundamental Proxy Server concepts via the Web. After registering for a five-day server training class, users were given the URL for the Proxy Server Training portion of the course and invited to visit the site

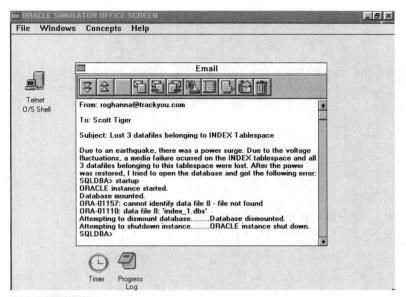

FIGURE 13.14 Customers send you any error messages related to their database situation via e-mail.

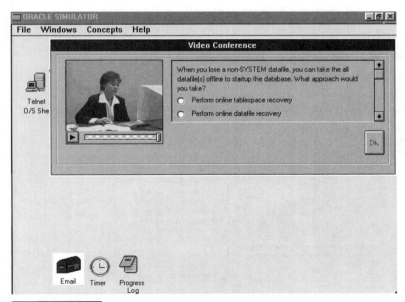

FIGURE 13.15 Video conference window.

Level 3 Courses: Interactive Multimedia

FIGURE 13.16 The software simulation includes a series of screens from the actual Oracle product.

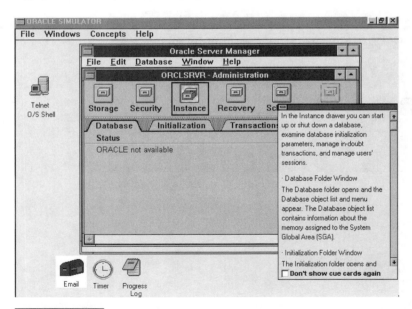

FIGURE 13.17 Oracle Server Manager.

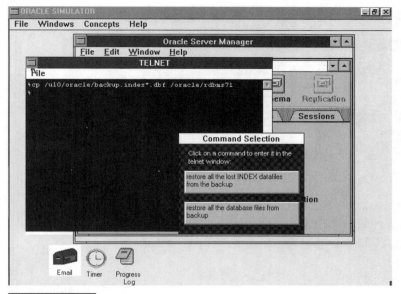

FIGURE 13.18 Telnet screen.

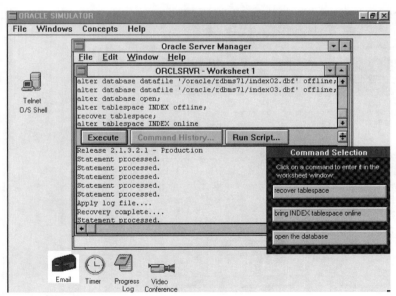

FIGURE 13.19 Command Selection.

Level 3 Courses: Interactive Multimedia

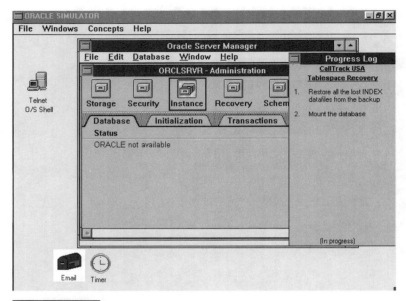

FIGURE 13.20 Progress Log.

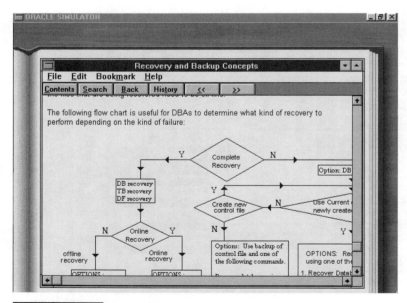

FIGURE 13.21 Recovery and Backup Concepts.

whenever their schedules allowed. It was hoped that with this preclass use, in-class training time for the Proxy Server could be reduced from two-and-a-half days to two days. Instructors could then devote the remaining three full days to Netscape's primary Web server, the Enterprise Server.

The target audience for the Netscape Proxy Server 2.0 training course was UNIX network administrators and corporate Webmasters. Because of the Proxy Server 2.0 training course, in-class training time for the Enterprise Server was able to be increased without short-changing in-class Proxy Server training time. The training course was developed using Netscape Navigator Gold 3.0 to create HTML and JavaScript for content pages. Graphics were created using Photoshop. In addition, Symantec Cafe was used to create a Java interface that allowed developers to generate a JavaScript quiz. Netscape Navigator 3.0 running on a Macintosh, PC or UNIX platform is required to view the course.

The table of contents page for the Netscape Proxy Server 2.0 program introduction allows the user to receive an overview and explanation of the program workings (Figure 13.22).

For companies that do business on the Internet or the Web, a proxy server can act as a transparent intermediary between individual users and

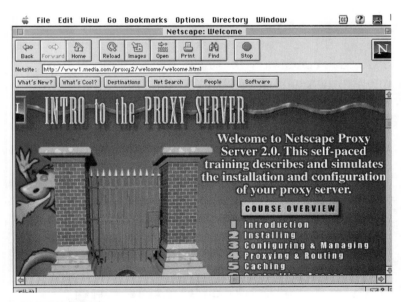

FIGURE 13.22 Table of contents.

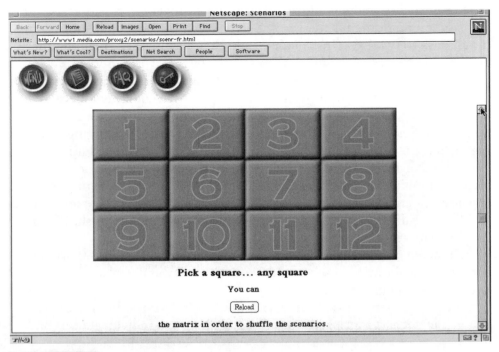

FIGURE 13.23 Scenarios.

the company's servers that contain the information users want. A proxy server also lets an organization or company provide controlled Internet accessibility for internal users who would otherwise be blocked by a security firewall; a proxy server working in reverse can also let the organization regulate access from external clients, as a refinement to firewall security protection.

The user is presented with 12 different scenarios that require applying the knowledge learned previously (Figure 13.23).

In scenario 2, the user is directed to create a template that will configure the proxy server to handle requests for all documents on the Web site (Figure 13.24). This type of activity has a gamelike element to it which helps with motivation.

DigitalThink's Commercial Offering

DigitalThink is a San Francisco-based commercial developer applying the latest Web technology to off-the-shelf technology training (Figure 13.25).

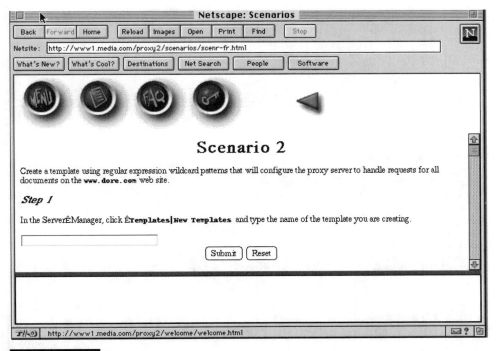

FIGURE 13.24 Scenario 2.

The company offers courses covering software titles, computer programming, multimedia tools, the Internet, and other topics. The training program allows students to connect with other classmates to exchange ideas and opinions about courses. Students can also go to the chat and discussion areas to talk with instructors, tutors, and classmates. Students engage in interactive learning activities and quizzes and are provided feedback and progress reports.

The Orientation Area instructs the user how to read descriptions of courses, learn more about instructors, and register courses. Students can preview the course syllabus and become acquainted with the course before deciding whether to purchase it. The company allows browsers to take a free course to see if it matches their needs.

The Course Area is where the user takes the courses and interacts with other students, instructors, and tutors and is open only to registered students. Students are provided a personal Locker page with links to their courses, instructors, tutors, and classmates. Course lessons are accessible here and include graphics, hypertext, and audio. There are quizzes, hands-on

FIGURE 13.25 The DigitalThink home page shows the courses offered and helps users register for courses.

Copyright 1997 DigitalThink, Inc.

exercises, course-specific discussion boards and live instructor-led chat sessions. If students need help in a course they may contact the instructor, tutor, or other classmates via e-mail, with a promised response within 24 hours.

Figure 13.26 shows the opening page of DigitalThink's Java for Programmers. At the left is the tool bar to connect the student with the chat lobby, discussion lobby, and orientation to the program.

Lesson overviews are available in the student locker under the course heading (Figure 13.27).

Registration for courses can be performed online with the secured server or via fax. Upon payment, the user receives a student ID and a password. These are used to access the courses through the student's locker (Figure 13.28).

Some of the courses offered through DigitalThink include: Java for Programmers, Object-Oriented Programming with C++, Hands-On

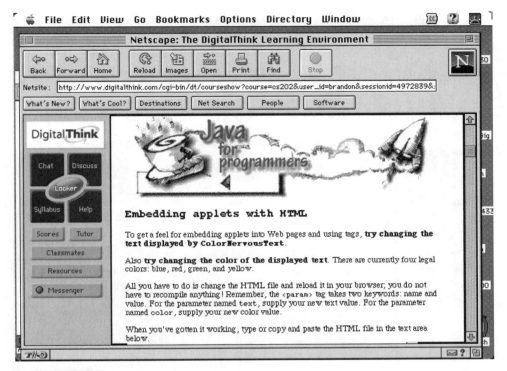

FIGURE 13.26 The opening page in the "Java for Programmers" course.

Copyright 1997 DigitalThink, Inc.

Photoshop, PageMaker to Perfection, Find It Faster! Power Searching on the Internet, Home Sweet Home Page, and Living with the Internet.

The technology behind DigitalThink's courseware is Java "on-the-fly," which means that a course is automatically customized for each student in real-time. This means that the course can change depending on what the user needs as the course is running. For example, if the user has a slower connection, less-media-intensive files can be downloaded and presented in the course, such as the smaller GIF format for graphics files instead of the larger JPEG format.

As another example, if a student answers a quiz question incorrectly, the course will incorporate the correct information into subsequent modules and quizzes to make sure the material is understood. DigitalThink's database keeps track of areas in which the student needs the most assistance and adjusts the courses accordingly.

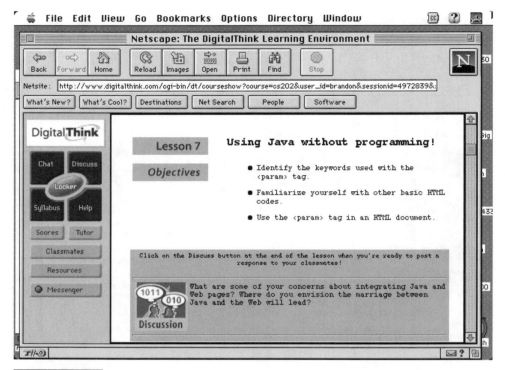

FIGURE 13.27 Lesson overviews.

Copyright 1997 DigitalThink, Inc.

Devon Lazarus, part of DigitalThink's Technology Team, says they are currently converting all of their courseware to Java (from Perl) because of its cross-platform compatibility. "We wanted to make sure that the student could run the course no matter what kind of computer he or she was running."

"Java also provides for more scaleability when you're talking about number of users," Lazarus continues. "As an example, with our previous system the code had to be compiled each time it was run. With a lot of users running courses at the same time, this can slow down the entire system. With Java, the code is already compiled in a way that the computer can understand, so the whole process is faster. This lets us support a number of users that goes into the millions without a significant loss of speed."

View DigitalThink's wares at www.digitalthink.com, accessible from the CD-ROM accompanying this book.

FIGURE 13.28 The student ID and password are entered to access the student locker.

Copyright 1997 DigitalThink, Inc.

Distance Learning and Computer-Based Training in One

In addition to the kinds of programs we've seen in this chapter there is another approach some companies are taking, that of blending the live-instructor aspects of distance learning with the self-instructional facilities of computer-based training. The two companies which have developed the premier examples of this combination of training are ILINC and Centra. Interestingly, the developers on the ILINC team have a background in distance learning while the developers at Centra, who were previously involved with Lotus Notes, have a background in collaboration software. Following is a description of each of these programs.

LearnLinc's Simulated Classroom Environment

LearnLinc from ILINC was created to mimic the classroom environment through the use of video conferencing, simulated hand-raising, shared applications, annotation, and a shared blackboard. There is no limit on the number of participants due to multicasting. The information is able to go from TCP/IP standard to WANs to LANs without much change to the content or sacrificing the communication quality. Communication is speeded up through the use of ISDN or T1 lines.

Video and audio casting allows attendees to see and hear what is going on as it happens. There are two ways to teach a class: Directed Discussion or Open Discussion. Directed Discussion is led by a Floor Holder. The Floor Holder is the instructor (and sometimes student) who is being seen/heard by the other attendees. Attendees may take control of the floor by "raising their hand" via the hand-raising icon. Hand raisers are then listed either chronologically or alphabetically. The Floor Holder may decide when to let the floor be taken as well as having the power to take control of the floor again. An Open Discussion is when participants can may take the floor at any time. The Floor Holder always has the capability to launch and share applications with everyone else.

LearnLinc provides a shared blackboard which allows the instructor and the students to participate in note taking, draw simple graphics, import pictures, and display Windows applications as screen captures. The blackboard is a full-shared application. LearnLinc is also equipped with a question-and-answer application (QNA) which allows the instructors to ask multiple-choice questions. The students receive immediate results.

For independent work there is a Library Browser available for anyone to browse through LearnLinc courses and resources. A potential student can open a selected course to review/preview the course or proceed to complete the course independently. The Session Browser lists all the upcoming courses. The Application Browser launches applications which are registered with the LearnLinc system. These applications may be launched during a session or independently.

LearnLinc has an assortment of options available for authoring through the Resource Editor and the LearnLinc Menu. The coursework may be new, old, or revised material as LearnLinc has the capability to take existing material and build it for the LearnLinc environment.

Administrators can control who is able to access what through the User Browser and Authority Control.

Centra Symposium

Symposium is a Java-based program that allows trainers to build and deliver Web-based training programs. Using Symposium, corporate training organizations can develop and deliver live, instructor-led training with real-time audio, as well as self-paced learning to geographically dispersed individuals.

Using Java-enabled browsers such as Netscape Navigator and Microsoft Internet Explorer, students participate in live, interactive instructor-led classes. In real-time, students engage in question-and-answer sessions, problem solve using a shared whiteboard, work in breakout sessions, converse with real-time audio, and dialog in text-based chat. Because this is a live, real-time environment, the instructor has the flexibility to adapt the class on-the-fly to meet student needs, and clarify content. The ability to quickly modify content and update training and to respond to people's questions immediately makes this a good delivery vehicle for urgent and critical content.

Other capabilities of the program include Web Safari, which allows the instructor to take the class to Web sites on the intranet and World Wide Web. Body Language is a tool that enables students to provide the kind of feedback instructors get from nonverbal clues. The student's interface has Body Language icons that provide the instructor with feedback on the pace and clarity of instruction, and an indicator to signal the instructor that the student has a question. The instructor's interface has icons that enable instructors to control the sequence of the lesson and monitor students' reactions and attendance. In addition, instructors can pass control of the audio portion of the program to the students, and they can then lead a discussion.

If organized collaboration is not possible due to time zone differences or students' schedules, self-paced training for individuals and groups is an option in Symposium. Students work independently to complete multimedia computer-based training programs, communicate via threaded discussions, engage in dialog with the facilitator, and take online quizzes. In this format, students work at their own pace but can draw on additional resources. Using Symposium communication tools, students can access subject matter experts and facilitators.

Symposium has a course assembly tool called Course Builder, with which developers can create programs that include multimedia modules, videos, text, animation, graphic presentations, and images. Course Builder allows the reuse of exiting course material, and the addition of new materials using tools such as Designer's Edge, PowerPoint, Aimtech IconAuthor, Macromedia Director, and Authorware. In addition to sequencing content, this tool helps the developer define the online environment to meet learning objectives. Course Builder lets the developer define course structure and control of interactions, quizzes, tests, text-based chat, audio-enabled breakout sessions, whiteboard interactions, threaded discussions, links to other Web sites, and libraries of resource materials.

Symposium courses are delivered across the existing intranet, and viewed at the student's desktop on standard multimedia PCs, UNIX stations, and other systems. Symposium does not require the installation of additional software or hardware such as boards and peripherals. No additional software is required to run Symposium.

PART 4

APPENDIXES

SAMPLE PROPOSAL

What follows is a proposal from Kevin Kruse of ACI that the American Management Association received after sending out its request for proposal (RFP).

ACI's PROPOSAL TO AMA

American Management Association

Nancy Bartlett

9 Galen Street

Watertown, MA 02172

Dear Nancy:

Thank you for the opportunity to propose on a proof of concept for the *AMA Training Network*. I am thrilled that the AMA is pursuing an Intranet-based training solution, and am excited by the prospect of working with you to make it a reality.

As you review our proposal I think you will see that we are uniquely qualified to partner with the AMA for the following reasons:

<u>ACI's Intranet-based Training (IBT) Experience</u>:

We have extensive experience developing Intranet-based training modules for several clients. We are currently near completion on 30 hours of Intranet-based, multimedia training for [*previous client*], which includes topics on Customer Service, Team Dynamics, Client Focus, Problem Solving, and Business Fundamentals.

<u>ACI's Instructional Design & Multimedia Development Expertise</u>:

The creativity and effectiveness of our multimedia design have been recognized recently with the 1996 *Blue Ribbon Award for Instructional Technology* from the American Society for Training and Development and the 1996 *Award of Excellence for an Instructional Intervention* from the International Society for Performance Improvement.

<u>Our Ability and Desire to Partner with the AMA</u>:

A key factor behind ACI's 100% annual growth rate (over the last five years) has been our ability to truly partner with our clients. You will see in our proposal that we are suggesting that the AMA forge a formal partnership with their multimedia vendor as a way to address some specific technological issues that are specific to IBT delivery. As a step in that direction, our budget for the Proof of Concept has been priced *below our cost of development*.

If you have any further questions, or if you would like to see samples of our work I'd be happy to come in for a visit. I have two scheduled trips to Newton in January already and would welcome the opportunity to discuss your plans further. Thanks again for the opportunity to propose.

Sincerely,

Kevin E. Kruse

The AMA Training Network

An Intranet-based Training Delivery System

AMA TRAINING PRODUCTS AND SERVICES

Prepared for:

_____

Nancy Bartlett

Director, Product Development & Ed. Services

Ann Beaton

Manager, Developmental Editing

Lynn Clifford

Product Development

Prepared by:

_____

Kevin Kruse

President

Advanced Consulting, Inc.

Green Brook, NJ

908-424-1785

I. Overview

Background

This proposal provides a plan for the development of a "proof of concept" for an Intranet-based online learning system. It is understood that the primary goals of this interactive learning environment will be to:

• transfer knowledge and develop skills

• provide performance support

•assess and/or certify learners' competencies

•track organizational use, and individual student history

This proposal was prepared at the request of the American Management Association, and is based on an RFP dated November 1 and an Addendum dated December 6.

Opportunity and Challenge

As corporations continue to build and expand their Intranet computer systems, there exists a tremendous opportunity for training suppliers to develop and market materials that will take advantage of this new medium. Recent surveys have indicated that over 50% of all training may be conducted online by the year 2000.

As high-bandwidth Internet access becomes available to homes in the next five years, the market for Internet-based self-study courses will also explode. Between corporate sponsorship and individuals interested in lifelong learning, Web-based training will likely become a multi-billion dollar industry.

However, while network technologies have created these new opportunities, they also present specific challenges. The challenges the AMA will face can be summarized with three points:

•Network servers are not standard. AMA clients will be running a variety of server operating systems including Windows NT/IIS, UNIX, and different derivative packages. The "infrastructure" of the AMA Training Network, including capabilities for chat, threaded discussion, and student tracking will need to be modified for each of these operating systems.

•The speed of change. The pace of change for Intranet technology will continue for the next ten years. These changes will effect audio and video compression and delivery, functionality of Web browsers, and server-side database access. The software developed by the AMA today, will probably have to be modified every year to keep up with these changes, even if the content remains the same.

•Tech support and custom installations. Due to the complexity of Intranet server software and firewall security systems, the AMA Training Network could require an experienced Intranet technician for installation. (A simple a:\install command will not suffice.) This installation procedure will either have to be performed by a client technician, AMA technician, or facilitated by the AMA's vendor's telephone technical support.

Because of the tremendous opportunity that is available for Intranet-based training, and due to the inherent technical challenges involved, ACI is proposing a "partnership" with the AMA. This partnership—outlined in the Investment Analysis portion of this proposal—will enable the AMA to focus on their core competencies which include instructional content and client relationships, without having to worry about long-term computer technology expertise.

II. Design

Overview

The AMA Training Network will actually consist of three distinct components. Each component will require a different type of programming language, support, and development roles. These components are:

•Network Infrastructure

•Communication Tools

•Interactive, multimedia content

Infrastructure

This component is the fundamental framework that will integrate all other modules. The Infrastructure is what will actually become integrated into AMA clients' Web page system.

The Infrastructure will include the Main Menu, which in turn will launch communication tools and/or content modules. Additionally, the Infrastructure is what will contain the software code that will handle student tracking and data flows to other modules like Registrar.

Communication Tools

The AMA Training Network will contain three separate applications to handle communication between students and instructors, other students, and/or the AMA.

•E-mail

The first communication tool will be standard electronic mail. This component will be scripted in HTML and will be designed to launch the Intranet's built-in e-mail system. This e-mail function can be customized so that it will be pre-addressed to the proper individual. For example, if a student clicked a button labeled "Submit a Writing Sample," the e-mail window could be pre-addressed to an individual at the AMA, or at the client's location, who is pre-designated to serve as a writing coach.

•Chat Rooms

The second communication tool will be real-time chat rooms. This application enables multiple participants, each using his/her own computer to discuss various issues. Typically, these chat sessions would be facilitated by an SME, training manager, or guest speaker.

Unlike many chat rooms that put all participants in a single window, ACI will create a chat room function that enables the moderator's text to appear in a separate content window. This will provide for easy distinction between questions and comments from the moderator/SME and those from the students.

Additionally, the chat room sessions will be recorded into a text file for future access by students. This "library" of previous sessions should provide an additional resource that will help to build a climate of continuous learning.

•Threaded Discussions

This feature, described in the AMA RFP as a "Bulletin Board" enables students to post questions, answers, or comments to an electronic messaging system. Unlike chat, where users are all speaking at the same time, threaded discussions enable participants to communicate at any time, individually. Questions and answers remain on the system until manually deleted by the system operator. Similar to chat sessions, these threaded discussions can always be saved for future reference.

Content

The instructional content for the *AMA Training Network* will consist of a series of brief modules, each 10–15 minutes in length and focused on a single topic (e.g., Coaching). (For the Proof of Concept only three modules will be developed at this time.)

These modules will be designed so that they can be completed as stand-alone units, or they can be linked together to create a curriculum around a single theme (e.g., Supervisory Skills).

Interactivity for Active Learning

The tutorials will be designed to provide a high degree of interactivity, which should make them superior in quality to most other Intranet-based training modules now available. Within each module students may encounter self-assessment questions, simulations, instructional games or puzzles, or other items that will force them to be *active learners*.

The structure around each module would likely be:

Pre-test (Level 2 Assessment Information)

Interactive Tutorial

Post-test (Level 2 Assessment Information)

Student Feedback Survey (Level 1 Evaluation)

Media Components

Each tutorial would include the following media elements: text, 2D and/or 3D illustrations, photographic images, animated sequences, and audio narration.

Standard Features of Instructional Modules

The instructional modules will also contain the following features, which will be available to the Learner at all times.

Glossary

Learner can pull up a glossary window at any time to get a complete definition of the term. Where appropriate, an audio pronunciation will be available.

Help

Online help will provide information about navigation, features, and general information. An e-mail button will enable Learners to ask for more specific help from a designated administrator or manager.

Clipboard

Learners can type in notes as they complete the module. These notes can then be saved for future reference or printing.

Reference (More Information)

All relevant online materials can be hyperlinked in a logical fashion. Learners could simply click the title to access it.

Bookmarks

Learners may "bookmark" individual screens for future reference. This will enable them to re-enter a module and quickly resume from where they left off, or to quickly review the material they found most beneficial.

Student Tracking

The pre- and post-test results will be presented to the Learner and will also be available to the training manager. These scores could be saved to a student tracking system (such as *Registrar*) or attached to an e-mail and forwarded to a specific individual. Additional information could also be tracked for management review (e.g., date and time course taken, number of times course taken, etc.).

III. Technical Specifications

Intranet Server Computer

The *AMA Training Network* will run on standard Intranet servers. However, the chat and bulletin board applications ideally should be written to specific operating systems—typically servers run either MS-Windows NT/IIS or a version of

UNIX. At the AMA's request, these communication applications can be created for both server platforms, or a single platform.

Development Language

The *AMA Training Network* will be developed with HTML and will likely use either Java or Shockwave. There are important differences between these languages, and the AMA will have to evaluate each option within the context of their long-term goals and strategies.

A brief description of the strengths and weaknesses of each language is outlined on the following page.

Development Language	Strengths	Weaknesses
HTML only	Runs on all machines and browsers Easy and fast to develop	Very limited interactivity (can't create simulations, instructional games, or complex questions like drag and drop) Limited control over screen design Limited audio and video capabilities (would require AMA client to purchase additional Server-side software like RealAudio) Limited security features
Java	Runs on most machines and browsers Good interactivity Very secure	Development time and costs 2–3 times higher than HTML or Shockwave Two different Java standards (100% pure vs. Microsoft) Limited audio and video capability at this time Young product; many known "bugs"

Authorware/ Shockwave	Development time is fast and costs are low Great capabilities for interactivity Excellent audio and video capabilities Source code can be used for BOTH Intranet-based training and CD-ROM Very secure Supported by the biggest multimedia vendor in the world, Macromedia	Requires Shockwave plug-in to be installed on each browser

ACI's recommendation is to use Authorware Shockwave for all instructional components. This provides the best Learner experience with the lowest development costs.

For chat and bulletin board (threaded discussion) capabilities, ACI recommends the use of Java (or customized API's if only Windows NT Servers will be supported). Java will provide greater control over the interface, and better presentation of the communication text. Alternate formats, such as HTML only or GIF-based chat/threaded, would be cheaper to create but would result in a less professional presentation.

Student Computers

If the above development languages are used, students will need the following system specifications:

•Computer connected to corporate Intranet, or to an AMA Internet site

•SoundBlaster-compatible sound card and speakers

•Standard Web browser (Internet Explorer or Netscape Navigator)

•Authorware Shockwave plug-in for browser

The Shockwave plug-in can be distributed free of charge, and is installed with a simple "setup" command. If the AMA's primary market segment is corporate users, it is likely that this plug-in can be installed on student machines by the corporate information technology department. Students without technical assistance can always download the plug-in from the main training site and complete the installation instructions themselves.

Macromedia has made announcements with Netscape and Microsoft indicating that Shockwave technology will be built in to future versions of browsers. However, no delivery date has been given for this technology.

IV. Work Process

Development will progress through the classic steps for Instructional Systems Design:

- Analysis
- Program Design
- Development
- Delivery
- Evaluation

Analysis

The analysis phase will clarify needs of the AMA and examine all resources and options for achieving project objectives. ACI will obtain all existing AMA materials and communicate with a designated project manager from the AMA to ensure a complete and clear understanding of the objectives for the program. Schedules will be confirmed, technical details will be defined, and program structure will be determined.

Program Design and Scripting

ACI will develop and deliver a treatment outline, script, and at least two sample user interfaces. All submissions will be revised after review and feedback from the AMA.

Development

During this phase, ACI will develop all artwork, record audio voiceovers, and program all components. Each module will be revised after review and feedback from the AMA.

Delivery

ACI will install all software components at the AMA, or the AMA's client's location. ACI will provide training in the use of the *AMA Training Network* and will provide ongoing technical support.

Evaluation

ACI will assist the AMA in its efforts to evaluate the effectiveness of the *AMA Training Network*, to evaluate the user interface, and to identify ways to enhance the software in the future.

V. Schedule

A complete and detailed schedule will be developed during Phase I of the work process.

At this time, ACI estimates that it will require approximately 8 weeks to complete the Proof of Concept components.

VI. Budget

Recommendation for Partnership

ACI acknowledges that the AMA's RFP is asking for a work-for-hire relationship, also known as fee-for-service. Most of ACI's clients work on this same basis, and we are certainly willing to work under this arrangement for the AMA.

However, due to the challenges inherent to intranet and Internet-based Training [see pages 388, 389] ACI recommends that the AMA forge a true partnership or alliance with the vendor they choose. This partnership, rather than revolving around a fee-for-service, would revolve around a royalty or revenue sharing system.

The benefits to the AMA in this arrangement are:

It would greatly reduce or eliminate the up-front costs of development (thereby reducing the AMA's financial risk, lowering breakeven points, and increasing short-term profits).

The AMA's vendor would be motivated to provide long-term, high-quality customer service, technical support, and product updates.

The AMA's vendor would be motivated to assist the AMA's sales and marketing staff in actually *making sales*. There may be many opportunities for the vendor to contribute technical expertise to the sales process during demonstrations, trial installations, trade shows, etc.

Although ACI does not yet know if the AMA would consider such a partnership, the budget for the Proof of Concept below has been priced *below the actual cost of development*. These prices are valid for six months, regardless of AMA's decision to proceed on a work-for-hire or royalty basis.

Budget for Proof of Concept:

Item	Fee

Three 10-minute Learning Modules:
  Instructional section
  Standard features (including glossary,
  clipboard, assessments, etc.)
  Levels 1, 2 evaluation
	$10,000

Chat using Java	$ 5,000
Threaded discussion (bulletin board) using Java	$ 5,000
Student Tracking Integration with *Registrar*	To be discussed
Ongoing end-user technical support	To be discussed

Fee Schedule
40% payable upon project initiation.
40% payable upon acceptance of beta review software.
20% payable upon completion of the project.

Notes and Assumptions:

Above costs do not include fees for duplication or packaging of materials, fulfillment or order processing, technical support, overnight express delivery, or travel requiring air transportation or overnight lodging. These items will all be billed at cost.

Unlimited office materials, telephone calls, faxes, and standard postage are included in the above costs.

All invoices are submitted Net 30 days.

VII. Why You Should Choose ACI?

Advanced Consulting, Inc., a Green Brook, New Jersey–based company founded in 1991, is a leader in the development of interactive multimedia for training and education. We are uniquely qualified to develop the *AMA Training Network* for four distinct reasons:

Intranet-based Training Experience

ACI is currently an industry leader in the development of Intranet-based training programs. Below are three separate projects that have been completed within the last year.

[*previous client*]

ACI developed 12 modules of almost 30 hours of Intranet-based, interactive, multimedia training for [*previous client*]. Topics included:

Customer Service

Team Dynamics

Client Focus

Problem Solving

Business 101

and several financial services related titles

These modules included text, graphics, animations, audio and even video clips.

Interactive components included:

self-assessment through exercises

questions (true or false, multiple choice, fill-in, matching, sequencing)

instructional Jeopardy game

instructional drag race game

instructional tic tac toe game

personal action plans

post-tests

Complete student tracking functionality was developed, including data output to an external tracking database (created with MS-SQL Server).

[*previous client*]

ACI developed Intranet-based instructional simulations to complement didactic materials for [*previous client*]. Topics were:

Time management

Objection handling

Conflict resolution

These modules, due to technical constraints of the [*previous client*] system, were created using HTML and CGI scripts.

[previous client]

ACI completed a network-based testing and assessment system for [*previous client*] pharmaceuticals, titled Digital Professor. This system has enabled trainers at [*previous client*] to quickly and easily administer exams to their 3,000 sales representatives around the country.

This project included the creation of a customized computer network server that now runs in the [*previous client*] home office. Six months of end-user tech support was also provided to all 3,000 employees.

Additional experience with Intranet-based programs includes ACI's work as a beta-test partner with Macromedia on the evaluation and testing of Shockwave for Authorware 3.5.

Expertise in Interactive Multimedia

ACI's core competency is the development of instructional, interactive, multimedia. Our designers, artists, and programmers are experienced in the subtleties involved in this unique medium. In 1996 ACI's work was recognized with two awards: the ASTD's *Blue Ribbon Award for Instructional Technology* and the ISPI's *Award of Excellence for an Instructional Intervention*.

Creativity in Instructional Design

ACI has been at the forefront of instructional design techniques that engage learners, maintain interest, and achieve measurable results. Techniques include the use of dynamic learning objectives, instructional games, and simulations.

Customer Service

The key factor behind ACI's 100% annual growth (for the last five years) has been our ability to truly partner with our corporate clients. We understand the long-term value each client represents, and invest considerable time and energy—at our own expense—learning about each client's culture, business, industry, and needs.

ACI's Awards and Distinctions

Winner of the American Society of Training and Development's *1996 Blue Ribbon Award for Instructional Technology.*

Winner of the International Society of Performance Improvement's *1996 Award of Excellence for an Instructional Intervention.*

Selected by Prentice Hall (a division of Simon & Schuster) to develop a combination book and software volume to teach multimedia developers how to use Authorware 3.5. This volume, titled *Authorware Projects 3.5*, was published in June, 1996.

ACI's President, Kevin Kruse, has been a featured speaker at leading industry conferences, including:

1996 ASTD International Conference

1996 ASTD-NJ Conference

1996 ASTD Satellite Video conference Program

1996 ISPI Conference

1996 Utilizing Technology in Training Conference

Seven confirmed conferences in 1997

ACI's work has been featured in leading publications, including:

Multimedia Training Newsletter

CBT Solutions

Training

Training and Development

Technical and Skill Training

Technology for Learning

Corporate University Review

Personnel Journal

Selling Power

Newspost

Pharmaceutical Sales Representative

Team Member Biographies

ACI has the capability to complete all required project tasks with in-house, full-time staff. No subcontracting will be required.

Using the definitions supplied by the AMA, the chart below depicts how individuals will fulfill project roles. Some individuals will fill more than one role. Complete biographies are included after the roles chart.

Project Role

Project Management
Instructional Design
Instructional Technologist
Writer/Editor
Programmers
Media Expert
Graphics Designer
Creation of chat rooms, bulletin boards
Product Implementation
Technical Support
Quality Control (ACI Category)

[ACI biographies included here]

Client List

ACI has over 100 clients worldwide. A partial list of clients includes: 3M, American Express, Arthur Andersen, Automatic Data Processing, Bank of Montreal, Bristol-Myers Squibb, Canada Trust, Deloitte & Touche, Du Pont Merck, Fidelity Investments, First Chicago Trust of NY, Fleet Financial Group, General Reinsurance, Glaxo Wellcome, IDS Financial Services, JP Morgan, KPMG Peat Marwick, Merck, [*previous client*], Northern Trust Company, Pfizer, Inc., Prudential Property & Casualty, Royal Bank of Canada, Seabury & Smith, The Chubb Group.

References

We strongly urge the AMA to contact our references to hear first hand about our dedication to customer service, and ability to exceed client expectations.

CRITERIA FOR EVALUATING PROGRAMS

One of the most daunting tasks for those responsible for providing training to their organization is the selection of a vendor for off-the-shelf course-ware or custom development. In the section below, we have provided suggestions for several different approaches to evaluating the good and bad qualities of training programs.

 ## The Multimedia and Internet Training Awards Criteria for Evaluating Web-Based Training

Over each of the last few years I have had the wonderful opportunity to present a session at the major training conferences on "The Best Examples of Multimedia Training." From that experience a number of criteria emerged which distinguish the best from the average programs. In addition, our newsletter's Multimedia and Internet Training Awards Program draws a wide range of entries including some of the best of technology-delivered instruction. In judging these programs, the panel of judges relies on their own professional experience, as well as our list of criteria for evaluating programs. Here is a high-level view of those ten criteria:

Content

- Does the program include the right amount and quality of information?

Instructional Design

- Is the course designed in such a way that users will actually learn?

Interactivity

- Are users engaged through the opportunity for their input?

Navigation

- Can users determine their own course through the program?
- Is there an exit option available?
- Is there a course map accessible?
- Is there an appropriate use of icons and/or clear labels so that users don't have to read excessively to determine program options?

Motivational Components

- Does the program engage the user through novelty, humor, game elements, testing, adventure, unique content, surprise elements, and so on?

Use of Media

- Does the program effectively employ video, animation, music, sound effects, and special visual effects?
- Is the gratuitous use of these media avoided?

Evaluation

- Is there some type of evaluation, such as:
    - Is mastery of each section's content required before proceeding to later sections?
    - Are section quizzes used?
    - Is there a final exam?

Aesthetics
- Is the program attractive and appealing to the eye and ear?

Record Keeping

- Are student performance data recorded, such as time to complete, question analyses, and final scores?

- Is the data forwarded to the course manager automatically?

Tone

- Is the program designed for professionals?

- Does it avoid being condescending, trite, pedantic, and so on?

When evaluating programs for your company, you may want to create your own job aid or list of criteria. Some organizations also establish a task force, including end-users, to review potential purchases so that several sets of eyes can rate the usefulness of a particular program. Sarah Porten has been evaluating programs for years from her position at Site Information & Learning Centers at Hewlett-Packard. In the following she discusses some of the issues she considers when selecting a program.

GUIDELINES FOR EVALUATING SELF-PACED COURSES

Sarah Porten, Hewlett Packard

Hewlett Packard offers employees extensive opportunities for continuous life-long learning. As such there are many internal training departments providing training in different subject areas and instruction types. I belong to an organization named The Site Information & Learning Centers (SILC). SILC provides self-paced training for employees located in the San Francisco Bay Area. At any one time SILC may offer 100 or more courses in a variety of subject areas (Technical; Computer Applications; Management Development; Individual Development and Environmental Health & Safety), media (Video; Laser Disc; CD-ROM; Diskette; and World Wide Web), and delivery channels (PCs; Portable PCs, LAN, and Web).

As an Education Technology Specialist at SILC I work on a variety of projects including: evaluating self-paced courses; piloting new technologies and their applicability to learning; integrating self-paced and instructor-led curricula; and designing and developing an online system which will increase employee accessibility to education opportunities at Hewlett Packard in this area.

In response to customer needs, course turnover is quite rapid. As a result I evaluate approximately 100 self-paced courses yearly for their instructional integrity. It is my role to ensure that the courses we offer our customers are well designed and truly facilitate learning. There are so many self-paced courses and vendors and I believe that our added value is in our ability to select the best-quality courses for our customers.

Self-paced learning is a specialization within Instructional Design and as such some of the criteria and parameters used to evaluate it differ from those used for traditional instructor-led courses. In the guidelines below I have tried to summarize those criteria so that anyone may use them when evaluating self-paced courses. I learned how to evaluate self-paced courses from my teacher and mentor Dr. Johanna Keirns, Department of Instructional Technology, San Jose State University. Many of the guidelines presented below are those learned in her classes and some of the examples and non-examples used are taken from her book *Designs for Self-Instruction*.

All the guidelines outlined below are applicable to most self-paced media, including video, print, computer-based diskette or CD-ROM, laser disk or Web delivered. However, the sections on user interface and navigation are most applicable to computer-based, laser disk, and Web-delivered courses.

Tell Them What You're Going to Tell Them:

What to look for: Objectives or an explanation at the beginning of the course which succinctly tells learners what they will learn in the course. This is very important since it helps to set learner expectations and aids him/her in deciding whether or not the course is suitable. This can be delivered via text or audio or both.

Motivation/Attention Grabbers:

What to look for: Apart from being told what they should learn, learners need to be motivated to proceed through the course. A good course will have some kind of motivational piece at the beginning of the course which really makes learners stand up and think about what they are about to learn, thereby giving them a reason to proceed.

Examples:

For an Ergonomics course: Starting with a video of a worker sitting in an ergonomically incorrect work area who progressively suffers from more and more aches and pains. The learner is then informed that in this course they will learn the principles of ergonomics so that they can avoid injury. Many learners will be able to identify with this situation, having perhaps experienced this themselves and they will be motivated to go on.

For a course on Teams: Starting with a video of an expert explaining why it is important to any organization to build effective teams. A powerful introduction from a renowned expert in the field of team dynamics will motivate learners to proceed.

For a course on Project Management: Starting with a written description of an employee who manages multiple projects but has been missing deadlines because she lacks skill in allocating resources. Learners are then informed that in this course they will learn how to allocate resources etc. Again learners may identify with this kind of situation and will be motivated to proceed.

User Interface:

What to look for:

Is the course intuitive to use, such that the learner needs little or no explanation to proceed through the course ?

Is the overall screen design consistent, consolidated, clean and clear ?

Are the graphics appealing and understandable ?

Navigation:

What to look for:

Are the navigational controls/icons intuitively meaningful? Can learners immediately understand the function of a particular navigational icon by looking at it or do they need a lengthy explanation? The more lengthy the explanation needed, the less intuitive the control or icon. For controls to be intuitively meaningful the graphic used should be very clear and easy to understand and if necessary labeled for good measure.

Example: Many programs use VCR or tape deck control bars as navigational controls so that a forward arrow means next and a backward arrow means previous. These are very intuitively meaningful.

Do users have COMPLETE control over the environment such that they can get anywhere they need to go and exit or quit anytime they need to? Learners must be able to EXIT or QUIT at anytime and feel that they have complete control. This functionality makes a course self-paced because complete control allows learners to pace themselves. This is VERY IMPORTANT. See below on self-pacing.

Do the navigational controls take learners where they logically expect to go? When driving on the highway we all hope that a signpost will take us where it says it will.

Example: A previous button which takes learners to the screen which immediately precedes the one they are on.

Nonexample: A previous button which takes learners back to the beginning of the section and not to the screen that precedes the one they are on.

Active Responding:

What to look for:

Learners should be given the opportunity to respond actively to the material being presented: Constant questions, choices, and interactions must be presented for learners to respond to. Just reading or observing is not sufficient to make the presentation of information function as instruction or learning. Active responding should make something happen in the learners' mind/brain which allows them to process the information presented.

Copy Screens/Frames: Though many self-paced courses provide lots of opportunities for learners to respond, the nature of these responses requires learners to merely copy information presented in that particular screen or the previous screen. However, just copying information does not really constitute an active response. There are times when it is important for learners to simply recall information. In this case copy frames would work. However, you must ask yourself the question: "Do learners really need to remember this information or can they look it up back on the job?" See the examples and nonexamples below.

Nonexample:

A course in database fundamentals introduces such basic terms as file, field, and record. A sample section might be:

Data is not information until it is organized in some meaningful and coherent fashion. Database systems group data into categories at three levels: the file, the field, and the record. A file is a collection of records, like your personal address book which consists of several items of information about each person in the book. The page of information about each person is a record; the specific items of information are the fields in the record.

An address book is a_____

Each page is a _____

Each piece of information on each is a _____

A more active response requires the learner to use these terms rather than simply copy them down as presented. See the following example.

Example:

Data is not information until it is organized in some meaningful and coherent fashion. Database systems group data into categories at three levels: the file, the field, and the record. A file is a collection of records, like your personal address book which consists of several items of information about each person in the book. The page of information about each person is a record; the specific items of information are the fields in the record.

How would you organize a family birthday list?

The file would be _____

Each record would be_____

Some fields you would need would be_____

Getting to the Point: Make sure that the response really gets at the main point being expressed in the information presented. See the nonexample and example that follow.

Nonexample:

Edmund Halley first observed the comet that would later bear his name in the winter of 1682–83. After years of calculating, he decided that the comet reported in 1531 and the comet seen in 1607 were probably identical to the 1682–83 comet. From his calculations, he decided his comet had an elliptical orbit and would return every 76 years. He asked young astronomers to watch the skies in 1758–59 and see if his figures would prove correct. They did prove out, and it is because of this great astronomer that we call the famous comet _____ _____.

Here the learner is told the main point, i.e., that there is a 76-year periodicity of the comet, and the response requested is trivial. It would be more effective to encourage the learners to process the information presented and generate the main idea themselves. See the example below.

Example:

Edmund Halley first observed the comet that would later bear his name in the winter of 1682–83. After years of calculating, he decided that the comet seen in 1531 and the comet reported in 1607 were similar and probably identical to the 1682–83 comet, returning regularly to our view as it moved in an elliptical orbit around the sun. In what year did he predict the return of what we now call "Halley's Comet"?_____

Guessing Games: Active responding also does NOT constitute asking your learner to take wild guesses because guessing does not really cause the learner to think or process the information being presented. See the two non-examples below:

Nonexample 1:

Halley's comet has an _____ _____ around the _____ and returns every _____ _____.

Nonexample 2:

Halley's comet was seen in   *a. 1531, 1607, 1683*

b. 1513, 1670, 1638

c. 1500, 1576, 1652

Page Turners: Active responding is more than "press return to go on" or "click the next arrow to proceed." Real learner interaction with the subject matter presented is fundamental to good self-instruction. If learners are just turning pages they could be reading a book on the subject which just presents information without any of the elements which make computer instruction unique.

Immediate Feedback:

What to look for:

Every response must be immediately followed by a consequence: The answer to a question is affirmed or corrected, a choice leads immediately to a result.

Example: In a self-paced work book on statistics the learner is asked to work out a problem using a stated formula. The learner is then asked to turn to page X for the answer. Seeing the correct solution will affirm the learner's correct calculation or clarify an incorrect answer by showing the learner where they went wrong.

Nonexample: In a self-paced interactive multimedia course on diversity learners are asked to distinguish between different cultural greetings and their meaning. Learners receive no feedback indicating whether or not their answers are correct.

An error should be identified and remediation identified: With an incorrect or inappropriate response, learners are moved to a reexplanation or clarification of the misunderstood point and offered a second opportunity to respond. It is important that remediation should take learners to a new screen, not ask them to "go back and try again." Going backward is quite a negative experience psychologically.

Wording for correction and remediation: Wording should be candid but positive, and should encourage learners to make the effort to understand.

Example: *Let's look at this another way.*

Nonexample*: Your response is incorrect. Go back and try again.*

Small Steps:

What to look for: Information must be presented in small enough increments to assure frequent response. Learners should not feel overwhelmed with information. We must remember that our brains can only process so much information at once. Overload it and it gets the equivalent of a stomach ache after a seven-course meal.

Self-Pacing:

What to look for: The pace at which the learner moves must be set and controlled by him/her. This is one of the unique characteristics of a self-paced course—allowing learners to decide and control how fast or slow they proceed through the course. Self-pacing also allows learners to repeat or skip units of a course as their specific needs dictate.

Opportunities for learners to practice or experience:

What to look for:

Practicing/Experiencing by the Student: This entails giving learners opportunities to practice skills learned so that they can then go back and use them on the job.

Example: For a course on Installing Microsoft NT the learner is given a hands-on opportunity to install NT onto a PC. This will probably be simulated so that the learner is "safe" to make mistakes without causing any damage. This gives learners a hands-on opportunity to experience what it is like to install Microsoft NT in an environment that mirrors the real world.

Contextualization:

In order for learners to truly experience what it would be like to use a skill learned in real life, the learning must be placed in the context within which the skill will be used. So in our example above it is important that the simulation of Microsoft NT installation looks and feels exactly as it would if the learner was actually installing NT on an actual PC.

Contextualizing learning also involves "setting the scene" so that the learner relates to skills being learned in terms of a real-world situation. This makes the skills being learned all the more applicable back on the job.

Example: For a course on Installing Microsoft NT the learner is told that he or she is a System Administrator and has been charged with installing NT on all the PCs in his or her division.

Assessing Student Learning/Student Monitoring Own Progress:

What to look for: In self-paced instruction, learners must be able to evaluate their own progress, since there is usually no instructor on hand to do so and no peers around to compare to.

This may be achieved via a simple test about the content for which the learners are graded.

Example: Learners are asked questions about the installation of Microsoft NT and then receive a grade which tells them if they know what they need to know about installing NT.

Alternatively this may be achieved by allowing learners to monitor their own progress through practice of skills learned in the course. Example: If learners successfully install Microsoft NT in a simulation presented in a course, than they themselves can recognize that they are progressing well through the course without the need for a formal test.

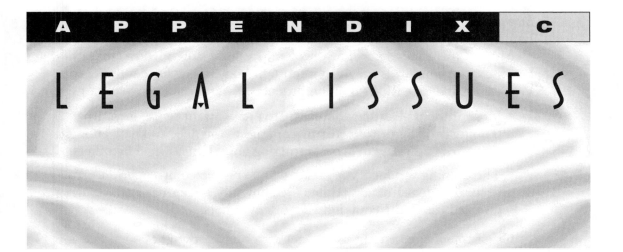

LEGAL ISSUES

Although the details are best left to lawyers, it is vital to have a basic understanding of the legal issues involved in using and developing Web-based technology. Ignorance of the law is no excuse, and violating other people's legal rights can be very costly. Copyright and licensing issues must therefore be a major concern for developers and publishers of Web-based training.

A major company in the computer industry recently developed a multi-media training program. The external vendor developing the program was unaware of the scope of copyright law. The developer didn't realize until too late that using copyrighted graphics and text without permission violates copyright law. In addition, no license was obtained for use of copyrighted technology in the program. Although completed, the product could not be sold and had to be shelved until all copyright owners could be located and permission—known as licenses—obtained. This appendix will give you an overview of some of the legal issues. Because the legal issues involved in developing Web-based training products are quite complex, we asked attorney Dianne Brinson to write this chapter for us. Brinson teaches "Law for Internet Users" at the Internet Education Institute at San Jose State University's Professional Development Center. She also teaches in-house seminars on Internet and multimedia legal issues, both online and live. The material which follows is based on her book *Multimedia Law and*

Business Handbook, copyright 1996 by J. Dianne Brinson and Mark F. Radcliffe, and available from Ladera Press, Menlo Park, California.

Most of this appendix will be devoted to a discussion of copyright law, because copyright law is the most important body of law for developers of Web-based and CD-ROM training products. That's true for two reasons:

- Most of the preexisting content that you will want to use in your training product is protected by copyright. You need to know enough about copyright law to avoid infringing copyrights owned by others.

- The training products you create will be protected by copyright. You need to understand what rights the copyright owner has against unauthorized use of the copyrighted work by others.

Other topics covered in this chapter are online copyright issues, licensing, publicity, and privacy rights.

Copyright Law Basics

When you start working on a training product, you're probably going to find music, text, graphics, film clips, and photographs that you'll want to use. Most of the preexisting material that you will want to use in your training product is protected by copyright. That's true because:

- Copyright protection is available for the types of material you will want to use—music, text, graphics, film, and photographs. This material is all "copyrightable subject matter."

- Copyright protection is easy to get—under current law, it attaches automatically when a work eligible for copyright protection (discussed below) is created.

- Copyright protection lasts a long time—50 years beyond the life of the author for works created by individuals.

Generally, you should not use copyrighted content in your training product without getting permission from the copyright owner. You are free to use uncopyrighted material—known as "public domain" material, which is discussed below—without getting permission. You are also free to use material for which you own the copyright, although copyright ownership rules are too complex to cover in this chapter.

Standards for Protection

For material to be copyrighted it must be "original" and "fixed." Certain types of works are not copyrightable.

The originality standard is easy to meet: A work is original in the copyright sense if it owes its origin to the author and was not copied from some preexisting work. A work can be original without being novel or unique.

> Betsy's training program, Management Skills, is original in the copyright sense so long as Betsy did not create her program by copying existing material—even if it's the zillionth program to be written on management skills.

Only minimal creativity is required to meet the originality requirement. No artistic merit is required.

A work may incorporate preexisting material and yet be original. For example, your training product can be original even if it incorporates music clips, photographs, and excerpts from several magazine articles.

Facts owe their origin to no one, and so are not original. However, a compilation of facts (a work formed by collecting and organizing data) can be protected by copyright.

According to the Copyright Act, a work is "fixed" when it is made "sufficiently permanent or stable to permit it to be perceived, reproduced, or otherwise communicated for a period of more than transitory duration." An author can "fix" words, for example, by writing them down, typing them on a typewriter, dictating them, or entering them into a computer.

Getting Protection

Copyright protection arises automatically when an original work is fixed in a tangible medium of expression. Registration with the Copyright Office is optional (but a copyright owner must register before filing a lawsuit for copyright infringement).

Copyright Notice

The use of copyright notice is optional for works distributed after March 1, 1989.

If you want to use material that does not contain a copyright notice, don't make the mistake of thinking that the material is uncopyrighted.

Copyright notice can take any of these three forms:

- A "C" in a circle followed by a date and a name.

- The word "Copyright" followed by a date and a name.
- The abbreviation "Copr." followed by a date and a name.

The Copyright Owner's Rights

A copyright owner has the right to control use of the copyrighted work. Here are the copyright owner's five exclusive rights:

- **Reproduction Right.** The reproduction right is the right to copy, duplicate, transcribe, or imitate the work in fixed form.

- **Modification Right.** The modification right (also known as the derivative works right) is the right to modify the work to create a new work. A new work that is based on a preexisting work is known as a "derivative work."

- **Distribution Right.** The distribution right is the right to distribute copies of the work to the public by sale, rental, lease, or lending.

- **Public Performance Right.** The public performance right is the right to recite, play, dance, act, or show the work at a public place or to transmit it to the public. In the case of a motion picture or other audiovisual work, showing the work's images in sequence is considered "performance."

- **Public Display Right.** The public display right is the right to show a copy of the work directly or by means of a film, slide, or television image at a public place or to transmit it to the public. In the case of a motion picture or other audiovisual work, showing the work's images out of sequence is considered "display."

Infringement

Anyone who violates any of the exclusive rights of a copyright owner is an infringer.

> Developer scanned Photographer's copyrighted photograph, altered the image by using digital editing software, and included the altered version of the photograph in a Web-based training product. If Developer used Photographer's photograph without permission, Developer infringed Photographer's copyright by violating the reproduction right (scanning the photograph), the modification right (altering

the photograph), and the distribution right (selling the altered photograph as part of the multimedia work).

A copyright owner can recover actual or, in some cases, statutory damages from an infringer. The federal district courts have the power to issue injunctions (orders) to prevent or restrain copyright infringement and to order the impoundment and destruction of infringing copies.

Duration of Copyright

For works created on and after January 1, 1978, the copyright term for works created by individuals is the life of the author plus 50 years.

The copyright term for "works made for hire" is 75 years from the date of first "publication" (distribution of copies to the general public) or 100 years from the date of creation, whichever expires first. Works made for hire are works created by employees for employers and certain types of specially commissioned works.

Limitations on the Exclusive Rights

The copyright owner's exclusive rights are subject to a number of exceptions and limitations that give others the right to make limited use of a copyrighted work. Here are the major exceptions and limitations.

Ideas

Copyright protects only against the unauthorized taking of a protected work's "expression." It does not extend to the work's ideas, procedures, processes, systems, methods of operation, concepts, principles, or discoveries.

> John's copyrighted training program explains a new system of bookkeeping created by John. While John's copyright protects his expression in the training program (his description of the system), it does not protect the system itself or the ideas that make up the system. Others are free to study John's training program, figure out and use the bookkeeping system, and even write their own training programs describing the system.

Facts

A work's facts are not protected by copyright, even if the author spent large amounts of time, effort, and money discovering those facts. Copyright protects originality, not effort or "sweat of the brow."

Susan spent months researching President Kennedy's assassination. She discovered a number of never-before-known facts about Lee Harvey Oswald. She reported her discoveries in a book. The copyright on the book does not protect the facts that Susan discovered.

Independent Creation

A copyright owner has no recourse against another person who, working independently, creates an exact duplicate of the copyrighted work. The independent creation of a similar work or even an exact duplicate does not violate any of the copyright owner's exclusive rights.

Fair Use

The "fair use" of a copyrighted work, including use for purposes such as criticism, comment, news reporting, teaching, scholarship, or research, is not an infringement of copyright. Copyright owners are, by law, deemed to consent to fair use of their works by others.

The Copyright Act does not define fair use. Instead, whether a use is fair use is determined by balancing these factors:

- The purpose and character of the use.
- The nature of the copyrighted work.
- The amount and substantiality of the portion used in relation to the copyrighted work as a whole.
- The effect of the use on the potential market for, or value of, the copyrighted work.

If you are creating a training product for purely noncommercial purposes—for example, for use by the American Red Cross for training—it is possible that you can justify copying small amounts of material as fair use. If your work is designed for commercial use of any sort—even for internal training within a for-profit corporation—it will be hard to succeed on a fair use defense. It is better to get a license (discussed later in this chapter).

International Protection

United States authors automatically receive copyright protection in all countries that are parties to the Berne Convention for the Protection of Literary and Artistic Works, or parties to the Universal Copyright Convention (UCC). Most countries belong to at least one of these conventions. Members of the two international copyright conventions have agreed to give nationals of member countries the same level of copyright protection they give their own nationals.

> Publisher has discovered that bootleg copies of one of its multimedia works are being sold in England. Because the United Kingdom is a member of the Berne Convention and the UCC, Publisher's work is automatically protected by copyright in England. When Publisher files a copyright infringement action in England against the bootlegger, Publisher will be given the same rights that an English copyright owner would be given.

Works of foreign authors who are nationals of Berne or UCC-member countries automatically receive copyright protection in the United States, as do works first published in a Berne Convention or UCC country. Unpublished works are subject to copyright protection in the United States without regard to the nationality or domicile of the author.

Public Domain

You don't need a license to use a public domain work. Public domain works—works not protected by copyright—can be used by anyone. Because these works are not copyrighted, no one can claim the exclusive rights of copyright for such works.

The rules regarding what works are in the public domain vary from country to country. A work in the public domain in the United States may be protected by copyright in Canada or other countries.

There are several ways in which works fall into the public domain in the United States:

- **Expiration of the copyright.** A copyright that was in existence before January 1, 1978, and was renewed, has a term of 75 years. All copyright terms run to the end of the calendar year in which they expire. Consequently, in 1997, all works first "published" before January 1, 1922 are in the public domain in the United States.

- **Failure of the copyright owner to renew the copyright.** Under the 1909 Copyright Act, copyright protection lasted 28 years. A copyright owner could obtain an additional term, known as a "renewal term," by filing an application to renew in the twenty-eighth year. The Copyright Renewal Amendment of 1992 eliminated the requirement of filing a renewal application for works published between 1964 and 1977, inclusive. Renewal is not required for works created after 1977. However, before 1992, a number of works entered the public domain because the copyright owner failed to file a renewal application. For works to which the renewal requirement applies, you can find out whether the owner renewed the copyright by ordering a Copyright Office renewal search. The provisions on renewal are complex, and you should get an experienced attorney or rights clearance agent to help you determine how those rules apply to a particular work.

- **Failure to use copyright notice of publicly distributed copies of a work (for works published before March 1, 1989).** Under prior law, the distribution of copies without copyright notice resulted in the forfeiture of copyright protection. For works distributed before January 1, 1978, forfeiture was automatic. For works publicly distributed after that date, the copyright law provided ways around the defect created by distribution without notice. A court recently found that most of the UNIX operating system is in the public domain because copies were publicly distributed without notice.

In the United States, works prepared by federal government officers and employees as part of their official duties are not protected by copyright. This rule does not apply to works created by state or local government officers and employees.

Finding Public Domain Works

The Copyright Office does not maintain a list of public domain works, nor does it publish annual lists of copyrights that will expire at the end of the year. You have to find these works yourself.

If the copyright notice on a work is dated more than 75 years ago, the work is in the public domain. It will be harder to determine expiration dates for works covered by the current Copyright Act: Except for works made for hire, the duration of copyright is 50 years beyond the life of the author rather than a set number of years.

The Copyright Office does not keep copies of works whose registrations have expired. Some content providers sell copies of public domain works, such as WPA photographs.

 Online Copyright Issues

Many think that copyright law and other laws do not apply to the Internet. Laws *do* apply. For example:

> If your Web-based training product contains copyrighted third-party content used without permission, you are opening yourself up to a lawsuit for copyright infringement—just as you would be if you used copyrighted content without permission in a book.

If you copy graphics from a Web site and use them in your Web-based training product, you could be sued for copyright infringement—just as you would if you found graphics in a magazine and scanned them to use in your product.

Copyright Myths

There are a number of myths out there about how copyright law applies to copying material from the Internet and posting material on the Internet. Here are a few:

Copying Material from the Internet

Don't make the mistake of believing these myths about copying material from the Internet:

Myth #1: If I find something on the Internet, it's okay to copy it and use it without getting permission.
Much public domain material is available on the Internet—government reports, for example. While you are free to copy public domain material that you find on the Internet, generally you should not copy copyrighted material without getting permission from the copyright owner.

Myth #2: Material on the World Wide Web is in the public domain if it is posted without a copyright notice.
Do not assume that material is uncopyrighted just because it doesn't contain a copyright notice. Remember, the use of notice is optional under current law.

Myth #3: Anyone who posts material on a Web server wants people to use that material, so I can do anything I want with material that I get from a Web server.

Individuals and organizations put material on a Web server to make it accessible by others. They do not give up their copyright rights by putting material on a Web server. Also, the person who posted the material may not be the copyright owner.

Posting Material on the Internet

And don't believe these myths about how copyright law applies to putting copyrighted material owned by others on the Internet:

Myth #4: It's okay to use copyrighted material in my Web site so long as no one has to pay to visit my Web site.

Unless your use of the copyrighted work is fair use (discussed earlier in this chapter), you need a license to copy and use the work in your Web site even if you don't charge viewers.

Myth #5: My training product will be a wonderful showcase for the copyright owner's song/graphics/text, so I'm sure the owner will not object to my use of the material.

Don't assume that a copyright owner will be happy to have you use his or her work. Even if the owner is willing to let you use the work, the owner may want to charge you a license fee.

Myth #6: Posting someone else's material on the Internet or putting it on a Web server is fair use, because the "culture" of the Internet is that it's okay to do these things.

Under current law, there is no absolute fair use right to post someone else's copyrighted material on the Internet. If copyrighted material is used on the Internet without the permission of the copyright owner, whether the use is fair use will be decided by considering the four factors discussed above, under "fair use." There is no blanket fair use exemption for the Internet.

 # Licensing

Every time you use a copyrighted work owned by a third party, you must determine whether it is necessary to obtain a license from the owner. For most uses, a license should be obtained.

You need a license to use a third party's copyrighted work if your intended use of the work would, without a license, infringe any of the copyright owner's exclusive rights. To use material from a copyrighted work owned by a third party, you will copy the work and possibly modify it. Therefore, you need a license unless "fair use" or one of the other exceptions to the owner's rights applies.

Licensing Myths

There are a number of myths out there concerning the necessity of getting a license. Here are a few.

Myth #1: I don't need a license because I'm using only a small amount of the copyrighted work.

It is true that *de minimis* copying (copying a small amount) is not copyright infringement. Unfortunately, it is rarely possible to tell where *de minimis* copying ends and copyright infringement begins. There are no "bright line" rules.

Copying a small amount of a copyrighted work is infringement if what is copied is a qualitatively substantial portion of the copied work. In one case, a magazine article that used 300 words from a 200,000-word autobiography written by President Gerald Ford was found to infringe the copyright on the autobiography. Even though the copied material was only a small part of the autobiography, the copied portions were among the most powerful passages in the autobiography.

Copying any part of a copyrighted work is risky. If what you copy is truly a tiny and nonmemorable part of the work, you may get away with it (the work's owner may not be able to tell that your work incorporates an excerpt from the owner's work). However, you run the risk of having to defend your use in expensive litigation. If what you are copying is tiny, but recognizable as coming from the protected work, it is better to get a license. You cannot escape liability for infringement by showing how much of the protected work you did not take.

Myth #2: I paid for the tape (compact disc, videotape) that I'm going to copy, so I already have the permission I need.

Copyright law distinguishes between ownership of the copyright in a work and ownership of a copy of the work. Purchasing a copy of a work (a tape, compact disc, videotape, book, photographic print) does not give you permission to exercise the exclusive rights of copyright. You can resell your copy, but that's all.

Myth #3: Since I'm planning to give credit to all authors whose works I copy, I don't need to get licenses.

If you give credit to a work's author, you are not a plagiarist (you are not pretending that you authored the copied work). However, attribution is not a defense to copyright infringement.

Myth #4: I don't need a license because I'm going to alter the work I copy.

You cannot escape liability for copyright infringement by altering or modifying the work you copy. You can use a copyrighted work's unprotected ideas and facts, but if you copy and modify protected elements of a copyrighted work, you will be infringing the copyright owner's modification right as well as the copying right.

Myth #5: Rather than just scanning in the copyrighted cartoon character I want to use, I'll hire an illustrator to create my own version of the cartoon character. That way, I won't need a license.

Using an illustrator's version of a character is copyright infringement if the illustrator copied the protected character. If you tell the illustrator, "Draw me a character that looks like Garfield," the illustrator's character will be a copy of Garfield (assuming the illustrator is competent). If you can't afford a license to use a protected character—or the owner will not grant you a license—create your own original characters.

Myth #6: We've used this song (photo, design, and so on) in our productions in the past, so we don't need to get a license to use the work now.

Don't assume that past use was licensed use. Even if the past use was licensed, the license may not cover your use now because the license may have authorized one-time use only, or may have been limited in duration, or there may have been other restrictions. If use has been licensed in the past, check the license to determine whether it authorizes the use you are planning.

The Licensing Process

There are three steps to the licensing process:

1. Determining who owns the copyrights in the works you want to use

2. Determining what rights you need

3. Obtaining licenses from the copyright owners

To shield you from an infringement suit, your license must authorize every type of use that you will be making of the licensed work.

Consequently, you need to determine how you will be using the work and what rights you need before you seek your license. A license is no protection for uses not authorized in the license.

> Developer obtained a license to reproduce Photographer's photograph of the Golden Gate bridge in Developer's multimedia work. Although the license did not authorize Developer to alter the photograph, Developer manipulated the image to eliminate cars and pedestrians and create an uncluttered image of the bridge. If Photographer sued Developer for unauthorized exercise of the modification right, Developer's license would be no defense.

Using a licensed work in ways not authorized in the license may be material breach of the license agreement. If it is, the licensor can terminate the license. In the previous example, Developer's alteration of the photograph is probably a material breach of Developer's license agreement with Photographer. If Photographer terminates the license, Developer will no longer have even the right granted to Developer in the license (the right to use the original photograph in Developer's multimedia work).

If you want the right to use the licensed work in more than one multimedia project, the license must explicitly give you that right.

> Developer obtained a license to use a five-second clip of Movieco's movie in Developer's work, *City Tour*. Developer later used the same film clip in another multimedia work, *Downtown*. Developer's second use of the film clip is copyright infringement.

The most important lesson in clearing rights to use copyrighted material is to start early. If you don't, you may find yourself unable to use material simply because you have not allowed enough time. Consider using an attorney or a rights clearance agency (discussed below) if you are creating a commercial product, particularly one with complex clearance issues.

To be successful, follow these four rules:

1. Identify your needs early. You may find that some of the material you want to use is not available and you may encounter unexpected delays. For example, in one clearance project, the owner of one of the works had declared bankruptcy several years before the clearance was being done. It took two months just to identify the new owner.

2. Always have an alternative. Don't plan your project around content owned by a third party unless you are confident that you can obtain the necessary rights. The rights may have been licensed already, or they may not be available at a reasonable price. For example, the owners of the copyright in the official anthem for one state wanted $10,000 to grant permission for use of the anthem in a CD-ROM atlas of the United States. The fee was simply too high, and the developer did not use the anthem.

3. Be creative. The content owner may be willing to settle for nonmonetary compensation—a "credit" on the packaging, for example.

4. Be frank. Be prepared to be frank about the nature of your project and the rights you will need in your first contact. Although you may consider your project to be confidential, you must be prepared to share your plans with the content owner in order to persuade the content owner to grant you a license.

Rights Clearance Agencies

To obtain the licenses that you need, you may want to use a rights clearance agency. A rights clearance agency will find out who owns the rights you need and negotiate licenses for you. Because these agencies perform rights clearance and licensing as their business, they can probably obtain licenses for you in far less time than it would take you to obtain them yourself.

These agencies are just beginning to handle licensing for Web-based products. They primarily handle rights clearance for movie and television production companies, ad agencies, and corporate video departments.

Most rights clearance agencies charge by the hour. An initial consultation is generally free (but you should ask). You should first determine whether the works you want to use are likely to be available (and for what fee) and whether the agent can suggest alternatives to unavailable or expensive material. Sometimes an agent can give you ideas if you need suggestions for works you might license and use.

These agencies frequently handle rights of publicity releases for photographs of celebrities (discussed below) as well as copyright licensing.

Stock Houses and Libraries

You can obtain film and video clips, photographs, illustrations, music, and sound effects from stock houses and from music and media libraries.

Stock houses and libraries frequently own the copyrights in works that they license (or they provide material that is in the public domain, such as WPA photographs). They will, for a separate fee, do research for you to help you find suitable material (or you can hire your own content specialist).

Rights of Publicity and Privacy

Web-based developers must make certain that they don't violate rights of publicity and privacy of individuals appearing in their works. This can usually be accomplished by getting releases from individuals before using illustrations, recordings, photographs, or film or video clips that include those individuals' names, faces, images, or voices.

Most states in the United States recognize that individuals have a right of privacy. The right of privacy gives an individual a legal claim against someone who intrudes on the individual's physical solitude or seclusion, and against those who publicly disclose private facts. Remedies for invasion of privacy include injunctions against continued intrusion and damages for mental distress.

Almost half the states in the United States recognize that individuals have a right of publicity. The right of publicity gives an individual a legal claim against one who uses the individual's name, face, image, or voice for commercial benefit without obtaining permission. The states recognizing the right are California, Connecticut, Florida, Georgia, Hawaii, Illinois, Kentucky, Massachusetts, Michigan, Minnesota, Missouri, Nebraska, Nevada, New Jersey, New York, Ohio, Oklahoma, Pennsylvania, Rhode Island, Tennessee, Texas, Utah, Virginia, and Wisconsin.

> Developer took a picture of Clint Eastwood standing on a street corner in Carmel. Developer used the picture in a multimedia work which was sold in California. Unless Eastwood gave Developer permission to use Eastwood's image, Developer's use of the image violated Eastwood's right of publicity (even though Developer, as "author" of the photo, owned the copyright in the photo).

Remedies for misappropriation of the right of publicity include injunctions against continued use of the misappropriated name, face, image, or voice, and damages based on the fair market value of the use or the profits earned by the infringer.

The law of publicity varies from state to state. In some states, the only unauthorized uses that violate the right of publicity are commercial uses (in advertising, for example). Since most multimedia works will be distributed nationwide, you should avoid trying to determine which states' laws you need to worry about. Instead, you should obtain releases from any person whose name, face, image, or voice is recognizable in your multimedia projects.

Newspapers and news magazines have a "fair use" privilege to publish names or images in connection with reporting a newsworthy event. Developers of Web-based training products are unlikely to be able to rely on fair use. Even if your project has no commercial benefit for you or anyone else—for example, if it's a public service project that you are doing for free—get releases to avoid violating the rights of publicity and privacy.

Experienced performers and models are accustomed to signing these releases. If a person won't sign a release, don't use their name, face, image, or voice in your multimedia project. If you are using a client's employees as actors, models, or narrators, make sure the employees sign releases. If you are using your own employees, make sure they sign releases.

If you want to use a photograph of a living person, get the person to sign a statement authorizing you to use his or her face or image as shown in the photograph. You also need a license authorizing you to use the photograph, unless you own the copyright in it.

Some photographers routinely obtain releases, but don't assume that this is the case. Even if the photographer did obtain a release, the release may not be broad enough to cover your use of the photograph in a multimedia work.

Deceased Individuals

In some states, an individual's right of publicity terminates when the individual dies. In other states, the right passes to the heirs of the deceased original owner. In California, Oklahoma, and Texas, the right passes on to the heirs only if the person's likeness has acquired some commercial value at the time of death. In Kentucky, the right is passed on to heirs for public figures only.

The right of publicity lasts 20 years beyond the year of death in Virginia, 40 years in Florida, 50 years in California, Kentucky, Nevada, and Texas, and up to 100 years in Oklahoma. In Tennessee, the right lasts as long as it is continuously exploited by the heirs.

As a rule of thumb, don't use the name, voice, face, or image of a celebrity who has been dead less than 50 years—for example, Marilyn Monroe or Martin Luther King, Jr.—without checking applicable state law on descendability. If state law provides for the right of publicity to descend to heirs, get permission from the current owners of the deceased celebrity's right of publicity before using the celebrity's name, voice, face, or image.

ONLINE CURRICULUM PROVIDERS

The training industry has long supported an infrastructure of commercial, prepackaged training programs available for purchase from third parties. Over the decades these have included everything from self-study booklets and videotapes, to videodiscs and CD-ROMs, not to mention student workbooks for live instruction. With the advent of the Web's popularity as a delivery medium for training, a number of companies are providing commercial, off-the-shelf programs. Some of these companies have long and well-respected histories in the industry; others have sprung up overnight to take advantage of this new wave. Some programs are licensed to be run on an intranet; others are available for pay-as-you-go on the Internet. In this chapter we present an overview of some companies that offer a curriculum of courses.

 MOLI

The Microsoft Network (MSN) has its own online training environment, the Microsoft Online Institute (MOLI), which is an interactive education service available on MSN and the Web (Figure D.1). Most of the courses offered through MOLI are designed to help students pass Microsoft certification exams to become Microsoft Certified Professionals.

MOLI courses are available to anyone with Web access and either Netscape 3.0 or Microsoft's own browser, Internet Explorer 3.0. Users can connect to http://moli.microsoft.com/ to view course descriptions and get a taste of the classroom atmosphere. Students can then register for courses via the Web.

MOLI courses include instructor guidance, self-study materials, developer advice, user forums, and other resources for Microsoft product and technology information. Students have online, real-time access to instructors and electronic self-paced learning materials. MOLI also has a "Student Union" where students can interact via e-mail, bulletin boards, and forums.

MOLI courses offer a flexible schedule for students to work through self-study materials at their own pace, then access the online classroom to complete labs, quizzes, or online assignments. Students can find supplementary learning materials or meet with a learning advisor or fellow students. Learning advisors work with students one-on-one via e-mail to evaluate labs and quizzes and to help students with questions or problems.

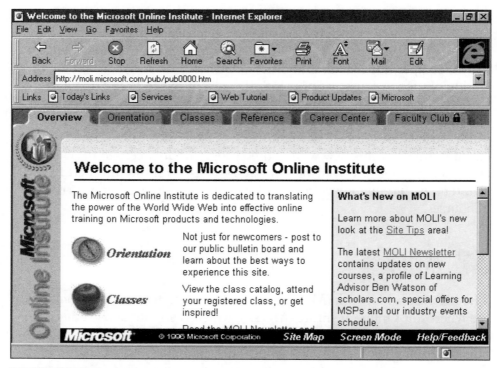

FIGURE D.1 Microsoft Online Institute.

Screen shot reprinted by permission from Microsoft Corporation.

Real-time "office hour" chats are scheduled for two hours each week with a learning advisor. Students thus have opportunities to interface "live" with their instructors. If students cannot attend a chat, they have the option of accessing a recorded transcript on their class bulletin board.

Most MOLI courses are based on Microsoft products and topics. Many of the larger courses are taught through self-study books and CD-ROMs offline, with portions of the course and labs and quizzes conducted online. Shorter courses are delivered entirely over the Web.

Staff at the Institute say the most popular MOLI courses are Microsoft's Networking Essentials, Supporting Windows '95, and Windows NT 4.0 Update. Students can also enroll in courses covering Microsoft Internet products including Supporting Microsoft Internet Information Server, Internet Application Development and Web Design, and Authoring with Microsoft Internet Explorer 2.0.

MOLI courses are currently priced between $225 for a two-week course and $425 for a five-week course. Some courses are offered about six times a year, while the most popular courses run almost once a month. All courses are taught by Microsoft Certified Professionals.

MOLI Case Study: Scholars.com

Online training companies like Scholars.com contract with Microsoft to provide MOLI training and certification (Figure D.2). Scholars.com is one of the few MOLI providers to devote its entire business to online training. The company offers online advising 12 hours a day, seven days a week and guarantees that if students take their courses and do not pass the Microsoft Certification exams, Scholars.com will pay for them to take the exam again. (Not bad, huh?)

Scholars.com specializes in technical training and offers courses for certification as Microsoft Certified Professionals (MCP) and Microsoft Certified Systems Engineers (MCSE). They also conduct training for IBM, Novell, Microsoft, and the military.

Once students receive the course materials, they have 12 weeks to complete the online course. But students may put their courses on hold at any time if they need to, which is attractive for managers or programmers who have looming project deadlines. Enrollment is continuous, with no structured course dates.

Students receive e-mail every day with a question or help-desk problem for them to solve; they can wait and answer all the questions at once, or e-mail teachers with questions.

FIGURE D.2 Scholars.com homepage.

Near the end of a course, students can download examination-prep materials (MCP Endeavor testing software). This helps get them used to the pace and nature of Microsoft exams. Students then go to a Sylvan testing center (the only location that administers Microsoft tests). Class fees (including all course materials) range from $695 for most single courses (i.e., NT Server), to $3250 for an entire engineering suite.

ZDU

The ZD Net division of Ziff-Davis Publishing operates an online university, ZDU, which uses the LOIS system (see Chapter 10) to maintain its online course catalog, generate course schedules, manage course enrollment, conduct online testing, monitor course usage, and provide other administrative functions (Figure D.3).

ZDU classes operate like regular college classes: They have an instructor and students, a course outline and often a textbook, and courses run for a set number of weeks. In other ways, ZDU classes are a bit different

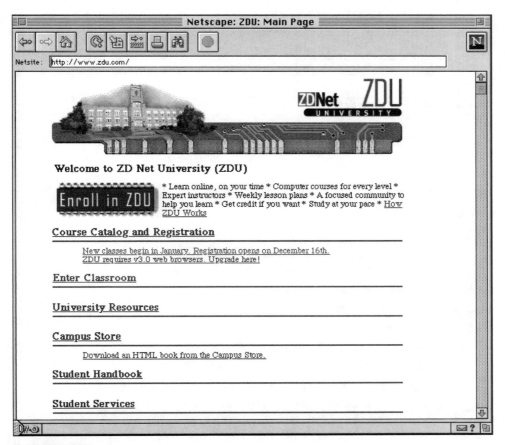

FIGURE D.3 ZDU main page.

because they take place through messages posted in the classroom—a discussion forum within ZDU's Web site (Figure D.4). In this forum, the instructor posts messages with instructions for the students, as well as information and explanations (the class "lectures"), homework and other assignments, and so forth. The students post messages with questions (for the instructor and for each other), comments, finished homework, and so on. Everybody in the class can read all the messages, and the messages remain visible even after they have been read.

Students log in when they have the time, read the class messages, and post their own messages. If students need to spend a few extra days on a particular assignment, or if they can't log in for a few days, all the

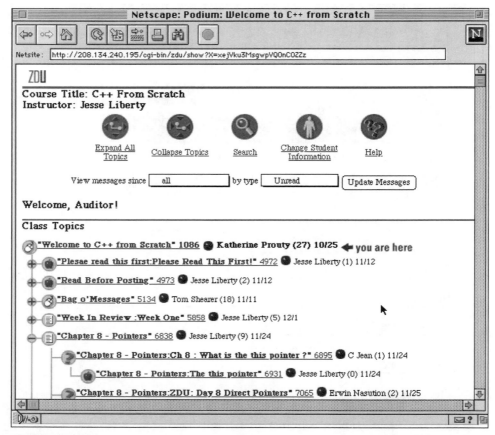

FIGURE D.4 Sample page from a ZDU discussion forum.

lectures and all the exchanges between the instructor and students will still be there when they get to them.

Through messages posted in the class discussion forum, the instructor provides lectures and background information, assigns homework and other projects, and answers questions from students. An instructor may also have one or more teaching assistants (TAs), especially if the class is large. The TAs are usually experienced students from previous sessions of the class and may tutor students one-on-one, post supplementary information, collect student assignments, maintain a class Web site, and so on.

Each class also has one or more sysops (short for SYStem OPerators). The sysops take care of the operation of the discussion forum to make sure that everything runs smoothly. Sysops also help students with more general questions about ZDU and the forum software, such as how to find and read messages, how to set up a browser properly for ZDU, or how to find out what other classes are available.

Some of the currently available courses include:

- Introduction to Java Applets
- Beginning Delphi
- Java for Managers
- Lotus Notes 4.0 for Executives
- Build Your Web Page with Hot Dog Pro
- How to Code with HTML
- Visual Basic 4.0
- Powerbuilder 5.0
- Windows Programming with Liberty BASIC
- Introduction to VRML
- And the ever-popular Build Your Own Duke Nukem 3D Level

The company is hoping the courses will have a wide appeal and are launching their curriculum at a very low cost per user of $4.95 a month. This fee allows a user to access any class offered during that month. Continuing Education Units can be earned for some courses. Classes last from four to eight weeks; the time required per week will vary with the intensity of the course. Clearly, this pricing is designed to appeal to a very broad, almost consumer, market. The depth of the content and the quality of the instructional design will determine whether the courses are a good fit for the corporate marketplace.

On the first day of class, the instructor begins posting messages to welcome students to the class, explains a bit about how the class operates, and begins the first lesson. Almost all interaction between the instructor and the students takes place through messages posted in the classroom—lectures, assignments, question-and-answer sessions, homework, and group discussions. Students also turn in homework by posting it online. In HTML-related classes, students may be posting homework as pages in their own Web site. In other classes, they may be posting homework as messages in the class discussion forum.

Instructors may schedule special real-time conferences as an addition to the normal class activity. Instructors hold office hours at least every two weeks, and sometimes more often. During scheduled office hours, the instructor will be online and available for live chat with students in the course.

↳ Logical Operations' LearnItOnline

LearnItOnline is an online learning site offered by Logical Operations, a well-respected company which has offered instructor-led courses for years on computer software topics (Figure D.5). To access the training courses the user needs Netscape Navigator or Microsoft Internet Explorer with LearnFlow. The program simulates a learning environment that is like running a live application through the Web browser.

LearnItOnline offers courses for corporate and training center users. Companies will purchase blocks of classes and will provide passwords to employees. Individual users will register and pay by credit card. Corporate users will be able to administer training through the Logical Operations Internet-based training program and employers can sign up their employees and monitor their training. A reporting system informs the employer how their employees are progressing in a course and gives departmental and course summaries.

Currently, LearnItOnline is offering the following courses:

- Excel 7.0
- Word 7.0
- Microsoft Internet Explorer 3.0
- Access 7.0
- Powerpoint 7.0
- Windows 95: Introduction

↳ Gartner Internet Training Group

Gartner Group Internet Learning Center (GGILC) is an Internet-based training provider that features 27 interactive courses for information technology. Some of the classes offered are Lotus Notes, Oracle, UNIX, and

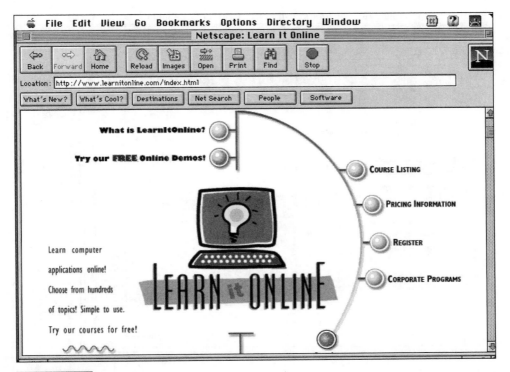

FIGURE D.5 LearnItOnline main page.

C++. Internet access and a browser are needed to access the courses. The classes are taught through the use of text and graphics, simulated practice, questions, and tests (Figure D.6).

GGILC uses the Shockwave plug-in to create interactive question and practice sections. Shockwave must be installed to complete the interactive activities, though not all activities are interactive (i.e., pretests and posttests). Participants can use the site's search engine to locate courses.

Users can search for a course by topic (Figure D.7), by full text search, or through the course library. For example, you might enter "C++ Programming" into the topic search and "video" into the full text search. The course library allows users to browse all available courses by curricula, by skill level, by job title, and alphabetically. The user can enter whether to search all the courses available or only the classes "licensed" to that individual or company.

There are two ways to become a registered user: as an organization or as an individual. Any individual user who desires to take a course through

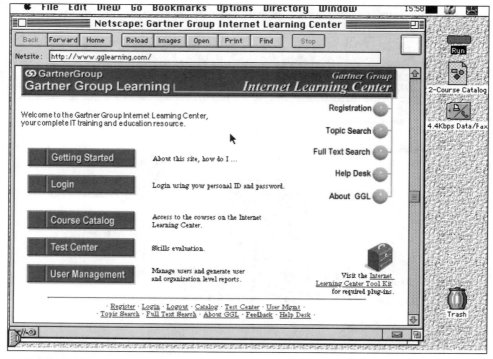

FIGURE D.6 Gartner Group main page.

GGILC needs to register, and can pay by credit card over the Internet. Individual users can browse through the courses, reading descriptions and taking pretests. Purchase information is available with each course.

The other way to register for GGILC courses is with an organization. When an organization registers with GGILC there are several advantages. The price structure is different for groups, and one member of the organization called the "Organization Authority" has full access to enrollment status and test results. The Organization Authority can use this information to track the progress of employees. The Organization Authority is responsible for giving out the password to the organization users. Both organization and individual users must enter the system by logging in on the home page. An organization user is able to access all courses the organization has been licensed for. Registration is done by giving the company name and password. Should an organization user wish to take more courses, the courses are paid for individually over the Internet.

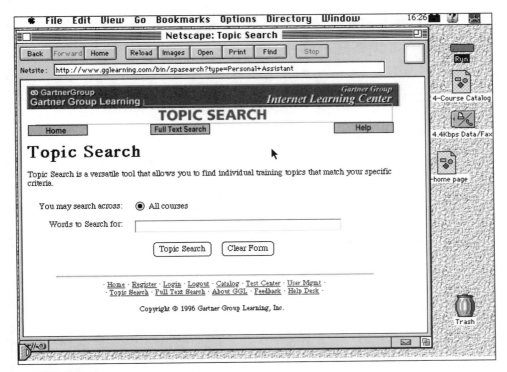

FIGURE D.7 Gartner Group Topic Search.

Registered users may take a pretest for every course offered. This exam allows users to test their knowledge on the information presented in the course and decide whether it is necessary to take the class. Only one pretest per course can be taken. Users can take a posttest after course completion to evaluate their understanding of the course content. These tests can be taken as many times as desired, but have a different makeup with each repetition. Scores are entered in the "user administration" database and can be viewed by the student at any time. The database can be used to update current registration information, change a password, check and track personal progress, view billing statements, order items from a product catalog, and log off.

See Appendix B for suggestions on how to evaluate commercial programs.

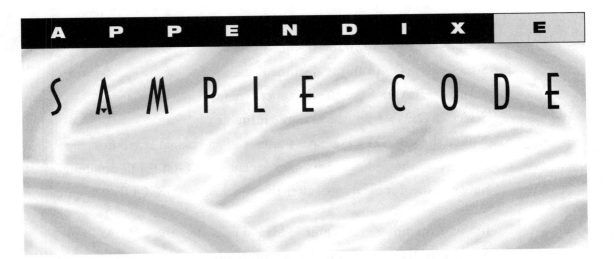

S A M P L E   C O D E

This appendix provides a description of several Web-based training programs discussed in this book, followed by sample pieces of source code for the program.

Randysoft's OPIE

The Online Programming Instruction Environment (OPIE) is an example of the Web-based training available from Randysoft (http://www .randysoft.com>. The program was written in HTML and JavaScript and requires a JavaScript and forms-aware Web browser, such as Netscape Navigator 3.0 or Microsoft Internet Explorer 3.0.

This product is not intended to compete with graphical Web document editors. It is part of a complete training package that teaches Web authoring at the source level. To use the HTML OPIE editor, simply select an HTML "tag" from the one of the popup menus. The HTML tag will be appended in the text editing area and will have all the attributes listed with the tag. You can fill in the attributes or delete them as needed.

To view the document that you created in the editor, click on the View button. This will bring up a separate window with your HTML document in it. The text can be cut and copied within the editor. To clear the contents of the editor, click on the Clear button.

Here is an example of a simple editing session:

1. Select <HTML> from the document menu.
2. Select <HEAD> from the document menu.
3. Select </HEAD> from the document menu.
4. Select <BODY> from the document menu.
5. Notice the <BODY> tag has a number of additional attributes.
6. Remove all the addition attributes except the BGCOLOR attribute.
7. Between the double quotes after the equal sign of BGCOLOR, enter green.
8. In the text editing area, enter 'This is a test' after the <BODY> tag.
9. Select </BODY> from the document menu.
10. Select </HTML> from the document menu.
11. Click on the View button.

To see how this technology is being used for interactive training, visit the Randysoft Web site and test the available courses. These demos allow you to take a limited subset of the lessons for an available course.

```
<BASE HREF="/home/randy/hopie/hopie.html">

<HTML>
<HEAD>
<META NAME="copyright" CONTENT="Randy Hootman 27 Sept. 1996">
<TITLE>
NEW HTML OPIE
</TITLE>
<SCRIPT LANGUAGE="JavaScript">

function docsAppendText(form) {
                    form.editor.value +=
form.docs.options[(form.docs.selectedIndex)].value;
                    return;
}

function emphasisAppendText(form) {
                    form.editor.value +=
form.emphasis.options[(form.emphasis.selectedIndex)].value;
                    return;
}
```

```
function offsetsAppendText(form) {
                form.editor.value +=
form.offsets.options[(form.offsets.selectedIndex)].value;
                return;
}

function headersAppendText(form) {
                form.editor.value +=
form.headers.options[(form.headers.selectedIndex)].value;
                return;
}

function imagesAppendText(form) {
                form.editor.value +=
form.images.options[(form.images.selectedIndex)].value;
                return;
}

function anchorsAppendText(form) {
                form.editor.value +=
form.anchors.options[(form.anchors.selectedIndex)].value;
                return;
}

function listsAppendText(form) {
                form.editor.value +=
form.lists.options[(form.lists.selectedIndex)].value;
                return;
}

function separatorsAppendText(form) {
                form.editor.value +=
form.separators.options[(form.separators.selectedIndex)].value;
                return;
}

function formsAppendText(form) {
                form.editor.value +=
form.forms.options[(form.forms.selectedIndex)].value;
                return;
}

function tablesAppendText(form) {
                form.editor.value +=
form.tables.options[(form.tables.selectedIndex)].value;
                return;
}
```

```
function miscAppendText(form) {
                form.editor.value +=
form.misc.options[(form.misc.selectedIndex)].value;
                return;
}

function ViewPage(form) {

msg=open("","HTML_Editor","scrollbars,toolbar=no,directories=no,menub
ar=yes");
                var source = form.editor.value;
                msg.document.write(source);
                msg.document.close();
                return true;
}

function ClearText(form) {
                form.editor.value="";
                return;
}

</SCRIPT>

</HEAD>
<BODY BGCOLOR="white" TEXT="blue">
<DIV ALIGN="center">
<FONT COLOR="red" SIZE="2">HTML Online Programming Instruction
Environment  &copy 1996 Mindscape Technologies</FONT><BR>
<FORM NAME="htmlopie">

<INPUT TYPE="button" NAME="View" VALUE="View"
onClick='ViewPage(this.form)'>
<FONT COLOR="black">Source</FONT>
<INPUT TYPE="button" NAME="Clear" VALUE="Clear"
onClick='ClearText(this.form)'><BR>

<TEXTAREA NAME="editor" ROWS=10 COLS=50>
</TEXTAREA>

<TABLE ALIGN="center" CELLSPACING=0 CELLPADDING=0>

<TR>
<TD ALIGN="center"><FONT COLOR="black" SIZE=2>Document</FONT></TD>
<TD ALIGN="center"><FONT COLOR="black" SIZE=2>Fonts</FONT></TD>
<TD ALIGN="center"><FONT COLOR="black" SIZE=2>Offsets</FONT></TD>
<TD ALIGN="center"><FONT COLOR="black" SIZE=2>Headers</FONT></TD>
<TD ALIGN="center"><FONT COLOR="black"
SIZE=2>Anchors/Images</FONT></TD>
```

```
</TR>

<TR>
<TD ALIGN="center">
<SELECT NAME="docs" onChange='docsAppendText(this.form)'>
<OPTION VALUE='<HTML>
'>&ltHTML&gt
<OPTION VALUE='</HTML>
'>&lt/HTML&gt
<OPTION VALUE='<HEAD>
'>&ltHEAD&gt
<OPTION VALUE='</HEAD>
'>&lt/HEAD&gt
<OPTION VALUE='<TITLE>
'>&ltTITLE&gt
<OPTION VALUE='</TITLE>
'>&lt/TITLE&gt
<OPTION VALUE='<BODY
    BGCOLOR=""
    BACKGROUND=""
    LINK=""
    ALINK=""
    VLINK=""
    TEXT=""
>
'>&ltBODY&gt
<OPTION VALUE='</BODY>
'>&lt/BODY&gt
<OPTION VALUE='<META NAME="" HTTP-EQUIV="" CONTENT="">
'>&ltMETA&gt
<OPTION VALUE='<LINK
    HREF=""
    REL=""
    REV=""
    TITLE=""
>
'>&ltLINK&gt
</SELECT>
</TD>

<TD ALIGN="center">
<SELECT NAME="emphasis" onChange='emphasisAppendText(this.form)'>
<OPTION VALUE="<B>
">&ltB&gt
<OPTION VALUE="</B>
">&lt/B&gt
<OPTION VALUE="<I>
">&ltI&gt
```

```
<OPTION VALUE="</I>
">&lt/I&gt
<OPTION VALUE="<TT>
">&ltTT&gt
<OPTION VALUE="</TT>
">&lt/TT&gt
<OPTION VALUE="<U>
">&ltU&gt
<OPTION VALUE="</U>
">&lt/U&gt
<OPTION VALUE='<FONT SIZE="" COLOR="">
'>&ltFONT&gt
<OPTION VALUE="</FONT>
">&lt/FONT&gt
</SELECT>
</TD>

<TD ALIGN="center">
<SELECT NAME="offsets" onChange='offsetsAppendText(this.form)'>
<OPTION VALUE='<PRE WIDTH="">
'>&ltPRE&gt
<OPTION VALUE="</PRE>
">&lt/PRE&gt
<OPTION VALUE='<ADDRESS>
'>&ltADDRESS&gt
<OPTION VALUE='</ADDRESS>
'>&lt/ADDRESS&gt
<OPTION VALUE='<BLOCKQUOTE>
'>&ltBLOCKQUOTE&gt
<OPTION VALUE='</BLOCKQUOTE>
'>&lt/BLOCKQUOTE&gt
</SELECT>
</TD>

<TD ALIGN="center">
<SELECT NAME="headers" onChange='headersAppendText(this.form)'>
<OPTION VALUE='<H1 ALIGN="">
'>&ltH1&gt
<OPTION VALUE='</H1>
'>&lt/H1&gt
<OPTION VALUE='<H2 ALIGN="">
'>&ltH2&gt
<OPTION VALUE='</H2>
'>&lt/H2&gt
<OPTION VALUE='<H3 ALIGN="">
'>&ltH3&gt
<OPTION VALUE='</H3>
'>&lt/H3&gt
```

```
<OPTION VALUE='<H4 ALIGN="">
'>&ltH4&gt
<OPTION VALUE='</H4>
'>&lt/H4&gt
<OPTION VALUE='<H5 ALIGN="">
'>&ltH5&gt
<OPTION VALUE='</H5>
'>&lt/H5&gt
<OPTION VALUE='<H6 ALIGN="">
'>&ltH6&gt
<OPTION VALUE='</H6>
'>&lt/H6&gt
</SELECT>
</TD>

<TD ALIGN="center">
<SELECT NAME="anchors" onChange='anchorsAppendText(this.form)'>
<OPTION VALUE='<A
    HREF=""
    NAME=""
    REL=""
    REV=""
    TITLE=""
>
'>&ltA&gt
<OPTION VALUE='</A>
'>&lt/A&gt
<OPTION VALUE='<IMG
    SRC=""
    ALIGN=""
    ALT=""
    WIDTH=""
    HEIGHT=""
    BORDER=""
    HSPACE=""
    VSPACE=""
>
'>&ltIMG&gt
</SELECT>
</TD>
</TR>

<TR>
<TD ALIGN="center"><FONT COLOR="black" SIZE=2>Lists</FONT></TD>
<TD ALIGN="center"><FONT COLOR="black" SIZE=2>Separators</FONT></TD>
<TD ALIGN="center"><FONT COLOR="black" SIZE=2>Forms</FONT></TD>
<TD ALIGN="center"><FONT COLOR="black" SIZE=2>Tables</FONT></TD>
<TD ALIGN="center"><FONT COLOR="black" SIZE=2>Misc</FONT></TD>
```

```
</TR>

<TR>

<TD ALIGN="center">
<SELECT NAME="lists" onChange='listsAppendText(this.form)'>
<OPTION VALUE='<UL TYPE="">
'>&ltUL&gt
<OPTION VALUE='</UL>
'>&lt/UL&gt
<OPTION VALUE='<OL TYPE="">
'>&ltOL&gt
<OPTION VALUE='</OL>
'>&lt/OL&gt
<OPTION VALUE='<LI TYPE="">
'>&ltLI&gt
<OPTION VALUE='<DL>
'>&ltDL&gt
<OPTION VALUE='</DL>
'>&lt/DL&gt
<OPTION VALUE='<DT>
'>&ltDT&gt
<OPTION VALUE='<DD>
'>&ltDD&gt
</SELECT>
</TD>

<TD ALIGN="center">
<SELECT NAME="separators" onChange='separatorsAppendText(this.form)'>
<OPTION VALUE='<DIV ALIGN="">
'>&ltDIV&gt
<OPTION VALUE='</DIV>
'>&lt/DIV&gt
<OPTION VALUE='<HR
    ALIGN=""
    SIZE=""
    WIDTH=""
>
'>&ltHR&gt
<OPTION VALUE='<BR CLEAR="">
'>&ltBR&gt
<OPTION VALUE='<P ALIGN="">
'>&ltP&gt
<OPTION VALUE='<CENTER>
'>&ltCENTER&gt
<OPTION VALUE='</CENTER>
'>&lt/CENTER&gt
</SELECT>
```

```
</TD>

<TD ALIGN="center">
<SELECT NAME="forms" onChange='formsAppendText(this.form)'>
<OPTION VALUE='<FORM ACTION="" METHOD="" ENCTYPE="">
'>&ltFORM&gt
<OPTION VALUE='</FORM>
'>&lt/FORM&gt
<OPTION VALUE='<INPUT
    TYPE=""
    NAME=""
    VALUE=""
>
'>&ltINPUT&gt
<OPTION VALUE='<SELECT
    NAME=""
    SIZE=""
>
'>&ltSELECT&gt
<OPTION VALUE='<OPTION VALUE="">
'>&ltOPTION&gt
<OPTION VALUE='<TEXTAREA NAME="" ROWS="" COLS="">
'>&ltTEXTAREA&gt
<OPTION VALUE='</TEXTAREA>
'>&lt/TEXTAREA&gt
</SELECT>
</TD>

<TD ALIGN="center">
<SELECT NAME="tables" onChange='tablesAppendText(this.form)'>
<OPTION VALUE='<TABLE
    BORDER=""
    ALIGN=""
    WIDTH=""
    CELLSPACING=""
    CELLPADDING=""
>
'>&ltTABLE&gt
<OPTION VALUE='</TABLE>
'>&lt/TABLE&gt
<OPTION VALUE='<TH
    ROWSPAN=""
    COLSPAN=""
    ALIGN=""
    VALIGN=""
    WIDTH=""
    HEIGHT=""
    BGCOLOR=""
```

```
>
'>&ltTH&gt
<OPTION VALUE='</TH>
'>&lt/TH&gt
<OPTION VALUE='<TR ALIGN="" VALIGN="">
'>&ltTR&gt
<OPTION VALUE='</TR>
'>&lt/TR&gt
<OPTION VALUE='<TD
    ROWSPAN=""
    COLSPAN=""
    ALIGN=""
    VALIGN=""
    WIDTH=""
    HEIGHT=""
    BGCOLOR=""
>
'>&ltTD&gt
<OPTION VALUE='</TD>
'>&lt/TD&gt
<OPTION VALUE='<CAPTION ALIGN="">
'>&ltCAPTION&gt
</SELECT>
</TD>

<TD ALIGN="center">
<SELECT NAME="misc" onChange='miscAppendText(this.form)'>
<OPTION VALUE='<MAP NAME="">
>
'>&ltMAP&gt
<OPTION VALUE='</MAP>
'>&lt/MAP&gt
<OPTION VALUE='<AREA
    HREF=""
    SHAPE=""
    COORDS=""
    ALT=""
>
'>&ltAREA&gt
<OPTION VALUE='<SCRIPT LANGUAGE="">
>
'>&ltSCRIPT&gt
<OPTION VALUE='</SCRIPT>
>
'>&lt/SCRIPT&gt
<OPTION VALUE='<APPLET
    CODEBASE=""
    CODE=""
```

```
        ALT=""
        NAME=""
        WIDTH=""
        HEIGHT=""
        ALIGN=""
        VSPACE=""
        HSPACE=""
>
'>&ltAPPLET&gt
<OPTION VALUE='</APPLET>
>
'>&lt/APPLET&gt
<OPTION VALUE='<PARAM NAME="" VALUE="">
'>&ltPARAM&gt
</SELECT>
</TD>

</TR>

</TABLE>

</FORM>
</DIV>
</BODY>
</HTML>
```

↰ Altos Education Network Questionnaire Code

Altos Education Network incorporates several different testing mechanisms into its courses for managers, professionals, and entrepreneurs. Following is a sampling of code for Altos' Entrepreneur Evaluation Questionnaire. This consists of multiple choice questions which are submitted to Altos after all selections have been made. Altos administrators then work with students to evaluate their capabilities and liabilities to be functioning entrepreneurs. Students also receive a copy of their results for their own personal study.

This questionnaire is differentiated from Altos' multiple choice type, which provides instant feedback and "branching." Branching means that the moment the selection is made we confirm if it is right or wrong, and we may then branch the student to other sections of the program to review material.

```
<!DOCTYPE HTML PUBLIC "-//W30/DTD HTML//EN">

<html>
<head>
<meta http-equiv="Content-Type"
content="text/html; charset=iso-8859-1">
<meta name="GENERATOR" content="Microsoft FrontPage 2.0">
<title>SProfile</title>
<meta name="FORMATTER" content="Microsoft FrontPage 1.1">
</head>
<body bgcolor="#FFFFFF">
<p><a href="sampler.htm">Sampler</a></p>
<blockquote>
    <blockquote>
        <p align="center"><a name="ALTOS SAMPLER"><font
        color="#408080" size="4"><strong><u>ALTOS
SAMPLER</u></strong></font></a><font
        color="#408080" size="4"><strong><u><br>
        </u></strong><strong>ENTREPRENEUR'S
PROFILE</strong></font></p>
    </blockquote>
</blockquote>
<form action="_vti_bin/shtml.exe/sprofile.htm" method="POST">
    <input type="hidden" name="VTI-GROUP" value="0"><input
    type="hidden" name="VTI-GROUP" value="0">
    <hr>
    <blockquote>
        <p><strong>Certain personal qualities are helpful for
        successful entrepreneuring or intrapreneuring (the
        characteristics needed to be a successful entrepreneur or
        intrapreneur are similar). This &quot;Entrepreneur's
        Profile Questionnaire&quot; will help define your
        characteristics vs. those of successful entrepreneurs.
</strong></p>
        <p><strong>You will find that some characteristics are
        out of your control, such as who your parents are, etc.
        In other areas, you have the opportunity to modify your
        behavior or build a team to cover your weak areas. Anyone
        can be an entrepreneur if they truly
</strong><strong><u>want
        to be</u></strong><strong>, but not everyone is cut out
        to be. Select </strong><font size="2" face="Arial"><img
        src="alink1g.if" width="80" height="15"></font><strong>
        for a demonstration of an Altos Link. </strong></p>
        <p><strong>Be as objective as possible in answering the
```

```
         following questions. </strong><font
color="#400040"><strong>Answer
         all the questions in order.</strong></font><strong> It's
         important that you think about the questions and make
         honest choices. You will be self-analyzing yourself in
         this Sampler, based on information which we will provide.
         Just follow the instructions at the end of the ques-
tions.</strong><font
         color="#FF0000"><strong> </strong></font></p>
     </blockquote>
     <hr>
     <blockquote>
         <p><em><strong>Questions 1-30: If you strongly agree
         select 5. If you strongly disagree select 1. Select other
         numbers for in-between feelings.</strong></em></p>
     </blockquote>
     <p><strong>1. I love to be with people I like even when there
     is nothing to be gained.<br>
     </strong>5<input type="radio" name="one" value="5">4<input
     type="radio" name="one" value="4">3<input type="radio"
     name="one" value="3">2<input type="radio" name="one"
     value="2">1<input type="radio" name="one" value="1"></p>
     <p><strong>2. In some situations, clarifying who is in charge
     is very important. <br>
     </strong>5<input type="radio" name="two" value="5">4<input
     type="radio" name="two" value="4">3<input type="radio"
     name="two" value="3">2<input type="radio" name="two"
     value="2">1<input type="radio" name="two" value="1"></p>
     <p><strong>3. When playing in a game, I am as concerned with
     how well I play in my own estimation as I am with whether or
     not I win. <br>
     </strong>5<input type="radio" name="three" value="5">4<input
     type="radio" name="three" value="4">3<input type="radio"
     name="three" value="3">2<input type="radio" name="three"
     value="2">1<input type="radio" name="three" value="1"></p>
     <p><strong>4. I believe it is most important to have the
     respect of others in your community. <br>
     </strong>5<input type="radio" name="four" value="5">4<input
     type="radio" name="four" value="4">3<input type="radio"
     name="four" value="3">2<input type="radio" name="four"
     value="2">1<input type="radio" name="four" value="1"></p>
     <p><strong>5. When I set a goal, there is a good chance I
     will make it even though it doesn't always happen.</strong> <br>
     5 <input type="radio" name="five" value="5">4<input
     type="radio" name="five" value="4">3<input type="radio"
     name="five" value="3">2<input type="radio" name="five"
     value="2">1<input type="radio" name="five" value="1"></p>
     <p><strong>6. It is important to have possessions that will
```

```
influence others to respect me.<br>
</strong>5<input type="radio" name="six" value="5">4<input
type="radio" name="six" value="4">3<input type="radio"
name="six" value="3">2<input type="radio" name="six"
value="2">1<input type="radio" name="six" value="1"></p>
<p><strong>7. Losing a friend is very upsetting to me. I work
hard to regain friends I have lost.<br>
</strong>5<input type="radio" name="seven" value="5">4<input
type="radio" name="seven" value="4">3<input type="radio"
name="seven" value="3">2<input type="radio" name="seven"
value="2">1<input type="radio" name="seven" value="1"></p>
<p><strong>8. I insist on the respect of people under me,
even if I have to push them around a bit to get it. <br>
</strong>5<input type="radio" name="eight" value="5">4<input
type="radio" name="eight" value="4">3<input type="radio"
name="eight" value="3">2<input type="radio" name="eight"
value="2">1<input type="radio" name="eight" value="1"></p>
<p><strong>9. I need lots of warmth from others, and I give
it back. <br>
</strong>5<input type="radio" name="nine" value="5">4<input
type="radio" name="nine" value="4">3<input type="radio"
name="nine" value="3">2<input type="radio" name="nine"
value="2">1<input type="radio" name="nine" value="1"></p>
<p><strong>10. I think about how what I am doing today will
affect my future five years from now. <br>
</strong>5<input type="radio" name="ten" value="5">4<input
type="radio" name="ten" value="4">3<input type="radio"
name="ten" value="3">2<input type="radio" name="ten"
value="2">1<input type="radio" name="ten" value="1"></p>
<p><strong>11. I like to set up measures of how well I am
progressing. <br>
</strong>5<input type="radio" name="eleven" value="5">4<input
type="radio" name="eleven" value="4">3<input type="radio"
name="eleven" value="3">2<input type="radio" name="eleven"
value="2">1<input type="radio" name="eleven" value="1"></p>
<p><strong>12. I am very concerned with the efficiency and
quality of my work.<br>
</strong>5<input type="radio" name="twelve" value="5">4<input
type="radio" name="twelve" value="4">3<input type="radio"
name="twelve" value="3">2<input type="radio" name="twelve"
value="2">1<input type="radio" name="twelve" value="1"></p>
<p><strong>13. Many people need advice, and someone should
give it to them whether they want it or not. <br>
</strong>5<input type="radio" name="thirteen" value="5">4<input
type="radio" name="thirteen" value="4">3<input type="radio"
name="thirteen" value="3">2<input type="radio"
name="thirteen" value="2">1<input type="radio"
name="thirteen" value="1"></p>
```

```
<p><strong>14. Strong actions are needed when people make
mistakes.<br>
</strong>5<input type="radio" name="fourteen" value="5">4<input
type="radio" name="fourteen" value="4">3<input type="radio"
name="fourteen" value="3">2<input type="radio"
name="fourteen" value="2">1<input type="radio"
name="fourteen" value="1"></p>
<p><strong>15. I enjoy social get-togethers and make time to
go to them.<br>
</strong>5<input type="radio" name="fifteen" value="5">4<input
type="radio" name="fifteen" value="4">3<input type="radio"
name="fifteen" value="3">2<input type="radio" name="fifteen"
value="2">1<input type="radio" name="fifteen" value="1"></p>
<p><strong>16. A key purpose in my life is to do things that
have not been done before.<br>
</strong>5<input type="radio" name="sixteen" value="5">4<input
type="radio" name="sixteen" value="4">3<input type="radio"
name="sixteen" value="3">2<input type="radio" name="sixteen"
value="2">1<input type="radio" name="sixteen" value="1"></p>
<p><strong>17. If I move to a new area, I imagine the first
thing I would do is develop new friends. Without close
friends, I'm like a plant without water.<br>
</strong>5<input type="radio" name="seventeen" value="5">4<input
type="radio" name="seventeen" value="4">3<input type="radio"
name="seventeen" value="3">2<input type="radio"
name="seventeen" value="2">1<input type="radio"
name="seventeen" value="1"></p>
<p><strong>18. I need to get strong emotional reactions out
of others because then I know I'm getting somewhere. <br>
</strong>5<input type="radio" name="eighteen" value="5">4<input
type="radio" name="eighteen" value="4">3<input type="radio"
name="eighteen" value="3">2<input type="radio"
name="eighteen" value="2">1<input type="radio"
name="eighteen" value="1"></p>
<p><strong>19. I need very much to be liked by others. <br>
</strong>5<input type="radio" name="nineteen" value="5">4<input
type="radio" name="nineteen" value="4">3<input type="radio"
name="nineteen" value="3">2<input type="radio"
name="nineteen" value="2">1<input type="radio"
name="nineteen" value="1"></p>
<p><strong>20. My friends may sometimes think it dull, but I
find myself talking about how to overcome future obstacles I
have anticipated. <br>
</strong>5<input type="radio" name="twenty" value="5">4<input
type="radio" name="twenty" value="4">3<input type="radio"
name="twenty" value="3">2<input type="radio" name="twenty"
value="2">1<input type="radio" name="twenty" value="1"></p>
<p><strong>21. My close relationships are very valuable to
```

```
me. <br>
</strong>5<input type="radio" name="twentyone" value="5">4<input
type="radio" name="twentyone" value="4">3<input type="radio"
name="twentyone" value="3">2<input type="radio"
name="twentyone" value="2">1<input type="radio"
name="twentyone" value="1"></p>
<p><strong>22. My reason for being in business is to become
rich, rich, rich!<br>
</strong>5<input type="radio" name="twentytwo" value="5">4<input
type="radio" name="twentytwo" value="4">3<input type="radio"
name="twentytwo" value="3">2<input type="radio"
name="twentytwo" value="2">1<input type="radio"
name="twentytwo" value="1"></p>
<p><strong>23. I don't like working on a project without
knowing how well I'm doing, so I make plans that allow me to
measure how fast I'm proceeding toward my goals.<br>
</strong>5<input type="radio" name="twentythree"
value="5">4<input
type="radio" name="twentythree" value="4">3<input
type="radio" name="twentythree" value="3">2<input
type="radio" name="twentythree" value="2">1<input
type="radio" name="twentythree" value="1"></p>
<p><strong>24. I like to get involved in community activities
because it gives me a chance to have influence where I live.
<br>
</strong>5<input type="radio" name="twentyfour"
value="5">4<input
type="radio" name="twentyfour" value="4">3<input type="radio"
name="twentyfour" value="3">2<input type="radio"
name="twentyfour" value="2">1<input type="radio"
name="twentyfour" value="1"></p>
<p><strong>25. The real meaning of life is the personal
relationships we form.<br>
</strong>5<input type="radio" name="twentyfive"
value="5">4<input
type="radio" name="twentyfive" value="4">3<input type="radio"
name="twentyfive" value="3">2<input type="radio"
name="twentyfive" value="2">1<input type="radio"
name="twentyfive" value="1"></p>
<p><strong>26. I do best when I have some room to choose my
own goals.<br>
</strong>5<input type="radio" name="twentysix" value="5">4<input
type="radio" name="twentysix" value="4">3<input type="radio"
name="twentysix" value="3">2<input type="radio"
name="twentysix" value="2">1<input type="radio"
name="twentysix" value="1"></p>
<p><strong>27. If people don't know you really appreciate
them, you can't expect them to do a good job.</strong> <br>
```

```html
5<input type="radio" name="twentyseven" value="5"> 4<input
type="radio" name="twentyseven" value="4">3<input
type="radio" name="twentyseven" value="3">2<input
type="radio" name="twentyseven" value="2">1<input
type="radio" name="twentyseven" value="1"></p>
<p><strong>28. In everything I do - work, sports, hobbies - I
try to set high standards for myself; otherwise where's the
fun of it? <br>
</strong>5<input type="radio" name="twentyeight"
value="5">4<input
type="radio" name="twentyeight" value="4">3<input
type="radio" name="twentyeight" value="3">2<input
type="radio" name="twentyeight" value="2">1<input
type="radio" name="twentyeight" value="1"></p>
<p><strong>29. It's people that make up a business, not a lot
of stock piled up on the shelves.<br>
</strong>5<input type="radio" name="twentynine"
value="5">4<input
type="radio" name="twentynine" value="4">3<input type="radio"
name="twentynine" value="3">2<input type="radio"
name="twentynine" value="2">1<input type="radio"
name="twentynine" value="1"></p>
<p><strong>30. I always dreamed about being a famous
politician, actor or athlete and living in the lap of luxury.
</strong><br>
5<input type="radio" name="thirty" value="5">4<input
type="radio" name="thirty" value="4">3<input type="radio"
name="thirty" value="3">2<input type="radio" name="thirty"
value="2">1<input type="radio" name="thirty" value="1"></p>
<hr>
<blockquote>
    <h4><font color="#FF0000"
size="4"><u>IMPORTANT</u></font></h4>
    <blockquote>
        <h4><font color="#FF0000" size="4"><u>Select the
        &quot;Submit Query&quot; button [below] and then
        print the &quot;Form Confirmation&quot; which
        automatically appears. You will need this page for
        your analysis.</u></font></h4>
        <h4><font color="#FF0000" size="4"><u>THEN return to
        this page and select the AltosLink button
below.</u></font></h4>
    </blockquote>
</blockquote>
<hr>
<p><input type="submit" name="Submit"><input type="reset"
name="Reset"></p>
</form>
```

```
<hr>
<blockquote>
    <blockquote>
        <p><strong>Select</strong> <a href="spexplai.htm"><font
        size="2" face="Arial"><img src="alink1g.if" border="0"
        width="80" height="15"></font></a><font color="#804040"
        size="3"> </font><font color="#400040" size="3"><strong>for
        further instructions AFTER the &quot;Submit Query&quot;
        button [above] has been selected and the &quot;Form
        Confirmation&quot; has been printed.</strong></font></p>
    </blockquote>
</blockquote>
<hr>
<blockquote>
    <blockquote>
        <p><strong>Example of data base summary -&gt; </strong><a
        href="spsummar.htm"><font size="2" face="Arial"><img
        src="alink1g.if" border="0" width="80"
height="15"></font></a></p>
    </blockquote>
</blockquote>
<hr>
<blockquote>
    <blockquote>
        <p><strong><u>ABOUT THE INSTRUCTOR <img src="sprofil.jpg"
        width="150" height="203"></u></strong></p>
        <blockquote>
            <p>K. Ry Smith has over 30 years experience in
            starting companies and in small business management.
            He is intimately familiar with the pitfalls and
            potential of entrepreneuring through his many
            companies and his own licensed products.</p>
        </blockquote>
    </blockquote>
</blockquote>
<hr>
<blockquote>
    <p>Here's the quick way to get on our mail list: Select <a
    href="mailto:mailist@altosnet.com"><font size="2"
    face="Arial"><img src="alink1g.if" border="0" width="80"
    height="15"></font></a> and enter under Subject: &quot;Mail
    List&quot;. In the body of the Email please tell us how you
    learned about our site. Thanks for thinking of the Altos
    Education Network for your learning needs.</p>
</blockquote>
<blockquote>
    <p><a href="#ALTOS SAMPLER"><img src="images/!altoslo.gif"
    border="0" width="72" height="50"></a></p>
```

```
</blockquote>
</body>
</html>
```

↳ Practising Law Institute Sample Code

The Practising Law Institute recently bought rights to a course for lawyers called "Keeping the Fire: From Burnout to Balance," developed by the CLE Group. Following is the source code for a portion of that course which demonstrates a basic use of audio programming in online courseware.

Here are a few salient features of the code:

1. This page uses "tables" (the TABLE, TR, and TD tags) to format the text and graphics in a way that makes the page look the same regardless of what browser or what size of monitor the user has.

2. The audio portions of the program are activated by user clicks on either a button (e.g., "The Downward Spiral" on this page) or the name of one of the two lawyers who provide testimonials (the mythical "Janet" or "Stuart"). RealAudio files are not triggered directly, but rather by "metafiles" (i.e., very simple text files with the ".ram" extension). Thus, on this page, this line of code

   "<A HREF="burnout2.ram"><IMG BORDER=0 SRC="../images/spiral.gif" ALT="The Downward Spiral" WIDTH=160 HEIGHT=30></A>"

   links the "The Downward Spiral" button to the "burnout2.ram" metafile. This metafile, in turn, calls the appropriate audio clip from our RealAudio server.

   You'll see lots of references to a graphic file called "dot_clear.gif." This is a one-pixel (hence "dot") graphic set to display transparently (hence "clear") so that it is invisible. It is used to regulate vertical and horizontal spacing in a much more flexible and attractive way than conventional <P> and <BR> tags do.

```
<HTML>
<HEAD>
```

```
<TITLE>&quot;Keeping the Fire&quot; Part 2</TITLE>
</HEAD>

<BODY BGCOLOR="#ffffff" BACKGROUND="../images/spine.gif"
LINK="000066"
ALINK="333366" VLINK="333333">

<TABLE BORDER=0>
<TR>
<TD WIDTH=90><IMG HSPACE=45 SRC="../images/dot_clear.gif"></TD>
<TD WIDTH=36><IMG HSPACE=18 SRC="../images/dot_clear.gif"></TD>

<TD WIDTH=432 ALIGN="center">
<IMG VSPACE=6 SRC="../images/dot_clear.gif"><BR>
<IMG SRC="../images/bo_title.gif" ALT="Keeping the Fire: From
Burnout to
Balance" HEIGHT=36 WIDTH=354><BR>
<IMG VSPACE=16 SRC="../images/dot_clear.gif"><BR>
</TD>
</TR>

<TR>
<TD WIDTH=90 ALIGN="right" VALIGN="top">
<IMG HEIGHT=8 SRC="../images/dot_clear.gif"><BR>
<IMG SRC="../images/part2.gif" HEIGHT=10 WIDTH=60></TD>

<TD WIDTH=36 VALIGN="top"><IMG HSPACE=18
SRC="../images/dot_clear.gif"></TD>

<TD ALIGN="center" VALIGN="top" WIDTH=432>
<A HREF="burnout2.ram"><IMG BORDER=0 SRC="../images/spiral.gif"
ALT="The
Downward Spiral" WIDTH=160 HEIGHT=30></A><BR>

<IMG VSPACE=6 SRC="../images/dot_clear.gif"><BR>
[ <A HREF="janet2.ram">Janet</A> | <A HREF="stuart2.ram">Stuart</A>
]<BR>
<IMG VSPACE=14 SRC="../images/dot_clear.gif"><BR>
</TD>
</TR>

<TR>
<TD WIDTH=90 ALIGN="right" VALIGN="top">
<IMG HEIGHT=1 SRC="../images/dot_clear.gif"><BR>
<IMG SRC="../images/experien.gif" HEIGHT=23 WIDTH=86></TD>

<TD WIDTH=36 VALIGN="top"><IMG HSPACE=18
SRC="../images/dot_clear.gif"></TD>
```

```
<TD ALIGN="left" VALIGN="top" WIDTH=432>
<B>Day-to-Day Experience of Burnout</B>
<UL>
<LI>Loss of self-esteem<BR>
<IMG VSPACE=2 SRC="../images/dot_clear.gif"><BR>
<LI>Dread of going to work<BR>
<IMG VSPACE=2 SRC="../images/dot_clear.gif"><BR>
<LI>Social withdrawal or isolation<BR>
<IMG VSPACE=2 SRC="../images/dot_clear.gif"><BR>
<LI>Lack of energy, chronic fatigue<BR>
<IMG VSPACE=2 SRC="../images/dot_clear.gif"><BR>
<LI>The feeling that &quot;my body is letting me down&quot;<BR>
<IMG VSPACE=2 SRC="../images/dot_clear.gif"><BR>
<LI>Operating from fear<BR>
<IMG VSPACE=2 SRC="../images/dot_clear.gif"><BR>
<LI>Efforts to deny what body, mind and spirit are signalling<BR>
<IMG VSPACE=2 SRC="../images/dot_clear.gif"><BR>
<LI>Spillover of above feelings into family relationships
</UL>

<IMG VSPACE=14 SRC="../images/dot_clear.gif"><BR>
</TD>
</TR>

<TR>
<TD WIDTH=90 ALIGN="right" VALIGN="top">
<IMG HEIGHT=1 SRC="../images/dot_clear.gif"><BR>
<IMG SRC="../images/symptoms.gif" HEIGHT=23 WIDTH=78></TD>

<TD WIDTH=36 VALIGN="top"><IMG HSPACE=18
SRC="../images/dot_clear.gif"></TD>

<TD ALIGN="left" VALIGN="top" WIDTH=432>
<B>Physical Symptoms</B>
<UL>
<LI>Low energy, chronic fatigue and weakness<BR>
<IMG VSPACE=2 SRC="../images/dot_clear.gif"><BR>
<LI>Nagging colds, increased susceptibility to illness<BR>
<IMG VSPACE=2 SRC="../images/dot_clear.gif"><BR>
<LI>Frequent headaches, nausea, muscle tension<BR>
<IMG VSPACE=2 SRC="../images/dot_clear.gif"><BR>
<LI>Changes in eating habits<BR>
<IMG VSPACE=2 SRC="../images/dot_clear.gif"><BR>
<LI>Sleep difficulties<BR>
<IMG VSPACE=2 SRC="../images/dot_clear.gif"><BR>
<LI>Changes in handwriting
</UL>
```

```
<IMG VSPACE=8 SRC="../images/dot_clear.gif"><BR>

<B>Emotional Symptoms</B>
<UL>
<LI>Feeling helpless, hopeless, trapped, often tearful<BR>
<IMG VSPACE=2 SRC="../images/dot_clear.gif"><BR>
<LI>Feeling empty, &quot;nothing left to give&quot;<BR>
<IMG VSPACE=2 SRC="../images/dot_clear.gif"><BR>
<LI>Easily irritated by friends, family, colleagues<BR>
<IMG VSPACE=2 SRC="../images/dot_clear.gif"><BR>
<LI>No pleasure from work or people in general<BR>
<IMG VSPACE=2 SRC="../images/dot_clear.gif"><BR>
<LI>Feeling lonely, discouraged, depressed<BR>
<IMG VSPACE=2 SRC="../images/dot_clear.gif"><BR>
<LI>No energy for everyday tasks
</UL>

<IMG VSPACE=8 SRC="../images/dot_clear.gif"><BR>

<B>Mental Symptoms</B>
<UL>
<LI>Negative attitude toward self, work, life in general<BR>
<IMG VSPACE=2 SRC="../images/dot_clear.gif"><BR>
<LI>Self-critical, pessimistic, cynical, indecisive<BR>
<IMG VSPACE=2 SRC="../images/dot_clear.gif"><BR>
<LI>Blame the problem on clients, colleagues — the very people you
previously served with pride<BR>
<IMG VSPACE=2 SRC="../images/dot_clear.gif"><BR>
<LI>Difficulty concentrating; feel scattered, no focus<BR>
<IMG VSPACE=2 SRC="../images/dot_clear.gif"><BR>
<LI>General feelings of incompetence, impotence
</UL>

<IMG VSPACE=14 SRC="../images/dot_clear.gif"><BR>
</TD>
</TR>

<TR>
<TD WIDTH=90><IMG HSPACE=45 SRC="../images/dot_clear.gif"></TD>
<TD WIDTH=36><IMG HSPACE=18 SRC="../images/dot_clear.gif"></TD>

<TD WIDTH=432 ALIGN="center">

<FONT SIZE=-1>[ <A HREF="part1.htm">Expectations vs. Reality</A> |
<A
HREF="part2.htm">Downward Spiral</A> | <A HREF="part3.htm">Wake-Up
Call</A> |
```

```
<A HREF="part4.htm">Strategies for Balance</A> ]<BR>
<IMG VSPACE=4 SRC="../images/dot_clear.gif"><BR>
[ <A HREF="facts.htm">Facts</A> | <A HREF="stats.htm">Statistics</A>
| <A
HREF="assess.htm">Self-Assessments</A> | <A HREF="author.htm">About
the
Author</A> ]
</FONT><BR>

</TD>
</TR>
</TABLE>

<IMG VSPACE=6 SRC="../images/dot_clear.gif"><BR>
</BODY>
</HTML>
```

NASA Kennedy Space Center WIT (Web Interactive Training)

The code for the normal distribution page consists of instructional text, formatting, graphic calls, and interactivity features. The instructional text is the bulk of the information on the page as it is represented in the Web browser. The formatting provides title, heading, colors, and positioning. The <image> tag calls graphics of the complex formulas that could not be accurately rendered in HTML.

The <embed> tag is used to call the normal distribution graphic calculator created in Macromedia Director and displayed using the Shockwave plug-in. The other interactive feature is the navigation area at the very end of the code. The code calls an image map with areas for navigating to other pages. The navigation is also duplicated in text for those users who do not have image map functions in their browsers.

```
<HTML>
<HEAD>
<TITLE>Visual Inspection</TITLE>
</HEAD><FRAMESET ROWS="*,60">

<NOFRAMES>
```

```
<body bgcolor="#FFFFFF">
<img src="visual.gif"><IMG SRC="newndemast2.gif">
<h1>Visual Inspection</h1>

<hr size=3>
<table cellpadding=0 cellspacing=0>
<tr><td>
<a href="visual.xdm"><img src="mpeg.gif"
border=0></a></td><td><i><font size=-1>Select this option if you
have downloaded the free StreamWorks player. </font></i></td></tr>
<tr><td><a href="visual.mov"><IMG SRC="quicktime.gif"
border=0></a></td><td><i><font size=-1>Select this option for a
QuickTime version of the video. <wrap>This may take several minutes
to download.</font> </i></td></tr>
<tr><td><a href="visual_video.html"><img src="transcript.gif" bor-
der=0></a></i></td><td><i><font size=-1>Select this option if you do
not have video capabilities.</font></i></td></tr></table><p>

<p>

Visual inspection is possibly the most widely used method of nonde-
structive evaluation.  From examining automobile tires for wear to
checking the condition of produce at the grocery store, people use
visual examination for a wide variety of reasons.<p>

Visual inspection is often the first method used in NDE.  NDE tech-
nicians inspect Shuttle and ground support equipment for surface
discontinuities using experience, lighting, and judgement. <p>

<a name="tools">Visual inspectors often use tools, ranging from mag-
nifiers and flashlights to borescopes and fiberscopes, to find sur-
face discontinuities. <p>
</a>
<a name="borescope"><img src="borescope.gif" width=288
height=120><p><i>The borescope is a rigid probe used to visually
inspect, for example, the interior of a straight length of
pipe.</i></a><p>

<img src="visual_01.gif"><p><i>An NDE inspector visually examines a
piece of flight hardware.</i><p>
<spacer type=vertical>



<hr size=4>
<table><th colspan=2><font size=+2>CCTV Inspection</font></th>
<tr><td valign=top><img src="cctv_fiberscope_01.gif"><p>
```

```
<i>A fiberscope with a closed circuit television (cctv) camera in
its tip enables the inspector to examine areas to which there is no
normal visual access. The inspector carefully examines the interior
of this canister for discontinuities.</i> <p></td>

<td valign=top><img src="cctv_fiberscope_03.gif"><p>
<i>If he concludes that the canister is unacceptable, the inspector
can videotape the discontinuity. Results of visual inspections can
be easily documented by video tape or
photographs.</i></td></tr></table>
<hr size=4>
<MULTICOL COLS=2 GUTTER=15>


<p>

<img align=left src="inclusion_small.gif" hspace=5>
<i>Computed tomography (slice picture) reveals an inclusion in the
part being examined. Interpreting a slice picture is an example of
indirect visual inspection.</i><br clear=left><p>

<a name="direct"><b>Direct</b></a> visual inspection methods, such
as the above inspection, involve  observing a condition in real-time
and judging it acceptable or unacceptable according to predefined
criteria.  However, judging a condition acceptable or unacceptable
by later interpreting a videotape, photograph, metallograph, or
radiograph is an <b>indirect</b> visual inspection method. <p>

Visual inspection is usually performed before other NDE methods.  It
can help pinpoint suspect areas where these methods should be
applied and possibly preclude the application of other time-consum-
ing methods.<p>

</multicol>

<p>
<hr size=3>

<a name="table"><table border=on><th colspan=2>Visual Inspection</th>

<tr><td valign=top>
<b>Advantages:</b><P>

<ul>
<li>Visual inspection is quick, simple, and economical, usually
requiring only lighting and simple tools.

<li>Inspection results are immediate and usually recordable on film
```

and/or videotape.

```
<li>Visual inspection can help pinpoint suspect areas where other
NDE tests should be applied.    </ul> </td>

<td valign=top>
<b>Disadvantages:</b>

<ul>

<li>The surface may require some preparation, cleaning, or removal
of paint, mill scale, or grease. These may obscure or fill in sur-
face cracks. However, care must be taken not to scratch or peen the
surface when preparing it.        <i>(For a more thorough discussion
of pretest cleaning, please see the Liquid Penetrant Testing sec-
tion.)</i>

<li>Visual inspectors must have acceptable eyesight, which must be
verified at specific intervals.

<li>Visual inspectors cannot adequately illuminate or even physi-
cally access all areas to be inspected. Some locations may even be
hazardous to humans.

<li>Visual inspection may require precise, time-consuming, segment-
by-segment viewing. In a large inspection area, a small, unaccept-
able discontinuity might be missed.

<li>Visual inspection is subjective. </ul></td></tr></table></a>

<hr size=3>

<CENTER>
<TABLE cellpadding=0 cellspacing=0>
<TR ALIGN=CENTER>
<TD>
<A HREF="welding.html"><IMG SRC="smallicons/navbarlsm.gif" BOR-
DER=0></A><A HREF="ndeoverview.html"><IMG
SRC="smallicons/navbarhsm.gif" BORDER=0></A><A
HREF="visual_inspect_sim.html"><IMG SRC="smallicons/navbarrsm.gif"
BORDER=0></A></TD>
<TD></TD>
<TD><A HREF="ndeintro.html"><IMG SRC="smallicons/mainhomesm.gif" BOR-
DER=0></A></TD>
<TD><A HREF="feedback.html"><IMG SRC="smallicons/feedbacksm.gif" BOR-
DER=0></A></TD>
<TD><A HREF="mailform.html"><IMG SRC="smallicons/bombsm.gif" BOR-
DER=0></A></TD>
```

```
<TD><A HREF="documentation"><IMG SRC="smallicons/docssm.gif" BOR-
DER=0></A></TD>
<TD><A HREF="search.html"><IMG SRC="smallicons/searchsm.gif" BOR-
DER=0></A></TD>
<TD><A HREF="help.html"><IMG SRC="smallicons/helpsm.gif"
BORDER=0></A></TD>
</TR>
</TABLE>

</NOFRAMES>

<FRAME SRC="visual_frames.html" NAME="_top">

<FRAME SRC="visual_navbar.html" NORESIZE NAME="_self"
scrolling="auto" marginheight="0">

</FRAMESET>

</body>
</html>
```

All of the simulation code pages share a common interface that consists of a header graphic, embedded Shockwave applet, and a navigation bar that can either be in a frame or on the page depending on the browser capability.

```
<HTML>
<HEAD>
<TITLE>Normal Distribution</TITLE>
</HEAD>
<body bgcolor="#FFFFFF">
<IMG SRC="spc.gif">


<h1> Normal Distribution</h1>
<hr size=3>
The normal distribution (also known as the Gaussian distribution or
the Bell Curve) is the most important distribution in statistics.
Walter Shewhart discovered that a large number of observed data tend
to be distributed in a bell shape. (The larger the data set is, the
closer the frequency distribution will approximate the bell curve.)
The peak of the bell represents the mean, around which the data
varies in a known, symmetrical dispersion. (The bell curve's mean,
median, and mode are identical.) Standard deviation is a measure of
how far data is dispersed from the mean. In a normal distribution,
68% of the population values will be within one standard deviation
(± 1 <img src="images/lcsigma.gif">), 95% of the population will be
within two standard deviations (± 2 <img src="images/lcsigma.gif">),
```

and 99.7% will be within three standard deviations (± 3 <img src="images/lcsigma.gif">).<p>
In the 1920's, Walter Shewhart also discovered that no matter the shape of the distribution of individual values, the <b> averages</b> of different-sized samples will be distributed in a bell shape. Known as the <b>Central Limit Theorem</b>, this idea implies that any process can be monitored and controlled over a period of time by sampling parts (sample size >4) from a population of data and calcu-lating the sample means. <p>

<img src = "images/static_normal_dist.gif"><p>

<i>How is the normal distribution useful? This curve tells you that if you randomly sample and measure products coming off the produc-tion line, you have: a 68% chance of picking one within ± one stan-dard deviation, a 95% chance of picking one within ± two standard deviations, and a 98% chance of picking one within ± three standard deviations.</i><p>

The normal distribution can be used to calculate the percentage of products inside or outside specification limits. Z values are used to estimate the area under the normal curve. The area to the left of the Z value represents the percentage of the population. <p>

The first step in finding the Z value is to calculate Z:<p>

<center>
<img src="images/normal_distribution.gif"></center><p>

The second step is to locate the Z value in a Z table. That value indicates the percentage of population items under the curve to left of the measured value.   <p>

Therefore, if you know the mean and standard deviation of a popula-tion, you can calculate the percentage of a population either less than or greater than a particular value or between two values.<p>

Rather than have you look up the Z value in a table, we've provided you a graphical calculator for finding (and visualizing) the area under the curve. <p>

<embed src="images/normaldist.dcr" height=300 width=480><p>

Use the above calculator to solve the following exercises. Enter the mean and standard deviation into the appropriate fields. If you're finding the percentage between two values (X1 and X2), enter

values in the appropriate fields. If you're finding the percentage
greater than or less than one value, click and hold the dot adjacent to the X2 field and select the appropriate operation from the
pull-down menu. Then, type in the X value and press enter. The calculator will show you the answer graphically and numerically. <p>

```
<hr size=3>
<h3>Exercise 8</h3>
```

For a normally distributed population, with a mean of 100 pounds and
a standard deviation of 10, calculate the percentage of the population:<ol>

```
<li>less than 94 pounds
<li>greater than 120
<li>between 80 and 120.</ol>

<a href="resources/exercise_8.pdf"><i>Check your answers.</a></i><p>
<center>
<img src = "spcline.gif"><p>
<a
href="http://kosh.ksc.nasa.gov/cgi-bin/imagemap/spc/imagemaps/nor-
mal_distribution.map">
<img src = "buttonbar.gif" border = 0 ISMAP></a><p>
<a href="discrete_conclusion.html">Back</a> - <a
href="overview.html">Home</a> - <a
href="exponential.html">Next</a> - <a href="search.html">Search</a> -
<a
href="resources.html">Resources</a>
</center>
</html>
```

ABOUT THE CD-ROM AND WEB SITE

There's no easier way of illustrating the multiple appearances and functions of Web-based training than to take you right to the Web sites where this training is already up and running. In the attached CD-ROM, we have included links to the Web site set up for this book (www.brandon-hall .com), links to sites mentioned in this book, and sample code from the book, so you don't have to retype code that would be useful to you.

The material on the CD-ROM includes code from Altos Education Network demonstrating the technology behind online testing and evaluation. Users can view the source code that creates these HTML pages and then view the page itself through the browser-based architecture of the CD.

Sample code and pages from multiple other training programs are also provided. Users can examine code from programs like the Practising Law Institute's online audio courseware and the Bureau of National Affairs text and graphics course describing the makeup of the U.S. government.. This course was developed with a budget of $0.00 by a staff of one! The final product is pretty impressive considering the restrictions Simonson worked under.

Viewers can look at code from NASA's Kennedy Space Center Web-based training and view Netscape's first foray into WBT — their Netscape Proxy Server 2.0 courseware.

Although code from every case study isn't accessible from the CD-ROM, URLs of products and companies listed in the book are hyperlinked. If your system is browser-ready, clicking on a URL link in the text of the CD will allow you to access that Web site online.

The CD can be used by both Macintosh and Windows systems.

User Assistance and Information

The software accompanying this book is being provided as is without warranty or support of any kind. Should you require basic installation assistance, or if your media is defective, please call the Wiley product support number at (212) 850-6194 weekdays between 9:00 A.M. and 4:00 P.M. Eastern Standard Time or via e-mail at: **wprtusw@wiley.com**.

To place additional orders or to request information about other Wiley products, please call (800) 879-4539.

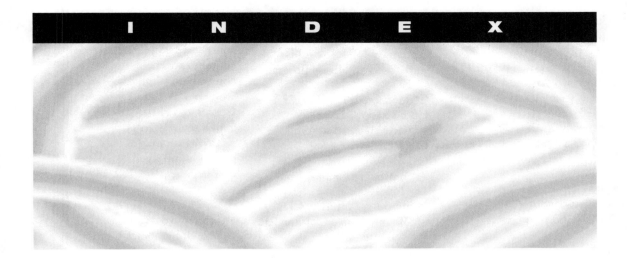

I N D E X

Software titles are indexed in most cases without the company name. For example look up "Acrobat," not "Adobe Acrobat."

Numerical Terms

327x terminal emulation, 123
3DS Max, 62

A

Acrobat, 27, 37, 46-47
Acrobat Reader, 37-38
Active Documents, 52
ActiveX, 49, 51-52, 208
    information resources, 56
ActiveX controls, 51, 52-53
administrative support, 98
Afterburner, 343-344
aiff (Apple Instrument File
    Format), 65
alpha testing, 243
Altos Education Network,
    301-303

sample code, 453-461
American Management
    Association, sample RFP,
    132-137
American Society for Training
    and Development (ASTD),
    100
analysis, 231
animated GIF files, 62-63, 64
animation, 152-153
animation files, 60-65
anonymous FTP, 35
anonymous ID, 32
Apache, 69
AppleTalk networks, 67, 74
art direction, 152
ASCII files, 41
asset management, 152

ATM (Asynchronous Transfer
    Mode) networks, 72
audience, *see* students
audio
    and download speed, 347-348
    keeping file size small, 89
    production, 152-153
audio files, 65-66
authoring storyboards, 86
authoring tools, 26, 27, 59-60.
    See also specific authoring
    tools
    checklist for selecting, 198
    choosing, 195-198, 226-230
    converting existing computer-
        based training, 25
    costs, 157
    for interactive multimedia
        training, 9

limitations, 199-200
program metaphors, 199
and programming WBT, 89
tradeoff in purchase of, 103
Authorware, 25, 26, 37, 226
converting files to Shockwave, 343-346
description, 200-207
TopClass integration, 271
Authorware Discussion listserv, 348
avatars, 54
AVI Constructor, 60
AVI files, 63-64

B

backbones, 73
Back button, 36
bandwidth, 16, 23, 28, 311
Bank of Montreal CenterPoint program, 6-7, 312-319
Berne Convention for the Protection of Literary and Artistic Works, 418
beta testing, 243
Body Language, 379
bookmarks, 36
Broadband technology, 121
browsers, see Web browsers
budget analyst, 98
budget estimation, 91
Bureau of National Affairs, 170-178
business case, 103-104
case study: Storage Technology, 112-117
concerns, 104-107
cost estimation, 149-158
market research, 117-131
proposals and, 131-149
ROI studies, 107-117
business drivers, 138-140
ButtonMaker, 52

C

C++, 48
camera (in VRML worlds), 54
card-based authoring programs, 199
CBIquick, 26, 168-169, 227
CBT Express, 227
CD-ROM-based training, 24
CD-ROM drives, 58
CD-ROMs
converting for Internet, 166-170
hybrid, see Internet CDs
and interactive multimedia training, 8-9
Internet CDs, 161-163
CenterPoint training program (Bank of Montreal), 6-7, 312-319
Centra, 377
Centra Symposium, 379-380
Charles Schwab (investment services company), 183-185
ClearFusionX, 52
Clearly Internet e-mail courses, 296-298
client, 49
client contact, 100
client/server networks, 67-68
CMX Viewer, 38
codes, HTML, 42, 43-47
colleges, as staffing source, 101
color HTML codes, 44, 46
color palettes, 243
Common Lisp Hypermedia Server, 69
communication, project manager's role, 93
CompUSA, 305
CompuServe GIFs, 63
computer-assisted instruction, 18
computer-based training, 17-18
computer requirements, 25, 57-59, 155

concerns, addressing in building business case, 104-107
content development, 152
content expert, 98
contextualization, 411-412
Control Pak 1, 53
Copfer and Associates, 349-354
copyright, 414-421
myths about, 421-422
copyright infringement, 416-417
cost benefits, 108-109, 143-144
cost estimation, 149-158
costs, 21-22, 109-117
interactive training, 312
text and graphics training programs, 289-290
Course Builder, 227, 380
CourseWorks, 228
CPC View, 53
creation
interactive multimedia training programs, 348-376
interactive training programs, 312-322
text and graphics training programs, 290-296, 300-301
cross-platform compatibility, 346-347
curriculum conversion
basic issues, 164-166
case study: Bureau of National Affairs, 170-178
case study: Charles Schwab, 183-185
CD-ROMs, 166-170
Cutler-Hammer training program, 349-354
Cyber Presence, 69
Cyber Travel Specialist, 4, 304-305

D

data-entry programmer, 98
DBMS, intranet linking to, 123

DBMS query/development
tools, 123
deceased individuals, publicity
rights, 428-429
Decision Aid, 179-182
Decisive Survey, 249-250
Dell University, 254-258
de minimis copying, 423
design. *See also* authoring tools
basic guidelines, 187-189
characteristics of good,
189-195
instructional, 189, 230-244
using Designer's Edge,
232-241
design document, 83-84, 91,
152
Designer's Edge, 232-241
design storyboards, 86
desktop training, 18
desktop video conferencing, 18
development, 231
costs of initial, 150-158
interactive multimedia
training, 343-348
process overview, 81-83
process steps, 83-93, 152-155
project team for, 93-100
and RFP process, 148
staffing for, 100-101
text and graphics courses,
291-293
development teams, 22-23,
93-100
DigitalThink training courses,
372-377
DigitalTrainer, 228
Director, 199, 200
TopClass integration, 271
discussion groups, *see* online
forums/discussion groups
distance learning, 18, 119
with computer-based training,
377-380

Distributed and Replicated
Learning Object Repository,
273, 277-279
distribution, 90
documentation, 154-155
intranet for sharing, 121
downloading, 35
speed, 347

E

EarthTime, 38
editor, 99
Electronic Distributive
Learning, 306
Electronic Workbook (Bank of
Montreal), 312-319
e-mail, 21, 41
e-mail courses, 15, 287
costs, 289
creating, 296-298
determining suitability, 289
planning, 298-300
employment agencies, 100
Encarta, 163
enterprisewide training, 121
enthusiasm building, 104
Envoy, 38
error messages, browsers,
40-41
Ethernet networks, 72-73
evaluation, 20-21, 231
criteria for, 403-412
Everest Authoring System, 228
executives, training concerns of,
105, 106
ExpressO, 69

F

facilitators, 24-25
facts, copyrightability, 415,
417-418
fair use, of copyrighted work,
418, 428

Internet myths about, 421,
422
FDDI (Fiber Distributed Data
Interface) networks, 73-74
file servers, 67
file transfers, 21
firewalls, 29, 75-76
Flash, 60
flowcharts, 85, 90
fonts, 46-47
forms, 43
Formula One/NET, 38
forums, *see* online
forums/discussion groups
Forward button, 36
frames, 42
FrontPage, 26, 27, 157, 161
FrontPage97, 293, 295
FTP (File Transfer Protocol),
34-35

G

Gartner Group Internet
Learning Center, 438-441
Georgia Tech, 101
GIFBuilder, 64
GIF Construction Set, 64
GIF files, animated, 62-63, 64
GIF89s, 63
graphic designer, 98-99
graphics, 34
production, 152-153
graphic user interfaces, 194

H

hackers, 29, 75
hard drive requirements, 58
hardware requirements, 25,
57-59, 155-156
Home button, 36
Home Page (Claris), 26, 157,
161
HTML (Hypertext Markup
Language), 26, 41-43,

HTML *continued*
293-295. *See also* authoring tools
coding, 42, 43-47
shortcomings for WBT, 229
using FrontPage97, 293, 295
HTTP (Hypertext Transfer Protocol), 32-34
hubs, 73
hybrid CDs, *see* Internet CDs
HyperCam, 60
hyperlinks, 33, 36
hypertext, 33

I

IBM Internet Connection Server, 69
IBTauthor, 26, 220-226
IconAuthor, 26, 226
description, 212-217
IconAuthor Present, 212
icon-based authoring programs, 199
ideas, copyrightability, 417
ILINC, 377, 378
Image Alchemy, 243
image maps, 191
image processing, 153
implementation, 231
text and graphics courses, 295-296
independent creation, 418
InfoSource Seminar-On-A-Disk programs, 326-329
Input Pro, 53
instructional design, 189, 230-244
instructional designer, 96-97
text and graphics courses, 293-296
interactive multimedia training, 8-14, 341-342
appropriate interactivity/ multimedia level, 23-24

creation case studies, 348-376
determining suitability, 342-348
needs for successful, 90-92
Interactive Patient (Marshall University), 348-349
interactive training, 5-7, 18, 119, 309-312
costs, 312
creation case studies, 312-322
external development, 332-340
off-the-shelf, 322-332
interactivity, 309-312
online vs. offline, 27
and training quality, 193, 289
interface design, 84-85, 152, 191
interface designer, 98
internal Web sites, 125-126
International Interactive Communications Society (IICS), 100
International Society for Performance and Improvement (ISPI), 100
Internet, 21. *See also* intranet; World Wide Web
adoption vs. intranet, 129-130
copyright myths, 421-422
future potential impact, 118
Internet Assistant for Word, 170-171
Internet-based training, 15, 17, 18. *See also* Web-based training
Internet CDs, 23, 161-163
creating with IconAuthor, 216-217
creating with ToolBook II, 210-211

Internet connection, 66
Internet Explorer, 43, 52
Internet Studio, 121
intranet, 25
adoption vs. Internet, 129-130
applications, 121-122, 125-126
download speed, 347
future applications, 121-122
market research, 122-129
intranet-based training, 18
intranet connection, 66
Introduction to Statistical Process Control course (NASA Kennedy Space Center), 9, 10-11, 354-356
IP address, 76
ISIM University online courses, 300-301

J

Jamba, 26
Java, 26-27, 47-49
cross-platform compatibility, 376
information resources, 56
Java applets, 46, 47, 48, 49-51
JavaScript, 46
Jigsaw, 69
justification, *see* business case

K

Keeping the Fire, 330-331
Kemet Electronics, 258-260

L

languages, 26, 41-55
LANs (Local Area Networks), 72
lead programmer, 97
Learning Junction, 279-284

Learning Organization
Information System (LOIS),
261-263
Learning Processor, 228
LearningSpace (Lotus), 263-265
LearnItOnline, 438
LearnLinc, 378-379
legal issues, 413-414
    copyright, 414-422
    licensing, 422-427
    privacy/publicity rights,
    427-429
libraries, 426-427
licensing, 413, 422-423
    myths about, 423-424
Lightning Strike, 38-39, 53
lists, 43
LocalTalk, 74
Logical Operations, 438
Lotus LearningSpace, 263-265
Lotus Notes, 129, 263
Lotus SmartSuite, 263

M

Macintosh computer
requirements, 58
Macintosh server software, 68,
69
mail servers, 67
maintenance costs, 158
managers, training concerns of,
105, 106
market research, 117-131
Marshall University Interactive
Patient, 348-349
mBED, 53
media, *see* multimedia
media design document, 83-84
media libraries, 426
MediaPro, Inc., 290-296
MediaStudio, 60
metaphors
    authoring programs, 199
    training programs, 190-191

Microsoft Internet Information
Server, 69
Microsoft Online Institute,
431-434
MIDI (Musical Instrument
Digital Interface), 65
MMX chip, 58
MocKingbird CBT, 228
modem limitations, 347, 348
motivation strategies, 22
Motorola programs, 332-335
MPEG audio files, 65-66
MPEGMaker, 61
MPEG video files, 58, 64-65
multimedia, 3, 23. *See also*
    interactive multimedia
    training
    acquisition, 88-89
    appropriate use, 188,
    189-190, 242
    authoring tools and, 196
    costs issues, 288
    determining suitability,
    140-142
    technology planning, 160
Multimedia and Internet
Training Awards Criteria,
403-405
multimedia authoring
programs, 196
multimedia developer, 99
*Multimedia Law and Business
Handbook*, 413-414
Multimedia Learning, 366,
371-372
Multimedia Learning Object
Broker, 273, 277
Multimedia Recruiters, 100
multimedia training, 17, 24. *See
also* interactive multimedia
training
*Multimedia and Internet
Training Newsletter*, 32
music libraries, 426

N

NASA Kennedy Space Center
training program, 8, 9, 10-11,
354-362
    sample code, 465-471
Nations Bank training
programs, 305-308
navigation, 407-408
Navus Gadget, 319-322
needs analysis, 151
Net-based training, 18
Netscape Navigator, 15, 43, 52
Netscape Navigator Gold, 27
Netscape Proxy Server 2.0
training course, 366, 371-372
NetShow, 350
Netware, 74
network computers, 160
network connections, 25, 28
    speed, 347
networking, 66-74
    Macintosh-PC connection, 74
    security, 75-77
Neuron, 25, 39, 208
New Media Strategies, 4,
303-305
NIIT, Ltd. training courses,
299-300
NOEMBED tag, 346
Nondestructive Evaluation
course (NASA Kennedy
Space Center), 8, 10-11,
354-356

O

OLE (Object Linking and
Embedding), 51
OmniTech, 301
online forums/discussion
groups, 288
    case study: Altos Education
    Network, 301-303
    costs, 290
    determining suitability, 289
    planning, 298-300

Online Learning Infrastructure (OLI), 272-279
Online Programming Instruction Environment (OPIE), 5-6, 329, 443-453
online testing, 245
  case study: Dell University, 254-258
  case study: Kemet Electronics, 258-260
  security aspects, 254
  using Decisive Survey, 249-250
  using Question Mark, 250-254
  using Web@ssessor, 245-249
online training, 18
OnNet, 69
OpenScript, 211
OpenServer, 69
Oracle Learning Architecture (OLA), 265-268
Oracle Simulator, 11-13, 14, 362-366, 367-370
Oracle WebServer, 69
Outbound Train, 322-326

P

packet filters, 75-76
page-based authoring programs, 199
PageMill, 271
pagination, 46-47
Pal Edit, 243
palettes, 63, 243, 345-346
palette shifting, 63
PC computer requirements, 57-59
PC Maclean, 74
PDF (Portable Document Format), 37, 46, 47
peer-to-peer networks, 67
Pentium chips, 57-58
performance support, 119
Personal AVI Editor, 61

planning
  e-mail courses, 298-300
  online forums/discussion groups, 298-300
  technology planning, 159-163
  text and graphics courses, 290-291
plug-ins, 37-40
  shortcomings for WBT, 229-230
PowerMedia, 228
PowerPC, 58, 68
PowerPoint, 53, 295
Practising Law Institute programs, 330-332
  sample code, 461-465
Premiere, 61
Price Waterhouse, 111
print servers, 67
privacy rights, 427
professional organizations, 100
program administration
  Learning Junction for, 279-284
  Learning Organization Information System (LOIS) for, 261-263
  Lotus LearningSpace for, 263-265
  Online Learning Infrastructure (OLI) for, 272-279
  Oracle Learning Architecture (OLA) for, 265-268
  TopClass for, 268-272
programmers, 97-98
programming, 89, 153-154
  expense of, 149
programming languages, 26, 41-55
project administration, 154-155
project management, 91-92
project manager, 93-96
project team, 244

for development, 22-23, 93-100
for text and graphics courses, 290
proof-of-concept, 89
proposals, 83
  RFPs, 131-149
  sample, 383-401
protocols
  file transfer, 31-34
  networking, 66-67
prototype, 89, 291-292
proxy servers, 76
public domain, 414, 419-420, 427
publicity rights, 427-429

Q

quality assurance, 90, 98
Quarterdeck WebServer, 69
Quest, 26, 217-220
  using Designer's Edge with, 235
Quest Internet Player, 217
Question Mark, 250-254
  case study applications, 255-260
Question Mark Guardian, 254
QuestNet+, 218
QuickSilver, 53
QuickTime files, 61, 64

R

RAM requirements, 58, 59
Randysoft courses, 5-6, 329-330
  sample code, 443-453
Rapid, 228
RealAudio, 39, 53, 66
RealAudio Server, 66
RealMagic Producer, 61
relational databases, 278-279
releases, 428
Reload button, 36-37

request for proposals (RFPs)
   procedure for, 145-149
   sample, 131-145
Return on Investment and Multimedia Training, 16
return on investment (ROI), 107-117
   determining, 117, 137-144
review, 242
revision costs, 158
rights clearance agencies, 425, 426

S

Sage Interactive, 335-340
San Francisco State University, 101
Scholars.com, 433-434
SCO OpenServer, 69
scripts, 85
search engines, 34, 191
security, 29
   and Java, 49
   networks, 75-77
   online testing, 254
self-paced training, 18
   guidelines for evaluating, 405-412
Seminar-On-A-Disk, 326-329
seminars (standup seminars), 288
servers, 28, 32, 67-68. *See also* Web servers
   costs, 155-156
   software for, 68, 69
Shockwave, 26, 37, 39, 53, 206-207
   converting Authorware files, 343-346
   Motorola application, 332-335
   using in interactive multimedia programs, 342-348
simulation, 190-191

interactivity with, 311
SiteMill, 271
slide-based authoring programs, 199
Society for Technical Communications (STC), 101
software quality assurance, 98
software requirements, 25, 59-66
   servers, 68, 69
sound, *see* audio
sound cards, 25, 58
Spry Web Server, 69
staffing
   for development process, 100-101
   text and graphics training programs, 290
standards, 84
static presentation programs, 196
stock houses, 426-427
Stop button, 37
Storage Technology, 109-111, 112-117
storyboard, 85-88
   PowerPoint for, 295
   tips for developing, 241-242
students
   and curriculum conversion, 164
   training concerns of, 105, 107
subject matter expert, 98
Superscape VR, 55
Surround Video, 53
Symposium (Centra), 379-380

T

tables, 42
tags, HTML, 41-42
teams, *see* project team
technical testing, 90

technology planning, 159-163. *See also* curriculum conversion
template pages, 294
327x terminal emulation, 123
testing
   alpha/beta testing, 243
   in development, 89-90, 154
   online, *see* online testing
text and graphics training, 4, 287-288. *See also* e-mail courses; online forums/discussion groups
   case study: ISIM University, 300-301
   costs, 289-290
   creating, 290-296, 300-301
   determining suitability, 288-290
   interactive, *see* interactive training
   with live training, 303-308
   staffing for, 290
timeline-based authoring programs, 199
time reduction, 108-109
Tobin Erdmann & Jacobsen, 332-335
token ring networks, 67, 73-74
ToolBook II, 26, 226
   description, 207-212
   TopClass integration, 271
ToolVox, 39
TopClass, 268-272
Train Depot (Outbound Train), 323, 325
training staff
   training concerns of, 105, 106-107
   transition to Web-based training, 22

U

Universal Copyright Convention, 418

Universal Media Access, 214
universities, as staffing source, 101
UNIX server software, 68, 69
UNIX viruses, 77
uploading, 35
URL (Uniform Resource Locator), 32, 33, 35-36
usability testing, 89

V

V-Active, 61
VDOLive, 39
VDOLive Player, 53
viability assessment, 19-20
video
 keeping file size small, 89
 production, 152-153
video accelerator cards, 58, 59
video files, 60-65
VideoShop, 62
VidWatch, 62
virtual office, 160
virus checkers, 77
viruses, 29, 77
Visual Basic, 51
Visual Home, 163
VivoActive Producer, 62
VRAM requirements, 58
VRML (Virtual Reality Modeling Language), 53-55
VR Scout VRML, 39

W

wave files, 66
Web-based training. *See also* business case; design; development; interactive multimedia training; interactive training; online testing; program administration; text and graphics training
 advantages, 15-16, 19
 cost benefits, 108-109
 cost estimation, 149-158
 curriculum conversion, *see* curriculum conversion
 Decision Aid for determining appropriateness, 179-182
 defined, 15
 disadvantages, 16-17
 evolutionary approach, 160
 examples, 3-14
 frequently-asked questions, 15-29
 legal and copyright issues, *see* legal issues
 market research, 117-131
 online vs. offline interactivity, 27
 terminology, 17-18
 tips for first, 241-244
 types, 4-9
Web-Based Training Market Research Report: Trends, Opportunities, and Risks, 117
Web browsers, 15, 26, 31, 35-36, 59
 error messages, 40-41
 navigation using, 36-37
 non-Shockwave-enabled, 346
 OLI architecture, 274
 plug-ins for, 37-40,
Web designer, 98-99
WebFX, 39
Web Interactive Training project (NASA Kennedy Space Center), 8, 9, 10-11, 354-362
 sample code, 465-471
Webmaster, 99-100, 158
Web Publisher, 27
Web Safari, 379
Web Server (Oracle), 69
Web Server (Quarterdeck), 69
WebServer (Spry), 69
Web servers, 67, 68, 69
 file ordering on, 294
 market research, 130-131
Web@ssessor, 245-249
WebStar, 69
WEBTRAINING-L, 17
Whip!, 53
wide-area learning, 120
Windows computer requirements, 57-59
Windows NT, 68
Windows server software, 68, 69
WIRL, 39
workbooks, 288
worlds, 53
World Wide Web, 21, 31-32. *See also* Internet; intranet
 copyright myths, 421-422
 information resources, 55-56
 information transfer on, 32-35
 internal Web sites, 125-126
World Wide Web Design Guide, 192
WPA photographs, 420, 427
writer, 99

Z

ZDU, 263, 434-438